CONTENTS

Bridging Differences

4th Edition

Bridging Differences

Effective Intergroup Communication

4th Edition

William B. Gudykunst
California State University, Fullerton

SAGE Publications
International Educational and Professional Publisher
Thousand Oaks ▪ London ▪ New Delhi

For information:

Sage Publications, Inc.
2455 Teller Road
Thousand Oaks, California 91320
E-mail: order@sagepub.com

Sage Publications Ltd.
6 Bonhill Street
London EC2A 4PU
United Kingdom

Sage Publications India Pvt. Ltd.
B-42, Panchsheel Enclave
Post Box 4109
New Delhi 110 017 India

Printed in the United States of America

Library of Congress Cataloging-in-Publication Data

Gudykunst, William B.
Bridging differences : effective intergroup communication /
William B. Gudykunst.— 4th ed.
p. cm.
Includes bibliographical references and index.
ISBN 0-7619-2936-3 — ISBN 0-7619-2937-1 (pbk.)
1. Intercultural communication. 2. Interpersonal communication.
I. Title.
HM1211.G82 2004
303.48′2—dc21

2003010527

03 04 05 06 07 10 9 8 7 6 5 4 3 2 1

Acquisitions Editor: Todd Armstrong
Editorial Assistant: Veronica Novak
Production Editor: Sanford Robinson
Copy Editor: Kris Bergstad
Typesetter: C&M Digitals (P) Ltd.
Proofreader: Scott Oney
Cover Designer: Michelle Lee

PREFACE

I became involved in studying intercultural communication in the United States Navy when I served as an Intercultural Relations Specialist in Japan. My job was to design and conduct training to help naval personnel and their families adjust to living in Japan. While conducting intercultural training in Japan, I thought intercultural communication (i.e., communication between people from different cultures) was different from intracultural communication (i.e., communication with members of our own cultures).

After getting out of the Navy, I went to the University of Minnesota to work on my Ph.D. While completing my Ph.D., I continued to see intercultural communication as different from intracultural communication and retained my interest in training. After accepting a position as an assistant professor, I initially focused on conducting research, and eventually turned to developing a theory to explain intercultural communication effectiveness.

In trying to develop a theory to explain communication between people from different cultures, I came to two conclusions. The first conclusion was that the processes operating when we communicate with people from other cultures (and races, ethnic groups, social classes, etc.) are the same as the processes operating when we communicate with people from our own cultures (and races, ethnic groups, social classes, etc.). To illustrate, our stereotypes affect our communication when we communicate on automatic pilot. Stereotypes, however, lead to ineffective communication when the person with whom we are communicating comes from another culture more than when the person comes from our own culture. One reason for this is that our stereotypes of groups in our cultures tend to be more accurate and favorable than our stereotypes of other cultures. Inaccurate and unfavorable stereotypes of other cultures and ethnic groups cause us to misinterpret the messages we receive from members of those cultures and ethnic groups. The second conclusion I reached was that a theory of intercultural communication must have direct application. To apply a theory there must be a focus on an applied "outcome" of our communication. I chose the effectiveness (i.e., minimizing misunderstandings) of our communication and adapting to new cultural environments as the foci of my work.

Given that the underlying process of communication is the same in intercultural (intergroup) and intracultural (intragroup) encounters, we need a way to refer to this common underlying process. I use "communicating with strangers" (Gudykunst, 1983b) to refer to this common process. Strangers, as I use the term, are members of outgroups approaching an ingroup. I write the book from the perspective of the ingroup members who are communicating with strangers, but virtually everything I say also applies to strangers' communication with ingroup members. Where there are differences due to the position of the ingroups strangers are approaching and strangers' groups in terms of power or numbers (e.g., "majority" and "minority" groups), I discuss these issues. I also discuss issues revolving around strangers having more experience communicating with ingroup members than ingroup members have communicating with strangers.

I have drawn on the work of Harry Triandis, Henri Tajfel, Howie Giles, Chuck Berger, Ellen Langer, Walter Stephan, Cookie Stephan, Edward T. Hall, and others to develop anxiety/uncertainty management (AUM) theory (Gudykunst, 1988, 1993, 1995, in press) to explain effective interpersonal and intergroup communication (intercultural communication is one type of intergroup communication; other types of intergroup communication include, but are not limited to, interracial communication, interethnic communication, intergenerational communication, disabled-nondisabled communication). I apply AUM theory to improving intergroup communication effectiveness in this book. I do not present the actual theory, but use it as a guide to material presented in the book. My emphasis is on improving communication effectiveness between people from different groups (e.g., culture, ethnicity, gender, disability, age, social class). The ideas presented, however, can be applied to communication with people from our own groups as well.

This edition of *Bridging Differences* is longer than the previous edition. In writing this edition, my goal was to provide sufficient content for the current edition to be used as a standalone text in courses or training programs designed to help participants improve their intergroup communication effectiveness. I have made several changes in this edition. First, I updated the research presented throughout the book. Second, I expanded the discussion of several topics: namely, changing intergroup expectations, cultural differences in attribution processes, cultural and ethnic differences in conflict, cultural differences in indirect messages, cultural differences in uncertainty management, empathy, ethnic and cultural identities, face and its relationship to conflict management, intergroup communication effectiveness, intergroup conflict, ingroup biases, negotiating meanings, perceptual processes, and prejudice. Third, I added new material on civic engagement, community in public life, diversity and community, the content of stereotypes, communication in romantic relationships, cultural differences in effective communication, and theoretical explanations for prejudice. Fourth, I have added study questions at the end of each chapter. Fifth, I added new self-assessment questionnaires (e.g., self construals, face-concerns). Sixth, I have added open-ended questions at the beginning of some sections to stimulate readers to think about their implicit theories. Seventh, I have added written skill exercises to increase readers' skill development.

The content of this edition reflects the state-of-the-art in our knowledge about intergroup communication. This edition also has a stronger focus on skills than previous editions. If readers complete the open-ended questions in many of the sections it will help them understand their implicit theories of communication. Understanding our implicit theories is necessary for us to improve the effectiveness of our communication and change how we behave on automatic pilot. If readers complete the self-assessment questionnaires, the written skill exercises, and the applications at the end of each chapter, it will help them improve their intercultural communication skills. While this edition has a strong skills focus, instructors do not have to emphasize skills to use this book. Answering the open-ended questions, completing the self-assessment questionnaires, and completing the written skill exercises also help readers understand the content of the book.

In addition to those people named earlier whose work has influenced the development of AUM theory, there are numerous people who have contributed, either directly or indirectly, to my thinking about communication and to this book. Exposure to Kurt Lewin's writing early in my graduate career convinced me that theories must have practical application. Tsukasa Nishida and I became friends as graduate students and we continue to work together today. Tsukasa and Gao Ge have worked with me on the vast majority of the cross-cultural studies of AUM theory, and have been constant sources of support. Stella Ting-Toomey served as a sounding board for AUM theory and its application, read drafts of earlier editions, and suggested the title. Harry Triandis and Michael Bond have provided valuable feedback on my work over the years (including earlier versions of this book) that I have incorporated in this edition. Participants in the "Applications of Intercultural Communication" course I teach at California State University, Fullerton tested many of the ideas presented in intergroup training programs they designed and implemented.

The book would not have been written without the gentle prodding and support of Ann West, my editor at Sage for the first edition. Sophy Craze facilitated the production of the second edition at Sage. Margaret Seawell, the current communication editor at Sage, provided support in the writing of the third edition. Margaret and Todd Armstrong, the interpersonal communication editor, arranged for this edition. Astrid Virding did excellent work overseeing the production of all editions. Sanford Robinson has done an outstanding job overseeing the production of this edition of the book. Finally, I want to thank Kristin Bergstad for her careful copyediting of this and the previous edition of the manuscript.

—Bill Gudykunst
Laguna Beach, CA

Greetings! I am pleased
to see that we are different.
May we together become greater
than the sum of both of us.

Vulcan Greeting
(Star Trek)

See at a distance an undesirable person;
See close at hand a desirable person;
Come closer to the undesirable person;
Move away from the desirable person.
Coming close and moving apart,
how interesting life is!

Gensho Ogura

CHAPTER 1

Communicating With Strangers

Elie Wiesel, a recipient of the Nobel Peace Prize, believes that hate directed toward members of different cultural and racial groups, as well as toward members of different political and ideological groups, is the major source of problems between people today.[1] Hate is being expressed toward, and conflict is occurring between people of different groups everywhere we look. To illustrate, nationality conflicts are taking place in the former Soviet Union, conflict between Neonazis and immigrants in Germany is leading to violence, conflict between Protestants and Catholics in Northern Ireland is still taking place, and conflict between Arabs and Jews in Israel continues, to name only a few of the intergroup conflicts occurring in the world today.[2] Recent international polls (i.e., Pew Research Centre, Chicago Council on Foreign Relations) indicate that a large percentage of people throughout the world (e.g., 60%-70% of respondents throughout Europe) view "religious and ethnic hatred" as major dangers to the world today (see *The Economist*, 2003, for a summary). There also is racial harassment on university campuses in the United States,[3] hate crimes are committed against members of different groups (e.g., ethnic groups, homosexuals), and there is conflict between pro choice and right to life groups at abortion clinics in the United States.[4]

While the specific causes of the conflicts occurring throughout the world differ depending upon the situation, all incidents share one thing in common, polarized communication. *Polarized communication* occurs when individuals have "the inability to believe or seriously consider one's view as wrong and the other's opinion as truth. Communication within human community becomes typified by the rhetoric of 'we' are right and 'they' are misguided or wrong" (Arnett, 1986, pp. 15-16). Polarized communication, therefore, exists when groups or individuals look out for their own interests and have little or no concern for others' interests. Polarized communication often stems from our everyday conversations:

> The devastating group hatreds that result in so much suffering in our own country and around the world are related in origin to the small intolerances in our everyday conversations—our readiness to attribute good intentions to ourselves and bad intentions to others; to believe there is one right way and ours is it; and to extrapolate from frustration with an individual in order to generalize to a group. (Tannen, 1993, p. B5)

We express these small intolerances in our everyday conversations, but we are not highly aware of doing so.

When we are not concerned for others' interests we are *morally exclusive.*

> Moral exclusion occurs when individuals or groups are perceived as outside the boundary in which moral values, rules, and considerations of fairness apply. Those who are morally excluded are perceived as nonentities, expendable, or undeserving; consequently, harming them appears acceptable, appropriate or just. (Optow, 1990, p. 1, italics omitted)

Lack of concern for others and moral exclusion are a function, at least in part, of the spiritual deprivation (i.e., the feeling of emptiness associated with separation from our fellow humans) that the late Mother Teresa saw as the major problem facing the world (Jampolsky, 1989). Our "inability to feel committed to others we see like us is matched by an equally strong tendency to diminish the humanity of those we see as different" (Tannen, 1993, p. B5).

One reason for our spiritual deprivation is the difficulties with which we must cope in our lives; "life is difficult" (Peck, 1978, p. 15). Most of us expect our lives to be easy, but they are not. The difficult conditions in our lives threaten our self-concepts (i.e., our views of ourselves; Staub, 1989). Also, anytime we perceive threats to achieving our goals, we perceive our self-concepts to be threatened (Lazarus, 1991). When our self-concepts are threatened, we try to improve the way we see ourselves. One way we accomplish this is by positively comparing ourselves to others or putting others down (Tajfel, 1978). When we feel superior to others or see others as inferior to us, we feel good about ourselves. Another way we deal with threats to our self-concepts is by becoming hostile or aggressive toward others, particularly those who are different from us in important ways (e.g., members of different cultures or ethnic groups, people with different gender orientations).

We also feel spiritually deprived and unconnected when we do not know how to communicate with others. This is especially true for our interactions with members of other cultures or ethnic groups in the United States, but it also is true for our interactions with people with disabilities, older/younger people, and members of different social classes. Since we have little contact with members of other groups (Rose, 1981), we do not have much practice in communicating with them. Many of us believe that our inabilities to communicate with members of other groups is due to one person not being competent in the other's language or dialect. Linguistic knowledge alone, however, is not enough to ensure that our communication with people from other groups will progress smoothly and/or be effective. "Human beings are drawn close to one another by their common nature, but habits and customs keep them apart" (Confucius). Misunderstandings in intergroup encounters often stem from not knowing the norms and rules guiding the communication of people from different groups. If we understand others' languages or dialects, but not their communication rules, we can make fluent fools of ourselves.

Language and culture are not the only factors that can contribute to misunderstandings in intergroup encounters. Our attitudes (e.g., prejudice, ageism, sexism) and stereotypes create expectations that often lead us to misinterpret messages we receive from people who are different *and* lead people who are different to misinterpret the messages they receive from us.

Our expectations regarding how people from other groups will behave are based on how we categorize them (e.g., he is Japanese; she is Mexican American; they are disabled). Our use of social categories, however, is not limited to our communication with people from different groups. We categorize others when we communicate with people from our own cultures or ethnic groups, but the categories are different (e.g., that person is a woman; he is a waiter; she or he is a "friend of a friend"). Until we get to know others, our interactions with them must be based on our expectations regarding how people in the categories in which we place others will behave. To be able to talk about the similarities in the underlying communication process, I refer to people who are not members of our own groups and who are different (on the basis of culture, ethnicity, gender, age, disability, social class, or other group memberships) as *strangers*[5] (based on Simmel's, 1950/1908, concept of "stranger").[6]

The concept of the stranger is important in understanding communication between members of different groups:

> It is the dialectic between closeness and remoteness that makes the position of strangers socially problematic in all times and places. When those

> who would be close, in any sense of the term, are actually close, and those who would be distant are distant, everyone is "in his [or her] place." When those who would be distant are close, however, the inevitable result is a degree of tension and anxiety which necessitates some special kind of response . . . group members derive security from relating in familiar ways to fellow group members and from maintaining distance from nonmembers through established insulating mechanisms. In situations where an outsider comes into the social space normally occupied by group members only, one can presume an initial response of anxiety and at least latent antagonism. (Levine, 1979, pp. 29-30)

To manage our antagonistic responses, we must understand the factors that influence our communication with strangers.

I wrote the book from the perspective of the ingroup members being approached by strangers. Almost everything I say, however, also applies to strangers' communication with ingroup members. There are some differences in ingroup members' and strangers' communication due to different amounts of power (e.g., ingroup members usually have more power than strangers), position in society (e.g., being members of "majority" and "minority" groups), and experience with intergroup communication (e.g., strangers have more experience than ingroup members). I point these differences out when they affect the communication process.

Throughout this book, I draw attention to those factors that are given more weight when we communicate with strangers than with people from our own groups. Our stereotypes, for example, affect our communication with people from our own groups and our communication with strangers. Stereotypes are, however, less problematic in our communication with people from our own groups because our stereotypes of our own groups usually are more favorable and accurate than our stereotypes of strangers' groups. In order to improve our effectiveness in communicating with strangers, we must understand how unfavorable and/or inaccurate stereotypes affect the way we communicate.

Improving our communication with strangers requires that we become aware of how we communicate. Throughout the book, I provide suggestions on how we can become consciously competent. We are most effective in communicating with strangers when we engage in mindful learning and we are aware of the processes occurring when we communicate with strangers (Langer, 1997).

I draw on a theory of effective interpersonal and intergroup communication (i.e., anxiety/uncertainty management [AUM] theory) that I have been developing (the most recent versions are Gudykunst, 1995, in press) in what is written in this book. "There is nothing so practical as a good theory" (attributed to Kurt Lewin). I agree and go a step farther: training and practical advice must be theoretically based. While the book is based on a communication theory, I do not present the theory in detail. Rather, I focus on practical applications of the theory. I translate the theory so that you can use it to improve your abilities to communicate effectively, manage conflict with strangers, and develop relationships with strangers.

Each of us has a responsibility to communicate as effectively as we can with each other. To communicate effectively, we must transmit our messages in a way that strangers can understand what we mean, and we need to interpret strangers' messages in the way they meant them to be interpreted. If strangers do not try to communicate effectively with us, it does *not* relieve us of our responsibility. We also have a responsibility to react when we see others put strangers down. If we say nothing when we hear someone make a racist or sexist remark, for example, we are equally culpable (see the discussion of responding to prejudice in Chapter 3 and the discussion of ethics in Chapter 10).

I do *not* mean to suggest that we try to communicate intimately or try to establish a personal relationship with all strangers we meet. This is impossible. We can, however, communicate as effectively as possible with strangers, whatever our relationship (e.g., acquaintance, neighbor, co-worker, superior, subordinate) with them is. I also am not advocating that we hit our head against a brick wall. No matter how hard we try, it may be impossible to communicate effectively or establish a cooperative relationship with some strangers. In cases like this, we each have to make an individual decision when it is time to stop trying. We do not have to learn to deal with everyone, sometimes it is best to learn how to walk around strangers with whom we cannot get along (Prather, 1986). The important thing is that we do our best to communicate effectively with the strangers we meet, before we decide to stop trying.

In order to understand how to improve our communication with strangers, we have to recognize our normal tendencies when we communicate with them (i.e., how we communicate when we do not think much about our behavior). When we are not highly aware of our behavior, our communication is based on our implicit theories of communication. Our *implicit personal theories of communication* are our unconscious, taken-for-granted assumptions about communication. As human beings, we "construct theories about social reality. [Our] theories have all of the features of the formal theories constructed by scientists. They employ concepts and relationships derived from observation; they provide a structure through which social reality is observed; they enable [us] to make predictions" about how other people will communicate with us (Wegner & Vallacher, 1977, p. 21). We are not, however, highly aware of the theories we use to guide our behavior.

Since we are not aware that we are using implicit, unconscious theories to guide our behavior, we do not question our theories or think about how they can be modified. Not questioning our implicit theories leads us to assume that the predictions we make about other people's behavior (based on our implicit theories) are accurate. The predictions we make based on our implicit theories, however, are not always accurate. To be able to improve our accuracy in predicting other people's behavior, we must become aware of the implicit theories we use to guide our behavior and think about how they can be improved.

Our implicit theories tell us with whom we should communicate, when we should communicate with others, what we should communicate, how we should communicate with others, how we should present ourselves when we communicate, what effective communication is, and how to interpret other people's communication behavior. Because we learned our implicit personal theories of communication as we were growing up, they are based on the cultures in which we were raised, our ethnic backgrounds, our genders, our social classes, the regions of the country in which we were raised, as well as on our unique individual experiences.

When we encounter new or novel situations, we become aware of our behavior (our behavior is enacted consciously). One difference to be expected between our communication with people from our own cultures and people from other cultures, therefore, is the level of awareness we have of our behavior. We are more aware of our behavior with people who are from other cultures than we are with people from our own cultures. This is the case because interaction with people from other cultures is less routine and involves new and novel situations compared with interaction with people from our own cultures.

To help you assess the implicit theories of communication you use when interacting with strangers, I include questions at the beginning of some sections that are designed to help you become aware of aspects of your implicit theories. There are no "right" or "wrong" answers to any of these questions. Your answers may be different from the answers I provide when discussing the topic. Understanding your answers will help you bring your implicit theory of communication into conscious awareness. My answers are designed to help you understand intergroup communication and improve the effectiveness of your communication. In other words, you can choose to change your implicit theories. This requires conscious effort initially, but the more you engage in new behavior, the more automatic it becomes (see the mindfulness section at the end of the chapter).

I also include written skill exercises that are designed to help you understand your implicit theories and think about what you might do differently. In addition, I present self-assessment questionnaires designed to assess your tendencies regarding the major ideas presented (e.g., your anxiety when communicating with members of other groups).[7] Completing the skill exercises and self-assessment questionnaires can help you cognitively understand the material presented, and it will assist you in improving the effectiveness of your communication with strangers. I, therefore, urge you to complete the questions at the beginning of sections, the skill exercises, and the self-assessment questionnaires presented, and to think about your typical behavior when communicating with strangers, as you read the book. When completing the questionnaires, please keep in mind that they will help you understand how you typically communicate and improve your communication only if you answer them honestly.

Given this summary of my approach and the purpose of the book, I will overview the process of communication. In the next section, I examine the role of symbols, messages, and meanings in communication. Following this, I isolate the aspects of communication (managing anxiety and uncertainty) that are central to the theory I use to guide the book. I conclude by looking at factors that have more influence on our behavior when we communicate with strangers than when we communicate with people from our own groups.

An Overview of the Communication Process

We all communicate and consider ourselves to be experts.[8] We think we know what the problems of communication are and know how to solve them. Unfortunately, many of the things we take for granted about communication lead to ineffective communication, especially when we communicate with strangers.

Symbols and Messages

Language often is equated with speech and communication.[9] There are, however, important differences. *Language* is a system of rules regarding how the sounds of the language are made, about how sentences are formed, about the meaning of words or combinations of words, and about how the language is used. Language is a medium of communication. When the rules of language are translated into a channel of communication (e.g., the spoken word) using symbols, messages are created.

Take a few minutes to answer the following questions designed to get you to think about your implicit theory of communication before you read the material in the next two sections.

What does it mean when you say that you communicated with someone?

____

____

____

Do others typically interpret your messages the way you intended? If yes, why? If no, why not?

____

____

____

How do you know when there have been misunderstandings when you communicate?

____

____

____

____

The answers to these questions should provide some beginning insight into how you view communication in your implicit theory. Keep your answers to these questions in mind as you read this section.

Symbols are things we use to represent something else. Virtually anything can be a symbol—words, nonverbal displays, flags, and so forth. Referents for symbols can include objects, ideas, or behavior. The word "flag," for example, is used to represent a piece of cloth with stars and stripes that is attached to a staff and serves as the "national banner" in the United States. As disagreements over the meaning of flag burning indicate, the symbol means different things to different people. For some, it is sacred and should not be burned or devalued under any circumstances. For others, it is not held in such high esteem and burning the flag is an expression of free speech. The point is that there is no natural connection between a specific symbol and its referent. **The relationship between a symbol and its referent is arbitrary and varies from culture to culture**. It also varies within cultures, as the example of the flag indicates. While there is not a direct relationship between the symbol and its referent, there are direct connections between our thoughts and a symbol and our thoughts and the symbol's referent (Ogden & Richards, 1923). If we think of the referent, the symbol comes to mind; if we think of the symbol, the referent comes to mind.

We combine a set of symbols into messages that we transmit to strangers. *Transmitting messages* involves putting our thoughts, feelings, emotions, and/or attitudes into a form recognizable by strangers. The messages we transmit are interpreted by strangers. *Interpreting messages* is the process of perceiving and making sense of the messages and other stimuli from the environment we receive through our senses (seeing, hearing, feeling, touching, smelling, and tasting). How we transmit and interpret messages is influenced by our life experiences (e.g., our experiences with strangers, the emotions we have felt). These life experiences include our unique individual experiences, as well as our shared ethnic and cultural experiences. The important point to keep in mind is that no two individuals have the same life experiences. **No two people interpret messages in the same way**.

There are several possible channels of communication through which messages can be transmitted. We can transmit our messages through the spoken word, use nonverbal cues, or write them. If one person cannot speak or hear, sign language can be used. Alternatively, messages can be transmitted through mathematics or through artistic forms of expression such as painting, photography, or music. Only when the channel is the spoken word does speech occur.

Messages and Meanings

The term *communication* refers to the exchange of messages and the creation of meaning (e.g., assigning significance to messages). **Meanings cannot be transmitted from one person to another**. Only messages can be transmitted. When we send a message we attach a certain meaning to that message and choose the symbols and channel of communication accordingly. We rely on more than the behavior that strangers display (e.g., they may laugh) when we construct our messages. We also rely on our interpretation of strangers' behavior (e.g., they assume we are funny *or* they are laughing at us). The way we construct and interpret messages is a function of our perceptions of ourselves, the strangers involved, their behavior, and the way they send their messages to us. The strangers who interpret our messages, however, attach their own meanings to the message. The meanings attached to the message are a function of the actual message transmitted, the channel used, the environment in which the message is transmitted, the people who receive it, the relationship between the people, and the way the message is transmitted.

We do not transmit and interpret messages independently of one another. We engage in both processes simultaneously. When we transmit messages we are affected by how we interpret messages we are receiving from strangers, and we may even modify our messages based on the feedback we receive when we are transmitting messages.

We can distinguish between the content and relationship dimensions of messages (Watzlawick et al., 1967). The *content dimension* of messages refers to the information in the messages (e.g., what is said). The *relationship dimension* of messages is inferred from how the messages are transmitted (including the specific words used), and it deals with how the participants are relating to each other. The way we communicate offers a definition of the relationship between us. If we say the same words in an angry and a "regular" tone, we are defining different relationships with strangers. The children's saying "sticks and stones may break my bones, but words will never hurt me" is not accurate. The words we choose and the way we say them to others can and do hurt.

When we communicate we present ourselves as we want strangers to see us and respond to how strangers present themselves to us. We modify how we see ourselves based on the feedback we receive from strangers.[10] If others consistently tell us we are incompetent, for example, we begin to see ourselves as incompetent. Through communication we can facilitate strangers' personal growth or destroy them. Our ability to destroy strangers by our communication as "symbolic annihilation" (Gerbner, 1978).

Sources of Communication Behavior

Our communication behavior is based on one of three sources.[11] We might behave in a particular way because it is habitual. Alternatively, we might communicate in a particular way because we are trying to accomplish certain objectives. Finally, we may react emotionally without much conscious thought.

Take a few minutes to answer the following questions designed to get you to think about your implicit theory of communication before you read the material in this section.

Do you have to intentionally send messages for communication to take place? If yes, why? If no, why not?

____

____

____

____

When are you highly aware of your communication and when are you not very aware of it?

____

____

____

How do your emotions influence the way you communicate?

____

____

____

Your answers to these questions should provide some insight into the sources of communication in your implicit theory. Keep your answers to these questions in mind as you read the remainder of this section.

Habits. We engage in much of our behavior out of habit. We are not always aware of making decisions about the routines we enact. When we are communicating habitually, we are following scripts—"a coherent sequence of events expected by the individual involving him [or her] either as a participant or an observer" (Abelson, 1976, p. 33). When we first encounter a new situation, we consciously seek cues to guide our behavior. As we have repeated experiences with the same event, we have less need to think consciously about our behavior. "The more often we engage in the activity, the more likely it is that we rely on scripts for the completion of the activity and the less likely there will be any correspondence between our actions and those thoughts of ours that occur simultaneously" (Langer, 1978, p. 39).

When we are engaging in habitual or scripted behavior, we are not highly aware of what we are doing or saying. To borrow an analogy from flying a plane, we are on automatic pilot. In other words, we are mindless (Langer, 1978). We do not, however, communicate totally on automatic pilot; we pay sufficient attention so that we can recall key words in the conversations we have (Kitayama & Burnstein, 1988). When we communicate on automatic pilot, we interpret incoming messages based on the symbolic systems we learned as children. A large part of our symbolic systems are shared with other members of our cultures, our ethnic groups, our religions, and our families, to name only a few of our group memberships. Parts of our symbolic systems, however, are unique and based on specific life experiences. No two people share the same symbolic systems.

Much of our habitual or scripted behavior involves superficial interactions with other members of our cultures or ethnic groups in which we rely mainly on group-based information about strangers. The meanings we attach to specific messages and the meanings other members of our culture attach to messages are relatively similar. This is due, in part, to the fact that the cultural scripts we enact provide us with shared interpretations of our behavior. While there are differences in our meanings, the differences are not large enough to make our communication ineffective. Under these conditions, we do not need to consciously think about our communication to be relatively effective.

The greeting ritual is one example of a script. The ritual for greeting others reduces the vast amount of uncertainty and anxiety present in initial interactions with people we do not know to manageable portions and allows us to interact with them as though there was relatively little uncertainty or anxiety. The rules for the ritual provide us with predictions about how others will respond in the situation. When someone deviates from the script or we enter a new situation, we cannot fall back on the ritual's implicit predictions. Under these circumstances, we have to actively reduce our uncertainty and anxiety before we can make accurate predictions and communicate effectively.

Intentions. The second basis for our communication behavior is the intentions we form.[12] *Intentions* are instructions we give ourselves about how to communicate (Triandis, 1977). When we think about what we want to do in particular situations, we form intentions. Intention, therefore, is a cognitive construct—it is part of our thought processes. We may not be able to accomplish our intentions, however. My intention, for example, may be to be nonjudgmental in my interactions with strangers, but in actuality I may be very judgmental. My ability to accomplish my intentions is a function, at least in part, of my motivation, knowledge, and skills (discussed in Chapter 7).

We often are not highly aware of what our intentions are. People may not intend to send messages to others, but others may perceive that a message has been sent and react based on their interpretations. This is particularly problematic when the people come from different cultures. Consider an example of U.S. American businesspersons negotiating a contract in an Arab culture. During the course of a meeting, the businesspersons from the United States cross their legs and in the process point the sole of their shoes toward an Arab. The U.S. Americans, in all likelihood, will not attach any meaning to this. The Arab, in contrast, will probably interpret this behavior as an insult and react accordingly. The U.S. Americans did not intend to send messages, but one was received.

Showing the sole of the foot does not mean anything in the United States. In Arab cultures, however, showing the sole of the foot to another person is considered an insult. The misunderstanding can be explained only by looking at behavior that was not intended to be meaningful.

Emotions. The final factor on which our communication behavior may be based is our affect, feelings or emotions. We often react to strangers on a strictly emotional basis. If we feel we were criticized, for example, we may become defensive and verbally attack strangers without thinking.

Emotions are our affective responses to changing relationships between ourselves and our environment (Lazarus, 1991). If we perceive that we are being threatened, for example, we feel anxiety. We cannot, however, understand the emotion anxiety without taking into consideration what led to the perception of threat and the person from whom we perceive the threats. Whether or not we perceive a threat depends on our appraisal of the situation. Our appraisals of "harm or benefit, actual or potential, real or imagined" (Lazarus, 1991, p. 92) influence the emotion that is generated in a particular situation.

Our appraisals of situations do not remain static, they are in flux (Lazarus, 1991). One of the reasons that our appraisals are in flux is that we constantly receive new information from the environment, which we must appraise. These appraisals can influence how we interpret the feelings we have. Some of the changes that occur in our appraisals are due to our ability to cope. *Coping* involves our cognitive and behavioral efforts to manage our appraisals (Lazarus, 1991). There are two ways of coping with emotions. One way to cope is to remove the problem. This form of coping is not highly successful in communication with strangers because we usually cannot remove the problem. Another way to cope involves changing the way we attend to or interpret our emotional responses. This involves managing our emotional reactions cognitively.[13] I argue later in this chapter that this is necessary for effective communication to occur, especially when we communicate with strangers.

Self-Concept and Communication

Our *self-concepts* are our views of ourselves. Our views of ourselves are derived from how we view ourselves in particular situations and from our views of ourselves as members of various groups, our identities. We have three general types of identities: human, social, and personal (Turner et al., 1987).

Before reading the remainder of this section, take a few minutes to write as many responses as you can to complete the following sentence:

I am a(an):

____________________	( )	____________________	( )
____________________	( )	____________________	( )
____________________	( )	____________________	( )
____________________	( )	____________________	( )
____________________	( )	____________________	( )
____________________	( )	____________________	( )
____________________	( )	____________________	( )

I'll ask you to look at your responses here later in the section to analyze which are human, social, or personal identities.

Our *human identities* involve those views of ourselves that we believe we share with all other humans. We need to keep in mind that "people and their cultures perish in isolation, but they are born or reborn in contact with other men and women, with men and women of another culture, another creed, another race. If we do not recognize our humanity in others, we shall not recognize it in ourselves" (Fuentes, 1992, back cover). To understand our human identities, we have to look for those things we share in common with all other humans.

Our *social identities* involve our views of ourselves that we share with other members of our ingroups (Turner et al., 1987). Ingroups are groups that are important to us, with which we identify, and for whom we will make sacrifices (Triandis, 1988). Our social identities may be based on the roles we play (e.g., student, professor, parent), our demographic categories (e.g., nationality, ethnicity, gender, age, social class), our membership in formal/informal organizations (e.g., political party, religion, organization, social clubs), our avocations or vocations (e.g., scientist, artist, gardener), or stigmatized groups to which we belong (e.g., being disabled, being homeless, having AIDS).

The degree to which we identify with these various groups varies from situation to situation. To illustrate, while I am a U.S. American, I do not think about being a member of my culture much in everyday life. When I visit another country, however, my U.S. American identity (my cultural identity) becomes important. I think about being a U.S. American, and my cultural identity plays a large role in influencing my behavior.

Our *personal identities* involve those views of ourselves that differentiate us from other members of our ingroups—those characteristics that define us as unique individuals (Turner et al., 1987). What we generally think of as our personality characteristics are part of our personal identities.[14]

Take a moment to look back at your responses at the beginning of this section. In the parentheses after your responses indicate whether your response is a human (H), social (S), or personal (P) identity. The responses you listed first are probably those that influence your behavior the most. They might, however, be influenced by where you were when you responded. If you were sitting with all members of the opposite sex, for example, your gender identity might have come first because of the situation. I discuss social identities in more detail in Chapter 3.

Our communication behavior can be based on our personal, social, and/or human identities. In a particular situation, we may choose (either consciously or unconsciously) to define ourselves communicatively mainly as unique persons or as members of groups. When our communication behavior is based mostly on our personal identities, interpersonal communication takes place. When we define ourselves mostly in terms of our social identities, in contrast, intergroup communication occurs. It is important to recognize, however, that **our personal and social identities influence all of our communication behavior, even though one predominates in a particular situation**. When our social identities have a greater influence on our behavior than our personal identities, there is an increased chance of misunderstandings occurring because we are likely to interpret strangers' behavior based on their group memberships. In order to overcome the potential for misunderstandings that can occur when our social identities predominate, we must recognize that we share common human identities with strangers. At the same time, we must acknowledge our differences and try to understand them and how they influence our communication.[15] I discuss issues of effective communication in more detail later in this chapter.

Communicative Predictions

"When people communicate they make predictions about the effects, or outcomes, of their communication behavior; that is, they choose among various communicative strategies on the basis of predictions about how the person receiving the message will respond" (Miller & Steinberg, 1975, p. 7). Sometimes we are very conscious of the predictions we make and sometimes we are not highly aware of them. When we meet someone we find attractive and whom we want to see again, for example, we may think of alternative ways to arrange a next meeting or date, and then select the strategy we think will work best. Under conditions like this, we are aware of the predictions we make.

Take a few minutes to answer the following questions, designed to get you to think about your implicit theory of communication before you read farther.

What type of information do you use to predict others' behavior? How does this vary depending on your relationship with the person?

____

____

____

____

When are you conscious of making predictions about others' behavior and when are you not highly aware of making predictions?

____

____

____

How are the predictions you make about members of your own group similar to and different from your predictions about members of other groups (e.g., cultures, ethnic groups)?

____

____

____

Your answers to these questions should provide some insight into the role of predictions in your implicit theory of communication. Keep your answers to these questions in mind as you read the remainder of this section.

We use three different types of information in making predictions about others: cultural, social, and personal (Miller & Steinberg, 1975).[16] People in any culture generally behave in a regular way because of the norms, rules, and values of their cultures. This regularity allows *cultural information* to be used in making predictions. "Knowledge about another person's culture—its language, beliefs, and prevailing ideology—often permits predictions of the person's probable response to messages. . . . Upon first encountering . . . [another person], cultural information provides the only grounds for communicative predictions" (Miller & Sunnafrank, 1982, p. 226). If we are introduced to U.S. Americans, we can make certain assumptions about their understanding introduction rituals. We implicitly predict, for example, that if we stick out our right hand to shake hands, they will do the same.

When we travel to another culture or interact with people from another culture in our culture, we cannot base our predictions of their behavior on our cultural rules and norms. This inevitably leads to misunderstandings. If we want to communicate effectively, we must use our knowledge of the strangers' cultures to make predictions. If we have little or no knowledge of the strangers' cultures, we have no basis for making predictions. "This fact explains the uneasiness and perceived lack of control most people experience when thrust into an alien culture; they not only lack information about the individuals with whom they must communicate, they are bereft of information concerning shared cultural norms and values" (Miller & Sunnafrank, 1982, p. 227).

Social predictions are based on our memberships in or aspirations to particular social groups or social roles (Miller & Sunnafrank, 1982). Social information is the principal kind we use to predict behavior of people from our culture. Group memberships based on ethnicity, gender, religion, social class, disabilities, gender orientation, and so forth are used to predict strangers' behavior. Roles such as professor, physician, clerk, or supervisor, among others, also provide a basis for the social predictions we make.

Our cultural and social predictions are based on the categories in which we place strangers (e.g., member of my culture, not member of my culture). *Social categorization* is the way we order our social environments (i.e., the people with whom we come in contact), by grouping people in a way that makes sense to us (Tajfel, 1978). We may, for example, divide people into women and men, white and nonwhite, black and nonblack, "Americans" and foreigners, to name only a few of the sets of categories we use. In categorizing strangers and ourselves, we become aware of being members of social groups. A *social group* can be thought of as two or more people who define themselves as sharing a common bond (Turner, 1982). Once we place strangers in social categories, our stereotypes of people in those categories are activated. *Stereotypes* are the mental pictures we have of a group of people. Our stereotypes create expectations about how people from our own and strangers' groups will behave. They may be accurate or inaccurate, and strangers may fulfill our expectations or violate them.

When we base our predictions on cultural or social information, we are assuming that the strangers within the category (e.g., the culture or ethnic group) are similar. Strangers within a category share similarities (e.g., there are similarities people born and raised in the United States share), but strangers within each of the categories also differ. When we are able to discriminate how strangers are similar to and different from other members of the same category, we are using psychological data to make predictions. The use of *personal information* involves taking the specific person with whom we are communicating and how she or he will respond to our messages into consideration when we make our predictions.

We rely on cultural and social information in the vast majority of the interactions we have (Miller & Steinberg, 1975). There is nothing wrong with this. It is natural and it is necessary to allow us to deal with the complexity of our social environment. Imagine going into a restaurant and having to get to know your servers so that you can make personal predictions about their behavior before you place your order. This would complicate our lives and is not necessary. We can communicate effectively with servers without using personal information about the individuals. Social information is all that is necessary to get our order correct. The same is true for most other role relationships that do not involve extended interaction (e.g., with clerks, mechanics).

When we communicate frequently with someone in a specific role relationship, using personal data becomes important. Physicians who treat all patients alike (e.g., use only social data) will not be very effective. Successfully treating patients requires knowledge of them both as patients and as individuals (e.g., specific information about the other person and how he or she is similar to and different from other members of her or his groups). Communicating effectively with strangers also requires differentiating individuals from the groups of which they are members. Relying completely on cultural and/or social information when communicating with strangers over an extended period of time inevitably leads to misunderstandings. Effective communication requires that some personal information be used to predict strangers' behavior.

Managing Anxiety and Uncertainty

Interacting with strangers is a novel situation for most of us.[17] "The immediate psychological result of being in a new situation is lack of security. Ignorance of the potentialities inherent in the situation, of the means to reach a goal, and of the probable outcomes of an intended action causes insecurity" (Herman & Schield, 1961, p. 165). Our attempts to deal with the ambiguity of new situations involves a pattern of information-seeking (uncertainty reduction) and tension (anxiety) reduction (Ball-Rokeach, 1973).[18]

Uncertainty

"What constitutes uncertainty depends on what we want to be able to predict, what we can predict, and what we might be able to do about it" (Marris, 1996, p. 16). Uncertainty arises from our inability to predict or explain strangers' behavior, attitudes, feelings, and so forth (Berger & Calabrese, 1975). We perceive uncertainty "in situations which lie between two extremes of determinacy. At one extreme, we are so confident of our predictions that we no longer experience doubt at all; at the other, what will happen is so absolutely unpredictable it can only be treated fatalistically" (Marris, 1996, p. 18). Between the two extremes, we have to deal with our uncertainties. We do not just perceive uncertainties and try to manage them. "The way we understand the world, our purpose in it and our power to control our destiny leads us to them. The structures of meaning which make the world orderly and predictable also define significant uncertainties" (Marris, 1996, p. 18).

Take a few minutes to answer the following questions designed to get you to think about the role of uncertainty in your implicit theory of communication before you read this section.

What causes you to be uncertain about others' behavior?

____

____

____

What type of information do you need to know in order to be able to predict the behavior of members of your own groups?

____

____

____

What type of information do you need to know in order to be able to predict the behavior of members of other groups?

____

____

____

Keep your answers to these questions in mind as you read the remainder of this section.

"Uncertainty is a fundamental condition of human life" (Marris, 1996, p. 1) and we can never have complete predictability about anything or anyone (Watts, 1951). Our desire to reduce our uncertainty has a tremendous influence on our behavior, especially when communicating with strangers. "Uncertainty reduction is perhaps the most fundamental motivational process underlying group membership and group behavior" (Grieve & Hogg, 1999, p. 928). When we experience uncertainty about the situations in which we find ourselves or the outcomes of our interactions, we often look to our ingroups to reduce our uncertainty (Hogg, 2001; Mullin & Hogg, 1998). Looking to our ingroups to reduce our uncertainty, however, can lead to discrimination against outgroup members (Mullin & Hogg, 1998).

Often when we meet people in our own culture, the norms and rules guiding our behavior in the situation provide sufficient information for us to be able to predict and explain strangers' behavior. This, however, is not always the case. When the situation does not reduce our uncertainties, we try to reduce uncertainty when the strangers we meet will be encountered in the future, provide rewards to us, or behave in a "deviant" fashion (Berger, 1979).[19] Given that strangers, especially those from other cultures or ethnic groups, are likely to behave in a deviant fashion, it is reasonable to say we try to reduce uncertainty when we communicate with strangers more than we do when we communicate with people who are familiar. We tend not to be conscious of our attempts to reduce our uncertainty.

Uncertainty and Communication. There are two types of uncertainty present in our interactions with strangers (Berger & Calabrese, 1975). First, there is *predictive uncertainty,* the uncertainty we have about predicting strangers' attitudes, feelings, beliefs, values, and behavior. We need to be able, for example, to predict which of several alternative behaviors strangers will choose to employ. The second type of uncertainty is *explanatory uncertainty,* the uncertainty we have about explanations of strangers' behavior. Whenever we try to figure out why strangers behave the way they do, we are engaging in explanatory uncertainty reduction. The problem we are addressing is one of reducing the number of possible explanations for the strangers' behavior. This is necessary if we are to understand their behavior and, thus, be able to increase our ability to predict their behavior in the future.

There is greater uncertainty in our initial interactions with strangers than with people from our ingroups (Gudykunst & Shapiro, 1996). This does not, however, mean that we will be more motivated to reduce uncertainty actively when we communicate with strangers than when we communicate with people from our own ingroups. Strangers may behave in a deviant fashion (e.g., they do not follow *our* norms or communication rules), but we rarely see them as sources of rewards and we may not anticipate seeing them again in the future. When we do not actively try to reduce our uncertainty regarding strangers' behavior, we rely on our categorizations to reduce our uncertainty and guide our predictions. As indicated earlier, this often leads to misunderstandings.

Thresholds for Uncertainty. Some degree of uncertainty exists in all relationships. We can never totally predict or explain strangers' behavior. We all have maximum and minimum thresholds for uncertainty.[20] If our uncertainty is above our *maximum thresholds,* we do not have enough information to predict or explain strangers' behavior comfortably. When our uncertainty is below our maximum thresholds, we have sufficient information to make *some* predictions and explanations. We may not be highly confident of our predictions and our predictions may not be highly accurate, but we have sufficient information to be able to interact with strangers with some degree of comfort. If our uncertainty is below our *minimum thresholds,* we see strangers' behavior as highly predictable. When this occurs, there may not be sufficient novelty in the relationship for us to sustain interest in interacting with strangers. We may also think that we can predict strangers' behavior, but our predictions may be inaccurate (e.g., we become overconfident in our predictions). When we see strangers' behavior as highly predictable we, therefore, are likely to misinterpret their messages because we do not consider the possibility that our interpretations are wrong.

When our uncertainty is below our minimum thresholds, we are very confident in our predictions of strangers' behavior and we feel in personal control. Uncertainty above our minimum thresholds "creates the freedom to discover meaning. If there are meaningful choices, there is uncertainty" (Langer, 1997, p. 130). Some degrees of uncertainty also enhance our creativity. When we are mindful, we do not see information we have about strangers as static (i.e., unchanging). Rather, we realize that there are always ambiguities present. Realizing that there are always ambiguities leads us to be observant of strangers' behavior, which, in turn, leads to effective communication.

Generally, as we get to know strangers, our uncertainty regarding their behavior tends to decrease. Uncertainty, however, does not always decrease as relationships change over time. It also can increase. When we find out that strangers are engaged in competing relationships, when we lose closeness in a relationship, as well as when we find out that strangers have deceived or betrayed us, our uncertainty may increase (Planalp et al., 1988). Depending on the nature of the event and how we handle the uncertainty, increases in uncertainty can have positive or negative consequences for our relationships with strangers.

TABLE 1.1 *Assessing Your Uncertainty**

The purpose of this questionnaire is to help you assess the amount of uncertainty you generally experience when you communicate with strangers. (NOTE: You can determine the amount of uncertainty you experience communicating with a specific person by substituting the person's name for "strangers" in each of the statements.) Respond to each statement by indicating the degree to which the statements are applicable when you interact with strangers. If you "Never" have the experience, answer 1 in the space provided; if you "Almost Never" have the experience, answer 2; if you "Sometimes" have the experience and sometimes do not, answer 3; if you "Almost Always" have the experience, answer 4; if you "Always" have the experience, answer 5.

_____ 1. I am not confident when I communicate with strangers.
_____ 2. I can interpret strangers' behavior when we communicate.
_____ 3. I am indecisive when I communicate with strangers.
_____ 4. I can explain strangers' behavior when we communicate.
_____ 5. I am not able to understand strangers when we communicate.
_____ 6. I know what to do when I communicate with strangers.
_____ 7. I am uncertain how to behave when I communicate with strangers.
_____ 8. I can comprehend strangers' behavior when we communicate.
_____ 9. I am not able to predict strangers' behavior when we communicate.
_____ 10. I know what to expect from strangers' behavior when we communicate.

To find your scores, first reverse the responses for the even numbered items (i.e., if you wrote 1, make it 5; if you wrote 2, make it 4; if you wrote 3, leave it as 3; if you wrote 4, make it 2; if you wrote 5, make it 1). Next, add the numbers next to each of the items. Scores range from 10 to 50. The higher your score, the more uncertainty you experience when interacting with strangers.

Adapted from Stephan and Stephan (1985).

Assessing Your Uncertainty. Before proceeding, I want you to think about your uncertainty in communicating with strangers for the first time. Take a moment to complete the assessment in Table 1.1 now.

Most of us experience some degree of uncertainty in communicating with strangers. Scores on this questionnaire range from 10 to 50. There are *not* specific scores that we can use to indicate minimum and maximum thresholds. These are different for each of us.

Anxiety

Anxiety refers to the feeling of being uneasy, tense, worried, or apprehensive about what might happen (Stephan & Stephan, 1985). It is an affective (i.e., emotional) response, not a cognitive or behavioral response like uncertainty. Anxiety is one of the fundamental problems with which all humans must cope (e.g., Lazarus, 1991; May, 1977). **The amount of diffuse anxiety we experience influences our motivation to communicate with strangers** (Turner, 1988). If our diffuse anxiety is too high, we are not motivated to communicate.

Take a few minutes to answer the following questions designed to get you to think about your implicit theory of communication before reading this section.

What causes you anxiety when you communicate with members of your own groups (e.g., cultures, ethnic groups)?

____

____

____

____

What causes you anxiety when you communicate with members of other groups (e.g., cultures, ethnic groups)?

____

____

____

____

How is your anxiety manifested physically (e.g., butterflies, sweaty palms)?

____

____

____

Your answers to these questions should provide some insight into the role of anxiety in your implicit theory of communication. Keep your answers to these questions in mind as you read the remainder of this section.

Anxiety in Intergroup Communication. When we communicate with strangers we not only have a high level of uncertainty, we also have a high level of anxiety. Interactions with strangers tend to lead to fear across cultures (Wallbott & Scherer, 1986). Actual or anticipated interaction with strangers leads to anxiety. Our anxiety tends to be higher in intergroup interactions than in intragroup interactions (Gudykunst & Shapiro, 1996). The amount and quality of contact we have with strangers influences the anxiety we experience when we interact with them; the more contact and the more positive the contact, the less anxiety we experience (Islam & Hewstone, 1993).

Experiencing anxiety leads us to engage in social categorizations (e.g., put people in categories that make sense to us; create ingroups and outgroups) (Greenland & Brown, 1999). The reasons we experience anxiety can vary widely (e.g., because we do not want to appear prejudiced, because we have hostile feelings toward the outgroup; Greenland & Brown, 2000). Sometimes, however, the reason we think we are anxious is not the real reason we are anxious. We may, for example, think our anxiety is due to hostile feelings toward strangers' groups when our anxiety is really due to not knowing how to behave in the situation in which we find ourselves (Britt et al., 1996).

Our anxiety tends to be high when we interact with strangers we perceive as stigmatized. Stigmatized individuals have (or are believed to have) "a social identity that is devalued in a particular social context" (Crocker et al., 1998, p. 505). Non-stigmatized individuals' "anxiety stems from not knowing whether the stigmatized person will behave stereotypically, whether their behavior will seem appropriate, or whether the stigmatized person will judge them to be prejudiced" (Crocker et al., 1998, p. 541). Our anxiety will occur most frequently with people we have never met before and when we care what the stigmatized person thinks of us.

The anxiety we experience interacts with the situation in which the interaction takes place to influence our reactions to strangers (Britt et al., 1996). European Americans who expect to interact with African Americans and have high levels of anxiety, for example, perceive African Americans as more dissimilar to themselves and interactions with African Americans to be more difficult than European Americans with low levels of anxiety who expect to interact with African Americans or European Americans expecting to interact with other European Americans, regardless of anxiety level.

The anxiety we experience when we communicate with strangers usually is based on negative expectations. We fear four types of negative consequences when interacting with strangers (Stephan & Stephan, 1985). First, we fear *negative consequences for our self-concepts.* In interacting with strangers, we worry "about feeling incompetent, confused, and not in control . . . anticipate discomfort, frustration, and irritation due to the awkwardness of intergroup interactions" (Stephan & Stephan, 1985, p. 159). We also may fear the loss of self-esteem, that our social identities will be threatened, and that we will feel guilty if we behave in ways that offend strangers.

Second, we may fear *negative behavioral consequences* will result from our communication with strangers (Stephan & Stephan, 1985). We may feel that strangers will exploit us, take advantage of us, or try to dominate us. We also may worry about performing poorly in the presence of strangers or worry that physical harm or verbal conflict will occur.

Third, we fear *negative evaluations by strangers* (Stephan & Stephan, 1985). We fear rejection, ridicule, disapproval, and being stereotyped negatively. These negative evaluations, in turn, can be seen as threats to our social identities. We perceive communication with people from our own groups as more agreeable and less abrasive than communication with strangers (Hoyle et al., 1989). Our anxiety may make us appear to be prejudiced to strangers. "Discomfort resulting from the desire to be nonprejudiced combined with a lack of confidence in one's ability to act appropriately may be misinterpreted [by strangers] as stemming from hostility and prejudice" (Crocker et al., 1998, p. 515).

Finally, we may fear *negative evaluations by members of our ingroups* (Stephan & Stephan, 1985). If we interact with strangers, members of our ingroups may disapprove. We may fear that "ingroup members will reject" us, "apply other sanctions," or identify us "with the outgroup" (Stephan & Stephan, 1985, p. 160).

The amount of anxiety we experience in intergroup interactions is partly a function of the degree to which we feel in control (Fiske & Morling, 1996). The less powerful we feel in a situation, the more anxious we are. The greater the anxiety we experience, the more intrusive thoughts we experience. These intrusive thoughts decrease our cognitive capacity (e.g., we tend to think in a simplistic fashion). When we are anxious, we see strangers as easier to control than ourselves and we, therefore, often try to control strangers when we are highly anxious. Our "discomfort resulting from a desire to be [viewed as] nonprejudiced combined with the lack of confidence in [our] ability to act appropriately, may be misinterpreted [by strangers] as stemming from hostility and prejudice" (Crocker et al., 1998, p. 515).

Thresholds for Anxiety. We have maximum and minimum thresholds for anxiety. If our anxiety is above our *maximum thresholds,* we are so uneasy that we do not want to communicate with strangers, and we are not capable of gathering accurate information about them. If our anxiety is below our *minimum thresholds,* there is not enough adrenaline running through our system to motivate us to communicate with strangers. To be motivated to communicate with strangers our anxiety has to be below our maximum thresholds and above our minimum thresholds. The role of anxiety in interpersonal communication is similar to its role in our performance on tests. If we are too anxious, we do not perform well on tests. Similarly, if we are not at all anxious, we do not perform well. There is an optimal level of anxiety that facilitates our having "flow" experiences (e.g., optimal experiences; Csikszentmihalyi, 1990).

Our minimum and maximum thresholds differ. One way that we can tell if our anxiety is above our maximum threshold is by paying attention to our physical reactions. My anxiety, for example, is manifested in "butterflies" in my stomach. If I feel *a few* butterflies in my stomach, my anxiety probably is not above my maximum threshold. A few butterflies probably indicate a normal amount of anxiety (i.e., an amount between my minimum and maximum thresholds). When I do not feel *any* butterflies or nervousness, my anxiety is probably below my minimum threshold. If, however, we have a stomachache, our heart is racing, we are short of breath, and the palms of our hands are sweating, our anxiety is probably above our maximum threshold. The physical indicators each of can use will differ. By paying attention to our physical reactions, we can figure out when our anxiety is so high that we do not feel comfortable communicating, and when it is so low that we do not care what happens. To illustrate, by paying attention over the years I know that I am approaching my maximum threshold for anxiety when the butterflies are about one inch below my sternum. Once we know where these points are, we can cognitively manage our anxiety. Anxiety management is discussed in Chapter 7.

When our anxiety is high (e.g., above our maximum thresholds), we tend to process information in a simplistic fashion (Wilder & Shapiro, 1989). One reason for this is that when our anxiety is high, we are aroused and tend to be self-focused (Wilder, 1993). The self-focused attention distracts us from what is happening in our interactions with strangers and makes it difficult to make differentiations regarding strangers. Our explanations for why we experience anxiety also may affect how we respond (Greenland & Brown, 2000). If we have a "positive" reason for experiencing anxiety (e.g., not wanting to appear prejudiced), we should be able to process information systematically. If we have a "negative" reason for experiencing prejudice (e.g., hostile feelings for the outgroup), in contrast, we will process information simplistically.

Generally, as we get to know strangers, the anxiety we experience in interacting with them tends to decrease. I do not mean to imply, however, that anxiety continually decreases. While there is a general trend for our anxiety to decrease the more we get to know strangers, our anxiety can increase or decrease at any particular point in a relationship depending on what is going on in the relationship and how we interpret it.

Assessing Your Anxiety. Before proceeding, I want you to think about your anxiety when communicating with strangers for the first time. Take a minute to complete the assessment in Table 1.2 now.

TABLE 1.2 *Assessing Your Anxiety**

The purpose of this questionnaire is to help you assess the amount of general anxiety you experience when you communicate with strangers. (NOTE: You can determine the amount of anxiety you experience communicating with a specific person by substituting the person's name for "strangers" in each of the statements.) Respond to each statement by indicating the degree to which the statements are applicable when you interact with strangers. If you "Never" have the experience, answer 1 in the space provided; if you "Almost Never" have the experience, answer 2; if you "Sometimes" have the experiences and sometimes do not, answer 3; if you "Almost Always" have the experience, answer 4; if you "Always" have the experience, answer 5.

_____ 1. I feel calm when I communicate with strangers.
_____ 2. I get frustrated when I communicate with strangers.
_____ 3. I do not get ruffled when I communicate with strangers.
_____ 4. I am insecure when I communicate with strangers.
_____ 5. I feel composed when I communicate with strangers.
_____ 6. I feel anxious when I communicate with strangers.
_____ 7. I do not get excited when I have to communicate with strangers.
_____ 8. I feel stress when I communicate with strangers.
_____ 9. I feel relaxed when I communicate with strangers.
_____ 10. I am worried when I communicate with strangers.

To find your scores, first reverse the responses for the odd numbered items (i.e., if you wrote 1, make it 5; if you wrote 2, make it 4; if you wrote 3, leave it as 3; if you wrote 4, make it 2; if you wrote 5, make it 1). Next, add the numbers next to each of the items. Scores range from 10 to 50. The higher your score, the more anxiety you experience when interacting with strangers.

Adapted from Stephan and Stephan (1985).

Scores on this questionnaire range from 10 to 50. There are *not* specific scores that we can use to indicate minimum and maximum thresholds. As indicated earlier, these are different for each of us. I would suggest, however, that very low scores (e.g., 10-15) would suggest little motivation to communicate with strangers. Similarly, very high scores (e.g., 45-50) probably suggest that we would avoid communicating with strangers.

Take a few minutes to answer the questions below, designed to get you to think about how you view effective communication in your implicit theory of communication, before reading the following section.

How would you define effective communication?

____

____

____

How do you know that your communication is effective?

___

___

___

How do you know when your communication is not effective?

___

___

___

Keep your answers to these questions in mind as you read the next section.

Effective Communication

In the movie *Cool Hand Luke,* Paul Newman plays Luke, a man put in prison for destroying parking meters. While in prison, Luke constantly gets into trouble with the prison staff. At one point when Luke had not done something that the Warden asked him to do, the Warden says to Luke, "What we have here is a failure to communicate." On the surface, the Warden's statement makes sense. It is, however, incomplete. The Warden and Luke communicated, but they did not communicate effectively.

Effective Communication Defined

To say we communicated does not imply an outcome. Communication is a process involving the exchange of messages and the creation of meaning (Barnlund, 1962). No two people ever attach the same meaning to a message. Whether or not a specific instance of communication is effective or not depends on the degree to which the participants attach similar meanings to the messages exchanged. Stated differently, **communication is effective to the extent that we are able to minimize misunderstandings**. "To say that meaning in communication is never totally the same for all communicators is not to say that communication is impossible or even difficult—only that it is imperfect" (Fisher, 1978, p. 257).

When we communicate, we attach meaning to (or interpret) messages we construct and transmit to strangers. We also attach meaning to (or interpret) messages we receive from strangers. We are not always aware of this process, but we do it nevertheless. To say that two people communicated effectively requires that the two attach relatively similar meanings to the messages sent and received (e.g., they interpret the messages similarly). This can be viewed as basic communication fidelity—"the degree of congruence between the cognitions [or thoughts] of two or more individuals following a communication event" (Powers & Lowrey, 1984, p. 58).

Why Misinterpretations Occur

Communication is effective to the extent that the person interpreting the message attaches a meaning to the message similar to what was intended by the person transmitting it. This, however, is not what happens most of the time. The vast majority of the time we interpret strangers' messages using our own frames of reference. There are problems that emerge when we interpret strangers' behavior based on our own frames of reference:

> We see all behavior from our own internal perspective: what would that mean if *I* did it? And, of course, if I, as a member of my own group, did what that person did in the presence of other members of my group, it would be strange or bad . . . we don't usually extrapolate, we don't say, "Yes, but in *his* [or *her*] frame of reference, what would it mean?" We assume the possibility of direct transfer of meaning, that a gesture or act in Culture A can be understood in the same way by members of Culture B. Often this is true: there are universals of behavior, but as often that is a dangerous assumption; and by cavalierly ignoring the need for translation, we are making misunderstanding inevitable. (Lakoff, 1990, pp. 165-166)

When we are communicating with strangers and base our interpretations on our symbolic systems, ineffective communication often occurs.

The misunderstandings that occur when we communicate with strangers may be due to many different sources, including, but not limited to: (1) the messages may be transmitted in a way that they cannot be understood by others (e.g., pronunciation or accents may hinder understanding), (2) the communication rules of the cultures from which the communicators come may differ and influence how messages are interpreted (e.g., one person is being indirect and the other person is interpreting the messages using direct rules for communication), (3) one of the communicators may not be able to speak the other's language adequately (e.g., one person is just learning the other's language and is not fluent), (4) one person may not understand how to accomplish a certain task or interpret a specific utterance within a social context (e.g., a person who does not speak English well may try to complain to an English speaker and actually apologize), (5) one person may make errors in attributions because of his or her group identity and/or intergroup expectations (e.g., a U.S. American expects a Japanese to be indirect and does not recognize a direct answer to a question when it is given), and (6) the communicators may not be familiar with the topic being discussed.[21]

The participants in intergroup encounters may or may not recognize that misunderstandings are occurring. When misunderstandings are recognized within a conversation, communicators have three options: (1) to stop the thread of conversation taking place by shifting topics, (2) to negotiate the misunderstanding, and (3) to ignore the misunderstanding and continue the conversation (Gass & Varonis, 1991).

To illustrate the misunderstandings that can occur, consider a European American teacher interacting with an African American student raised in the lower-class subculture. The teacher asks the student a question. In answering the question, the student does not look the teacher in the eyes. The teacher, in all likelihood, would interpret the student's behavior as disrespectful and/or assume that the student is hiding something. Establishing eye contact is expected in the European American, middle-class subculture in the United States when you are telling the truth and being respectful. The student's intent, on the other hand, may have been to show respect to the teacher given that children in the lower-class African American subculture in the United States often are taught not to make eye contact with people they respect. Situations like this lead to misunderstanding and ineffective communication.

To further illustrate the misunderstandings that can occur when we communicate with strangers, consider the following example that involves a segment of interaction between a supervisor from the United States and a subordinate from Greece. In the segment, the supervisor wants the employee to participate in decisions (a norm in the United States), while the subordinate expects to be told what to do (a norm in Greece):

Behavior	*Attribution*
[U.S.] American: How long will it take you to finish this report?	[U.S.] American: I asked him to participate. Greek: His behavior makes no sense. He is the boss. Why doesn't he tell me?
Greek: I do not know. How long should it take?	[U.S.] American: He refuses to take responsibility. Greek: I asked him for an order.

[U.S.] American: You are in the best position to analyze time requirements.	[U.S.] American: I press him to take responsibility for his own actions. Greek: What nonsense! I better give him an answer.
Greek: 10 days.	[U.S.] American: He lacks the ability to estimate time; this estimate is totally inadequate.
[U.S.] American: Take 15. It is agreed you will do it in 15 days?	[U.S.] American: I offer a contract. Greek: These are my orders.

In fact the report needed 30 days of regular work. So the Greek worked day and night, but at the end of the 15th day, he still needed one more day's work.

[U.S.] American: Where is my report?	[U.S.] American: I am making sure he fulfills his contract. Greek: He is asking for the report.
Greek: It will be ready tomorrow.	(Both attribute that it is not ready.)
[U.S.] American: But we agreed it would be ready today.	[U.S.] American: I must teach him to fulfill a contract. Greek: The stupid, incompetent boss! Not only did he give me wrong orders, but he does not appreciate that I did a 30-day job in 16 days.
The Greek hands in his resignation.	The [U.S.] American is surprised. Greek: I can't work for such a man. (Triandis, 1975, pp. 42-43)

Clearly, the Greek and the U.S. American are attributing different meanings to the same behavior.

As these two examples illustrate, our cultures and ethnicities influence our explanations of the causes we make about strangers' behavior. The unique aspects of our symbolic systems also can be problematic when we are communicating with people we know reasonably well. In fact, it appears that we have as many misunderstandings with people we know well as with strangers.[22] One reason for this is that we *assume* that people we know well have meanings that are similar to ours (i.e., our uncertainty is below our minimum threshold). Since the topics of conversations we hold with people we know (including co-workers) are often more important than those we hold with strangers, small differences in meanings attached to messages may lead to misunderstandings.

It is important to recognize that **the misunderstandings that we have with strangers are the result of our interpretations of their behavior, not their behavior per se.**[23] I may say, for example, "You make me angry." This is not an accurate statement. While it is true I would not have experienced anger if you had not behaved in a certain way, my anger is based on how I interpreted your behavior, not your actual behavior.

To decrease the chance of misinterpretations of strangers' messages based on our unconscious interpretations, we must be aware of our normal tendencies. There are five principles that are useful in understanding how misinterpretations occur:

1. We can never know the state of mind—the attitudes, thoughts, and feelings—of other people.
2. We depend on signals, which are frequently ambiguous, to inform us about the attitudes and wishes of other people.
3. We use our own coding system, which may be defective, to decipher these signals.
4. Depending on our own state of mind at a particular time, we may be biased in our method of interpreting other people's behavior, that is, how we decode.
5. The degree to which we believe that we are correct in divining another person's motives and attitudes is not related to the actual accuracy of our belief. (Beck, 1988, p. 18)

Understanding these principles can help us improve the quality of our communication with strangers. Using the principles, however, requires that we be mindful.

Mindfulness

We must become aware of our communication behavior in order to correct our tendency to misinterpret strangers' behavior and to communicate effectively. Social psychologists refer to this as becoming mindful of our behavior.[24] There are three qualities of *mindfulness:* "(1) creation of new categories; (2) openness to new information; and (3) awareness of more than one perspective" (Langer, 1989, p. 62). One condition that contributes to being mindless is the *use of broad categories.* Categorization often is based on physical (e.g., gender, race, etc.) or cultural (e.g., ethnic background) characteristics, but we also can categorize strangers in terms of their attitudes (e.g., liberal-conservative) or approaches to life (e.g., Christian or Buddhist). "Categorizing is a fundamental and natural human activity. It is the way we come to know the world. Any attempt to eliminate bias by attempting to eliminate the perception of differences is doomed to failure" (p. 154).

What we need to do is learn to make more, not fewer, distinctions (Langer, 1989). To illustrate, consider an example of people who are in the category "cripple." If we see all people in this category as the same, we start treating the category in which we place strangers as their identities. If we draw additional distinctions within this category (e.g., create new categories), on the other hand, it stops us from treating the stranger as a category. If we see strangers with "lame legs," we do not necessarily treat them as "cripples."

Mindfulness involves being *open to new information* (Langer, 1989). When we behave on automatic pilot in a particular situation, we tend to see the same thing occurring in the situation as we saw the previous time we were in the same situation. If we are consciously open to new information, we see the subtle differences in our own and strangers' behavior that may take place. The more we think about how to behave in situations, the more appropriate and effective our behavior tends to be (Cegala & Waldron, 1992).

Being open to new information involves focusing on the process of communication that is taking place, not the outcome of our interactions with strangers:

> An outcome orientation in social situations can induce mindlessness. If we think we know how to handle a situation, we don't feel a need to pay attention. If we respond to the situation as very familiar (as a result, for example, of overlearning), we notice only minimal cues necessary to carry out the proper scenarios. If, on the other hand, the situation is strange, we might be so preoccupied with the thought of failure ("what if I make a fool of myself?") that we miss nuances of our own and others' behavior. In this sense, we are mindless with respect to the immediate situation, although we may be thinking quite actively about outcome related issues. (Langer, 1989, p. 34)

Focusing on the process (e.g., how we do something) allows us to be mindful of our behavior and pay attention to the situations in which we find ourselves. **It is only when we are mindful of the process of our**

communication that we can determine how our interpretations of messages differ from strangers' interpretations of those messages.

To be mindful, we must also recognize that there is *more than one perspective* that can be used to understand or explain our interaction with strangers (Langer, 1989). When we communicate on automatic pilot, we do not recognize strangers' perspectives. The mindset we bring to communication situations limits our abilities to see the choices we actually have about how to behave in most situations (Langer, 1989). When we communicate mindfully, however, we can look for the options that are available to us and not be limited by only those that came to mind in the situation. "In a mindful state, we implicitly recognize that no one perspective optimally explains a situation" (Langer, 1997, p. 108). When we are communicating mindfully, we can use all of the communication resources available to us rather than limit ourselves to those we use when we communicate on automatic pilot.

Recognizing alternative perspectives is critical to effective communication. Effective communication requires recognizing that strangers use their own perspectives to interpret our messages, and they may not interpret our messages the way we intended them. The problem is that when we communicate on automatic pilot, we assume strangers use the same perspective as we do. It is only when we are mindful of the process of our communication that we can determine how our interpretations of messages differ from strangers' interpretations of those messages.

Sometimes we become mindful of our communication without any effort on our part because of the circumstances in which we find ourselves. We become mindful of our communication: "(1) in novel situations where, by definition, no appropriate script exists, (2) where external factors prevent completion of a script, (3) when scripted behavior becomes effortful because substantially more of the behavior is required than is usual, (4) when a discrepant outcome is experienced, or (5) where multiple scripts come into conflict" (Berger & Douglas, 1982, pp. 46-47).

We often are mindful of our behavior when we communicate with strangers because they may act in a deviant or unexpected fashion, or we do not have scripts to guide our communication with them. The problem is that we usually are mindful of the outcome, not the process. Since we tend to interpret strangers' behavior based on our own frames of reference, to communicate effectively with strangers we need to become mindful of the process of our communication, even when we are engaging in habitual behavior. I am not suggesting that we try to be mindful at all times. That would be impossible. Rather, I am suggesting that when we know there is a high potential for misunderstanding, we need to be mindful and consciously aware of the process of communication that is taking place.

Uncertainty, Anxiety, Mindfulness, and Effective Communication

In general, as our uncertainty and anxiety decrease, the better we get to know strangers. Uncertainty and anxiety, however, do not increase or decrease consistently over time. Uncertainty, for example, is not reduced every time we communicate with strangers. We may reduce our uncertainty the first time we communicate, but something may occur the second time we communicate (e.g., strangers do something we did not expect) and our uncertainty might increase. Once we have established relationships with strangers, we can expect that our uncertainty and anxiety regarding strangers will fluctuate over time. As the relationships become more intimate, nevertheless, there should be a general pattern for uncertainty and anxiety to decease. To illustrate, there tends to be less uncertainty and anxiety in acquaintance relationships than in relationships with people we meet for the first time, and there is less uncertainty and anxiety in friendships than in acquaintance relationships. At the same time, within any stage (e.g., acquaintance, friend) of a particular relationship, uncertainty and anxiety will fluctuate over time.

We do not want to try to reduce our anxiety and uncertainty totally. At the same time, we cannot communicate effectively if our uncertainty and anxiety are too high. If uncertainty and anxiety are too high (e.g., above our maximum thresholds), we cannot accurately interpret strangers' messages or make accurate predictions about strangers' behavior. If anxiety is above our maximum thresholds, as it often is when we first meet strangers, we are too anxious to communicate effectively. When anxiety is above our maximum thresholds, the way we process information becomes very simple, thereby decreasing our ability to predict strangers' behavior (Wilder & Shapiro, 1989). When uncertainty is above our maximum thresholds, we do not think we can predict strangers' behavior. In many situations, however, there are sufficiently clear rules for communication that our uncertainty and anxiety are reduced below our maximum thresholds.

Even if our uncertainty and anxiety are below our maximum thresholds, either or both may still be too high for us to communicate effectively. To communicate effectively our anxiety needs to be sufficiently low so that we can accurately interpret and predict strangers' behavior. When anxiety is too high, we communicate on automatic pilot and interpret strangers' behavior using our own frames of reference (which leads to inaccurate interpretations and predictions). When our anxiety is too high, we must mindfully manage it (see Chapter 8).

If uncertainty and anxiety are low (e.g., below our minimum thresholds), we may not be motivated to communicate. If both uncertainty and anxiety are consistently below our minimum thresholds in particular relationships, for example, the relationships will become boring. When uncertainty is below our minimum thresholds, we also become overconfident about our predictions for strangers' behavior and we do not question whether our predictions are accurate. To communicate effectively, our uncertainty and anxiety both must be above our minimum thresholds.

Uncertainty and anxiety do not necessarily increase and decrease at the same time. We may reduce our uncertainty and be highly anxious. Consider, for example, a situation in which we predict very confidently that something negative is going to happen. We also may reduce our anxiety and have high uncertainty. To communicate effectively, our anxiety must be sufficiently low (well below maximum threshold, but above minimum) that we can reduce our explanatory uncertainty. If our anxiety is high, we must cognitively manage our anxiety (i.e., become mindful) if we are to communicate effectively.

When we have managed our anxiety, we need to try to develop accurate predictions and explanations for strangers' behavior. This requires we be mindful of our communication. When we communicate on automatic pilot, we predict and interpret strangers' behavior using our frames of reference. When we are mindful, in contrast, we are open to new information and aware of alternative perspectives (e.g., strangers' perspectives; Langer, 1989). If we focus on the process of our communication with strangers and try to understand how they are interpreting messages, we can increase the accuracy of our predictions and explanations for strangers' behavior.

When we are mindful, we want to negotiate meanings with strangers. That is, we need to try mindfully to understand strangers' meanings and ensure that they understand ours. The collaborative model of language usage suggests that meanings emerge in our interactions with others (Clark, 1996). We try to make sure that we share similar meanings for each utterance with others before proceeding. When we perceive a problem in our conversations that we think may lead to misunderstandings, we try to repair the problem (Clark, 1996). We use various conversational mechanisms (e.g., repetition) to ensure that meanings are negotiated (e.g., that they establish a common ground). Negotiating meanings with others involves creating and reflecting our identities in the situation in which we are communicating (Tracey, 2002).

When we are communicating with strangers, we tend to interpret their messages using our own frames of reference when we are not mindful. This frequently leads to miscommunication. When we are mindful, we can take strangers' perspectives into consideration (e.g., trying to understand strangers' meanings for their messages rather than using our frames of reference to interpret strangers' messages). This inevitably increases the effectiveness of our communication with strangers.

Study Questions

1. What leads to polarized communication with strangers?
2. How does being morally exclusive influence our communication with strangers?
3. Why is there always a difference in the meanings we attach to messages and the meanings others attach to messages?
4. What are the different sources of our communication behavior and how does our awareness of our communication vary as a function of the source?
5. How is our communication different depending on whether we communicate using social or personal identities?
6. Why do we experience greater uncertainty communicating with people from other ethnic groups or cultures than when communicating with members of our own ethnic groups or cultures?
7. What contributes to our anxiety when communicating with strangers?
8. How do our thresholds for anxiety and uncertainty influence our communication with strangers?
9. When we are mindful, what do we need to do to improve the effectiveness of our communication with strangers?

Applications

At the end of each chapter, I provide suggestions for ways that you can become more aware of your behavior when you communicate with strangers. I suggest that you do as many of the activities as possible and write your responses in a communication journal.

1. Over the next week, pay attention to the identities you use to guide your communication. Under what conditions (e.g., interacting with clerks in stores) is your communication guided by your social identities? Under what conditions (e.g., interacting with your best friend) is your communication guided by your personal identities? How do you communicate similarly and differently when your communication is guided by different identities (e.g., how is your anxiety, uncertainty, effectiveness of communication similar and/or different)?

2. Over the next week, pay attention to the times you think you communicated effectively and ineffectively with strangers. What did you do when you thought you communicated effectively (e.g., how did you communicate)? What did the strangers do when you thought you communicated effectively (e.g., how did they communicate)? What did you do when you thought you communicated ineffectively? What did the strangers do when you thought you communicated ineffectively?

3. Over the next week, pay attention to when you are mindful of your communication. Under what conditions are you highly aware of your communication? How is the outcome different when you are mindful of the outcome (e.g., the decision that will be made, what the other person will think of you), as opposed to being mindful of the process? Under what conditions do you tend to communicate on automatic pilot?

Notes

1. See Bill Moyer's PBS program "Beyond Hate" for a summary of Wiesel's position on hate.

2. The *Los Angeles Times* (June 8, 1993, p. H8) estimates that there are over 50 places in the world where ethnic conflict is occurring today. This estimate counts the ethnic conflict in the United States as one spot where tensions exist. See Ignatieff (1994, 1998a, 1998b) for discussions of ethnic hatred and ethnic wars and what might be done about them.

3. There are, for example, still instances of white students painting their faces black at fraternity parties in the United States (see Bartlett, 2001).

4. The animosity among the various groups is aggravated by the hate programs appearing on public access cable television in the United States (e.g., "Race and Reason"; see Zoglin, 1993).

5. This idea originally was used in *Communicating With Strangers* (Gudykunst & Kim, 1984, 1992). This book is much more "applied" than the earlier text. My focus here is on presenting material that can be used to improve communication effectiveness. I take a "culture general" approach; that is, I present general strategies for reducing uncertainty and anxiety that can be applied when you communicate with people from a variety of cultural and ethnic groups.

6. Stranger is a figure-ground phenomenon. Who is the stranger depends on the context. To simplify application of the material presented here I use the perspective of a person being approached by a stranger. In presenting the material, I arbitrarily use either the perspective of the "sender" or "receiver." I believe that these processes occur simultaneously, but separating the processes simplifies the presentation.

7. Most of the questionnaires presented are adapted from reliable and valid measures used in research. Some I developed for the purpose of the book. While I have not assessed the psychometric properties of the questionnaires, I believe they are all reasonable measures of the concepts under discussion.

8. Some of the ideas for this introduction were drawn from Fisher (1978).

9. My view of the nature of communication draws upon many different sources (e.g., Barnlund, 1962; Berger & Bradac, 1982; Berlo, 1960; Miller & Steinberg, 1975). It is influenced most by Miller and Steinberg (1975). I disagree with them in one important area, however. They argue that communication is an intentional activity. I will argue that communication can occur unintentionally. Here and throughout the book I will attempt to keep references to a minimum. The general sources for this section are specified above. When I use a specific scholar's position, I will cite the source in the text.

10. See Stewart (1990) for a detailed discussion of the transactional model of communication.

11. The sources of behavior discussed below are based originally on the work of Harry Triandis (1977, 1980, 1984). The specific discussion here is drawn from my extension of his work (Gudykunst, 1987; Gudykunst & Ting-Toomey, 1988).

12. Some scholars (e.g., Miller & Steinberg, 1975) argue that we must have intentions to call our messages communication. Obviously, I think this is only one of the sources of our communication behavior.

13. I will draw on models of cognitive therapy throughout the book, especially Beck (1988).

14. Deaux (1993) argues that the distinction between social and personal identity is somewhat arbitrary. "Personal identity is defined, at least in part, by group memberships, and social categories are infused with personal meaning" (p. 5). Trafimow, Triandis, and Goto (1991), however, demonstrated that personal and social aspects of the self are stored in different "baskets" in memory.

15. See Boulding (1988) for a discussion of "species identity."

16. Miller and Steinberg's actual terms are cultural, sociological, and psychological.

17. Intergroup encounters probably will continue to be novel for many people given the public school resegregation that is occurring (see Winter, 2003).

18. These two functions are drawn from my theory of interpersonal and intergroup communication (Gudykunst, 1988, 1993, 1995). I extended the work of Charles Berger and his associates (e.g., Berger & Bradac, 1982; Berger & Calabrese, 1975) on uncertainty reduction and Stephan and Stephan (1985) on anxiety reduction.

19. Kellermann (1986) has presented research questioning the anticipated interaction assumption. Kellermann and Reynolds (1990) provide data supporting the deviance and incentive (reward) value assumptions.

20. Kellermann and Reynolds (1990) found that tolerance for uncertainty influences our communication. This finding indirectly supports the argument made here. The minimum and maximum thresholds are catastrophe points. That is, there are sudden changes in other variables (e.g., effectiveness) when uncertainty or anxiety goes above or below either threshold.

21. Some of the sources presented are drawn from Banks, Gao, and Baker (1991).

22. Beck (1988) cites research on marital communication (e.g., Noller, 1980) to support this claim.

23. See Chapter 7 in Beck (1988) for an extended discussion of this process.

24. See Langer (1989). Langer's work provides the conceptual foundation for most of this section.

CHAPTER 2

Understanding Cultural Differences

Our cultures have a tremendous influence on the way we communicate, whether we are aware of it or not. We generally are not aware of how our cultures affect our behavior. To communicate effectively with strangers, we must understand how our cultures influence our communication. In this chapter, I examine how cultural similarities and differences influence the way we communicate with strangers. We can use our knowledge of cultural similarities and differences in communication to make accurate predictions of and explanations for strangers' behavior. There also are several other sources of diversity that affect our communication every day. I, therefore, discuss how ethnicity, gender, disability, age, and social class influence our communication in the next chapter.

Culture

Culture has been viewed as including everything that is human made (e.g., Herskovits, 1955) and as a system of shared meanings (e.g., Geertz, 1973), to name only two possible conceptualizations. Culture also has been equated with communication; "culture is communication and communication is culture" (Hall, 1959, p. 169).

Defining Culture

While there are many definitions of culture, it is necessary to select one to guide our analysis. I find the following definition useful because it treats culture as an implicit theory that guides our behavior:

> Culture, conceived as a system of competence shared in its broad design and deeper principles, and varying between individuals in its specificities, is then not all of what an individual knows and thinks and feels about his [or her] world. It is his [or her] theory of what his [or her] fellows know, believe, and mean, his [or her] theory of the code being followed, the game being played, in the society into which he [or she] was born. . . . It is this theory to which a native actor [or actress] refers in interpreting the unfamiliar or the ambiguous, in interacting with strangers (or supernaturals), and in other settings peripheral to the familiarity of mundane everyday life space; and with which he [or she] creates the stage on which the games of life are played. . . . But note that the actor's [or actress's] "theory" of his [or her] culture, like his [or her] theory of his [or her] language may be in large measure unconscious. Actors [or actresses] follow rules of which they are not consciously aware, and assume a world to be "out there" that they have in fact created with culturally shaped and shaded patterns of mind. We can recognize that not every individual shares precisely the same theory of the cultural code, that not every individual knows all the sectors of the culture . . . even though no one native actor [or actress] knows all the culture, and each has a variant version of the code. Culture in this view is ordered not simply as a collection of symbols fitted together by the analyst but as a system of knowledge, shaped and constrained by the way the human brain acquires, organizes, and processes information and creates "internal models of reality." (Keesing, 1974, p. 89)

Culture, therefore, is our implicit theories of the "game being played" in our societies.

We generally are not highly aware of the rules of the game being played, but we behave as though there was general agreement on the rules (Keesing, 1974). To illustrate, if we met a stranger from Mars and the Martian asked us to explain the rules of our cultures, we probably would not be able to describe many of the rules because we are not highly aware of them. We, nevertheless, use our theories of the game being played to interpret unfamiliar things we come across. We also use our theories in interacting with the other people we encounter in our societies. Members of cultures do *not* all share exactly the same view of their cultures. **No one individual knows all aspects of a culture, and each person has a unique view of a culture**. The theories that members of cultures share, however, overlap sufficiently so that they can coordinate their behavior in everyday life.

Cultural Norms and Rules

We learn to be members of our cultures from our parents, from teachers in schools, from our religious institutions, from our peers, and from the mass media. Originally, we learn about our cultures from our parents. Our parents begin to teach us the norms and communication rules that guide behavior in our cultures. *Norms* are guidelines of how we should behave or should not behave that have a basis in morality. *Rules*, in contrast, are guidelines for the ways we are expected to communicate. Rules are not based in morality (Olsen, 1978). Our parents do *not* explicitly tell us the norms and rules of our culture. They do not, for example, tell us that when we meet someone for the first time we should stick out our right hands and shake three times. Rather, they teach us the norms and rules by modeling how to behave and correcting us when we violate a norm or rule.

Once we are old enough to interact with other children, they reinforce the norms and rules we learned from our parents. We also learn additional norms and rules of our cultures from them. We learn how to be cooperative and how to compete with others from our peers. When we attend religious services or school we learn other norms and rules of our culture. The other way we learn about our cultures is through the mass media, especially television. Television teaches us many of the day-to-day norms of our cultures and provides us with views of reality. Television has become the medium through which most of us learn what others' expectations are for our behavior. It appears that the more television we watch, the more our views of reality overlap with others (Gerbner et al., 1980).

Cultures and Subcultures

As indicated earlier, the definition of culture I am using emphasizes that our cultures provide us with a system of knowledge that allows us to know how to communicate with others and how to interpret their behavior. The term *culture* usually is reserved to refer to the systems of knowledge used by relatively large numbers of people. The boundaries between cultures *usually* coincide with political, or national, boundaries between countries. To illustrate, we can speak of the culture of the United States, the Mexican culture, the Japanese culture, and so forth. In some countries, however, there is more than one culture.[1] Consider Canada as an example; there is the Anglophone (i.e., English speaking) culture derived from England and there is the Francophone culture derived from France.

I do *not* mean to imply that cultures are homogeneous (i.e., that the members are alike). All cultures are heterogeneous to some degree. The heterogeneity is due, at least in part, to the existence of subcultures within the larger cultures. *Subcultures* are groups within cultures whose members share many of the values of the cultures, but also have some values that differ from the larger cultures.[2] We can talk about ethnic subcultures, a subculture of the disabled, a Deaf subculture, an elderly subculture, social class subcultures, a student subculture, a business subculture, a medical subculture (people who work in medicine), a gay/lesbian subculture, and so forth. The subcultures of which we are members have norms and rules that we use to guide our behavior. These norms and rules share some similarities with the larger cultures, but they also are different from the norms and rules of the larger cultures (if they were not different, there would not be subcultures).

The norms and rules used to guide communication in the various subcultures overlap to some extent in every culture. If they did not overlap, people would not be able to coordinate their actions. While the United States is not highly homogeneous, there clearly is sufficient homogeneity for most people to know how to behave and coordinate their communication in most situations.

Throughout this book, I focus on how our cultures influence our communication. The relationship between our cultures and our communication, nevertheless, is reciprocal. Our cultures influence our communication *and* our communication influences our cultures. The influence of our communication on our cultures, however, does not take place over short periods of time. If people begin to communicate differently, over time, this will change their cultures. Most of the time we automatically follow the rules and norms of our cultures when we communicate because this does not require effort. Not following the rules and norms of our cultures, in contrast, requires effort.

How Cultures Differ

In order to understand similarities and differences in communication across cultures, it is necessary to have a way of talking about how cultures differ. It does not make any sense to say that "Masako communicates indirectly because she is Japanese" or that "Kimberly communicates directly because she is from the United States." This does not tell us *why* there are differences between the way people communicate in the United States and Japan. There has to be some aspect of the cultures in Japan and the United States that are different and this difference, in turn, explains why Japanese communicate indirectly and U.S. Americans communicate directly. In other words, there are dimensions on which cultures can be different or similar that can be used to explain communication across cultures. I refer to these as dimensions of cultural variability.

It is important to recognize that communication is unique within each culture and, at the same time, there are systematic similarities and differences. The similarities and differences can be explained and predicted theoretically using dimensions of cultural variability (e.g., individualism-collectivism). In individualistic cultures, for example, individuals take precedence over groups; while in collectivistic cultures, groups take precedence over individuals (Triandis, 1988). There are systematic variations in communication that can be explained by cultural differences in individualism and collectivism. To illustrate, members of individualistic cultures emphasize person-based information to predict each other's behavior, and members of collectivistic cultures emphasize group-based information to predict each other's behavior (Gudykunst & Nishida, 1986a).

There are general patterns of behavior that are consistent in individualistic cultures, and there are general patterns of behavior that are consistent in collectivistic cultures. Individualism and collectivism, however, are manifested in unique ways in each culture. In the Japanese culture, for example, collectivism involves a focus on contextualism (Hamaguchi, 1985), and the concepts of *wa* (roughly translated as harmony), *amae* (roughly translated as dependency), and *enryo* (roughly translated as reserve or restraint) are critical to understanding Japanese collectivism (Gudykunst & Nishida, 1994). Other collectivistic cultures emphasize different cultural constructs as part of their collectivistic tendencies (e.g., Latin cultures emphasize the family, African cultures emphasize the community). Understanding communication in any culture, therefore, requires culture general information (i.e., where the culture falls on the various dimensions of cultural variability) and culture specific information (i.e., the specific cultural constructs associated with the dimension of cultural variability).

Understanding where cultures fall on the various dimensions of cultural variability alone has tremendous practical value in improving the quality of our communication. To illustrate, if people from individualistic cultures are interacting with people from collectivistic cultures but do not know anything about the specific collectivistic cultures, the individualists can use general information about collectivism to make predictions about collectivists' behavior. Examples of how the information is useful will be presented throughout the chapter.

There are several different conceptualizations of how cultures differ. In this chapter, I emphasize the two dimensions of cultural variability that I have found most useful in understanding similarities and differences in communication across cultures: individualism-collectivism and low- and high-context communication.[3] I also discuss three other dimensions of cultural variability that influence our communication more briefly: uncertainty avoidance, power distance, and masculinity. I selected these three dimensions because we have data on where many cultures fall on each dimension (e.g., Hofstede, 2001).

Individualism-Collectivism

Individualism-collectivism is the major dimension of cultural variability used to explain cross-cultural differences in behavior.[4] This dimension of cultural variability has been isolated by theorists across disciplines, and by theorists in eastern and western cultures.

Cultural Individualism-Collectivism

At the cultural level, emphasis is placed on individuals' goals over group goals in individualistic cultures, and group goals have precedence over individuals' goals in collectivistic cultures (Triandis, 1988). Members of individualistic cultures, for example, promote self-realization:

> Chief among the virtues claimed by individualist philosophers is self-realization. Each person is viewed as having a unique set of talents and potentials. The translation of these potentials into actuality is considered the highest purpose to which one can devote one's life. The striving for self-realization is accompanied by a subjective sense of rightness and personal well-being. (Waterman, 1984, pp. 4–5)

Individuality is more important than group memberships in individualistic cultures.

Collectivistic cultures require that individuals fit into their groups. This is illustrated by the culture in Kenya:

> In Kenyan tribes nobody is an isolated individual. . . . First, and foremost, he [or she] is several people's contemporary. His [or her] life is founded on these facts economically, socially and physically. In this system group activities are dominant, responsibility is shared and accountability is collective. . . . Because of the emphasis on collectivity, harmony and cooperation among the group tend to be emphasized more than individual function and responsibility. (Saleh & Gufwoli, 1982, p. 327)

Group memberships are more important than individuality in collectivistic cultures.

"People are supposed to look after themselves and their immediate family only" in individualistic cultures, while "people belong to ingroups or collectivities which are supposed to look after them in exchange for loyalty" in collectivistic cultures (Hofstede & Bond, 1984, p. 419). The "I" identity has precedence over the "we" identity in individualistic cultures, and the "we" identity takes precedence over the "I" identity in collectivistic cultures. The emphasis in individualistic societies is on individuals' initiatives and achievement, and emphasis is placed on belonging to groups in collectivistic societies. People in individualistic cultures tend to be universalistic and apply the same value standards to all. People in collectivistic cultures, in contrast, tend to be particularistic and apply different value standards for members of their ingroups and outgroups.

Importance of Ingroups. The relative importance of ingroups is one of the major factors that differentiates individualistic and collectivistic cultures (Triandis, 1988). Ingroups are groups that are important to their members, in which members look out for each other's welfare, and will make sacrifices for each other. Individualistic cultures have many specific ingroups (e.g., family, religion, social clubs, profession, to name only a few) that might influence behavior in any particular social situation. Since there are many ingroups, individual ingroups, therefore, exert relatively little influence on behavior. In collectivistic cultures, there are few general ingroups (e.g., work group, university, family, to name the major ingroups that influence behavior in collectivistic cultures) that have a strong influence on behavior across situations.

The ingroup may be the same in individualistic and collectivistic cultures, but the sphere of its influence is different. The sphere of influence in an individualistic culture is very specific (e.g., the ingroup affects behavior in very specific circumstances), and the sphere of influence in a collectivistic culture is very general (e.g., the ingroup affects behavior in many different aspects of a person's life).

Collectivistic cultures emphasize goals, needs, and views of the ingroup over those of the individual; the social norms of the ingroup, rather than individual pleasure; shared ingroup beliefs, rather than unique individual beliefs; and a value on cooperation with ingroup members, rather than maximizing individual outcomes. Ingroups have different rank-orders of importance in collectivistic cultures; some cultures, for example, put family ahead of all other ingroups, and other cultures put their companies ahead of other ingroups (Triandis, 1988). To illustrate, the company often is considered the primary ingroup in Japan (Nakane, 1970), the family is the primary ingroup in many other collectivistic cultures (e.g., Latin America), and the community is the most important ingroup in other collectivistic cultures (e.g., most African cultures).

Self-Ingroup Relationships in Collectivistic Cultures. In most writing on collectivism, the self-ingroup relationship is portrayed one way. There are, however, three types of self-ingroup relationships that operate in collectivistic cultures: undifferentiated, relational, and coexistence (U. Kim, 1994).

The *undifferentiated facet* of collectivism "is defined by firm and explicit group boundaries, coupled with undifferentiated self-group boundaries" (U. Kim, 1994, p. 33). This form of self-ingroup relationship develops in one of two ways. First, some individuals have not developed separation from their ingroups and view themselves as "enmeshed" with their ingroups. Second, some individuals choose to give up their self-identities and immerse themselves in their ingroups (e.g., cult members). In this form of collectivism, individuals are "governed and defined" by their ingroups. Most discussions of collectivism (e.g., Triandis, 1995) are based on this type of collectivism. This form of collectivism is relatively rare and often is confused with the other two forms of self-ingroup relationships (U. Kim, 1994).

The *relational facet* of collectivism "is depicted by porous boundaries between in-group members that allow thoughts, ideas, and emotions to flow freely. It focuses on the relationship shared by in-group members" (U. Kim, 1994, p. 34). This form of collectivism requires "the willingness and ability to feel and think what others are feeling and thinking, to absorb this information without being told, and to help others satisfy their wishes and realize their goals" (Markus & Kitayama, 1991, p. 229). The qualities of this type of collectivism have been discussed in terms of *amae* ("dependence") in Japan and *chong* ("affection") in Korea.

The *coexistence facet* of collectivism separates the public self and the private self (U. Kim, 1994). The public self is "enmeshed with collectivist values" (e.g., ingroup solidarity, family loyalty) and "coexists with the private self, which maintains individualist values" (e.g., personal striving) (U. Kim, 1994, p. 36). In this form of collectivism, individuals follow group norms and fulfill their roles because collective actions "need to be orchestrated cooperatively and harmoniously" (p. 37). If individuals' goals are not compatible with the ingroup's goals, those individuals are expected to make sacrifices for the harmony of the group. This does not mean that individuals agree with the social norms or rules, however (U. Kim, 1994). This form of collectivism relates to the notion of *tatemae* ("conventions") and *honne* ("true intentions") in Japan. In Japan, individuals are expected to behave on the basis of *tatemae* (e.g., what is expected of them), not *honne* (e.g., what they want to do).

As indicated earlier, most analyses of collectivism focus on the undifferentiated facet of collectivism. The relational and coexistence facets of collectivism are used in Southeast Asian cultures (U. Kim, 1994). The relational facet is used in the Mexican culture, traditional African cultures, and Pacific Island cultures. The coexistence facet is used in the Bedouin Arab culture and Moroccan culture. The undifferentiated facet of collectivism is used in the United States more than it is in Japan

(Yuki & Brewer, 1999). The interdependent and distinct relational facet of collectivism is used in Japan.

Horizontal Versus Vertical Cultures. Individualistic and collectivistic cultures can differ in whether relations among people in the culture are horizontal or vertical (Triandis, 1995). People are not expected to stand out from others in horizontal cultures. In horizontal cultures, people tend to see themselves as the same as others, and there is an emphasis on valuing equality. People are expected to try to stand out from others in vertical cultures. In vertical cultures, people tend to see themselves as different from others, and equality is not valued highly.

In the horizontal, collectivistic cultures there is high value placed on equality, but little value placed on freedom (Triandis, 1995). To illustrate, in Japan there is a saying, "The nail that sticks out, gets hammered down," which illustrates that members of the culture are expected to not stand out. In vertical, collectivistic cultures (e.g., India) individuals are expected to fit into the group and, at the same time, they are allowed or expected to try to stand out in the group. People in vertical collectivistic cultures do not value equality or freedom. In vertical, individualistic cultures (e.g., United States, Britain, France, Germany), people are expected to act as individuals and try to stand out from others. People in these cultures place low value on equality and high value on freedom. In horizontal, individualistic cultures (e.g., Sweden, Norway), people are expected to act as individuals but, at the same time, not stand out from others. People in these cultures place high value on equality and freedom.

Summary. Before proceeding, think about how you can use the information about individualistic and collectivistic cultures to improve the quality of your communication. Assume that individualists are interacting with collectivists. After being introduced, the collectivists ask individualists questions like "Where do you work?," "Where did you go to school?," and "How old are you?" Some of these questions may seem inappropriate to individualists in initial interactions, and individualists may be "put off" by the collectivists' questions. If the individualists understand collectivism, however, they may realize that the collectivists are trying to understand the individualists' group memberships. This should allow the individualists to respond more positively to the collectivists than if they did not understand what the collectivists were doing.

Individualism-collectivism has been used widely to explain cultural differences in different types of behavior (see Triandis, 1990, 1995, for a summary). There are, however, problems with using dimensions of cultural variability to explain individual-level behavior (Kashima, 1989).

One area where there are problems is the area of developing causal explanations; it is impossible to test causal explanations of behavior based on cultural-level explanations (e.g., culture cannot be controlled in an experiment). The second area where there are problems is that not all members of individualistic and collectivistic cultures are individualists and collectivists, respectively. In other words, there are collectivists in individualistic cultures and individualists in collectivistic cultures. To overcome these problems, it is necessary to study individualism-collectivism at the individual level.

There are individual-level changes occurring in some collectivistic cultures. In Japan, for example, college students tend to be less collectivistic and more individualistic than working adults (e.g., those 30 or older; see Matsumoto et al., 1996, for an example study). These tendencies have been occurring for a decade or more. Similar patterns are occurring in other collectivistic cultures. The question is whether corresponding changes are taking place at the cultural level. There is no clear direct evidence that cultural changes are occurring in Japan (e.g., less emphasis placed on harmony in ingroups than traditionally occurs).[5] It probably will take a generation or two for the culture to change (e.g., when the younger people who are more individualistic and less collectivistic than working adults today are in positions of authority), assuming that the culture does not change the young people when they begin to work in organizations emphasizing collectivism.[6]

Individual Factors That Mediate the Influence of Cultural Individualism-Collectivism on Individuals' Behavior

Cultural individualism-collectivism has a direct effect on our communication behavior in that it affects the communication rules that we use to guide our behavior. Cultural individualism-collectivism also has an indirect effect on our communication in that it influences the way that we are socialized. Since members of a specific culture are not all socialized in the same way, they do not all learn the same general tendencies. There are at least three different individual characteristics that mediate the influence of individualism-collectivism on our communication: our personalities, our values, and our self construals.[7] Figure 2.1 illustrates how the influence of cultural individualism-collectivism on communication is mediated by these factors.

Personality Orientations. The effect of cultural individualism-collectivism on communication is mediated by our personalities. Idiocentrism and

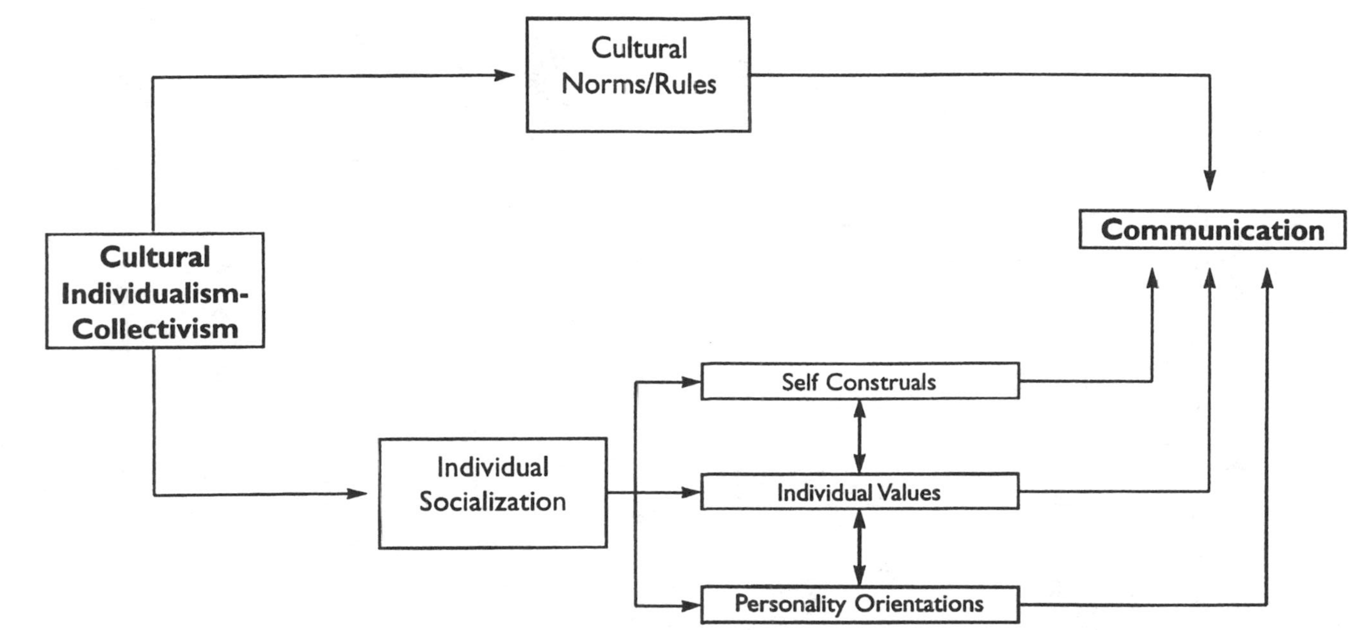

FIGURE 2.1 *Cultural- and Individual-Level Influences of Individualism-Collectivism on Communication*

allocentrism, for example, can be viewed as the personality orientations we learn as a function of individualism and collectivism, respectively (Triandis et al., 1985). Allocentrism is associated positively with social support, and negatively with alienation and anomie in the United States. Idiocentrism, in contrast, is associated positively with an emphasis on achievement and perceived loneliness in the United States.

The more idiocentric people are in the United States, the less sensitive they are to others' behavior (Gudykunst, Gao, Nishida, et al., 1992). The more idiocentric Japanese are, the less sensitive they are to others' behavior, the less they pay attention to others' status characteristics, and the less concern they have for behaving in a socially appropriate fashion. The more idiocentric Chinese and English are, the less they pay attention to others' status characteristics and the less concerned they are with behaving in a socially appropriate fashion (Gudykunst, Gao, & Frankly-Stokes, 1996).

Idiocentric individuals in individualistic cultures see it as natural to "do their own thing" and disregard needs of their ingroups, while allocentric individuals in individualistic cultures are concerned about their ingroups (Triandis et al., 1988). Allocentric individuals in collectivistic cultures "feel positive about accepting ingroup norms and do not even raise the question of whether or not to accept them," while idiocentric individuals in collectivistic cultures "feel ambivalent and even bitter about acceptance of ingroup norms" (Triandis et al., 1988, p. 325).

Collectivism at the individual-level involves the tendency to give priority to the collective self over the private self, especially when the two are in conflict (Yamaguchi, 1994). The more collectivistic Japanese are, the more sensitive they are to others and the less they have a tendency to want to be unique. These tendencies extend to people in Korea and the United States (Yamaguchi et al., 1995).

Individual Values. The second way that the influence of cultural individualism-collectivism on communication is mediated is through the values we hold. Our values are the central core to our personalities (Ball-Rokeach et al., 1984). Our values serve as the major component of our personalities that help us maintain and enhance our self-esteem. The type of values we hold influences the valences (positiveness/negativeness) we attach to different behavior (Feather, 1995). Our values influence the way we define situations, but they are not tied to specific situations (Feather, 1990).

Value domains specify the structure of values and consist of specific values (Schwartz, 1992). The interests served by value domains can be individualistic, collectivistic, or mixed. The value domains of stimulation, hedonism, power, achievement, and self-direction serve individual interests; the value domains of tradition, conformity, and benevolence serve collective interests; and the value domains of security, universalism, and spirituality serve mixed interests.

Individualistic and collectivistic values do not necessarily conflict. With respect to individualistic values, "hedonism (enjoyment), achievement, self-direction, social power, and stimulation values all serve self interests of the individual, but not necessarily at the expense of any collectivity. . . . These same values might be promoted by leaders or members of collectivities as goals for their ingroup" (Schwartz, 1990, p. 143). With respect to collectivistic tendencies, "prosocial, restrictive conformity, security, and tradition values all focus on promoting the interests of others. It is other people, constituting a collective, who benefit from the actor's [or actress'] concern for them, self-restraint, care for their security, and respect for shared traditions. But this does not necessarily occur at the expense of the actor [or actress]" (Schwartz, 1990, p. 143). We, therefore, can hold both individualistic and collectivistic tendencies. Even though we hold both individualistic and collectivistic values, one tends to predominate. In the United States, for example, there are collective tendencies and some subcultures tend to be collectivistic, but most U.S. Americans hold more individualistic values than collectivistic values.

In addition to the differences in values discussed here, there also are similarities in value priorities across cultures. "Benevolence, self-direction, and universalism values are consistently most important; power, tradition, and stimulation values are least important; and security, conformity, and hedonism [are] in between" (Schwartz & Bardi, 2001, p. 268). These similarities in values "can be understood as reflecting adaptive functions of values in meeting three basic requirements of successful societal functioning, ordered by importance: cooperative and supportive primary relations, productive and innovative task performance, and gratification of self-oriented needs and desires" (p. 287).

The questionnaire in Table 2.1 is designed to help you assess the degree to which you hold individualistic and/or collectivistic values. Take a few minutes to complete the questionnaire now.

Scores on the questionnaire range from 10 to 50 for both individualistic and collectivistic tendencies. The higher your scores, the greater your individualistic and collectivistic tendencies. While you probably have a tendency toward one orientation more than the other, you can have high or low scores on both. The important thing to keep in mind is that your tendencies affect your communication with people who have different tendencies.

TABLE 2.1 *Assessing Your Individualistic and Collectivistic Values**

The purpose of this questionnaire is to help you assess your individualistic and collectivistic tendencies. Respond by indicating the degree to which the value reflected in each phrase is important to you: "Opposed to My Values" (answer 1), "Not Important to Me" (answer 2), "Somewhat Important to Me" (answer 3), "Important to Me" (answer 4), or "Very Important to Me" (answer 5).

_____ 1. Having an exciting life
_____ 2. Being helpful
_____ 3. Having a sense of accomplishment
_____ 4. Being obedient
_____ 5. Being capable
_____ 6. Being polite
_____ 7. Being independent
_____ 8. Having harmony with others
_____ 9. Being intellectual
_____ 10. Being obedient to my parents
_____ 11. Having self-respect
_____ 12. Being cooperative with others
_____ 13. Being self-directed
_____ 14. Having solidarity with others
_____ 15. Being imaginative
_____ 16. Observing social rituals
_____ 17. Being ambitious
_____ 18. Being interdependent with others
_____ 19. Experiencing pleasure
_____ 20. Ordering relationships by status and observing this order

To find your individualism score, add your responses to the odd numbered items. To find your collectivism score, add your responses to the even numbered items. Both scores will range from 10 to 50. The higher your scores, the more individualistic and/or collectivistic your values are.

*Adapted from Gudykunst, Matsumoto, et al. (1996).

Self Construals. The third way the influence of cultural individualism-collectivism on communication is mediated is through the way we conceive of (think about) ourselves (e.g., Kashima, 1989; Markus & Kitayama, 1991, 1994a, 1994b; Triandis, 1989). The focus on self construal is important because how we conceive of ourselves is one of the major determinants of our behavior. The most widely used conceptualization of self construal is the distinction between independent and interdependent self construals (Markus & Kitayama, 1991, 1998; Markus et al., 1997).[8]

The independent construal of self involves the view that an individual's self is a unique, independent entity. Individualists' "goal of independence requires construing oneself as an individual whose behavior is organized and made meaningful primarily by reference to one's own internal repertoire of thoughts, feelings, and action, rather than by reference to the thoughts, feelings, and actions of others" (Markus & Kitayama, 1991, p. 226). The important tasks for people emphasizing an independent self construal are to be unique, strive for their own goals, express themselves, and be direct (e.g., "say what you mean"; Markus & Kitayama, 1991). Individuals' self-esteem is based on their abilities to express themselves, and their abilities to validate their internal attributes (e.g., have others see them as competent if they think they are competent; Markus & Kitayama, 1991).

"Experiencing interdependence entails seeing oneself as part of an encompassing social relationship and recognizing that one's behavior is determined, contingent on, and, to a large extent organized by what the actor [actress] perceives to be the thoughts, feelings, and actions of *others* in the relationship" (Markus & Kitayama, 1991, p. 227). The self-in-relation to specific others guides behavior in specific social situations. Depending on the situation, different aspects of the interdependent self will guide people's behavior. If the behavior is taking place at home, the family interdependent self guides behavior; if the behavior is taking place on the job, the co-worker interdependent self guides behavior. The important tasks for people emphasizing an interdependent self construal are to fit in with the ingroup, act in an appropriate fashion, promote the ingroup's goals, occupy their proper place, to be indirect, and read other people's minds (Markus & Kitayama, 1991). "Giving in is not a sign of weakness, rather it reflects tolerance, self-control, flexibility, and maturity" (p. 229). Self-esteem is based on people's abilities to adjust to others, and their abilities to maintain harmony in the social context when an interdependent self construal predominates (Markus & Kitayama, 1991).

When the interdependent self construal predominates, individuals try to maintain harmony in their ingroups. "Strong social bonds of interdependence do not imply actual harmony or affection, however. People may be extremely empathic, polite, gracious, and generous without loving and trusting each other" (Fiske et al., 1998, p. 925). Collectivistic cultures in which interdependent self construals predominate may be "characterized by extreme social tension" because "interdependence may make it difficult to express differences and resolve or escape conflict" (Fiske et al., 1998, p. 925).

Independent construals of the self *predominate* in individualistic cultures and interdependent construals of the self *predominate* in collectivistic cultures (Gudykunst, Matsumoto et al., 1996). By this I mean that members of individualistic cultures use independent self construals to guide their behavior more than members of collectivistic cultures, and members of collectivistic cultures use interdependent self construals to guide their behavior more than members of individualistic cultures. It is important to recognize, however, that everyone has both an independent and interdependent construal of the self. Further, people who emphasize interdependent self construals exist in individualistic cultures and people who emphasize independent self construals exist in collectivistic cultures. The critical issue is which self construal predominates to influence individuals' behavior in specific situations.

Situations prime us to activate our independent or interdependent self construals (e.g., Gardner et al., 1999). "The content of the working self-concept is determined by the social situation at a given time and by the person's current goals, affect, and motivational states. Once activated, the working self-concept orients and directs an individual's behavior so as to facilitate adaptation to a given social context" (Kanagawa et al., 2001, p. 91).

Table 2.2 contains short self-assessments of the strength of your independent and interdependent self construals. Take a moment to complete the scale now.

Scores on both scales range from 6 to 42. The higher your score on each scale, the more you emphasize this self construal. If you score high on both self construal scales, you tend to use the two self construals in different situations (e.g., you may use your independent self construals when interacting with your friends, and your interdependent self construals when interacting with your family).

Summary. Our personality orientations, individual values, and self construals mediate the influence of cultural individualism-collectivism on our communication. Our individual-level individualistic and collectivistic tendencies vary depending on the particular ingroup involved (e.g., Uleman et al., 2000). That is, we may have different tendencies with our families, co-workers, friends, relatives, or other ingroups to which we belong. This is true for our personality orientations (e.g., Hui, 1988), individual values (e.g., Matsumoto et al., 1997), or our self construals (e.g., Gudykunst & Nishida, 2002; Rhee et al., 1996).

TABLE 2.2 *Independent and Interdependent Self Construals**

The purpose of this questionnaire is to find out how you generally think about yourself and your relationship with members of groups to which you belong. Please answer each question by indicating the degree to which you agree or disagree with the item. If you strongly disagree with the item, answer 1. If you strongly agree with the item, answer 7. Feel free to use any number between 1 and 7.

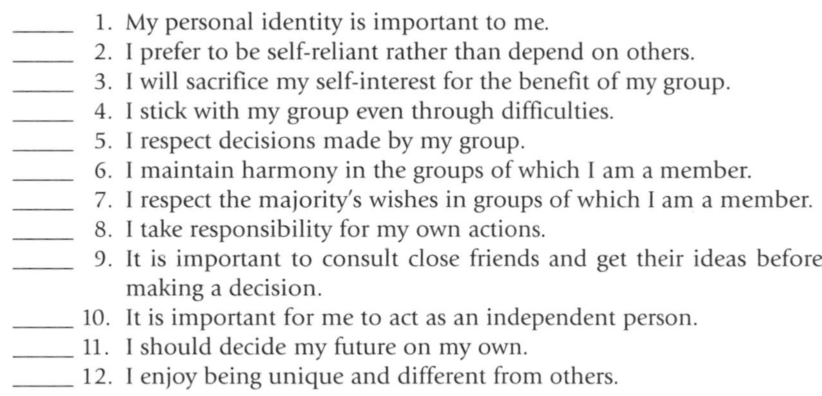

_____ 1. My personal identity is important to me.
_____ 2. I prefer to be self-reliant rather than depend on others.
_____ 3. I will sacrifice my self-interest for the benefit of my group.
_____ 4. I stick with my group even through difficulties.
_____ 5. I respect decisions made by my group.
_____ 6. I maintain harmony in the groups of which I am a member.
_____ 7. I respect the majority's wishes in groups of which I am a member.
_____ 8. I take responsibility for my own actions.
_____ 9. It is important to consult close friends and get their ideas before making a decision.
_____ 10. It is important for me to act as an independent person.
_____ 11. I should decide my future on my own.
_____ 12. I enjoy being unique and different from others.

To find your independent self construal, add items 1 + 2 + 8 + 10 + 11 + 12. To find your interdependent self construal, add items 3 + 4 + 5 + 6 + 7 + 9. Scores range from 6 to 42 for each scale. The higher your score on each scale, the stronger the self construal.

*These are short versions of scales developed by Gudykunst, Matsumoto, et al. (1996).

Low- and High-Context Communication

Individualism-collectivism provides a powerful explanatory framework for understanding cultural similarities and differences in behavior. While individualism-collectivism defines broad differences between cultures, the low- and high-context scheme focuses upon cultural differences in communication processes (Hall, 1976). A *high-context message* is one in which "most of the information is either in the physical context or internalized in the person, while very little is in the coded, explicit, transmitted part of the message" (Hall, 1976, p. 79). A *low-context message,* in contrast, is one in which "the mass of information is vested in the explicit code" (p. 70).

Low- and high-context communication are the predominant forms of communication in individualistic and collectivistic cultures, respectively (Gudykunst & Ting-Toomey, 1988). Both forms of communication, however, are used in both individualistic and collectivistic cultures.

Members of collectivistic cultures, for example, may use low-context communication in everyday communication, but anytime the harmony of the relationship (e.g., what they are saying might be perceived as face-threatening) or the ingroup might be threatened, they will use high-context communication. Similarly, members of individualistic cultures tend to use low-context communication most of the time, but they often use high-context communication to express emotions in intimate relationships (to name only one example).

The level of context influences all other aspects of communication:

> High-context [systems] make greater distinction between insiders and outsiders than low-context cultures do. People raised in high-context systems expect more of others than do the participants in low-context systems. When talking about something that they have on their minds, a high-context individual will expect his [or her] interlocutor to know what's bothering him [or her], so that he [or she] doesn't have to be specific. The result is that he [or she] will talk around and around the point, in effect putting all the pieces in place except the crucial one. Placing it properly—this keystone—is the role of his [or her] interlocutor. (Hall, 1976, p. 98)

To understand high-context communication fully, we must be raised in the culture in which it is used.

Members of individualistic cultures who use low-context communication tend to communicate in a direct fashion, while members of collectivistic cultures who use high-context communication tend to communicate in an indirect fashion. Communication in the Amhara culture in Ethiopia (a collectivistic culture) can be described as follows:

> The Amhara's basic manner of communicating is indirect, often secretive. Amharic conversation abounds with general, evasive remarks, like *Min yeshallal?* ("What is better?") when the speaker has failed to indicate what issue he [or she] is referring to, or *Setagn!* ("Give me!") when the speaker fails to specify what it is he [or she] wants. When the speaker then is quizzed about the issue at hand or the object he [or she] desires, his [or her] reply still may not reveal what is really on his [or her] mind; and if it does, his [or her] interlocutor will likely as not interpret that response as a disguise. (Levine, 1985, p. 25)

High-context communication tends to be indirect, and it often is ambiguous.

Communication in the United States (an individualistic culture) can be described in this way: "The [U.S.] American way of life, by contrast, affords little room for the cultivation of ambiguity. The dominant

[U.S.] American temper calls for clear and direct communication. It expresses itself in such common injunctions as 'Say what you mean,' 'Don't beat around the bush,' and 'Get to the point'" (Levine, 1985, p. 28). Low-context communication tends to be direct, precise, and clear.

People raised in cultures in which low-context communication predominates (e.g., the United States) tend to assume that high-context communication is ineffective. This is not necessarily the case. Indirect messages can be very effective in collectivistic cultures because members of the cultures understand how to interpret the contextual cues that tell them what the indirect messages mean. Outsiders (e.g., people raised to use low-context communication), in contrast, generally are not able to interpret the contextual cues and, therefore, assume that the indirect messages are ineffective.

Understanding differences in low- and high-context communication can help improve the quality of our communication with strangers. To illustrate, assume that individualists and collectivists are communicating and the individualists ask the collectivists a question expecting a direct answer (e.g., a U.S. American asks a Japanese "How do you feel about Americans writing the Japanese constitution?"). The collectivists, however, give an ambiguous answer to the question (e.g., the Japanese responds "People should write their own constitutions"). If the individualists do not understand high-context communication, the individualists may be angry that the collectivists were evasive. If the individualists understand high-context communication, in contrast, the individualists can try to interpret the ambiguous answer to the question rather than get angry. Depending on the relationship between the individuals and the situation, individualists can make an educated guess (e.g., in the example here, it easily can be inferred that the Japanese is not happy that Americans wrote the Japanese constitution). Low- and high-context communication is discussed in more detail in Chapters 5 and 6.

Individualism and collectivism exist in all cultures, but one tends to predominate. Table 2.3 contains a summary of the characteristics of individualistic and collectivistic cultures, and examples of cultures in which each predominates.

Other Dimensions of Cultural Variability

Individualism-collectivism is the major dimension of cultural variability used to explain similarities and differences in communication across cultures. There are, however, many other dimensions that also can be

TABLE 2.3 *Individualistic and Collectivistic Cultures*

Individualism	*Collectivism*
Major Characteristics	
Focus on individuals' goals	Focus on group's goals
"I" identity emphasized	"We" identity emphasized
Universalistic	Particularistic
Many ingroups influence behavior	Few ingroups influence behavior
Little difference between ingroup and outgroup communication	Large differences between ingroup and outgroup communication
Individual Level	
Idiocentric personalities	Allocentric personalities
Value stimulation, hedonism, power, self-direction	Value traditions, conformity, benevolence
Independent self construal	Interdependent self construal
Communication	
Low-context messages: direct, precise, clear	High-context messages: indirect, ambiguous, implicit
Example Cultures*	
Australia	Argentina
England	Brazil
Belgium	China
Canada	Egypt
Denmark	Ethiopia
France	Greece
Germany	Guatemala
Ireland	India
Italy	Japan
New Zealand	Korea
Sweden	Mexico
United States	Saudi Arabia

*Example cultures are based on predominate tendencies (Hofstede, 2001).

used (see Gudykunst & Ting-Toomey, 1988; Gudykunst & Kim, 2003; for dimensions other than those discussed here). In this section, I examine three other dimensions that have been linked to communication (i.e., those derived by Hofstede, 1980, 2001). These dimensions were selected because we know where a large number of cultures fall on each dimension. This is not the case for the vast majority of dimensions not discussed here.

Uncertainty Avoidance

In comparison to members of cultures low in uncertainty avoidance, members of cultures high in uncertainty avoidance have a lower tolerance "for uncertainty and ambiguity, which expresses itself in higher levels of anxiety and energy release, greater need for formal rules and absolute truth, and less tolerance for people or groups with deviant ideas or behavior" (Hofstede, 1979, p. 395). There is a strong desire for consensus in high uncertainty avoidance cultures, therefore, deviant behavior is not acceptable. People in high uncertainty avoidance cultures tend to display emotions more than people in low uncertainty avoidance cultures. People in low uncertainty avoidance cultures have lower stress levels, weaker superegos, as well as accept dissent and taking risks more than people in high uncertainty avoidance cultures.

Uncertainty avoidance should not be equated with risk avoidance. People in "uncertainty avoiding cultures shun ambiguous situations. People in such cultures look for a structure in their organizations, institutions, and relationships which makes events clearly interpretable and predictable. Paradoxically, they are often prepared to engage in risky behavior to reduce ambiguities, like starting a fight with a potential opponent rather than sitting back and waiting" (Hofstede, 1991, p. 116). The view of people in high uncertainty avoidance cultures can be summarized as "what is different, is dangerous" (p. 119), and the credo of people in low uncertainty avoidance cultures as "what is different, is curious" (Hofstede, 1991, p. 119).

There are several differences between low and high uncertainty avoidance cultures that influence intergroup communication. First, there are more "critical attitudes toward younger people" and a larger "generation gap" in high uncertainty avoidance cultures than in low uncertainty avoidance cultures (Hofstede, 2001, p. 160). Second, there is "suspicion of foreigners as managers" in high uncertainty avoidance cultures and "acceptance of foreigners as managers" in low uncertainty avoidance cultures (p. 160). Third, members of high uncertainty avoidance cultures reject members of other races as neighbors and believe that "immigrants should be sent back" home (p. 160). Members of low uncertainty avoidance cultures, in contrast, accept members of other races as neighbors, tolerate immigrants, and are prepared to live abroad.

Uncertainty avoidance is useful in understanding differences in how strangers are treated. People in high uncertainty avoidance cultures try to avoid ambiguity and, therefore, develop rules and rituals for virtually every possible situation in which they might find themselves, including interacting with strangers. Interaction with strangers in cultures high in uncertainty avoidance may be highly ritualistic and/or very polite. If people from high uncertainty avoidance cultures interact with strangers in a situation where there are not clear rules, they may ignore the strangers—treat them as though they do not exist.

Understanding uncertainty avoidance can help improve the quality of our communication with strangers. To illustrate, assume that individuals from low uncertainty avoidance cultures are communicating with people from high uncertainty avoidance cultures for the first time. The people from the high uncertainty avoidance culture appear to be highly anxious and nervous. If the people from the low uncertainty avoidance culture do not understand cultural differences on this dimension, they will probably assume that the other person is timid or shy. If the people from the low uncertainty avoidance culture understand this dimension, however, they will recognize that the anxiety probably stems from not understanding the rules operating in the situation or that the situation contains too much uncertainty for the people from the high uncertainty avoidance culture. By understanding differences on this dimension, members of low uncertainty avoidance cultures can increase the accuracy of their predictions about members of high uncertainty avoidance cultures.

The individual level factors that mediate the influence of cultural uncertainty avoidance on communication are uncertainty-certainty orientation (e.g., Sorrentino & Short, 1986; see Chapter 6 for a discussion of this concept) and tolerance for ambiguity (e.g., Budner, 1962; see Chapter 7 for a discussion of this concept). A certainty orientation at the individual level predominates in high uncertainty avoidance cultures, and an uncertainty orientation predominates in low uncertainty avoidance cultures. Low tolerance for ambiguity predominates in high uncertainty avoidance cultures, and high tolerance for ambiguity predominates in low uncertainty avoidance cultures.

Different degrees of uncertainty avoidance exist in every culture, but one tends to predominate. Table 2.4 contains a summary of the two types of cultures and example cultures.

Power Distance

Power distance is "the extent to which the less powerful members of institutions and organizations accept that power is distributed unequally" (Hofstede & Bond, 1984, p. 419). Individuals from high power distance cultures accept power as part of society. As such, superiors consider their subordinates to be different from themselves and vice versa. People in high power distance cultures see power as a basic

TABLE 2.4 *Low and High Uncertainty Avoidance Cultures*

Low Uncertainty Avoidance	*High Uncertainty Avoidance*
Major Characteristics	
Low stress and anxiety	High stress and anxiety
Dissent accepted	Strong desire for consensus
High level of risk taking	Low levels of risk taking
Few rituals	Many rituals
Small generation gap	Large generation gap
Acceptance of foreign managers	Suspicion of foreign managers
Members of other races accepted as neighbors	Members of other races rejected as neighbors
What is different is curious	What is different is dangerous
Individual-Level	
Uncertainty orientation	Certainty orientation
High tolerance for ambiguity	Low tolerance for ambiguity
Example Cultures*	
Canada	Egypt
Denmark	Argentina
England	Belgium
Hong Kong	Chile
India	France
Jamaica	Greece
Sweden	Japan
United States	Mexico

*Example cultures are based on the predominate tendencies in each culture (Hofstede, 2001).

fact of life in society, and stress coercive or referent power, while people in low power distance cultures believe power should be used only when it is legitimate and prefer expert or legitimate power. "In small power distance countries there is limited dependence of subordinates on bosses, and a preference for consultation, that is, *interdependence* between boss and subordinate. The emotional distance between them is relatively small: subordinates will quite readily approach and contradict their bosses. In large power distance countries there is considerable dependence of subordinates on bosses" (Hofstede, 1991, p. 27). The power distance dimension clearly focuses on the relationships between people of different statuses (e.g., superiors and subordinates in organizations).

There is "latent conflict between the powerful and the powerless" in high power distance cultures and there is "latent harmony between the powerful and the powerless" in low power distance cultures (Hofstede, 2001, p. 98). In high power distance cultures, "older people are respected and feared" (p. 98). In low power distance cultures, in contrast, "older people [are] neither respected nor feared" (p. 98).

Power distance is useful in understanding strangers' behavior in role relationships, particularly those involving different degrees of power or authority. People from high power distance cultures, for example, do not question their superiors' orders. They expect to be told what to do. People in low power distance cultures, in contrast, do not necessarily accept superiors' orders at face value; they want to know why they should follow them. When people from the two different systems interact, misunderstanding is likely unless one, or both, understands the other person's system.

Understanding cultural differences in power distance can help improve the quality of our communication with strangers. If members of low power distance cultures are working in a high power distance culture, they will probably interpret their supervisor telling them what to do at work as a personal trait (e.g., the supervisor is authoritarian) if they do not understand cultural differences on this dimension. If they do understand differences on this dimension, however, they will recognize the supervisor telling them what to do as a characteristic of high power distance cultures, not a personal trait. This, in turn, will allow them to interact more effectively with the supervisor than if they did not recognize the cultural differences.

The individual-level factor that mediates the influence of cultural power distance on communication is egalitarianism (Gudykunst, 1995). Egalitarianism involves viewing others as equals. High egalitarianism is related to low power distance and low egalitarianism is related to high power distance. Another individual-level factor that should mediate cultural power distance is social dominance orientation (Pratto et al., 1994; Sidanius & Pratto, 1999). Individuals who are high in social dominance orientation view social hierarchies (e.g., power differences) as natural and desirable and, therefore, predominate in high power distance cultures.

Low and high power distance tendencies exist in all cultures, but one tends to predominate. Table 2.5 contains a summary of the two types of cultures, and examples of the cultures in which the tendencies predominate.

TABLE 2.5 *Low and High Power Distance Cultures*

Low Power Distance	*High Power Distance*
Major Characteristics	
Individuals viewed as equals	Individuals viewed as unequal
Emphasis on legitimate power	Emphasis on coercive/referent power
Superiors and subordinates are interdependent	Subordinates are dependent on superiors
Obedience of children to parents not valued	Obedience of children to parents valued highly
Old people not respected or feared	Old people respected and feared
Individual Level	
High egalitarianism	Low egalitarianism
Low social dominance orientation	High social dominance orientation
Example Cultures*	
Australia	Egypt
Canada	Ethiopia
Denmark	Ghana
Germany	India
Ireland	Malaysia
Israel	Nigeria
New Zealand	Panama
Sweden	Saudi Arabia
United States	Venezuela

*Example cultures are based on the predominate tendencies in each culture (Hofstede, 2001).

Masculinity-Femininity

The focus of the cultural masculinity-femininity dimension of cultural variability is on the gender roles in cultures. "*Masculinity* pertains to societies in which social gender roles are clearly distinct (i.e., men are supposed to be assertive, tough, and focused on material success whereas women are supposed to be more modest, tender, and concerned with the quality of life); *femininity* pertains to societies in which social gender roles overlap (i.e., both men and women are supposed to be modest, tender, and concerned with the quality of life)" (Hofstede, 1991, pp. 82–83). People in highly masculine cultures value things, power, and assertiveness, while people in cultures low on masculinity or high on femininity value quality of life and nurturance (Hofstede, 1980). Members of highly masculine cultures emphasize differentiated sex roles, performance, ambition, and independence. Members of cultures low on masculinity, in contrast, value fluid sex roles, quality of life, service, and interdependence.

Masculinity-femininity is useful in understanding cultural differences and similarities in opposite-sex and same-sex relationships. People from highly masculine cultures, for example, tend to have little contact with members of the opposite-sex when they are growing up. They tend to see same-sex relationships as more intimate than opposite-sex relationships. For people from a feminine culture to communicate effectively with strangers from a masculine culture, especially if they are male and female, they must understand the others' orientation toward sex-roles.

Understanding cultural differences in masculinity-femininity can help improve the quality of our communication with strangers. If people from feminine cultures, for example, are working in masculine cultures, they are likely to interpret a relatively low level of communication between husbands and wives as lack of love if they do not understand this dimension. If they understand this dimension, however, they will recognize that the sex-role specialization in masculine cultures leads to little open communication between husbands and wives.

The individual-level factor that mediates the influence of cultural masculinity-femininity on communication is psychological sex-roles (Gudykunst, 1995; see Bem, 1974; discussed in Chapter 3). Androgyny and undifferentiated sex-roles predominate in feminine cultures, and high masculinity and high femininity sex-roles predominate in masculine cultures.

As with the other dimensions of cultural variability, both masculinity and femininity tendencies exist in all cultures. One tendency, however, tends to predominate. Table 2.6 contains a summary of this dimension and examples of cultures in which masculinity and femininity predominate.

Cultural Identity

Our *cultural identities* are our social identities that focus on our membership in our cultures. Take a few minutes to answer the following questions designed to help you understand your implicit theory of communication before reading the remainder of this section. Think of

TABLE 2.6 *Masculine and Feminine Cultures*

Masculine	*Feminine*
Major Characteristics	
Differentiated gender-roles	Overlapping gender-roles
Values power, assertiveness, performance	Values quality of life, service, nurturance
Sympathy for strong	Sympathy for weak
"Live in order to work"	"Work in order to live"
Emphasis on performance and ambition	Emphasis on quality of life and service
Individual Level	
Masculine/feminine sex-roles	Androgyny/undifferentiated sex-roles
Example Cultures*	
Arab cultures	Chile
Austria	Costa Rica
Germany	Denmark
Italy	East African cultures
Jamaica	Finland
Japan	Netherlands
Mexico	Norway
New Zealand	Portugal
Switzerland	Sweden
Venezuela	Thailand

*Example cultures are based on predominate tendencies in each culture (Hofstede, 2001).

being a member of your culture (e.g., being an "American") when you answer the questions.

What does it mean to you to be a member of your culture?

____

____

____

How does being a member of your culture influence your communication?

____

____

____

In what situations does being a member of your culture influence your behavior the most? The least?

____

____

____

Your answers to these questions should provide some insight into the importance of your cultural identity in your implicit theory of communication. Keep your answers to these questions in mind as you read the remainder of this section.

Our cultural identities have a tremendous influence on our communication in everyday life, but we generally are not highly aware of their influence. We become aware of the influence of our cultural identities on our communication when we find ourselves in another culture or in a situation in our cultures where we are interacting with members of other cultures.

There are two issues that need to be addressed with respect to our cultural identities. First, how strongly do we identify with our cultures? Second, what is the content of our cultural identities?

Strength of Cultural Identity

The strength of our cultural identities involves the degree to which we see our cultures as important in the way we define ourselves.[9] U.S. Americans' cultural identities, for example, involve the degree to which they identify with being "Americans." We tend to see our cultures as more important in how we define ourselves when we are in another culture than when we are in our own cultures. People who have lived in other cultures see themselves as more similar to others sharing their cultural identities and rate the content of their cultural identities more positively than people who have not lived abroad (Kosmitzki, 1996). Asian Americans, European Americans, and Latino(a) Americans identify with the U.S. culture more than African Americans (Ting-Toomey et al., 2000).

Table 2.7 contains a questionnaire designed to assess the strength of your cultural identity. Take a few minutes to complete it now.

Scores on the cultural identity questionnaire range from 10 to 50. The higher your score, the stronger you identify with your culture. As I indicated earlier, we are more aware of our cultural identities when we find ourselves in another culture than when we are in our own

TABLE 2.7 *Assessing the Strength of Your Cultural Identity**

The purpose of this questionnaire is to help you think about the degree to which you identify with being a member of your national culture. Respond to each statement by indicating the degree to which the statement is true regarding the way you typically think about yourself. When you think about yourself, is the statement "Always False" (answer 1), "Mostly False" (answer 2), "Sometimes True and Sometimes False" (answer 3), "Mostly True" (answer 4), or "Always True" (answer 5)?

_____ 1. Being a member of my culture is important to me.
_____ 2. Thinking about myself as a member of my culture is not central to how I define myself.
_____ 3. I have a positive view of my culture.
_____ 4. I rarely think about being a member of my culture.
_____ 5. Being a member of my culture plays a large role in my life.
_____ 6. It does not bother me if others do not recognize me as a member of my culture.
_____ 7. I enjoy being a member of my culture.
_____ 8. I rarely choose to express my culture in the way I communicate.
_____ 9. I like the things that make me a member of my culture and different from people in other cultures.
_____ 10. If I were born again, I would want to be born as a member of a different culture.

To find your score, first reverse the responses for the even numbered items (i.e., if you wrote 1, make it 5; if you wrote 2, make it 4; if you wrote 3, leave it as 3; if you wrote 4, make it 2; if you wrote 5, make it 1). Next, add the numbers next to each of the statements. Scores range from 10 to 50. The higher your score, the more you identify with your culture.

*Adapted in part from Hofman (1985).

culture. If your score is low, it may not mean that you do not identify strongly with your culture, but only that you are not aware of how important your culture is to you. If you visit another culture and complete this questionnaire after you have been there for a day or two, you will probably see that your score is higher than when you completed it just now.

Content of Cultural Identities

The second aspect of our cultural identities is the content of our cultural identities. Each of the dimensions of cultural variability discussed in this chapter contributes to the content of our cultural identities. The one that influences our communication with strangers the most, however, appears to be individualism-collectivism. I, therefore, focus on this dimension here.

Individualistic and collectivistic tendencies exist in all cultures, but one tends to predominate. Everyone, however, has individualistic and collectivistic thoughts. It is possible, therefore, for there to be collectivists in an individualistic culture and individualists in collectivistic cultures. Individuals' collectivistic tendencies involve three factors: subordinating individual goals to group goals, viewing the ingroup as an extension of the self, and having a strong ingroup identity (Triandis et al., 1985). As indicated earlier, individualistic and collectivistic values do not necessarily conflict (Schwartz, 1990). We, therefore, can hold both individualistic and collectivistic tendencies.[10]

The strength with which we identify with our cultures influences the content of our cultural identities (e.g., the values we hold). U.S. Americans who strongly identify with their culture, for example, value freedom, social recognition, and independence more than U.S. Americans who weakly identify with their culture and more than Japanese who strongly identify with their culture. Japanese who strongly identify with their culture, in contrast, value self-sacrifice, harmony, and accepting traditions more than Japanese who weakly identify with their culture and U.S. Americans who strongly identify with their culture (Gudykunst & Nishida, 1999). Asian Americans who strongly identify with the U.S. culture emphasize their independent self construals and hold individualistic values more than those who weakly identify with the U.S. culture (Gudykunst, 2001).

When we communicate with people from other cultures, we start from the assumption that the members of the other culture are similar. People from individualistic cultures, for example, assume that people in collectivistic cultures act collectively. This provides valuable information on how to communicate with people from collectivistic cultures. To illustrate, it allows us to predict that people in collectivistic cultures emphasize their social identities over their personal identities when they communicate.[11] To communicate effectively with specific members of collectivistic cultures, however, we must also recognize that not all people in collectivistic cultures emphasize their collectivistic tendencies; some are highly individualistic. In other words, we must know whether people identify with their cultures to be able to predict whether their behavior will be based on the dimensions of cultural variability discussed in this chapter.

Study Questions

1. What does it mean to say that culture is our theory of the game being played in our society?
2. How are cultural norms and rules similar and how are they different?
3. How are dimensions of cultural variability (e.g., individualism-collectivism) useful in explaining similarities and differences in communication across cultures?
4. What are the major differences between individualistic and collectivistic cultures?
5. How do personality orientations, individual values, and self construals mediate the influence of cultural individualism and collectivism on communication?
6. What is the relationship between cultural individualism-collectivism and low- and high-context communication?
7. What are the major differences between low and high uncertainty avoidance cultures?
8. What are the major differences between low and high power difference cultures?
9. What are the major differences between masculine and feminine cultures?
10. Why is it important to understand strangers' cultural identities when we communicate with them?

Applications

1. Over the next week, pay attention to when your communication is based on your individualistic and collectivistic tendencies. Under what conditions do you act as an individualist? Under what conditions do you act as a collectivist? Why do you act the way you do in these situations?

2. Over the next week, pay attention to the cultural rules that guide your communication. What rules do you follow without any thought when you interact with strangers and acquaintances? Try to isolate as many rules guiding your communication as you can.

3. Over the next week, pay attention to how your cultural identity influences your communication. Under what conditions does your cultural identity influence your communication?

Notes

1. There are other ways of talking about culture. Joel Garreau (1981), for example, isolates nine nations of North America (Mexamerica, Dixie, Quebec, The Islands, New England, The Foundry, The Breadbasket, Ecotopia, The Empty Quarter). He argues that each of the nine nations shares a common culture.

2. Some writers have used the term "coculture" instead of subculture. This term implies that all subcultures are equal. This is not the case. Some are more similar to the larger culture than others; some have more power than others.

3. For a complete discussion of the various dimensions that could be used see Gudykunst and Ting-Toomey (1988).

4. See Hofstede (1980), Kluckhohn and Strodtbeck (1961), and Triandis (1988) for extended discussions of this dimension of cultural variability. It should be noted that this dimension is not only isolated by theorists in "western" cultures, but is also isolated by theorists from "eastern" cultures (see Chinese Culture Connection, 1987, for an example).

5. There is some indirect evidence of cultural change in Japan. To illustrate, elementary school teachers are complaining of not being able to control their students (which was never a problem in the past). There also is an increasing crime rate (e.g., thieves breaking into houses) and divorce rate; both of which may suggest a decline in collectivism.

6. See the A&E "Being Japanese" episode of the series *Nippon Since 1945* for an excellent example of new employees being socialized in a collectivistic organization. This episode follows new employees of Fuji Film as they start their new careers with the organization.

7. See Oyserman et al. (2002) for reviews of research on individual-level mediators of cultural individualism-collectivism. Also see responses to this article and Oyserman et al.'s response to the responses.

8. Kashima et al. (1995) and Kashima and Hardie (2000) argue that there are three self construals: (1) the individual, which is based on viewing the self as unique and separate, similar to Markus and Kitayama's independent; (2) the collective, which is based on individuals' group memberships, similar to Markus and Kitayama's interdependent; and (3) the relational, which is based on connections with specific individuals. I use Markus and Kitayama's for two reasons: Kashima et al.'s research suggests that the relational self construal is related to gender differences more than cultural differences, and the independent and interdependent clearly relate to cultural individualism-collectivism. The two-dimensional self construal construct has been criticized recently (e.g., see Levine et al., 2003, for criticisms, but also see Gudykunst & Lee, 2003, for supporting arguments).

9. See Fitzgerald (1993) for a discussion of the interrelated meanings of culture, communication, and identity.

10. Greeley (1989) argues that individualism-collectivism differences can be applied to religious denominations; Protestants are individualistic and Catholics are collectivistic.

11. Triandis, Brislin, and Hui (1988) provide concrete suggestions for individualists interacting with collectivists and collectivists interacting with individualists.

CHAPTER 3

Understanding Group Differences

In the previous chapter, I discussed how cultural differences influence our communication with strangers. Culture, however, is only one of our group memberships that influences our communication with strangers. We have many other group memberships that also affect our communication. In this chapter, I examine how our social identities based on our ethnicities, our genders, our ages, our social classes, and whether or not we have disabilities influence our communication. My emphasis is on how our ethnic identities influence our communication with strangers. In order to understand how these group memberships influence our communication, it is necessary to begin with how we form social identities based on our memberships in ingroups.

Social Identities

We are members of many groups that are important to us (i.e., ingroups), and we form social identities based on our memberships in these groups. In order to understand why social identities are important, we need to begin with our memberships in ingroups and the affect ingroups have on our communication.

Ingroups and Outgroups

The most important component of our self-concepts influencing our communication with strangers is our social identities, which are based on our group memberships. We define ourselves regarding the world in which we live (Tajfel, 1978). We do this, in part, by creating social categories. *Social categorization* is "the ordering of social environment in terms of groupings of persons in a manner which makes sense to the individual" (Tajfel, 1978, p. 61); for example, men and women, students and professors, Vietnamese Americans and African Americans.

As part of our socialization into our cultures, we are taught to interact with members of certain groups of people because of their ethnic heritage, religion, or social class, to name only a few group memberships. Belonging to groups is an important motive for behavior because it removes ambiguity about ourselves and others, and helps us plan our actions (Stevens & Fiske, 1995). The groups of people with whom we are taught to associate are our ingroups. *Ingroups* are "groups of people about whose welfare [we are] concerned, with whom [we are] willing to cooperate without demanding equitable returns, and separation from whom leads to discomfort or even pain" (Triandis, 1988, p. 75). The groups of people with whom we are taught *not* to associate, in contrast, are outgroups. *Outgroups* are groups of people about whose welfare we are not concerned, and groups with whom we require an equitable return in order to cooperate. The tendency to draw a distinction between ingroups and outgroups is universal among humans (Brewer & Campbell, 1976).

Before reading farther, take a moment and think about what the major ingroups are that influence your communication.

What are your major ingroups? How does being a member of these groups influence your communication?

____

____

____

Your answers to these questions should provide some insight into the role of ingroups in your implicit theory of communication. Keep these major ingroups in mind as you read the remainder of this section.

Members of collectivistic cultures draw a firmer distinction between ingroups and outgroups than members of individualistic cultures (Triandis, 1995). When collectivists encounter people who are unknown but who are members of one of their ingroups, they are "inclined to help, support, cooperate, and even self-sacrifice" (Triandis & Trafimow, 2001, p. 372). When collectivists encounter people who are unknown and who are members of outgroups, in contrast, "distrust, competition, and hostility can be typical responses. Individualists do not show such strong differences in behavior when they deal with ingroup and outgroup members" (p. 372).

We identify and evaluate ourselves in terms of the ingroups to which we belong and the characteristics of those groups (e.g., their status; Tajfel,

1978). Our ingroup memberships can contribute either positive or negative aspects to our social identities. We tend to maintain positive identities associated with our ingroups by evaluating our ingroups positively when we compare them with outgroups (e.g., Tajfel & Turner, 1979). This leads to an ingroup bias.

One consequence of the ingroup bias is that discriminating against outgroup members increases ingroup members' self-esteem (Rubin & Hewstone, 1998). Categorization alone, however, is not sufficient to lead to discrimination against outgroup members. Outgroup discrimination occurs when individuals categorize themselves as members of ingroups in order to reduce subjective uncertainty about outgroup members (Grieve & Hogg, 1999). "People strive to feel certain that they are correct so they may ascribe meaning to their world and their place within it" (p. 927).

The ingroup bias does not always occur when we compare our ingroups and outgroups. The ingroup bias occurs when we compare ingroups and outgroups on the same dimension (e.g., intelligence, competency of behavior). If we use different dimensions to evaluate ingroups and outgroups, however, the ingroup bias does not necessarily occur. Further, how we view the way that outgroups differ from our ingroups influences our responses. "If the outgroup's difference is judged as non-normative and inferior, devaluation, discrimination, and hostility are likely responses to the outgroup. Judging the outgroup's difference to be normative or positive leads to acceptance and appreciation of the group" (Mummendey & Wenzel, 1999, p. 158; italics omitted).

The ingroup bias also is less likely to occur in intergroup encounters when ingroup members categorize outgroup members using more than one category than when ingroup members categorize outgroup members using only one category (Crisp et al., 2001). When ingroup members use more than one category, they treat outgroup members "more like individuals than group members" (p. 85), and this reduces ingroup members' tendencies to exhibit the ingroup bias.

The ingroup bias is the major consequence of dividing people into ingroups and outgroups. There are, nevertheless, other consequences of dividing people into members of ingroups and outgroups. First, we have a tendency to expect members of our ingroups to behave and think similarly to the way we do (Tajfel, 1969). Second, individualists tend to perceive outgroups as relatively homogeneous and see more variability in their ingroups than outgroups (Tajfel, 1969). Third, we have less anxiety about interacting with members of our ingroups than about interacting with members of outgroups (Stephan & Stephan, 1985). Fourth, we tend to be more accurate in predicting the behavior of members of our ingroups than we are in predicting the behavior of members of outgroups (Gudykunst, 1995). Fifth, there are greater differences in ingroup and outgroup communication in collectivistic cultures than in individualistic cultures (e.g., Gudykunst, Gao, Schmidt et al., 1992; Gudykunst, Yoon, & Nishida, 1987).

Characteristics of Social Identities

Once we become aware of belonging to one or more ingroup, our social identities begin to form. *Social identities* are those parts of an "individual's self-concept which derive from his [or her] knowledge of his [or her] membership in a social group (or groups) together with the value and emotional significance attached to that membership" (Tajfel, 1978, p. 63). Our social identities can be based on our memberships in demographic categories (e.g., nationality, ethnicity, gender, age, social class), the roles we play (e.g., student, professor, parent), our memberships in formal or informal organizations (e.g., political parties, social clubs), our associations or vocations (e.g., scientist, artist, gardener), or our memberships in stigmatized groups (e.g., homeless, people with AIDS). The degree to which we assert our social identities varies from situation to situation, but the general degree to which we identify with particular groups appears to remain relatively stable over time. You isolated many of the social identities important to you in Chapter 1 when you completed the sentence "I am a(an)."

Our social identities emerge from the tension between our need to be seen as similar to and fit in with others, and our need to be seen as unique (Brewer, 1991). Our need to be seen as similar allows us to identify with different groups and involves the general process of *inclusion.* Our need to be seen as unique is based on the general process of *differentiation,* or making ourselves stand out from others. In individualistic cultures, like the United States, balancing these two tensions usually involves emphasizing differentiation more than inclusion. In collectivistic cultures, in contrast, balancing the tensions usually involves emphasizing inclusion more than differentiation.

People with individualistic value orientations identify with larger and more inclusive social groups than people with collectivistic value orientations (Brewer & Roccas, 2001). Whether we see our ingroups as distinct or overlapping influences how we view our social identities. "To the extent that individuals see their multiple group identities as different and nonoverlapping, they will have complex, differentiated social identities and will conceptualize their in-groups as heterogeneous and inclusive" (p. 233). This leads to high identity complexity. "To the extent that individuals perceive their ingroups as highly similar and overlapping, their conceptualization of their in-groups will be simple, homogeneous, and exclusive" (p. 233). This leads to low identity complexity. Individualists' identity complexity tends to be higher than collectivists' identity complexity.

Some of our social identities, such as our ethnicities and our genders, are important in most situations (Smith & Bond, 1993). Other social identities, in contrast, are important only when they are distinctive; that is, when there are only a few people holding the social identities present in the situation. To illustrate, if a lower-class person is alone in a group of upper-middle-class people, his or her social class identity will be activated. If there are an equal number of lower-class and upper-middle-class people present, on the other hand, social class identities tend not to be activated.

The degree to which we perceive strangers to be typical members of their groups also influences whether we activate our social identities (Smith & Bond, 1993). If we are interacting with members of another ethnic group and perceive them to be typical members of their group, for example, we tend to activate our ethnic identities. If we do not perceive strangers to be typical members of their groups, on the other hand, we tend not to activate our ethnic identities. Rather, we will use another of our social identities or our personal identities to guide our behavior.

The social relations between our ingroups and outgroups also affects whether we activate our social identities (Smith & Bond, 1993). If there are good relations between our ethnic groups and other ethnic groups, for instance, our ethnic identities may not be activated when we interact with members of different ethnic groups. If there are hostile relations between our ethnic groups and other ethnic groups, in contrast, our ethnic identities will be activated when we interact with members of different ethnic groups.

Table 3.1 contains a questionnaire designed to assess the extent to which your social identities influence you when you communicate with others. Take a few minutes to complete the questionnaire now.

Scores on the questionnaire range from 10 to 50. The higher your score, the more your social identities influence your communication. If your score is 35 or greater, your social identities probably influence your communication in a lot of your interactions with others.

Collective Self-Esteem

We try to achieve positive social identities in our interactions with strangers (Tajfel, 1978). Take a few minutes to answer the following questions designed to help you think about your implicit theory of communication before reading the remainder of this section.

TABLE 3.1 *Assessing the Importance of Your Social Identities*

The purpose of this questionnaire is to help you assess how much your social identities influence your communication with others. Respond to each statement by indicating the degree to which the statement is true regarding the way you typically think about yourself. When you think about yourself, is the statement "Always False" (answer 1), "Mostly False" (answer 2), "Sometimes True and Sometimes False" (answer 3), "Mostly True" (answer 4), or "Always True" (answer 5)?

_____ 1. I think of myself as a man or a woman when I communicate with others.
_____ 2. I think of myself as a unique person when I communicate with others.
_____ 3. My memberships in social clubs (e.g., fraternities, sororities, campus clubs) influence the way I communicate with others.
_____ 4. My personality influences my behavior when I communicate with others.
_____ 5. My ethnicity influences my communication when I communicate with others.
_____ 6. I communicate with others as though they are unique individuals.
_____ 7. My age influences the way I communicate with others.
_____ 8. I assume others are like me when we communicate.
_____ 9. I see people as similar to other members of their group when I communicate with them.
_____ 10. My group memberships are not important to me when I communicate with others.

To find your score, first reverse the responses for the even numbered items (i.e., if you wrote 1, make it 5; if you wrote 2, make it 4; if you wrote 3, leave it as 3; if you wrote 4, make it 2; if you wrote 5, make it 1). Next, add the numbers next to each of the statements. Scores range from 10 to 50. The higher your score, the more your social identities influence your communication.

Which of the groups of which you are a member do you evaluate positively? Negatively?

____

____

____

Which of the groups of which you are a member do you think others evaluate positively? Negatively?

____

____

____

Which of the groups of which you are a member are central to how you define yourself?

____

____

____

Your answers to these questions should provide some insight into the role of collective self-esteem in your implicit theory of communication. Keep your answers to these questions in mind as you read the remainder of this section.

There are individual differences in the degree to which we have positive social identities. Our *collective self-esteem* is the degree to which we generally evaluate our social groups positively (Luhtanen & Crocker, 1992). Our level of collective self-esteem moderates the degree to which we try to protect or enhance our social identities when they are threatened (Crocker & Luhtanen, 1990). When our social identities are threatened and we put down the outgroup threatening our social identities, our collective self-esteem increases (Branscombe & Wann, 1994).

When we are engaged in competition with members of other groups (e.g., other ethnic groups) and we successfully discriminate against them, our social identities associated with the relevant group membership (e.g., our ethnic identities) are enhanced (Rubin & Hewstone, 1998). Our collective self-esteem associated with the relevant social identities (e.g., our collective self-esteem associated with our ethnic identities) increases when our social identities are enhanced. The reverse process also can occur. If our collective self-esteem associated with specific social identities is low, this may lead us to engage in discrimination against members of other groups to increase our collective self-esteem associated with those social identities.

There are four components to our collective self-esteem (Luhtanen & Crocker, 1992). First, private collective self-esteem involves the degree to which we evaluate our social groups positively. Second, membership esteem involves the degree to which we evaluate ourselves as good members of the social groups to which we belong. Third, public collective self-esteem involves our perceptions about how others evaluate our social groups. Fourth, the importance of our group memberships involves the degree to which our group memberships are central to how we define ourselves.

We can have different levels of collective self-esteem for the different social identities we have. We may, for example, have high collective self-esteem for our ethnic identities and low collective self-esteem for our gender or family identities. Our level of collective self-esteem is associated with the strength of our self construals (Ogawa et al., 2004). The stronger our interdependent self construals, the greater our collective self-esteem. This holds for our general self construals and general collective self-esteem, as well as for our family-specific self construals and our family-specific collective self-esteem in Japan and the United States.

Ethnicity and Ethnic Identity

Our ethnicities influence our behavior to some degree any time we interact with members of other ethnic groups. Ethnicity can be based on national origin, race, or religion (Gorden, 1964). Race is based on biological characteristics, and ethnicity is based on cultural characteristics shared by people of a particular race, national origin, or religion. Both race and ethnicity are socially constructed categories, but it is the shared cultural characteristics that influence communication, not the biological characteristics associated with race.[1] My focus here, therefore, is on ethnicity, not race.

Ethnicity

There are many ways to define ethnicity. Ethnicity, for example, can be viewed as involving individuals using some aspect of a group's cultural background to separate themselves from others (DeVos, 1975). It also can be viewed as "those individuals who identify themselves as belonging to the same ethnic category" (Giles & Johnson, 1981, p. 202). Take a few minutes to think about your ethnicity and answer the following questions before proceeding. Think about your ethnicity, not your culture (e.g., being an African American, Vietnamese American), when answering the questions.

What does it mean to you to be a member of your ethnic group?

____

____

____

How does being a member of your ethnic group influence your communication?

____

____

____

In which situations does your ethnicity have a strong influence on your communication? When does it not have much of an influence?

____

____

____

Your answers to these questions should provide some insight into the role of ethnicity in your implicit theory of communication. Keep your answers in mind as you read the remainder of this section.

There are three primary ingredients that can be used in defining ethnic groups: "(1) The group is perceived by others in the society to be different in some combination of the following traits: language, religion, race, or ancestral homeland with its related culture; (2) the members also perceive themselves to be different; and (3) they participate in shared activities built around their (real or mythical) common origin and culture" (Yinger, 1994, pp. 3–4). If any one of these three ingredients is present in an interaction, ethnicity is influencing what is happening.

The way we react toward strangers often is based on our assumptions about their ethnicities; for example, we impose ethnic labels on strangers. When we impose ethnic labels on strangers, however, we may not impose the ethnic labels strangers would use to describe themselves (Barth, 1969). We impose ethnic labels on strangers *and* they identify with ethnic groups. Anytime we categorize ourselves as members of ethnic groups, we also categorize strangers as not members of our ethnic groups and, therefore, members of other ethnic groups (Turner et al., 1987). Problems occur in our interactions with strangers if we categorize them based on their ethnicities when they do not see their ethnicities as relevant to the interactions (e.g., interaction between a superior and a subordinate in an organization). Problems also occur if we do *not* categorize strangers based on their ethnicities when they see their ethnicities as important to the interactions.

Interactions between members of different ethnic groups can be complicated when their ethnicities are clear, but it is even more complicated when one person's ethnicity is ambiguous. A black woman who appears white points out that

> when you look like what you are, the external world mirrors back to you an identity consistent with your idea of yourself. However, for someone like me, who does not look like what I am, those mirrors are broken, and my consciousness or lack of consciousness takes on serious implications.

> . . . All of my life I have passed invisibly into the white world, and all my life I have felt that sudden and alarming moment of consciousness when I remember I am black. It may feel like I'm emerging too quickly from deep in the ocean, or touching an electric fence, or like I'm a deer stuck in the headlights of an oncoming car. Sometimes in conversation with a white person who doesn't know I'm black, suddenly a feeling comes over me, a precursor—though nothing has been said about race—and I either wait helplessly for the other shoe to drop, try desperately to veer the conversation in another direction, or prepare myself for painful distinctions. (Derricotte, 1997, p. B11)

Ethnicity may, therefore, be an issue in our interactions with others, even when we are not aware of it.

Assimilation Versus Pluralism

There have been changes in recent years in the way people in the United States view ethnicity.[2] *Assimilation* refers to the process of giving up one culture and taking on the characteristics of another. Approximately 10 percent of the population in the United States is foreign born (Current Population Reports, 1999). Foreign born people are going through the process of acculturating to the U.S. culture. These people may or may not want to assimilate to the U.S. culture. The alternative process is cultural pluralism, which involves immigrants acculturating to the U.S. culture but, at the same time, maintaining their ethnicity.

Take a few minutes to answer the following questions designed to get you to think about the role of immigrants in the United States before reading further.

How do you know whether someone is an "American"?

___

___

___

What are you attitudes toward immigrants in the United States? Are your attitudes different for different immigrants?

___

___

___

How should immigrants adapt to the U.S. culture (e.g., give-up their native cultures or maintain them)?

____

____

____

Keep your answers to these questions in mind as you read the remainder of this section.

Many believe that the "cycle of contact, competition, accommodation, and eventual assimilation [among ethnic groups] is apparently progressive and unreversible" (Park, 1950, p. 13).[3] One metaphor often used for assimilation is the "melting pot" (e.g., the School House Rock cartoon "The Great American Melting Pot"). Virtually all discussions of assimilation in the United States prior to World War II, however, focused on immigrants of European ancestry (Glazer, 1993). "The chief obstacle to assimilation [of African Americans] seems to be not cultural differences, but physical traits" (Park, 1930, p. 282). Perceptions of immigrants of European ancestry are more positive than perceptions of immigrants of nonEuropean ancestry (see Simon, 1993, for survey results).

The assimilation view often leads to the use of "race" as a metaphor, with "Americanness" being defined as "white" (Morrison, 1992, p. 42). One illustration of this is Asian Americans being asked "Where do you come from?" by European Americans. Asian Americans may answer "San Francisco" or "New York." To many European Americans these are not acceptable answers and they ask "No, where does your family come from?" Usually when this happens the European Americans are assuming that Asian Americans are not "Americans." When the question "Where do you come from?" is repeated in some form, it implies "*you couldn't be from here!* It equates the Asian with the alien" (Lee, 1999, p. ix).

Explaining the culture of the United States by equating being "American" with white will not work when whites become a numerical minority in the United States sometime in this century (and it will not work in California now where whites make up less than 50 percent of the population). The changes in the ethnic composition of the United States are redefining what it means to be an "American." "The deeper significance of Americans becoming a majority nonwhite society is what it means to the national psyche, to individuals' sense of themselves and their nation—their idea of what it is to be an American" (Henry, 1990, p. 30).

U.S. Americans are ambivalent toward foreigners (Honig, 2002). Both xenophobia (i.e., fear of foreigners) and xenophilia (i.e., attraction to foreigners) exist in the United States simultaneously. Foreign immigrants who come to the United States and choose to become citizens reinforce that the United States is a good place to live. Foreign immigrants also reinforce that being an "American" is voluntary; people are "Americans" because they agree to be "Americans."

Pluralism is as an alternative form of relations between ethnic groups to assimilation. In *pluralism,* ethnicity is viewed as "an internal attitude which predisposes, but does not make compulsory, the display of ethnic identification in interaction. When it facilitates self-interest, ethnic identity will be made self-evident; it is left latent when it would hinder" (Hraba & Hoiberg, 1983, p. 385). When members of ethnic groups decide to exert their ethnicities depends upon the particular circumstances in which they find themselves (Glazer & Moynihan, 1975). In the pluralistic view, maintaining ethnic identity is valued or accepted. The metaphor often used for a pluralistic view of society is the "tossed salad" where all of the ingredients (e.g., lettuce, tomatoes) make up the whole when combined, but continue to be separate.

Ethnic pluralism does not necessarily lead to divisions in the U.S. society. A large majority of middle-class U.S. Americans from all ethnic groups strongly disagree or disagree with the statement "There are times when loyalty to an ethnic group or to a race should be valued over loyalty to the country as a whole" (Wolfe, 1998, p. 158). Identifying with ethnic groups does not take away identifying with the U.S. culture (Gaertner & Dovidio, 2000).

U.S. Americans do not think of "themselves as a single people as the Germans do. Although white, English-speaking Christians of European decent have set the norms for [U.S.] American society, there is still no sense of *Volk* (a group that shares a common ancestry and culture that embodies the national identity)" (Suro, 1998, p. 303). It is ideas that "generate oneness and homogeneity in the United States" (p. 303). There are not large differences among the ethnic groups in the United States with respect to values and aspirations (e.g., "the American dream") (see Etzioni, 2001, for a summary of studies).

Ethnic Identity in the United States

Asserting our ethnic identities helps us define who we are. Our ethnicities offer

> communality in language, a series of customs and symbols, a style, rituals, and appearance, and so forth, which can penetrate life in many ways. These trappings of ethnicity are particularly attractive when one is continually confronted by others who live differently. . . . If I see and experience myself

> as a member of an ethnic category or group, and others—fellow members and outsiders—recognize me as such, "ways of being" become possible for me that set me apart from the outsiders. These ways of being contribute to the *content* of my self-perceptions. In this sense, I *become* my ethnic allegiance; I experience any attack on the symbols, emblems, or values (cultural elements) that define my ethnicity as an attack on myself. (Roosens, 1989, pp. 17–18)

In this view, our ethnicities are important social identities that influence the way we view ourselves and others.

European Americans' Ethnic Identities. There has been a transformation regarding how ethnic identity is manifested for nonimmigrants of European descent in the United States (Lieberson, 1985).[4] Ethnic distinctions based on ancestry from specific European countries are fading and people recognize being white, but do not have a "clearcut identification with and/or knowledge of a specific European [country of] origin" (p. 159).[5] The tremendous intermarriage among people from different European countries is evidence of this change—three of every four marriages involve marrying someone from a different country of origin (Alba, 1990). Individuals in marriages where the couple trace their origins to different European countries, however, do not perceive their partners to be from different ethnic groups. I refer to whites who trace their heritage to Europe as *European Americans* throughout the book.

People from Europe as a group do not generally recognize a specific country of origin, but it is important to note that there are places in the United States where European Americans clearly differentiate their country of origin (e.g., usually in large cities such as Boston, New York, Chicago).[6] There are differences in patterns of communication among European Americans with different countries of origin. The differences, nevertheless, are relatively small when European Americans are compared with members of other ethnic groups.

European Americans often do not recognize their ethnicities or do not strongly identify with their ethnic groups (Kleg, 1993). The reason for this is that European Americans are members of the largest ethnic group in the United States. "The popular notion that ethnics are somewhat different or exotic, along with the fact that members of the national ethnos [European Americans] do not perceive anything special about their own [ethnicity], probably contribute to the lack of identification. The cliché of not being able to see the forest for the trees is quite appropriate in this case" (Kleg, 1993, p. 52). European Americans also may feel disassociated from their ethnic group because nonEuropean Americans' ethnicities are stressed and romanticized (Kleg, 1993).

European Americans can choose whether to express their ethnic identities and European Americans vary in the degree of importance they attach to their ethnicity (Alba, 1990). Symbolic ethnicity describes the manifestation of ethnicity among European Americans today (Gans, 1979). *Symbolic ethnicity* refers to "the desire to retain a sense of being ethnic, but without any deep commitment to the ethnic social ties and behavior" (Alba, 1990, p. 306). "The reality is that white ethnics have a lot more choice and room for maneuver than they themselves think they do. The situation is very different for members of racial minorities, whose lives are strongly influenced by their race or national origin regardless of how much they choose not to identify themselves in ethnic or racial terms" (Waters, 1990, p. 157). European Americans, however, do not necessarily recognize the differences between their experience of ethnicity and the way nonEuropean Americans experience it.[7] The voluntary aspect of European Americans asserting their ethnicities and the enjoyment they receive from it (e.g., it is asserted at ethnic celebrations) make it difficult for European Americans to understand the way ethnicity affects nonEuropean Americans (Waters, 1990).

NonEuropean Americans' Ethnic Identities. Ethnicity tends to be a more important aspect of nonEuropean Americans' identities than European Americans' identities (e.g., Chin, 1983). Ethnic identities, for example, are more important to Asian Americans who are geographically or psychologically close to other Asian Americans than to those who are not close to other Asian Americans (e.g., Hayano, 1981). For European Americans, cultural and ethnic identities are associated positively. For Asian Americans, in contrast, cultural and ethnic identities are associated negatively (Sinclair et al., 1998). NonEuropean Americans' ethnic identities are associated positively with their individual self-esteem (e.g., Lay & Verkuyten, 1999) and their collective self-esteem (e.g., Gudykunst, 2001).

One recent national survey conducted by The Market Segment Group with representative samples of Latino(a) Americans (LAs) and Asian Americans (AAs) asked respondents about their cultural and ethnic identities (Ward, 2002).[8] This survey asked respondents the degree to which they emphasize their cultural or ethnic identities. The results are as follows: American, not ethnic: LAs = 2 percent, AAs = 2 percent; American first, ethnic second: LAs = 12 percent, AAs = 15 percent; American and ethnic equally: LAs = 34 percent, AAs = 48 percent; ethnic first, American second: LAs = 25 percent, AAs = 16 percent; and ethnic, not American: LAs = 22 percent, AAs = 13 percent. These findings suggest that Asian Americans identify with the U.S. culture more than Latino(a) Americans. They also suggest, however, that at least 80 percent of both groups view their ethnic identities as equal to or more important than their "American" identities.

European Americans often use nonEuropean Americans' race as a way to categorize them. NonEuropean Americans' race, therefore, cannot be separated from their ethnicities. This is referred to as "racialized ethnicity" (Omi & Winant, 1986). Racial identities may be more important than ethnic identities for nonEuroprean Americans raised in predominately European American neighborhoods (Tuan, 1998). Asian Americans raised in European American neighborhoods, for example, are "made aware to varying degrees of being racially different and [are] reminded in both inadvertent and meanspirited forms" (p. 104). These individuals feel constrained to identify themselves as Asian Americans because European Americans constantly categorize them in this way, but they resist this categorization. Ultimately, "they struggle to work within imposed limitations and fashion an identity that resonates for them" (p. 151).

Ethnic identity based on race is multidimensional and involves four components: ethnic salience, ethnic centrality, ethnic regard, and ethnic ideology (Sellers et al., 1998).[9] *Ethnic salience* involves the extent to which our ethnicities are an important part of our self-concepts in a specific situation. *Ethnic centrality* involves the extent to which we usually think about ourselves in terms of our ethnicities. *Ethnic regard* involves two aspects: public and private regard. Private regard is the extent to which we have positive or negative feelings about our ethnic groups (e.g., private collective self-esteem), and public regard is the extent to which we think others view our ethnic groups positively or negatively (e.g., public collective self-esteem). *Ethnic ideology* involves holding one of four alternative ideologies: nationalist, oppressed minority, assimilationist, or humanist. A nationalist ideology involves stressing the uniqueness of being members of specific ethnic groups. An oppressed minority ideology involves stressing the oppression shared by members of different ethnic "minorities." An assimilationist ideology involves stressing the similarities between our ethnic groups and the mainstream U.S. culture (e.g., emphasizing our cultural identities). Finally, a humanist ideology involves stressing the common characteristics that all humans share (e.g., emphasizing our human identities).

The development of ethnic identities among nonEuropean Americans is based on where they were born; their family experiences; their personal experiences, especially experiences of prejudice and discrimination; where they live; where their extended families live; their interactions with European Americans; the situation; and so forth. NonEuropean Americans born in the United States, for example, tend to identify with their ethnic groups less than those born outside the United States (e.g., Gudykunst, 2001).

NonEuropean Americans' families play a large role in the development of their ethnic identities. Do their families, for example, stress maintaining their ethnic heritage or assimilating into the larger U.S. culture? A 22-year-old Vietnamese teacher who came to the United States when she was five illustrates some of the problems when the family emphasizes maintaining ethnicity:

> I've always battled with the two sides of me. Always at home, I was the Vietnamese daughter and sister; at school I was supposed to be like everyone else: I'm a student, I'm supposed to be independent and think for myself. But when I'm at home, [I was] expected to act within the tradition, right. Do what your parents expect of you. I always had problems when the two values conflicted. And for a while, my father and I didn't get along because of that, especially when my father let my brother do something and not me. Back then, I didn't think it was because of the culture, I thought it was because we were different and my parents were old fashioned. I always said that the American kids at school get to do this and that. I thought it was a generation thing, and not a cultural thing. (Thai, 1999, p. 62)

The family's emphasis on collectivistic familial ideologies plays a large role in how individuals negotiate their ethnic identities.

As indicated earlier, where nonEuropean Americans live plays a large role in the development of their ethnic identities. In New York City, for example, Puerto Rican young people live among African Americans and the two groups share their music and dance. This has facilitated their "growing together," which has led to the development of "AmeRican" and "Nuyorican" identities among the Puerto Rican youth (Flores, 1977).

Living where ethnic stores are available also affects nonEuropean Americans' ethnic identities. "The nostalgic practice of shopping eases the trauma of immigration experienced by [nonEuropean Americans] by giving them some degree of comfort or security in being/feeling *at home*" (Bonus, 1997, pp. 655–656). This facilitates maintaining ethnicity.

The area where nonEuropean Americans live also may or may not provide opportunities to interact with other members of their ethnic groups and live their lives in ethnic terms. To illustrate, third-generation Japanese Americans who are raised in neighborhoods of mostly Asian Americans have stronger ethnic preferences than those raised in mostly European American or equally European American and Asian American neighborhoods (Nagata, 1993).

One consequence of living mainly among European Americans for nonEuropean Americans' ethnic identities is illustrated by the way a Japanese American playwright describes his experiences. The playwright was raised in the United States, but lived in Japan. Living in Japan helped the playwright understand his ethnicity:

> After I'd been living in Japan for about a year, I had an extraordinary experience. . . . I was walking down the streets and I looked over to my left and I saw a bank of televisions all lined up, and they were filled with a Japanese newscaster. I looked up at the billboard and there was a Japanese face, I looked at the magazines on display and they were filled with Asian faces; I looked ahead and I saw a sea of people coming toward me, all about my same height, with black hair, with skin that looked exactly like mine. . . . What I experienced for the first time was this extraordinary thing called anonymity—the sense of being able to be part of a group, of everything around me reinforcing what I was. I didn't have to second guess my obviousness, to be constantly aware that I was different . . . in that instant in Tokyo something lifted from me, and I as able to move freely. . . . Of course, the longer I was in Japan the more I became aware of the fact that I wasn't strictly Japanese either, that I would never be Japanese Japanese—that I was Japanese-American. (Gotanda, 1991, pp. 9–10)

These experiences clearly illustrate that **ethnicity is not symbolic for nonEuropean Americans in the United States**. It is something they must address every day of their lives.

Some nonEuropean Americans' experiences with their ethnicities are linked to the cultures from which they emigrated. When this occurs, ethnicity is a diaspora. *Diasporas* "are formed by the forcible or voluntary dispersion of people to a number of countries. They constitute a diaspora if they continue to evince a common concern for their 'homeland' (sometimes an imagined homeland) and come to share a common fate with their own people, wherever they happen to be" (Cohen & Kennedy, 2000, p. 32). Not all nonEuropean Americans experience their ethnicity as a diaspora; it depends on their connection to their homeland. Diasporas fill the space between "where you're from" and "where you're at" (Ang, 1993, p. 41). Immigrants who experience their ethnicities as diasporas may not plan to stay in the country to which they immigrated; they may plan to return to their homelands. This clearly influences how they communicate in the country to which they immigrated.

The situations in which nonEuropean Americans find themselves influence the activation of their ethnic identities. There are structural and cognitive dimensions of the situational activation of identities (Okamura, 1981). The structural dimension involves where the interaction is taking place and which group is in the majority (e.g., Vietnamese Americans interacting with European Americans in Little Saigon or in a place where Vietnamese Americans are in the numerical minority). The cognitive dimension "pertains to the actor's [or actress'] subjective perception of the situation in which he [or she] finds himself [or herself] and to the salience he [or she] attributes to ethnicity as a relevant factor in that situation" (p. 454).

The preceding discussion focuses on individuals from one racial group. Biracial identities (e.g., those of children with one black and one white parent) appear to be different than those based on one race. Biracial individuals tend to use one of four alternative identities: "(a) a border identity, (b) a singular identity, (c) a protean identity, and/or (d) a transcendent identity," which are not mutually exclusive (Rockquemore & Brunsma, 2002, p. 41). A *border identity* involves individuals viewing themselves on the border between two identities (e.g., between black and white identities) and it is the most widely used identity. A *singular identity* involves individuals viewing themselves as exclusively one race or the other. A *protean identity* involves individuals changing how they view themselves depending on the context. This is the least frequently used of the four identities. A *transcendent identity* involves individuals who "claim to opt out of the [race] categorization game altogether" (p. 50). In other words, they do not view themselves in terms of race. Several factors influence which biracial identity individuals use to define themselves. These include "individual factors (such as physical appearance) and structural factors (such as socioeconomic status, social network composition, and racial socialization)" (p. 56).

Language and Ethnic Identity

The language we speak is a major way we mark boundaries between our ethnic groups and strangers' ethnic groups.[10] This is true in informal conversations with strangers, acquaintances, and friends, as well as in formal communication situations (e.g., when we talk to our supervisors at work) (see Pavlenko & Blackledge, 2003, for a discussion of negotiating identities in multilingual contexts).

One recent national survey conducted by The Market Segment Group with representative samples of Latino(a) Americans (LAs) and Asian Americans (AAs) asked about the language(s) spoken at home (Ward, 2002). The results were as follows: native language exclusively: LAs = 28 percent, AAs = 12 percent; primarily native language with some English: LAs = 26 percent, AAs = 23 percent; both native language and English equally: LAs = 22 percent, AAs = 36 percent; primarily English with some native language: LAs = 14 percent, AAs = 13 percent; and English exclusively: LAs = 8 percent, AAs = 8 percent. These findings suggest that Latino(a) Americans rely on their native languages more than Asian Americans. At least 75 percent of both groups, however, use their native languages the same amount or more than English (see Morales, 2002, for a discussion of the role of English and Spanish in Latino[a] American identities).

There are at least four reasons why language is an important aspect of ethnic identities (Giles & Coupland, 1991). First, language often is considered a criterion for ethnic group membership (e.g., people who do not speak the language may not be considered members of the ethnic group by those who do). Second, language is used by outgroup members to categorize individuals as members of the ethnic group. Third, language provides the emotional component to ethnic identities (e.g., members of ethnic groups feel closer to each other speaking their native language than when speaking English in the United States; see below). Fourth, ethnic languages facilitate cohesion among members of ethnic groups.

The emotional component of language can be seen in the way one Latino American writer describes the effect of hearing his father speak English to a European American gas station attendant when he was growing up: "I cannot forget the sounds my father made as he spoke. At one point his words slid together to form one word—sounds as confused as the threads of blue and green oil in the puddle next to my shoes. His voice rushed through what he had left to say. And, toward the end, reached falsetto notes, appealing to his listeners' understanding. I looked away to the lights of passing automobiles. I tried not to hear anymore" (Rodriguez, 1982, p. 15).

In contrast to the alienation he felt when he heard his father speaking English, the Latino American writer felt comfort when members of his family spoke to him in Spanish: "A family member would say something to me and I would feel specially recognized. My parents would say something to me and I would feel embraced by the sounds of their words. Those words said: I am speaking with ease in Spanish. I am addressing you in words I never use with los gringos. I recognize you as someone special, close, like no one outside. You belong with us. In the family" (Rodriguez, 1982, p. 15). The language spoken clearly is linked to how we feel about ourselves and others.

Ethnic Labels

Another way language affects our ethnic identities is through the labels we use for our ethnic groups. Before reading further, take a moment to answer the following questions.

What label do you prefer for your ethnic group?

____

____

What label do you typically use to refer to people who trace their heritages to Africa?

____

____

What labels do you typically use to refer to people who trace their heritages to Mexico? To China?

____

____

Keep your answers to these questions in mind as you read the remainder of this section.

It appears that the majority of blacks prefer to use the label African American when they refer to themselves.[11] Two individuals provide the reasons for the use of this term:

> I grew up in a time when "black" was the accepted term. It was used on application forms and among family and friends. I changed to African American because it seemed more accurate and more enduring to our culture.
>
> [In the past] I didn't prefer "black," it was just used. However, when I began to realize that the term "black" was just making us be seen in terms of skin color (and not including our ethnic heritage), I embraced the term African American. After all, a "white, American, Irish person" is Irish American. We've done just as much for the country, and we have a heritage from *our* mother land, so why not express it! (Larkey et al., 1993, p. 311)

Note that there is *not* a hyphen in the label African American. In fact, most nonEuropean Americans no longer use a hyphen for their ethnicities (e.g., Japanese American, Mexican American). While it may seem like a minor point, omitting or including a hyphen may be interpreted as providing self-concept support (omitting) or denying a self-concept (including it). (The issue of self-concept support is discussed in more detail in Chapter 7.) We, therefore, need to pay attention to the labels strangers use to refer to themselves.

Concern over the use of ethnic labels is not limited to African Americans. Ethnic labels also are an issue for whites as well. Respondents in one study

(Martin et al., 1996), for example, indicated that their preferences were (from most selected label to least selected): "White," "Caucasian," "white American," "European American," "Euro American," "Anglo," and "WASP" (White Anglo-Saxon Protestant). With the exception of European American and Euro American, all of the labels focus on race rather than ethnicity. My use of European American in this book is meant to emphasize ethnicity rather than race.

Many people born in Mexico, Puerto Rico, and Cuba find the panethnic term Hispanic (i.e., a term used for all of these cultures combined) archaic and offensive (e.g., see Gonzalez, 1992). Participants in a survey of Latino(a) Americans report that they prefer the term "Latino" over Hispanic if a panethnic term is used (summarized in Gonzalez, 1992).[12] Even the pronunciation of the term can be a statement of identity (the preferred pronunciation is lah-TEEN-oh). "To say Latino is to say you came to my culture in a manner of respect" (Cisneros quoted by Gonzalez). People who prefer the term Hispanic want to fit into the mainstream culture (i.e., give up their original culture), while people who use Latino want to maintain their ethnicity (Cisneros quoted by Gonzalez).

All panethnic terms (e.g., Latinos, Asian Americans) are misleading since they imply homogeneity across the groups included under the term. People who come from Mexico, Cuba, and Puerto Rico, for example, share some similarities based on a common language, but there are many cultural differences among the three groups that cannot be ignored. Respondents in a survey of Latino(a) Americans indicate that they prefer labels based on their country of origin (e.g., Mexican American, Cuban American), rather than panethnic terms like "Latino" (Gonzalez, 1992). Similarly, first-generation Asian Americans may share a collectivistic upbringing, but there are many differences among Chinese Americans, Japanese Americans, Korean Americans, and Vietnamese Americans, to name only a few of the Asian groups often lumped together. For people who trace their heritage to different Chinese countries, Chinese American is preferred over labels such as Hong Kong Chinese or Taiwanese Chinese (Kang, 1997).

The labels individuals use regarding their ethnic group memberships can tell us a lot about them. People who trace their heritage to Mexico, for example, might use several different terms to refer to themselves. To illustrate, people who label themselves as Chicanos or Chicanas tend to define themselves differently than people who label themselves Mexican Americans. The people who define themselves as Chicanos or Chicanas probably have political goals (e.g., promoting La Raza and community solidarity), while people who define themselves as Mexican Americans do not (Gonzalez, 1992). To communicate effectively with members of either group, it would be important to know that they prefer one label or another. This is important, as indicated earlier, because **effective communication requires that we support strangers' self-concepts, including their preferred ethnic identities**.

Personal and social identities are both important in how we view ourselves, how we view strangers, and how strangers view us. We need "(1) respect for the unique identities of each individual, regardless of gender, race, or ethnicity [personal identities], and (2) respect for those activities, practices, and ways of viewing the world that are particularly valued by or associated with members of disadvantaged groups, including women, Asian-Americans, African-Americans, Native Americans, and a multitude of other groups in the United States [social identities]" (Gutmann, 1992, p. 8). We need to respect the identities others claim for themselves if we want to develop relationships with them. I discuss this issue in detail in Chapter 7.

Strength and Content of Ethnic Identities

The labels we use for our ethnicities influence our communication. To understand fully how our ethnicities influence our communication, however, we must also take into consideration the strength and content of our ethnic identities. As with our cultural identities, we vary in the degree to which we identify with our ethnic groups (see Root, 1995, for how people with multiple identities deal with these issues). Some of us strongly identify with our ethnic groups and some of us weakly identify with our ethnic groups. Recognizing this difference is critical to effective communication with strangers.

Often someone will say that we should ignore ethnic differences and strive for a "color blind" society. If everyone weakly identified with their ethnic groups this might make sense. We may be able to ignore ethnic group differences when interacting with strangers who weakly identify with their ethnic groups. If strangers strongly identify with their ethnic groups, in contrast, we cannot ignore their ethnicities. When strangers strongly identify with their ethnic groups and we ignore their ethnicities when we interact with them, we are *not* supporting their self-concepts. This is a problem because self-concept support is necessary for strangers to be satisfied with their communication with us (Hecht et al., 1989).

The content of our ethnic identities can be described similarly to the content of our cultural identities (see Chapter 2). In other words, the content of our ethnic identities may be highly individualistic or highly collectivistic, masculine or feminine, low or high in power distance, and low or high in uncertainty avoidance. The content of our ethnic identities depends on our national heritages, and the strength of our identities. To illustrate, if strangers' national heritages can be traced to collectivistic cultures and they strongly identify with their ethnic identities, then the content of their identities will tend to be collectivistic values.[13] If strangers do not strongly identify with their ethnic groups, in contrast, the content of their identities would not involve holding collectivistic values. Whether strangers will hold individualistic values depends on their cultural identities. If strangers are U.S. Americans who strongly identify with the U.S. culture, then their values will probably be individualistic. If they do not strongly identify with the U.S. culture, however, their values will not necessarily be individualistic.

It appears that African Americans, Asian Americans, and Latino(a) Americans are more collectivistic than European Americans; for example, nonEuropean Americans emphasize interdependent self construals and hold collectivistic values more than European Americans (e.g., Gudykunst, 2001; Rhee et al., 1996). NonEuropean Americans, however, are not necessarily less individualistic than European Americans. This would not be expected since nonEuropean Americans are raised in the United States and have learned to view themselves as independent from others and learned individualistic values.

In order to understand strangers' communication, we must understand their cultural and ethnic identities. Strangers who weakly identify with their cultures and strongly identify with their ethnic groups will tend to base their communication on their ethnic identities. Strangers who strongly identify with their cultures and weakly identify with their ethnic groups, in contrast, will tend to base their communication on their cultural identities. Strangers who strongly identify with both their cultural identities and their ethnic identities will choose which identity to use to guide their behavior in specific situations. To illustrate, they may choose to base their communication at work on their cultural identities, and base their communication at home on their ethnic identities. Strangers who weakly identify with both their cultural identities and their ethnic identities will tend to base their communication on other social identities or their personal identities. These people, however, may base their communication on their cultural or ethnic identities if others categorize them on the basis of these identities and act on the basis of that categorization.

We all identify to some degree with our ethnic groups. The stronger we identify with our ethnic groups, the more our ethnicities influence our behavior. Strongly identifying with our ethnic groups, however, does *not* necessarily mean that we put members of other groups down or are biased toward our ethnic groups. The degree to which we are biased toward our ethnic groups is a function of our collective self-esteem. As indicated earlier, collective self-esteem is the extent to which we evaluate our group memberships positively (Crocker & Luhtanen, 1990). If we strongly identify with our ethnic groups and only derive collective self-esteem from our ethnicities, we will be biased toward our ethnic groups and, therefore, we may have problems in interacting with members of other ethnic groups. If we strongly identify with our ethnic groups and we derive collective self-esteem from group memberships other than our ethnicities (e.g., our religions, occupations), we will not necessarily be biased toward our ethnic groups. Throughout the book, when I discuss ethnic differences in communication behavior there should always be a caveat; **ethnic differences in communication may only occur between individuals who strongly identify with their ethnic groups**.

Table 3.2 contains a questionnaire designed to assist you in assessing the strength of your ethnic identity. Take a few minutes to complete the questionnaire now.

The scores on the questionnaire range from 10 to 50. The higher your score, the more you identify with your ethnic group. Keep your scores in mind. In later chapters, I will discuss how the strength of your identification with your ethnic group can influence your communication with strangers. The questionnaire only assesses the strength of your identification with your ethnic group. It does not assess what it means to be a member of this group.

Identities Based on Gender, Disability, Age, and Social Class

Our cultural and ethnic identities are only two of the social identities that influence the way we communicate. We have many other social identities that can be sources of misinterpretations and ineffective communication; for example, identities based on gender, disability, age, social class, gender orientation, occupation, religion, and so forth. Religion can be used as a basis for determining ethnicity if the religion provides a distinct subculture. Jews and Muslims are the main religious groups that meet this criterion in the United States, and these groups are the targets of negative intergroup attitudes (e.g., anti-Semitism).[14] In this section, I discuss four major social identities that affect our behavior. I begin with the most obvious and discuss the four in decreasing order of our awareness of how they influence our behavior.

TABLE 3.2 *Assessing the Strength of Your Ethnic Identity**

The purpose of this questionnaire is to help you think about the degree to which you identify with being a member of your ethnic group. Respond to each statement by indicating the degree to which the statement is true regarding the way you typically think about yourself. When you think about yourself, is the statement "Always False" (answer 1), "Mostly False" (answer 2), "Sometimes True and Sometimes False" (answer 3), "Mostly True" (answer 4), or "Always True" (answer 5)?

_____ 1. If I were born again, I would want to be born as a member of a different ethnic group.
_____ 2. Being a member of my ethnic group is important to me.
_____ 3. I rarely think about being a member of my ethnic group.
_____ 4. Being a member of my ethnic group plays a large role in my life.
_____ 5. Thinking about myself as a member of my ethnic group is not central to how I define myself.
_____ 6. I like the things that make me a member of my ethnic group and different from people in other ethnic groups.
_____ 7. I rarely choose to express my ethnicity in the way I communicate.
_____ 8. I have a positive view of my ethnic group.
_____ 9. I do not enjoy being a member of my ethnic group.
_____ 10. If others do not recognize me as a member of my ethnic group, it upsets me.

To find your score, first reverse the responses for the odd numbered items (i.e., if you wrote 1, make it 5; if you wrote 2, make it 4; if you wrote 3, leave it as 3; if you wrote 4, make it 2; if you wrote 5, make it 1). Next, add the numbers next to each of the statements. Scores range from 10 to 50. The higher your score, the more you identify with your ethnic group.

*Adapted in part from Hofman (1985).

Gender

One of the major social identities affecting our communication is our gender and the way we define our gender roles. There are differences in the way men and women relate to the world that affect their social identities. Women's gender identities are based more on communal processes than differentiation processes, and men's gender identities are based more on differentiation processes than communal processes (e.g., Williams, 1984).[15]

Take a few minutes to answer the following questions regarding your feelings about being male or female before reading the remainder of this section.

What does it mean to you to be a male or female?

____

____

How does being a male or female influence the ways you communicate?

____

____

Are there situations in which you define yourself as a male or female more than others? Less than others? What characteristics do these situations share in common?

____

____

Your answers to these questions provide some insight into the role of gender in your implicit theory of communication. Keep your answers in mind as you read the remainder of the section.

Women are socialized to develop close relationships with others and to be involved with others (Maltz & Borker, 1982; Tannen, 1990). As part of their socialization, women learn to view talk as an important aspect of developing and maintaining relationships. Men, in contrast, are socialized to assert their dominance and to be independent. Men learn to see talk as a way of asserting their dominance, and to view talk as weakening intimate relationships. These differences in socialization suggest that "women are more inclined [than men] to value relationships with other people from groups other than their own" (Skevington, 1989, p. 56). This implies that men and women engage in intergroup behavior differently.[16]

Members of social groups can derive positive social identities in two different ways (Williams, 1984). People can develop positive social identities by differentiating or comparing their groups with other groups. This appears to be the method of developing positive social identities commonly used by men. People also can derive positive social identities by developing relations with members of other groups. This appears to be the method preferred by women.

There are differences in the ways men and women communicate (Beck, 1988). Women, for example, tend to see questions as a way of keeping a conversation going. Men, in contrast, see questions as requests for information. Women tend to make connections between what their partner said and what they have to say. Men, on the other hand, do not use conversational bridges as much and may appear to ignore what their partners just said in a conversation. Men tend to view aggressiveness as a way of communicating, while women tend to interpret aggressiveness as an attack. Women may discuss problems and only be looking for reassurances. Men, on the other hand, interpret the discussion of a problem as a request for a solution.[17] These differences in communication patterns suggest that there are subcultural

> differences between men and women . . . in their conceptions of friendly conversation, their rules for engaging in it, and, probably most important, their rules for interpreting it. We argue that [U.S.] American men and women come from different sociolinguistic subcultures, having learned to do different things with words in a conversation, so that when they attempt to carry on conversation with one another, even if both parties are attempting to treat one another as equals, cultural miscommunication results. (Maltz & Borker, 1982, p. 200)

Male-female communication, therefore, can be considered a form of intergroup communication.

The differences in men's and women's communication are not due to biological sex, but their gender identities (Bem, 1974). Before reading further, write as many adjectives (e.g., smart, funny) as come to mind to describe yourself:

____

____

____

I will provide some guidelines for you to get a rough idea of your gender identity below.

We have *masculine gender identities* if we exhibit a high degree of stereotypical masculine traits and behavior (e.g., aggressive, competitive, dominant) and a low degree of stereotypical feminine traits and behavior (e.g., compassionate, sensitive, warm) (Bem, 1974). We have *feminine gender identities* if we exhibit a high degree of stereotypical feminine traits and behavior and a low degree of stereotypical masculine traits and behavior. We have *androgynous gender identities* if we exhibit a high degree of stereotypical masculine *and* a high degree of stereotypical feminine traits and behavior. We have *undifferentiated gender identities* if we exhibit a low degree of stereotypical masculine and low degree of stereotypical feminine traits and behavior.

Stereotypical masculine traits include, but are not limited to: acts as leader, aggressive, ambitious, analytical, assertive, athletic, competitive, dominant, forceful, independent, risk taking, self-reliant, self-sufficient, and strong (Bem, 1974). Stereotypical feminine traits include, but are not limited to: affectionate, cheerful, compassionate, gullible, helpful, loyal, sensitive, shy, soft-spoken, sympathetic, tender, understanding, warm, and yielding. Look back at the adjectives you used to describe yourself earlier. Count the number of stereotypical masculine and stereotypical feminine traits you used. Use the descriptions in the previous paragraph to determine your sex-role identity.

Traditional gender oriented individuals (high masculine men, high feminine women) tend to organize and recall information about others on the basis of their genders (Bem, 1993). Also, traditional gender oriented individuals tend to follow the cultural definition of appropriate behavior. To illustrate, "conventionally masculine men [are] independent but not nurturant, and conventionally feminine women [are] nurturant but not independent" (Bem, 1993, p. 157). Gender differences discussed earlier in this section, therefore, should be considered as applying to masculine men and feminine women (not to masculine women, feminine men, androgynous or undifferentiated men or women).

Disability

We categorize others based on their physical appearance and evaluate novel appearances negatively (McArthur, 1982). When nondisabled people communicate with people who are disabled visibly in some way, they tend to experience uncertainty and anxiety, and avoid interaction when possible (e.g., there is a bias toward the ingroup).[18] Nondisabled people communicating with people in a wheelchair, for example, predict more negative outcomes and are less aware of the person in a wheelchair than when communicating with other nondisabled individuals (Grove & Werkman, 1991). Similar observations can be made about interactions with other people we view as stigmatized (e.g., blind, Deaf, AIDS victims, mentally ill; see Goffman, 1963). The bias toward the ingroup is a two-way street, and many of the groups classified as "disabled" are biased toward their group. To illustrate, there is a sign in the American Sign Language with the right index finger circling forward in front of the forehead that indicates a deaf person who thinks like a hearing person. This sign is *not* meant as a compliment and its use demonstrates a bias against the Deaf ingroup (Barringer, 1993; see Ladd, 2002, for a recent discussion of the Deaf culture).

Before reading the remainder of this section, take a few minutes to think about your communication with people who are disabled, assuming you are not disabled; or your communication with nondisabled, if you are disabled.

How do you think of yourself in terms of disabilities?

____

____

What is your stereotype (mental image) of people in wheelchairs? People who are blind? People who are deaf? Nondisabled people?

____

____

____

____

How do your stereotypes influence your communication with people with disabilities, assuming you are not disabled? With nondisabled people, if you are disabled?

____

____

____

Keep your answers to these questions in mind as you read the remainder of this section.

The visability of others' conditions influences whether we see them as disabled. "External markers of a disability, such as the use of sign language by the deaf, canes and guide dogs by the blind, and wheelchairs by amputees and paraplegics, render those special conditions even more salient. However, even conditions almost completely invisible can be perceived as disabling and can engender miscommunications if they are known to others" (Coleman & DePaulo, 1991, p. 64). Conditions that are not physically disabling (e.g., facial scars, burns) may be psychologically disabling.

Both nondisabled and disabled individuals contribute to miscommunication when they interact (Coleman & DePaulo, 1991). The nondisabled, for example, have negative stereotypes of the disabled. Disabled people are seen as "dependent, socially introverted, emotionally unstable, or depressed, hypersensitive, and easily offended, especially with regard to their disability" (p. 69). Nondisabled people may expect that disabled people will view them as prejudiced against the disabled. When nondisabled people interact with the disabled, they may experience anxiety, fear, and surprise. These reactions often are displayed nonverbally (e.g., in the voice or on the face), even though the nondisabled may try to control their reactions.

If nondisabled individuals become aware of a disabled person's disability after they begin communicating, it often changes the way they communicate. A blind person, for example, tells what happened when a taxi driver became aware of the blindness: "I could tell that at first the taxi driver didn't know that I was blind because for a while he was quite a conversationalist. Then he asked me what these sticks were for (a collapsible cane). I told him it was a cane, and then he got so different . . . He didn't talk about the same things as he did at first" (Davis, 1977, p. 85). Changes in communication like this clearly have an effect on the disabled person.

Disabled people also contribute negative expectations to their interactions with nondisabled individuals. Disabled people may be "bitter and resentful about their disability" (Coleman & DePaulo, 1991, p. 75). Disabled people also may expect to be perceived negatively by nondisabled individuals; "for example, blind people think that sighted persons perceive them as slightly retarded and hard of hearing" (p. 75). It is important to recognize that disabled persons' disabilities may affect their communication with nondisabled people. To illustrate, blind people cannot make eye contact and hearing impaired people who read lips cannot pick up nuances of communication in tone of voice.

There are idioms in English such as "the blind leading the blind" and "that's a lame excuse" to which disabled individuals react negatively (Pogrebin, 1987). Also, the labels that nondisabled use to refer to disabled can cause problems in communication. To illustrate, "A man who wears leg braces says the issue is accuracy. I'm not handicapped, people's attitudes about me handicap me" (Pogrebin, 1987, p. 218). "Differently abled" and "physically challenged" also do not appear to be accepted widely by disabled individuals either.

A psychotherapist with cerebral palsy says: "Friends who care most sometimes think they're doing you a favor by using euphemisms or saying 'I never think of you as disabled.' The reason they don't want to acknowledge my disability is that they think it is so negative. Meanwhile, I'm trying to recognize it as a valued part of me. I'm more complex than my disability and I don't want my friends to be obsessed by it. But it's clearly there, like my eye color, and I want my friends to appreciate and accept me with it" (Russo, quoted by Pogrebin, 1987, p. 219). Some disabled prefer the label "cripple" or "gimp" because they are not euphemisms and recognize the realities facing the disabled. As with members of different ethnic groups, it is important for us to know what the individuals with whom we are communicating want to be called, and how their disabilities contribute to their identities (e.g., are their disabilities important parts of their identities).

Age

Members of other groups do not have to be visibly disabled for us to experience uncertainty and anxiety and want to avoid communicating with them; for example, young people often avoid communicating with old people, and old people often avoid interacting with young people. We categorize others based on age when we guess their age based on their physical appearance, when they tell us their age, when they make references to age categories (e.g., indicating they are retired), and when others talk about experiences in the past, to name only a few of the cues we use for categorizing others based on age. Age-based identities can take place at the beginning of our interactions with others or emerge out of our communication with others (Coupland et al., 1991).

Before reading the remainder of this section, take a moment to answer the following questions designed to get you to think about how age influences your communication with people of different ages.

How would you describe your age identity?

____

____

What is your stereotype (mental image) of "young" people? "Middle-aged" people? "Old" people?

____

____

____

How do your age-based stereotypes influence your communication with members of other age-groups?

____

____

____

Keep your answers to these questions in mind as you read the remainder of this section.

There are several factors that have contributed to the development of age-based identities in the United States: (1) the growing number of old people, (2) the development of retirement communities that segregate old people, (3) the increase in retirement, which decreases interaction between young and old on the job, (4) the amount of money available to older people, and (5) the emergence of groups and organizations exclusively for old people (Rose, 1965). Older people demonstrate "all of the signs of group identification. There is a desire to associate with fellow-agers, especially in formal associations, and to exclude younger adults from these associations. There are expressions of group pride. . . . There are manifestations of a feeling of resentment at 'the way older people are being mistreated,' and indications of their taking social action to remove the sources of their resentment" (Rose, 1965, p. 14). Intergenerational interaction, therefore, is clearly a form of intergroup communication.

Young people view elderly people as less desirable interaction partners than other young people or middle-aged people (Tamir, 1984). When young people are communicating with the elderly they use several different strategies to adapt their behavior (Coupland et al., 1988). First, young people adapt their behavior by over accommodating to the elderly because they assume the elderly are handicapped (e.g., hard of hearing). Second, young people communicate with the elderly in ways that reflect the attitude that the elderly are dependent on the young. This allows young people to control the elderly. Third, young people may speak differently than elderly to establish their identities as young people (e.g., using slang the elderly do not understand). Fourth, young people may over accommodate to the elderly to nurture them (e.g., young people might use baby talk when talking to the elderly). Fifth, young people may not adapt their behavior to the elderly. The elderly, in turn, may perceive this as lack of interest in them.

The elderly also use strategies in adapting their behavior to the young (Coupland et al., 1988). First, the elderly may not accommodate their behavior to the young. One reason for this is that the elderly may have little contact with young people and not know how to adapt their behavior. Second, the elderly may use self-protecting strategies because they anticipate negative interactions with young people. Third, the elderly may anticipate that they will not perform well when they communicate with young people. Fourth, the elderly may engage in self-stereotyping (e.g., they may have negative stereotypes of being old). Fifth, the elderly may speak differently from the way young people do because they want to establish their social identities.

Young people view their conversations with older people as dissatisfying when older people do not accommodate to them and stereotype them (Williams & Giles, 1996). Young people are reluctant to accommodate to older people when this occurs. Young people view their conversations with older people as satisfying when older people are supportive, tell interesting stories, and are not stereotypical of older people. Young people's communication with older people is affected by whether or not the older people are family members (Ng et al., 1997). Young people have more satisfying conversations with older family members than with older people who are not family members.

Self-concept support is necessary for effective intergenerational communication. One of the major concerns of older people is maintaining healthy self-concepts. Older people's self-concepts are threatened by the process of aging and attitudes toward old people (Tamir, 1984). "Lack of self-affirmation by others can lead to a vicious circle of decreasing self-worth and continued negative and self-effacing encounters" (p. 36). Older people will find interactions with younger people who support the older people's self-concept more satisfying than interactions with younger people who do not support their self-concepts.

Social Class

We all identify with a social class, whether we are aware of it or not. Social class

> is much more than a convenient pigeonhole or merely arbitrary divisional unit—like minutes, ounces, I.Q. points or inches—along a linear continuum. It is a distinct reality which embraces the fact that people live, eat, play, mate, dress, work, and think at contrasting and dissimilar levels. These levels—social classes—are the blended product of shared and analogous occupational orientations, educational backgrounds, economic wherewithal, and life experiences. Persons occupying a given level need not be conscious of their class identity. But because of their approximately uniform backgrounds and experiences and because they grew up perceiving or "looking at things" in similar ways, they will share comparable values, attitudes, and life-styles. (Hodges, 1964, p. 13)

The social class to which we belong may be the class with which we identify if we are satisfied with our position in society. Alternatively, if we are seeking upward mobility, our class identities may be based on the social class to which we aspire.

Before reading further, answer the following questions designed to get you to think about your communication with members of different social classes.

How would you describe your own social class?

____

____

What is your stereotype (mental image) of "upper-class" people? "Middle-class" people? "Lower-class" people?

____

____

____

How do your stereotypes influence your communication with members of different social classes?

____

____

Keep your answers to these questions in mind as you read the remainder of this section.

Sociologists tend to divide the social classes in the United States into upper class, upper middle class, middle class, lower middle class, and lower class. No matter how we divide up the class structure, we sort ourselves and others into social classes when we interact. The criteria we use for sorting ourselves and others is usually based on income, occupation, education, beliefs/attitudes, style of life, or kind of family (Jackman & Jackman, 1983).[19] We also can tell people's social classes by their hometowns, their houses, their yards, the decorations in their houses, as well as the clothes they wear and the cars they drive (Fussell, 1983).

Social class appears to influence our individualistic tendencies. At the cultural level, individualism is associated with gross national product (Triandis, 1995). At the individual level, the higher our social classes, the more individualistic we tend to be (Marshall, 1997).

Our class identities influence the way we communicate. We can tell others' class background from the way they speak. Using the standard dialect (e.g., the dialect used by newscasters on national broadcasts) is attributed higher social status than using a nonstandard dialect (see Chapter 6 for more on dialect). The use of double negatives (e.g., "I can't get no satisfaction") and grammatical numbers (e.g., "He don't," "I wants it"), for example, distinguishes lower-class speakers from middle-class speakers (Fussell, 1983). The way we pronounce words and the vocabulary we use distinguish between middle-class and upper-middle/upper-class speakers.

Lower- and middle-class speakers learn to emphasize different communication codes and these codes reinforce class identities (Bernstein, 1973).[20] Middle-class speakers are taught to speak using an elaborated code. An *elaborated code* involves the use of (1) verbal explicitness (e.g., direct messages), (2) being verbally elaborate, (3) a focus on verbal aspects of messages, (4) not relying on shared meanings, (5) not taking others' intentions for granted, (6) being oriented toward individuals, and (7) planning messages. Lower-class speakers, in contrast, are socialized to speak using restricted codes. A *restricted code* involves (1) using metaphors and indirectness, (2) not being verbally elaborate, (3) stressing nonverbal aspects of communication, (4) relying on shared identities and meanings between communicators, (5) taking others' intentions for granted, (6) being oriented toward the group, and (7) not engaging in much planning. Class differences in the use of these codes is one of frequency. Middle-class speakers use elaborated codes more than restricted codes, but they also use restricted codes. Similarly, lower-class speakers use restricted codes more than elaborated codes, but they also use elaborated codes.

Our class identities and our statuses in particular communication situations (e.g., are we superiors or subordinates, teachers or students, physicians or patients) influence our communication. Class identification tends to be stronger in the lower classes than in the middle or upper classes (Jackman & Jackman, 1983). Our communication in particular situations, in turn, influences how we define particular situations and the social identities we choose to emphasize in the particular situations. Our class identities interact with other identities, particularly our ethnic identities. It can be argued, for example, that there is little difference between the way middle-class European Americans and middle-class African Americans communicate. There are, however, significant differences between the ways middle-class European Americans and lower-class African Americans communicate (see Gudykunst & Lim, 1985).

In addition to ways of living and language usage, upper- and middle-class individuals' lack of respect for members of lower social classes inhibits effective intergroup communication. U.S. Americans assign value to each other based on their socioeconomic status (Sennett, 2003). In the United States, the emphasis is on the skills individuals have and individuals' potential. This focus on skills and potential devalues people who are perceived to not have them (e.g., members of lower social classes). This leads to members of lower social classes not receiving social respect from members of the middle and upper social classes. Respect for the individuals with whom we are communicating is necessary for effective communication to take place.

To conclude, no matter what the criteria for strangers' group memberships, we do not have scripts to follow when communicating with them. The only basis we have for communicating with strangers is their group memberships and our stereotypes about their groups. Strangers' communication may be based on any one (or more) of their social identities. To communicate effectively, we need to understand which social identities are influencing strangers' behavior and how they define themselves with respect to these identities.

Our stereotypes tend to provide us with negative expectations and we, therefore, try to avoid (either consciously or unconsciously) communicating with strangers. In the next chapter, I discuss the role of expectations in communication. Specifically, I examine positive versus negative expectations and how they influence our predictions of strangers' behavior and our interpretations of the messages we receive from them. I also look at specific factors on which our expectations are based including strangers' group memberships, our stereotypes, and intergroup attitudes (e.g., prejudice, ethnocentrism, sexism, ageism).

Study Questions

1. What are the consequences of dividing ourselves into ingroups and outgroups?
2. How can we decrease our tendency to engage in the ingroup bias?
3. What factors influence whether we activate our social identities?
4. What is the relationship between social identities and collective self-esteem?
5. How does desiring assimilation or pluralism influence intergroup communication?
6. What are the differences between European Americans' and nonEuropean Americans' experiences with their ethnic identities?
7. How does language influence individuals' ethnic identities?
8. How do the strength and content of our ethnic identities influence intergroup communication?
9. How do our gender identities influence intergroup communication?
10. How do ablebodied and disabled identities influence communication?

11. How do our age identities influence intergroup communication?
12. How do our social class identities influence intergroup communication?

Applications

1. Over the next week, pay attention to how your ethnicity influences your communication. When do you activate your ethnic identity? How does your communication differ when you activate your ethnic identity and when you do not?

2. Over the next week, pay attention to how your gender identity influences your communication. When do you activate your gender identity? How does your communication differ when you activate your gender identity and when you do not?

3. Over the next week, pay attention to how your age identity influences your communication. When do you activate your age identity? How does your communication differ when you activate your age identity and when you do not?

Notes

1. The Human Genome project suggests that there are not major genetic differences attributable to race. See the PBS program *Race—The Power of an Illusion* (Episode 1: "The Difference Between Us"; Episode 2: "The Story We Tell"; Episode 3: "The House We Live In") for a discussion of why race is not based on physical traits, and how it is socially constructed.

2. I do not mean to say that everyone's ideas of ethnicity have changed. The predominate view, however, has changed from assimilationist to pluralistic.

3. Park actually used the term "race," not ethnic group. I am avoiding the use of the term race throughout the book. There are several reasons for this. The major reason is that the term race is emotionally loaded for many people, while ethnicity is not as emotionally loaded. Moreover, it is the shared cultural characteristics of a racial group (i.e., their ethnicity) that influence their communication patterns.

4. People who directly immigrate to a country tend to maintain their identifications with their home countries, but this tendency decreases with future generations.

5. See Omi and Winant (1986) for a discussion of how racial categories form and change over time. There is the beginning of a movement for European Americans to reassert their identities associated with their countries of origin (e.g., see Hayden, 2002).

6. See Hegi (1997) for oral histories of immigrant German American experiences in the United States.

7. There is no good term to use to refer to nonEuropean Americans (e.g., African Americans, Japanese Americans). Some writers use "people of color," but this term has problems because European Americans are "of color" too. While it is an awkward usage, I have chosen nonEuropean Americans.

8. The survey was conducted in the late summer and early fall of 2001. Unfortunately the survey used the U.S. Census method of assessing ethnicity, which does not separate the two.

9. The model being described was designed to explain African American identity, but the components should generalize to other groups as well.

10. Edwards (1985) makes the point that language is not necessary for an ethnic group to survive as a unique group.

11. This should not be taken to suggest that all blacks prefer the label African Americans. Other labels, including black, are still used widely.

12. The Latino Political Survey "Latino Voices" was conducted by Rodolfo de la Garza and Chris Garcia.

13. See Wink (1997) for a study that relates Chinese and Korean ethnicities to collectivism.

14. With respect to religion, anti-Semitism is on the rise in recent years. See Rubin (1990) for an excellent discussion of anti Semitism. Tempest's (1990) article also provides a summary of recent examples of anti-Semitism.

15. This position is consistent with Gilligan's (1982) work on differences in moral development between men and women.

16. To the best of my knowledge there is no specific research supporting this contention. For a complete elaboration of the logic and suggestions for research, see Skevington (1989).

17. Beck also indicates there are differences in the intimacy of the topics men and women discuss. I have not included this difference because the research findings are mixed.

18. For a review of this research, see Dahnke (1983). See Shearer (1984) for disabled persons' views of their communication with the nondisabled.

19. There is disagreement among sociologists today regarding the effect of social class in the United States (e.g., Lee, 2003). Some argue that there are not class differences in things like watching television, listening to music, voting, and recreation when class is defined by income (e.g., Kingston, 2000). Some argue that social mobility has decreased in recent years (e.g., Perrucci & Wysong, 2002) or that 20 percent of the population are "privileged" and have security, high wages, and "skills" while the other 80 percent do not have these same privileges (e.g., Wright, 1997). I believe that there are class differences based on

education, occupation, and where we live that lead to different lifestyles and ways of communicating. We, therefore, cannot ignore social class when we want to communicate effectively.

20. Bernstein's distinction is similar to Hall's low- and high-context messages discussed in Chapter 2: low-context messages are similar to elaborated codes and high-context messages are similar to restricted codes. See Haslett (1990) for a summary of research supporting Bernstein's distinction.

CHAPTER 4

Having Expectations for Strangers

In the previous chapters, I indicated that we have expectations about how strangers are going to communicate. Sometimes we are highly aware of our expectations for strangers' behavior and sometimes we are not. In this chapter, I discuss expectations in detail. I begin by examining the nature of expectations. I then look at specific sources of our expectations for strangers' behavior focusing on those sources that contribute to misinterpretations and misunderstandings when we communicate with strangers.

The Nature of Expectations

Expectations involve our anticipations and predictions about how strangers will communicate with us. Our expectations are derived from social norms and communication rules. Expectations also emerge from our stereotypes of strangers' groups and our intergroup attitudes toward strangers.

Expectations Are Culturally Based

"People who interact develop expectations about each others' behavior, not only in the sense that they are able to predict the regularities, but also in the sense that they develop preferences about how others *should* behave under certain circumstances" (Jackson, 1964, p. 225). **Our cultures and ethnicities provide guidelines for appropriate behavior and the expectations we use in judging competent communication**. To illustrate, in the European American middle-class subculture[1] "one expects normal speakers to be reasonably fluent and coherent in their discourse, to refrain from erratic movements or emotional outbursts, and to adhere to politeness norms. Generally, normative behaviors are positively valued. If one keeps a polite distance and shows an appropriate level of interest in one's conversational partner, for instance, such behavior should be favorably received" (Burgoon & Hale, 1988, p. 61). The problem is that the norms and rules for what is a polite distance and what constitutes an emotional outburst vary across cultures and subcultures within a culture.

An example illustrates the potential problems with expectations that can occur when people from different cultures communicate. In the European American middle-class subculture, we expect that friends will stand an acceptable distance away from us when talking (e.g., an arm's length away). Arabs, in contrast, expect friends to stand close enough so that they can smell each other's breath (Almaney & Alwan, 1982). To deny the smell of your breath to a friend is considered an insult in most Arab cultures. If a European American and an Arab are following their own cultural communication rules and are not aware that the other person's communication rules are different, they will inevitably violate each other's expectations and misinterpret each others' behavior.

Strangers' "novelty makes people feel uncomfortable because they do not know which expectations for behavior and interaction are shared" (Fiske et al., 1996, p. 119). Not knowing which expectations are shared threatens our needs for social acceptance, perceiving ourselves as fundamentally good, perceiving ourselves as competent and effective. When this occurs, we feel anxious and we try to cope with our anxiety. Our anxiety leads us to seek control over the situations in which we find ourselves. "When the powerless feel anxious, one coping strategy is to seek vicarious control by affiliating with the group in power" (p. 120).

Evaluating Violations of Our Expectations

If strangers violate our expectations to a sufficient degree that we recognize the violations, we become aroused and have to assess the situation (Burgoon & Hale, 1988). The degree to which strangers provide us with rewards affects how we evaluate the violations and the strangers committing the acts. As used here, rewards do not refer to money (although it might be a consideration if the other person is our boss or a client). Rather, *rewards* include the benefits we obtain from our interactions with strangers (e.g., status, affection). If strangers provide us with rewards, we choose the most positive of the possible interpretations of violations available to us; "for example, increased proximity during conversation may be taken as a sign of affiliation if committed by a high reward person but as a sign of aggressiveness if committed by a low reward person" (Burgoon & Hale, 1988, p. 63).

Positively evaluated violations of our expectations have positive consequences for our communication with violators (e.g., they do not lead to misinterpretations, increase intimacy). Negatively evaluated violations, in contrast, lead to negative outcomes (e.g., misinterpretations, decreases in intimacy). There are, however, exceptions for negative violations. If the other person provides rewards and commits an extreme violation of our expectations, positive outcomes (e.g., higher credibility and/or interpersonal attraction) are possible (Burgoon & Hale, 1988).

We often believe our expectations have been fulfilled when we communicate with strangers, regardless of how strangers behave (Stephan, 1985). We often do not change our behavior when strangers disconfirm our expectations. "Confirmation of positive expectancies and disconfirmation of negative expectancies would be expected to elicit favorable affective responses to the behavior, such as pride and happiness. Disconfirmation of positive expectancies and confirmation of negative expectancies may lead to negative affect, such as sadness or low self-esteem or resentment and hostility directed toward the self or the holder of the expectancy" (Stephan, 1985, p. 637). Whether strangers can provide rewards, however, influences how we interpret the confirmation or disconfirmation of our expectations.

Strangers usually are not viewed as potential sources of rewards. Rather, we tend to see the costs as outweighing the rewards when we communicate with strangers. There are exceptions, however. Interacting with strangers "is enjoyable when the interaction is brief, when the differences are few and on peripheral beliefs, and when the chance of rejection is small, that is, when the costs of pursuing dissimilar relations are negligible relative to the rewards" (Knapp, cited in Crockett & Friedman, 1980, p. 91).

Negative Intergroup Expectations

Both strangers and non-strangers bring expectations to intergroup encounters. We expect interpersonal interactions (e.g., interactions with members of our ingroups) to be more agreeable and less abrasive than our interactions with strangers (Hoyle et al., 1989). Our communication with strangers usually is based on negative expectations. Actual or anticipated interaction with strangers, for example, leads to anxiety.[2] "Intergroup anxiety often has a basis in reality. People sometimes do make embarrassing mistakes, are taken advantage of, and are rejected by ingroup and outgroup members" when communicating with strangers

(Stephan & Stephan, 1985, p. 160). One of the emotional reactions we have to our expectations of strangers being disconfirmed is that we become frustrated. "Frustration involves feelings of intense discomfort stemming from the blockage of paths toward goals. . . . Frustration, in turn, often leads to aggressive behavior when people try to vent their negative feelings" (Brislin et al., 1986, p. 250).

Several factors are associated with the amount of intergroup anxiety we experience when communicating with strangers. Thinking about the behavior in which we need to engage when communicating with strangers, for example, can reduce our anxiety about interacting with them (Janis & Mann, 1977). Further, if we focus on finding out as much as we can and forming accurate impressions of strangers, the biases we have based on our anxiety and our negative expectations will be reduced (Neuberg, 1989). The less intergroup contact we have had, the less ethnocentric we are, and the more positive our stereotypes are, the less the intergroup anxiety we experience (Stephan & Stephan, 1989).

Members of "majority" groups tend to have negative expectations for interacting with members of "minority" groups. Members of "minority" groups also have negative expectations for interacting with members of "majority" groups. Members of "minority" groups, for example, often mistrust European Americans and are suspicious of their intentions (Devine et al., 1996). One reason that members of "minority" groups are suspicious is that they are aware that their groups often are the targets of prejudice and discrimination. To illustrate, homosexuals may not tell others their gender orientation because they fear physical abuse or discrimination. Another reason that members of "minority" groups are suspicious is that they are not sure about the meaning of others' behavior. Members of "minority" groups do not know whether majority group members' behavior toward them is a response to their group memberships, their personal qualities, or majority group members' prejudice (Major & Crocker, 1993).

Members of "minority" groups who are stigmatized (e.g., looked down on) because of their group memberships (e.g., ethnicity, gender orientation) or other characteristics (e.g., having AIDS, paralysis) tend to be uncertain how others will respond to them. Because of the uncertainty, members of "minority" groups often become mindful of their interactions with others (Frable et al., 1990). When they are mindful, members of "minority" groups pay attention to their interactions with others and imagine different ways the interaction might proceed. This strategy can be adaptive because it allows members of "minority" groups to be responsive to the demands of the interaction. Being mindful, however, is only helpful if members of "minority" groups are not biased against the people with whom they are interacting (Devine et al., 1996). Members of "minority" groups who expect biases tend to see biases.

The extent to which expectations lead to miscommunication is, at least in part, a function of the match between strangers' (e.g., members of a group in the numerical "minority") and non-strangers' (e.g., members of a group in the numerical "majority") match or clash in expectations:

> An interaction between a high prejudiced majority group member and a suspicious minority group member may go relatively smoothly, if not positively. In this case, the majority group member may plan his or her interaction strategy so as to terminate the interaction as soon as possible. The minority group member may set in motion attributional biases to protect his or her self-esteem. . . . Under these circumstances, little miscommunication occurs, but tension is likely to be high. Alternatively, the majority group member may be a low prejudiced person who possesses the requisite skills to convey his or her standards [e.g., beliefs about minority group member], and the minority group member may not be suspicious of majority group members. Under these circumstances, miscommunication also is unlikely, and we can anticipate a smooth and positive exchange between the interactants. (Devine et al., 1996, pp. 453–454)

Miscommunication is most likely when interaction occurs between highly prejudiced "majority" group members and non-suspicious "minority" group members, as well as between low prejudiced "majority" group members and suspicious "minority" group members.

Stereotypes

Stereotypes are the pictures we have in our heads for the people we place in the various social categories we use (Lippmann, 1922). Stereotyping is a natural result of the communication process. We stereotype strangers immediately upon meeting them, and this occurs "within milliseconds after first encounters" (Operario & Fiske, 2001b, p. 33). There are three essential aspects of stereotypes: (1) we categorize others based on easily identifiable characteristics; (2) we assume that certain attributes apply to most or all of the people in the category, and that people in the category are different than people in other categories with respect to these attributes; and (3) we assume that individual members of the category have the attributes associated with their groups (Hewstone & Brown, 1986).

Take a few minutes to answer the following questions designed to get you to think about your stereotypes before reading the remainder of this section.

Of the groups with which you have contact, for which groups do you have "positive" stereotypes (list specific groups)?

___

___

___

Of the groups with which you have contact, for which groups do you have "negative" stereotypes (list specific groups)?

___

___

___

How do your "positive" and "negative" stereotypes influence your communication with members of these groups?

___

___

___

Your answers to these questions should provide some insights into the role of stereotypes in your implicit theory of communication. Keep your answers in mind as you read the remainder of the section.

Nature of Stereotypes

There is a distinction between stereotypes and social stereotypes. Some of our stereotypes are unique and based on our individual experiences, but some are shared with other members of our ingroups. The stereotypes we share with others are our social stereotypes. Stereotypes "become *social* only when they are shared by large numbers of people within social groups" (Tajfel, 1981, pp. 146–147). Social stereotypes often are used in the media and we learn many of our stereotypes from the media. Anyone who watches Saturday morning cartoons, for example, knows that villains are nonEuropeans. With respect to ageing, the "dirty old man" is used frequently in the media and ageing is depicted as involving evil, failures, and unhappiness in television dramas (Arnoff, 1974). Similarly, disabled people often are presented as bitter, self-pitying, and maladjusted, while nondisabled are portrayed as *not* having trouble accepting the disableds' identities (Longmore, 1987).

Virtually all stereotypes of the old, disabled, and nonEuropeans presented in the media are negative and inaccurate.

Stereotypes also are used in advertising. To illustrate, I received an advertisement for a cleaning service in the mail that indicated that the company had "German thoroughness, Swedish spotlessness, Polish flexibility, Discreet as a Swiss bank, Cheap as Russian promises." Some of these are positive stereotypes, but others are negative and are offensive to members of those groups.

Our stereotypes are multidimensional images.[3] They vary in terms of their complexity (e.g., the number of traits included), specificity (e.g., how specific the traits are), favorability (e.g., the positive or negative valence of the traits), the degree of consensus there is on the traits (i.e., social vs. individual stereotypes), and whether or not they are valid (i.e., the degree to which our stereotypes of a group coincide with the stereotypes members of those groups have of themselves; Vassiliou et al., 1972).

The size of the groups we are stereotyping influences the way we think about the groups (Mullen, 1991). In general, the smaller the group, the more simple our stereotypes. Group size also influences how we form our stereotypes. The smaller the group, the more likely we are to create stereotypes based on what we consider the average or typical member to be like. The larger the group, the more likely we are to base our stereotype on the group members with whom we have interacted.[4]

Appearance also contributes to the formation of stereotypes (Zebrowitz, 1996). We are attuned to strangers' physical appearances. Strangers' physical appearances provide information about their identities (e.g., ethnicities, ages), emotions, and health. Appearance is used to categorize strangers and it influences "the content of stereotypes about groups who are identified by their appearance. . . . Such stereotypes may be accurate, since appearance can provide accurate information about people's traits" (Zebrowitz, 1996, p. 108).

Our moods influence our tendency to stereotype. Negative moods clearly have an influence on our tendencies to stereotype. Positive moods, however, also can create problems. The more positive our moods, the more we perceive strangers' groups to be homogeneous, the more we perceive strangers to be typical members of their groups, and the more stereotypic judgments we make (Mackie et al., 1996). One reason for this is that the more positive our moods, the less we process information in a careful and thorough manner. This suggests that we need to be mindful when we interact with strangers when we are in extremely negative and extremely positive moods.

Content of Stereotypes

Stereotypes provide the content of our social categories. We have social categories in which we place people and it is our stereotypes that tell us what people in the categories are like.[5] Three basic principles underlie stereotype content: "(a) stereotypes contain ambivalent beliefs reflecting relationships between groups, (b) stereotypes augment perceptions of negative and extreme behavior, and (c) stereotypes maintain divisions between ingroup ('us') and outgroup ('them')" (Operario & Fiske, 2001b, p. 24).

Competence and niceness are core dimensions of stereotype content (Fiske et al., 1999). The relative status of the group being stereotyped determines whether its members are perceived as competent. The interdependence (cooperation vs. competition) between the groups influences whether members are seen as nice. Blind people, disabled people, the elderly, retarded people, and housewives are perceived as "nice, but incompetent." African American professionals, Jews, Asians, feminists, and businesswomen, in contrast, are perceived as "competent, but not nice." "The beliefs associated with these two clusters reflect the relationship with the dominant majority (white, male, middle-class, able-bodied). The first group [nice, but incompetent] present no threat to the majority, whereas the second group [competent, but not nice] presents a significant threat" (Operario & Fiske, 2001b, p. 25).

Since 1933, a series of studies have traced the content of U.S. American college students' stereotypes of several groups (i.e., "Americans," African Americans, Chinese, English, Germans, Irish, Italians, Jews, Japanese, Turks).[6] Over the years, the content of most of the stereotypes has remained relatively stable when the same adjectives are used. The one stereotype to change the most is that of African Americans (different labels were used in early studies). This stereotype became more positive between 1933 and 1969, but it has remained relatively stable since 1969 when the same adjectives are used (Madon et al., 2001). The most recent study looked at European Americans' and nonEuropean Americans' stereotypes:

> The European American sample most often perceived Germans as liking to drink beer, Italians as loyal to family ties, African Americans as listening to a lot of music and noisy, Irish as liking to drink beer, English as competitive, Jews as very religious and wealthy, Americans as diverse, Chinese as disciplined, Japanese as scientifically minded and disciplined, and Turks as very religious. The non-European American sample most often perceived Germans as liking to drink beer; Italians as macho; African Americans as musical and tough; Irish as liking to drink beer; English as egotistical, proud, and liberal; Jews as proud; Americans as diverse; Chinese and

Japanese as loyal to family ties; and Turks as cultural. (Madon et al., 2001, p. 1003)

These results suggest there is general agreement in the content of European Americans' and nonEuropean Americans' stereotypes of these groups.

Another recent study examines the stereotypes of African Americans, Asian Americans, European Americans, and Latino(a) Americans at 28 colleges and universities (Charles & Massey, 2003). All groups generally have favorable stereotypes of European Americans with one exception; African Americans, Asian Americans, and Latino(a) Americans see themselves as more "hard-working" than European Americans. Asian Americans, European Americans, and Latino(a) Americans perceive African Americans as "poor and violence prone," and they also perceive African Americans as more "lazy, unintelligent, and preferring welfare dependence" than themselves. African Americans, Asian Americans, and European Americans perceive Latino(a) Americans as "violence prone and poor." Asian Americans and European Americans perceive Latino(a) Americans to be more "lazy, unintelligent, and to prefer welfare dependence" than themselves. Asian Americans are perceived to be "hard-working, intelligent, preferring to be self-sufficient, and tending to stick to tasks." African Americans and Latino(a) Americans who identify mainly with the U.S. culture are more likely to stereotype their groups as "tending to be lazy, unintelligent, hard to get along with, to give up easily, and to discriminate against others" than those who identify mainly with their ethnic groups.

Stereotypes and Communication

Stereotypes and language are interlinked closely (Maas & Arcuri, 1996). It is difficult, for example, to imagine a stereotype that does not involve language. Language is the medium through which stereotypes are transmitted and maintained. Most of the process, however, takes place at very low levels of awareness (i.e., we do it mindlessly).

Stereotyping is the result of our tendencies to overestimate the degree of association between group memberships and psychological attributes. While there may be some association between group memberships and psychological characteristics of members, it is much smaller than we assume when we communicate on automatic pilot. Only 28 to 37 percent of the people in a culture, for example, have the traits attributed to them (Wallace, 1952). In some cases, there is more similarity between people in the same occupation across cultures than there is between people in different occupations within a culture (Inkeles, 1974).

Our stereotypes influence the way we process information. We remember more favorable information about our ingroups and more unfavorable information about outgroups (Hewstone & Giles, 1986). This, in turn, affects the way we interpret incoming messages from members of ingroups and outgroups. Our processing of information is "biased in the direction of maintaining the preexisting belief systems. . . . These processes, then, can produce the *cognitive confirmation* of one's stereotypic beliefs" (Hamilton et al., 1992, p. 138). Our stereotypes create expectations regarding how strangers will behave. Since they create expectations, stereotypes provide us with ways to predict and explain strangers' behavior. When we base our predictions of strangers' behavior on our stereotypes, we tend to have *confidence* in our predictions and explanations. Predictions and explanations based on stereotypes, however, are not necessarily accurate (see discussion of accuracy below).

Our stereotypes of strangers can influence strangers' views of themselves. Strangers may not generally view themselves as stigmatized (e.g., shamed or discredited), but when they interact with members of other ethnic groups and they expect to be evaluated by these people they feel stigmatized (e.g., Brown, 1998). To illustrate, nonEuropean American students may not feel stigmatized in general, but when they interact with European American instructors who will be evaluating them, they may feel stigmatized, especially if they expect a negative evaluation.

Our stereotypes tend to be activated automatically when we have contact with strangers (Devine, 1989). Unconsciously, we assume that our expectations are correct and behave as though they are:

> stereotypes operate as a source of expectancies about what a group as a whole is like (e.g., Hispanics) as well as about what attributes individual group members are likely to possess (e.g., Juan Garcia). Their influence can be pervasive, affecting the perceiver's attention to, encoding of, inferences about, and judgments based on that information. And the resulting interpretations, inferences, and judgments typically are made so as to be consistent with preexisting beliefs that guided them. (Hamilton et al., 1992, p. 142)

We, therefore, unconsciously try to confirm our expectations when we communicate with strangers.

Our stereotypes constrain strangers' communication and often lead us to engage in stereotype-confirming communication. Stated differently, stereotypes create self-fulfilling prophecies. We tend to see behavior that confirms our expectations, even when it is absent. We ignore disconfirming evidence when communicating on automatic pilot. "Perceivers can influence a person with whom they interact by constraining the person's behavior. However, perceivers typically do not recognize this influence or take it into consideration when interpreting the target's behavior. Although a target person's behavior may be affected by perceiver-induced constraints, it is often interpreted by the perceiver as a manifestation of the target's personality" (Hamilton et al., 1992, p. 149). To illustrate, if we assume strangers are not competent and communicate with them based on this assumption, they will appear incompetent (even if they are actually competent). We do not recognize our influence on strangers' behavior, and we judge them to be incompetent. We often do this when we communicate with disabled and older people.

Our tendency to engage in stereotype confirming behavior depends on our goals in the interaction (Snyder & Haugen, 1995). If our goal is to adjust to strangers and have smooth interactions, we tend to engage in stereotype confirming behavior. If our goal is to gather information about strangers, in contrast, we do not necessarily engage in stereotype confirming behavior. We also do not engage in stereotype confirming behavior when our expectations for strangers' behavior are weak or when there is a large difference between our expectations and what we observe (Operario & Fiske, 2001b).

There is an alternative explanation for stereotype confirming behavior. We may confirm others' stereotypes because of stereotype vulnerability. *Stereotype vulnerability* does not involve consciously or unconsciously accepting a stereotype; rather, it emerges from having to contend with stereotypes when mental capabilities are taxed.

> Much of what is mistaken for racial animosity in America today is really stereotype vulnerability. Imagine a Black man and a White man meeting for the first time. Because the Black knows the stereotype of his group, he attempts to deflect the negative traits, finding ways of trying to communicate, in effect, "Don't think of me as incompetent." The White, for his part, is busy deflecting the stereotype of his group: "Don't think of me as a racist." Every action becomes loaded with the potential of confirming the stereotype, and you can end up with two people struggling with phantoms they're only half aware of. The discomfort and tension is often mistaken for racial animosity. (Steele quoted by Watters, 1995, p. 47)

The problem is that both parties are mindful of the outcome, not the process of communication that takes place between them.

When strangers do not confirm our expectations, we are likely to see them as "exceptions to the rule." Our stereotypes will not change if we "group together disconfirming members into a subtype and treat them as exceptions, unrepresentative of the group as a whole" (Richards & Hewstone, 2001, p. 53). Alternatively, we can create subgroups within the broad categories in which we put strangers. This involves creating subgroups that are similar in some way and different from the other subgroups in some other ways. This process is similar to creating new categories in mindfulness (see Chapter 1; Langer, 1989). When we create subgroups, members of different subgroups confirm or disconfirm the general stereotype of the groups as a whole. Creating subgroups increases our perception of variability in the group as a whole, which can lead to changes in our stereotypes.

We are likely to stereotype strangers when we have power over them (Operario & Fiske, 2001b). One reason for this is that we do not pay attention to individuating information (e.g., how strangers are different from other members of their groups) about strangers when we have power over them. "Not only does power perpetuate beliefs associated with social subordinates and minority groups, it also enables people to act upon stereotypic beliefs through legislation, economic policies, and institutional practices" (p. 37). Members of low power groups may recognize their group's disadvantaged status, but tend to "minimize perceptions of personal vulnerability to discrimination" so they can maintain self-esteem and a sense of control (p. 37).

Stereotypes, in and of themselves, do not lead to miscommunication and/or communication breakdowns. If, however, inaccurate or negative stereotypes are held rigidly, they lead to inaccurate predictors of strangers' behavior and misunderstandings. In addition to inaccurate stereotypes, simple stereotypes (e.g., stereotypes with only a few traits) of strangers can lead to misunderstandings. In order to increase our effectiveness in communicating with strangers, we need to increase the complexity of our stereotypes (e.g., include a large number of traits in the stereotype and differentiate subgroups within the group being stereotyped) and question our unconscious assumption that most, if not all, members of a group fit a single stereotype (Stephan & Rosenfield, 1982).

We may try to avoid the influence of stereotypes on our behavior. One way we do this is by trying to suppress our stereotypes. This approach, however, usually does not work and frequently results in more stereotyping than when we do not try to suppress our stereotypes (Bodenhausen & Macrae, 1996). When we try to suppress stereotypes, the rebound effect (i.e., more, not less stereotyping) occurs most frequently for those of us who are highly prejudiced. It also occurs, however, in those of us who *want* to be low in prejudice, but still react negatively to members of other ethnic groups. The rebound effect occurs least frequently in those of us who are low in prejudice (Monteith et al.,

1998). The extent to which we are able to process complex information also influences the extent to which the rebound effect will occur. When something inhibits our abilities to process complex information (e.g., high levels of anxiety, cognitive overload), the rebound effect takes place.

As indicated at the beginning of the discussion of stereotypes, they tend to be activated automatically when we categorize ourselves or strangers. There are, however, some factors that moderate the activation of our stereotypes (Blair, 2002). First, our "motivation to maintain a positive self-image or have positive relationships with others" can moderate the activation of negative stereotypes (p. 255). We can, for example, choose to look at strangers in a positive manner if it supports our self-image or if we want to have positive interactions with them. Second, we can make "strategic efforts to reduce stereotypes or promote counterstereotypes" (p. 255). To illustrate, we can consciously decide to expect to see behavior that is inconsistent with our stereotypes. Third, our focus of attention influences the activation of our stereotypes. If we are preoccupied with something else, we may not automatically stereotype strangers. Alternatively, we could choose to focus on different identities and not activate our stereotypes of strangers' ethnicities. Fourth, contextual cues influence the activation of our stereotypes. Whether strangers are making eye contact with us or looking away affects whether our stereotypes of strangers' groups are activated. Also, different stereotypes of strangers' groups are activated depending on whether we meet strangers in church or on the street, and depending on what we are doing (e.g., eating dinner or working on a task).

When negative stereotypes are activated, we tend to react in a prejudiced fashion. People very low in prejudice, however, do not necessarily act on their "automatically activated stereotypes" (VonHippel et al., 1995, p. 224). Conscious control of our reactions when our stereotypes are activated is necessary for the rest of us to control our prejudice: "Nonprejudiced responses are . . . a function of intentional controlled processes and require a conscious decision to behave in a nonprejudiced fashion. In addition, new responses must be learned and well practiced before they can serve as competitive responses to the automatically activated stereotype-congruent response" (Devine, 1989, p. 15). This suggests that mindfulness is a successful strategy to reduce our prejudice.

Accuracy of Predictions Based on Stereotypes

There are many reasons that stereotypes are inaccurate (see Ryan et al., 1996). We have a tendency, for example, to overestimate or underestimate the major traits associated with strangers' groups. The positiveness or negativeness of our views of strangers' groups is influenced by our prejudice, ethnocentrism, ageism, sexism, and so forth (see next section). We also tend to assume that strangers from one group are more alike than they actually are. Our stereotypes of our ingroups are more accurate than our stereotypes of strangers' groups.

Strangers may or may not fit our stereotypes of their groups. There are four possible options between how strangers identify with their groups and the way they behave: (1) strangers may see themselves as typical group members and behave typically, (2) strangers may see themselves as typical group members and behave atypically (i.e., not typically), (3) strangers may see themselves as atypical group members and behave atypically, and (4) strangers may see themselves as atypical group members and behave typically (Ting-Toomey, 1989). It is actually more complicated than this, however, because our perceptions of strangers as typical or atypical members of their groups may not be the same as theirs.

The accuracy of our predictions of strangers' behavior depends on whether the traits that we include in our stereotypes of strangers' groups are similar to the ones in the strangers' stereotypes of their groups (i.e., are our stereotypes valid). If the traits we apply to strangers' groups agree with the traits strangers apply to their group, our stereotype should lead to accurate interpretations of the behavior of strangers who are typical members of their groups. Valid stereotypes, however, lead to misinterpretations of the behavior of atypical members of strangers' groups.

When we place strangers' behavior in a category our stereotypes help us predict strangers' behavior if we perceive strangers are typical members of their groups.[7] We are able to reduce our uncertainty because we *assume* that our stereotypes tell us how typical group members communicate (Krauss & Fussell, 1991). If strangers have informed us of their category memberships, our predictions may be accurate. To illustrate, if we are communicating with a woman who traces her heritage to Mexico and she tells us she is a Chicana, not a Mexican American, we can make some accurate predictions of her behavior if our stereotypes of people from Mexico differentiate Chicanos/Chicanas from Mexican Americans. If our stereotypes do not include this differentiation, then our predictions will probably not be accurate. It is rare, however, for strangers to tell us their group memberships directly (Kellermann, 1993).

Rather than using strangers' self-categorizations (the group memberships they announce), we tend to base our categorizations on their skin color, dress, accents, the cars they drive, and so forth (Clark & Marshall, 1981). The cues we use, however, are not always accurate ways to categorize strangers (i.e., an inaccurate categorization occurs when we put strangers in categories into which they would not place themselves). This is true for all social categories, including ethnicity. To illustrate, recall from Chapters 2 and 3 that we vary in the degree to which we identify with our ethnic groups and cultures. If we categorize strangers based on ethnicity and they do *not* identify strongly with their ethnic groups, our predictions will, in all likelihood, be inaccurate. Predictions based on ethnicity will probably only be accurate for strangers who identify strongly with their ethnic groups and do not identify strongly with their cultures.

Another source of inaccuracy in our predictions based on our stereotypes is that the boundaries between many social groups are fuzzy (Clark & Marshall, 1981). What, for example, is the boundary between educated and uneducated people? or between young and old? Even skin color may not be a good predictor of category membership. To illustrate, there are light-colored African Americans who look like European Americans. These individuals may be categorized as European Americans based only on skin color. They may, however, identify strongly with being African American. Obviously, predictions about their behavior based on skin color will be inaccurate.[8]

Even if strangers are typical members of the groups in which we categorize them, the inferences we make about them based on their group memberships may *not* be accurate. One reason for this is that our stereotypes are not valid (i.e., our stereotypes of strangers' groups are different from their stereotypes of their groups). Another reason our predictions may not be accurate is that the group memberships we are using to categorize strangers may not be affecting their behavior in specific situations. We are all members of many social groups that influence our behavior and provide us with different social identities. When communicating with strangers, we might categorize them based on one group membership (e.g., ethnicity) and assume that their social identities based on this category are influencing their behavior. The strangers, however, may be basing their behavior on different social identities (e.g., social class, gender, role). To increase our accuracy in making predictions, we must try to understand which social identities are guiding strangers' behavior in a particular situation.

Stereotypes and Communication Breakdowns

Stereotypes influence intergroup communication breakdowns. A *communication breakdown* is a feeling of dissatisfaction that detracts from the full potential of an encounter (Hewstone & Giles, 1986). For the breakdown to be intergroup in nature, the individuals must attribute their dissatisfaction as being due to memberships in contrasting social groups.

The context in which we interact with strangers influences whether communication breakdowns occur (Hewstone & Giles, 1986). *Context* involves the historical and changing relationship between social groups.

It includes the past efforts that members of different groups have made toward mutual social and linguistic accommodation. *Accommodation* refers to our tendency to adapt our behavior to strangers' behavior. We can move toward strangers (convergence) or move away from them (divergence). Using our own language when around people who do not speak it (divergence), for example, is one way we may exert positive social identities (Giles et al., 1977). We tend to react favorably to strangers who linguistically move toward us (e.g., speak our language or dialect).[9] Our reaction, however, depends upon the intent we attribute to the strangers. If we perceive strangers' intent to be positive, we will evaluate their convergence positively. As mutual convergence increases, there is less of a likelihood of communication breakdowns occurring. Also, as we perceive that strangers are making evaluative comparisons with our groups, there is an increased potential for communication breakdowns to occur.

Our perceptions of the situation and of the characteristics of the strangers with whom we are communicating (e.g., are there more strangers than members of our own groups present? are the strangers typical of their groups?) affect how important our social identities are in the encounter (Hewstone & Giles, 1986). Our stereotypes of strangers lead us to depersonalize them (i.e., think of them as members of a group and not as individuals). When this occurs, we place little emphasis on strangers' individual characteristics since the stereotypes associated with the strangers' groups are guiding our behavior. We use our stereotypes of strangers' groups to explain communication difficulties and, therefore, confirm our negative feelings associated with strangers' groups. Participants in intergroup breakdowns are likely to seek advice and consolation from members of the ingroup and, therefore, they will ultimately attribute the cause of the breakdown to the strangers.

Assessing Your Stereotypes

To get an idea of what your stereotypes are, take a few minutes and complete the questionnaire in Table 4.1. To complete this questionnaire you need to think of a specific group to which you belong (e.g., your culture or ethnic group) and another group (e.g., another culture or ethnic group). Take a few minutes to complete the questionnaire now.

The specific adjectives you checked constitute the content of your stereotype. The content of your stereotypes can vary in complexity (i.e., the number of traits). The content also can vary in terms of the degree of consensus (i.e., do other members of your group assign the same traits to your group) and validity (i.e., do members of the other group assign the same traits to themselves as you assign to them).

TABLE 4.1 *Assessing Your Stereotypes**

The purpose of this questionnaire is to help you understand what your stereotypes of your own and other groups are. Several adjectives are listed below and there is space for you to add adjectives if the ones you want to use are not listed. Since stereotypes are specific to particular groups, you will have to think of specific groups. Think of one group of which you are a member (e.g., your cultural or ethnic group) and an outgroup (e.g., another culture or ethnic group). Put a check mark in the column "My Group" next to the adjectives that apply to your group. Put a check mark in the column marked "Other Group" next to the adjectives that apply to the outgroup you have selected. After you make your check marks, go back through the list and rate each adjective you checked in terms of how favorable the quality described by the adjective is: 1 = very unfavorable, 2 = moderately unfavorable, 3 = neither favorable nor unfavorable, 4 = moderately favorable, and 5 = very favorable. Put these ratings in the column to the right of the adjectives.

My Group	Other Group		Favorableness
_____	_____	Intelligent	_____
_____	_____	Materialistic	_____
_____	_____	Ambitious	_____
_____	_____	Industrious	_____
_____	_____	Compassionate	_____
_____	_____	Deceitful	_____
_____	_____	Conservative	_____
_____	_____	Practical	_____
_____	_____	Shrewd	_____
_____	_____	Arrogant	_____
_____	_____	Aggressive	_____
_____	_____	Warm	_____
_____	_____	Sophisticated	_____
_____	_____	Conceited	_____
_____	_____	Neat	_____
_____	_____	Alert	_____
_____	_____	Friendly	_____
_____	_____	Cooperative	_____
_____	_____	Impulsive	_____
_____	_____	Stubborn	_____
_____	_____	Conventional	_____
_____	_____	Progressive	_____
_____	_____	Sly	_____
_____	_____	Tradition-loving	_____
_____	_____	Pleasure-loving	_____
_____	_____	Competitive	_____
_____	_____	Honest	_____
_____	_____	Modern	_____

(Continued)

TABLE 4.1 (Continued)

_____	_____	Emotional	_____
_____	_____	Logical	_____
_____	_____	Sincere	_____

The adjectives you checked constitute the content of your stereotypes. To find out how favorable the stereotypes are add the numbers next to the adjectives you checked and divide by the number of adjectives you checked. Compute separate favorableness scores for the stereotype of your group and the other group. Scores range from 1 to 5. The higher the score, the more favorable your stereotype.

*Adapted in part from Katz and Braly (1933).

Intergroup Attitudes

"An attitude is a learned predisposition to respond in an evaluative (from extremely favorable to extremely unfavorable) manner toward some attitude object" (Davidson & Thompson, 1980, p. 27). Attitudes, therefore, create expectations for others' behavior. I focus on four specific attitudes that affect our communication with strangers in this section: ethnocentrism, prejudice, sexism, and ageism.

Ethnocentrism

Ethnocentrism is "the view of things in which one's own group is the center of everything, and all others are scaled and rated with reference to it" (Sumner, 1940, p. 13). Two facets of ethnocentrism can be isolated (LeVine & Campbell, 1972). One involves our orientation toward our ingroups. If we are highly ethnocentric, we see our ingroups as virtuous and superior, and we see our ingroups' values as universal (i.e., applying to everyone). The second facet of ethnocentrism involves our orientation toward outgroups. If we are highly ethnocentric, we see outgroups as contemptible and inferior, we reject outgroups' values, we blame outgroups for ingroup troubles, and we try to maintain social distance from outgroups.

Take a few minutes to answer the following questions about your attitudes toward members of cultures before you read this section.

Think about behavior of people from other cultures with which you are familiar. What do you do when you generally think that their behavior is very different from yours?

____

____

____

How do you try to make sense of the behavior of people from other cultures?

____

____

____

How do you judge the behavior of people from other cultures?

____

____

____

Your answers to these questions provide some insights into the role of ethnocentrism in your implicit theory of communication. Keep your answers in mind as you read the remainder of this section.

We can think about ethnocentrism as the tendency to interpret and evaluate strangers' behavior using our own standards. This tendency is natural and unavoidable. **Everyone is ethnocentric to some degree**. It is possible to have a low degree of ethnocentrism, but it is impossible to be nonethnocentric. Ethnocentrism leads us to view our ways of doing things as the natural and right ways of doing things. The major consequence of this in an intergroup context is that we tend to view our ingroup's ways of doing things as superior to outgroups' ways of doing things. In other words, ethnocentrism is a bias toward the ingroup that causes us to evaluate different patterns of behavior negatively, rather than try to understand them.

The opposite of ethnocentrism is cultural relativism. *Cultural relativism* involves trying to understand strangers' behavior in the context of the cultures or groups of the strangers engaging in the behavior. We cannot understand strangers' behavior if we use our own cultural or ethnic frames of reference to interpret their behavior.

> I didn't learn until I was in college about all other cultures, and I should have learned that in first grade. A first grader should understand that his or her culture isn't a rational invention; that there are thousands of other cultures and they all work pretty well; that all cultures function on faith rather than truth; that there are lots of alternatives to our own society. Cultural relativity is defensible and attractive. It also is a source of hope. It means we don't have to continue this way if we do not like it. (Kurt Vonnegut Jr.)[10]

Some degree of cultural relativism is necessary to understand strangers' behavior. Cultural relativism, however, should not be extended to moral relativism (this issue is discussed in detail in Chapter 10).

The more ethnocentric we are, the more trouble we have making accurate predictions of and explanations for strangers' behavior (Gudykunst, 1995). Also, the more ethnocentric we are, the greater our anxiety when we interact with strangers (Stephan & Stephan, 1985). When we are culturally relative, in contrast, we try to understand strangers' behavior from their perspectives. This allows us to make accurate predictions of and explanations for strangers' behavior.

The attitudes we hold influence the way we speak to strangers. The speed with which we talk or the accent we use may be varied in order to generate different feelings of distance between us and the strangers with whom we are communicating (i.e., to make the distance seem smaller or greater). The concept of *communicative distance* can be used to explain this linguistic diversity: "our awareness of a communicative distance in the midst of a conversation depends to a large extent on certain linguistic devices which serve, from the speaker's point of view, to set up the communicative distance, or from the hearer's point of view, to let the hearer know that it has already been set up by the speaker" (Peng, 1974, p. 33). This conceptualization of communicative distance can be extended to *ethnocentric speech,* communicative distance based on our ethnocentrism (Lukens, 1978) and communicative distances based on cultural relativism (Gudykunst & Kim, 1984).[11]

The *distance of disparagement* involves very high levels of ethnocentrism and very low levels of cultural relativism. This distance reflects animosity of the ingroup toward strangers (Lukens, 1978). It arises when the two groups are in competition for the same resources. This level is characterized by the use of pejorative (e.g., negative) expressions about the outgroup and the use of ethnophaulisms (i.e., ethnic name-calling).[12] Imitation and mockery of speech styles are characteristic of this distance.

The *distance of avoidance* is based on high levels of ethnocentrism and low levels of cultural relativism. It is established in order to avoid or minimize contact with strangers (Lukens, 1978). One technique commonly used to accomplish this is the use of an ingroup dialect. "The emphasizing of an ethnic dialect and other linguistic differences between the in-group and outsiders may be purposefully used by in-group members to make themselves appear esoteric to the out-group thus lessening the likelihood for interaction" (p. 45). At this distance, members of the ingroup also may use terms of solidarity (e.g., "black pride"). Feelings of ingroup pride and solidarity are increased through the use of such terms. In establishing the distance of avoidance, jargon common to the ingroup is used extensively.

The *distance of indifference* is based on moderate levels of ethnocentrism and moderate levels of cultural relativism. It is the speech form used to "reflect the view that one's own [group] is the center of everything" (Lukens, 1978, p. 42). This distance, therefore, reflects an insensitivity to strangers' perspectives. One example of the speech used at this distance is "foreigner talk," the form of speech we use when talking to people who are not native speakers of our languages. It usually takes the form of loud and slow speech patterns, exaggerated pronunciations, and simplifications (e.g., deletion of articles). "We tend to believe that, if we speak slowly enough or loudly enough, anyone can understand us. I have done this myself quite without realizing it, and others have tried to reach me in the same way in Japanese, Chinese, Thai, Punjabi, Navajo, Spanish, Tibetan, and Singhalese" (Downs, 1971, p. 19). The distance of indifference also is characterized by the use of idiomatic expressions like "Indian giver," "Jew them down," "Mexican standoff," "the blind leading the blind," "Russian roulette," "black sheep," "blacklist," and "low person on the totem pole" that suggest indifference to strangers' feelings.

The *distance of sensitivity* is based on low ethnocentrism and high cultural relativism. This distance reveals a sensitivity to group differences (Gudykunst & Kim, 1984). Our speech at this level reflects our desire to decrease the communicative distance between ourselves and strangers. When speaking at this level with members of a different ethnic group, for example, we would use the label for their ethnic group that they prefer, even if it is different from the one we typically use. When men are speaking with women at this distance, for example, they will avoid using the term "lady" if it causes offense to the women with whom they are speaking.

The *distance of equality* is based on very high cultural relativism and very low ethnocentrism. It reflects our desire to minimize the distance between ourselves and strangers (Gudykunst & Kim, 1984). This distance involves an attitude of equality, one where we demonstrate we are interpreting the language and behavior of strangers in terms of their groups' standards. Speech at this distance avoids evaluations of strangers. Men's use of nonsexist language (e.g., using "his or her" instead of using "he" as a generic pronoun), for example, would reflect a distance of equality between men and women.

Assessing Your Ethnocentrism. Table 4.2 contains a brief questionnaire designed to help you assess your level of ethnocentrism. Take a moment to complete the questionnaire. In responding to the statements, please keep in mind it will not help you to understand your communication behavior if you answer the questions as you think you should. For the questionnaire to be useful, the questions must be answered honestly.

Scores on the questionnaire range from 10 to 50. The higher your score, the more ethnocentric you are. I will not provide average scores

TABLE 4.2 *Assessing Your Ethnocentrism**

The purpose of this questionnaire is to assess your ethnocentrism. Respond to each statement by indicating the degree to which the statement is true regarding the way you typically think about yourself. When you think about yourself, is the statement "Always False" (answer 1), "Mostly False" (answer 2), "Sometimes True and Sometimes False" (answer 3), "Mostly True" (answer 4), or "Always True" (answer 5)? Answer honestly, not how you think you should.

_____ 1. I do not apply my values when judging strangers.
_____ 2. I see people who are similar to me as virtuous.
_____ 3. I cooperate with strangers.
_____ 4. I prefer to associate with people who are like me.
_____ 5. I trust strangers.
_____ 6. I am obedient to authorities.
_____ 7. I do not fear strangers.
_____ 8. I try to maintain distance from members of other groups.
_____ 9. I do not blame strangers for troubles I have.
_____ 10. I believe that my values are universal values.

To find your score, first reverse the responses for the odd numbered items (i.e., if you wrote 1, make it 5; if you wrote 2, make it 4; if you wrote 3, leave it as 3; if you wrote 4, make it 2; if you wrote 5, make it 1). Next, add the numbers next to each of the statements. Scores range from 10 to 50. The higher the score, the more ethnocentric you are.

*Based on Brewer's (1981) description of ethnocentrism.

because they would not be useful in helping you improve your communication. The thing to keep in mind is that the more ethnocentric you are, the more likely you are to misinterpret strangers' messages. You can manage the effect of ethnocentrism on your communication when you are mindful.

Prejudice

Prejudice involves making a prejudgment based on membership in a social category. While prejudice can be positive or negative, there is a tendency for most of us to think of it as negative. Consistent with this view, *negative ethnic prejudice* is "an antipathy based on a faulty and unflexible generalization. It may be felt or expressed. It may be directed toward a group as a whole, or toward an individual because he [or she] is a member of that group" (Allport, 1954, p. 10).

Take a few minutes to answer the following questions about your prejudices before reading the remainder of this section.

With members of which ethnic groups do you like to associate (list specific groups)?

___

___

___

With members of which ethnic groups do you not like to associate (list specific groups)?

___

___

___

How do your preferences to associate or not associate with members of specific ethnic groups influence your communication?

___

___

___

Your answers to these questions should begin to provide some insight into the role of prejudice in your implicit theory of communication. Keep your answers in mind as you read the remainder of this section.

Dimensions of Prejudice. We tend to think of prejudice in terms of a dichotomy; either I am prejudiced or I am not. It is more accurate, however, to think of the strength of our prejudice as varying along a continuum from low to high. This suggests that **we all are prejudiced to some degree**. We also are all racist, sexist, ageist, and so forth to some degree. As with ethnocentrism, this is natural and unavoidable. It is the result of our being socialized as members of our ingroups. Even people with low levels of prejudice prefer to interact with people who are similar to themselves because such interactions are more comfortable and less stressful than interactions with strangers.

The amount of our prejudices (e.g., low to high) is related to our personal standards for how to treat strangers (Devine et al., 1996). People who are low in prejudice want to behave in ways that are consistent with their standards for treating strangers. These standards are important parts of their self-concepts. People who are low in prejudice, therefore, are motivated to interact with strangers in non-prejudiced ways. People who are low in prejudice, however, sometimes respond with more prejudice than they find acceptable. When this occurs they feel guilty and criticize themselves. People who are high in prejudice do not have well-defined standards for treating strangers, and the standards are not particularly important to them. They, therefore, do not feel guilty when their behavior does not meet their standards for treating strangers.

We also can think of prejudice as varying along a second continuum ranging from very positive to very negative. We tend to be positively prejudiced toward our ingroups and negatively prejudiced toward outgroups. There has been a tendency for European Americans' prejudice to decrease from the 1950s to now, but there is still resistance to government programs to eliminate discrimination. "While White approval of the principles of equality and integration was steadily advancing over the last four decades, White support for the policies that might bring such principles to life was not" (Kinder & Sanders, 1996, p. 270). Surveys taken in the late 1980s and early 1990s suggest that 35 percent of European Americans support school desegregation and 46 percent of European Americans support equal opportunity programs. The corresponding percentages for African Americans are 83 and 90 percent, respectively. "By the 1980s, most Americans no longer considered it appropriate to express prejudice openly. Prejudice was becoming more covert, and the people who harbored negative feelings toward other racial, ethnic, and religious groups were increasingly reluctant to express them in public. However, prejudice did not disappear" (Stephan & Stephan, 2001, p. 11).

Prejudice often is expressed as a pro-white bias now (Greenwald et al., 1998). The pro-white bias is related to the "aversive" form of racism in the United States today (e.g., Gaertner & Dovidio, 1986).[13] Aversive racists' reactions "to minorities is not one of overt dislike or hostility, but rather one of anxiety or discomfort. As a consequence, aversive racists tend to avoid interracial interactions whenever possible. And although they try not to behave in overtly negative ways toward blacks (which would threaten their self image as unbiased), they frequently express their bias indirectly, by favoring whites rather than discriminating against blacks and other minorities" (Dovidio, 1997, p. A60). Aversive racists endorse egalitarian values, but discriminate (intentionally or unintentionally) when they can rationalize that their behavior is not based on race. Aversive racists discriminate against minorities by favoring people like themselves (e.g., through promotions, mentoring). "Because aversive racists are unaware of their own prejudice and discriminate only when they can justify their behavior on grounds other than race, they tend to underestimate the continuing impact of race" (Dovidio, 1997, p. A60). There is no such thing as reasonable racism (see Armour, 1997).

One recent survey also suggests the trend for younger European Americans to have more positive attitudes toward African Americans than older European Americans may be on the decline. An Anti-Defamation League survey reports that 35 percent of European Americans over age 50 are highly prejudiced against African Americans, while 23 percent between 30 and 49, and 31 percent of those between 18 and 29 are highly prejudiced.[14] Some writers argue that there is a "new white nationalism" emerging in the United States today (e.g., Swain, 2002).

Viewing prejudice as varying along continua from low to high and favorable to unfavorable does not capture the complexity of our intergroup attitudes. There actually may be two different types of intergroup prejudice: one based on strong negative affect toward outgroups, the other based on the absence of positive feelings toward outgroups (Brewer & Brown, 1998). "Ultimately, many forms of discrimination and bias may develop not because outgroups are hated, but because positive emotions such as admiration, sympathy, and trust are reserved for the ingroup and withheld from outgroups" (Brewer & Brown, 1998, p. 575).

There are at least four aspects of ingroup identification and intergroup comparisons that influence the type of bias that occurs (Brewer, 2002). First, social categorization leads to the formation of ingroups and outgroups. Second, we positively value our ingroups and want to maintain cooperative relations with members of our ingroups. Third, intergroup comparisons often lead us to view our ingroups as superior to outgroups. Fourth, when there are antagonistic relations between ingroups and outgroups, outgroup hostility occurs. Recognizing our ingroup memberships and valuing them does not necessarily lead to prejudice. Prejudices emerge from intergroup comparisons and antagonistic relations between groups.

It often is assumed that young children (e.g., between three and seven) develop prejudices against outgroup members (e.g., Aboud, 1988). It is clear that young children recognize racial differences and show a preference for their own races, but it is not clear that young children develop prejudices against outgroups (Cameron et al., 2001). Whether or not young children develop prejudices against outgroups depends on the relations between their ingroups and outgroups in their neighborhoods and schools.

It also appears that some people in the United States today experience inner conflict regarding members of other ethnic groups. Some people have both favorable and unfavorable attitudes that are not necessarily related to each other. Both attitudes are important to these people. With respect to African Americans, for example, the majority of European

Americans are disposed "(a) to be in sympathy with [African Americans] as a group that is unfairly disadvantaged by past and present discrimination but also (b) to be critical of them for not doing enough to help themselves" (Hass et al., 1992, p. 787). When we are aware of our incompatible beliefs regarding other ethnic groups, we experience psychological discomfort and stress. Recognizing our incompatible beliefs may damage our self-images as humane people (Hass et al., 1992). We, therefore, try to manage the way we present ourselves to strangers in the way we talk when we are worried about the outcome of our interactions.

There is a potential explanation for our holding and expressing both tolerant and prejudiced attitudes toward a particular group. It appears that the extent to which we hold or express our prejudices at any particular time is a function of the identities we have activated in the situation (Verkuyten & Hagendoorn, 1998). To illustrate, if I think of myself in terms of one of my personal identities when interacting with a member of another ethnic group, my prejudices toward that person's ethnic group are not manifested. If I think of myself in terms of my ethnic identity, in contrast, my prejudices toward members of the other person's ethnic group will be manifested if I communicate on automatic pilot.

We tend to respond to intergroup interactions in self-focused ways (Vorauer & Kumhyr, 2001). That is, we tend to worry about how others are evaluating us. This occurs for both European Americans and nonEuropean Americans. Others' prejudices tend to be perceived in terms of "self-directed negative affect." Perceptions of personal discrimination (as opposed to group discrimination), however, tend to be moderated by ethnic identities for nonEuropean Americans but not for European Americans (Operario & Fiske, 2001a). NonEuropean Americans who strongly identify with their ethnic groups perceive personal vulnerability to discrimination. NonEuropean Americans who weakly identify with their ethnic groups, in contrast, perceive that it is the group that is being discriminated against, not themselves personally. NonEuropean Americans' strength of ethnic identity also moderates responses to subtle prejudice. Those who strongly identify with their ethnic groups react more strongly to subtle prejudice than those who weakly identify with their ethnic groups.

Most research on prejudice has focused on whites' attitudes toward blacks. One recent study, however, isolates four dimensions of anti-white attitudes among blacks (Johnson & Lecci, 2003). The first dimension is "ingroup-directed stigmatization/discriminatory expectations." This dimension involves blacks perceiving that whites see blacks as inferior and that whites discriminate against blacks. The second dimension is "outgroup-directed negative beliefs," or blacks' negative beliefs about whites (e.g., that whites are racists). The third dimension is "negative views toward ingroup-outgroup relations." This dimension involves blacks viewing relations with whites negatively (e.g., looking at interracial romances negatively). The final dimension, "negative verbal expression toward the outgroup," includes calling whites names (e.g., "honkey") and insulting whites.

An Explanation for Overt Prejudice. There are numerous explanations for prejudice that have been posited over the years (e.g., scapegoating, authoritarian personalities). One recent theory, integrated threat theory (Stephan & Stephan, 1996, 2000; see Stephan et al., 2002, for a recent study), incorporates intergroup anxiety as a major factor explaining our prejudice. Integrated threat theory suggests that there are four "threats" that cause our prejudices: intergroup anxiety, realistic threats, symbolic threats, and negative stereotypes.

Intergroup anxiety leads to "amplified cognitive, affective, and behavioral responses, most of which are negative in intergroup contexts" (Stephan et al., 1999, p. 619). *Realistic threats* are threats to the existence of our ingroups and/or threats to our well-being or the well-being of our ingroups. "The perception of threat can lead to prejudice, regardless of whether or not the threat is real" (p. 619). *Symbolic threats* involve perceived differences in values, customs, attitudes, morals, and so forth between our ingroups and strangers' outgroups. These are threats because we tend to see our ingroups' ways of doing things as the right ways to do things, especially when we are on automatic pilot. *Negative stereotypes* are the final threat leading to prejudice. These are threats because they lead to negative expectations for strangers' behavior.

Several factors influence whether we perceive that these four threats exist. The more positive our prior contact with strangers, the less likely we are to perceive the threats (Stephan & Stephan, 1996). Status inequalities between our ingroups and strangers' groups heighten our tendency to perceive these threats. The less knowledge we have about strangers and their groups, the more likely we are to perceive threats. Finally, the stronger our identification with the relevant ingroup (e.g., ethnicity if we categorize strangers based on this), the more we perceive the four threats. I believe, however, that this only occurs if we are insecure in our ingroup identities.

Forms of Prejudice. Prejudice can take many forms. When our prejudice is based on race, the relevant attitude is racism. *Individual racism* is prejudice against members of other races. Racism usually is associated with European Americans' prejudice against African Americans. African

Americans, however, can hold racist attitudes toward European Americans. Racism can involve other races as well.[15] There is a difference between individual racism and institutional racism. *Institutional racism* involves racial bias that is embedded in institutions (e.g., business, government). At the institutional level, racism involves the group in power discriminating against those that do not have power (e.g., in hiring decisions, university admissions, housing). At the individual level, we are all racists to some extent. This is a natural result of being socialized as members of our races.

There also are other forms of prejudice. When our prejudice is based on sex, the relevant prejudice is sexism (discussed later in this chapter). When our prejudice is based on age, the prejudice is ageism (discussed later in this chapter). When our prejudice is based on gender orientation, the relevant prejudice is homophobia. Other forms of prejudice can be based on religion (e.g., anti-Semitism) or social class, to name only a few.

Prejudice and Communication. Our prejudice is reflected in our communication with members of the groups against which we are prejudiced.

> Communication that is prejudiced or stereotypic specifically involves the explicit or implicit conveyance of stereotypic beliefs, prejudiced attitudes, or discriminatory intentions. Although prejudiced communication includes blatant forms such as hate speech, written discriminatory policies, and extreme symbolism (e.g., swastikas), a good portion of prejudiced communication is subtle. . . . Communicators may not always be consciously aware that these behaviors transmit beliefs that the outgroup is unworthy of greater consideration or is simply inferior, or even that they are conveying feelings of disdain or distrust. Indeed, without a direct comparison between how individuals treat ingroup and outgroup members, on-lookers may fail to recognize subtle behaviors as reflecting prejudice. (Ruscher, 2001, pp. 2–3)

Prejudiced communication can occur at the individual level, or at the institutional or societal levels (e.g., members of the ingroup demand that members of outgroups use the ingroup's language).

It generally is not acceptable to make overt prejudiced or racist comments in public.[16] It may be acceptable within some ingroups (e.g., Ku Klux Klan, Skinheads), but in public talk most people try to present themselves as nonprejudiced. If we are going to make a negative comment about strangers, for example, we preface our comment with a claim of not being prejudiced. To illustrate, one person responds in this way:

> Interviewer: Did you ever have any unpleasant experiences [with foreigners]?
>
> Interviewee: I have nothing against foreigners. But their attitude, their aggression is scaring. We are no longer free here. You have to be careful. (van Dijk, 1984, p. 65)

An African American law professor reports that a European American woman approached her after a meeting saying that "the media have made such monsters of black men that I find myself afraid when I meet two black men on the street" (Nayo, 1995, p. B7). The blame for her feelings, therefore, is placed on the media, not her prejudice.

Prejudiced communication clusters in four categories: (1) "they are different (culture, mentality)"; (2) "they do not adapt themselves"; (3) "they are involved in negative acts (nuisance, crime)"; and (4) "they threaten our (social, economic) interests" (van Dijk, 1984, p. 70).[17] We communicate our prejudice and racism in our everyday talk or behavior and we usually are not aware of doing it (Essed, 1991). To illustrate, a clerk in a store may follow an African American customer around the store, but not watch a European American. If the African American has not done anything suspicious, this is a clear case of racism. Prejudice and racism occur frequently and we often do not recognize them because we are so used to hearing them. After Martin Luther King Jr. was shot, for example, European American reporters asked African American leaders questions like "Who is going to hold your people together?" Some reporters said things like "When our leader died (referring to John F. Kennedy), his widow held us together." Many people hear reporting like this but do not recognize the racism inherent in it.[18]

The presence of ingroup members leads us to identify with our ingroups and see outgroup members as typical members of their groups (Wilder & Shapiro, 1991). The way we talk about and to people who are different is, in large part, a function of how we want to be seen by our ingroups, not strangers' groups.

> People "adapt" their discourse to the rules and constraints of interaction and communication social settings. Especially when delicate topics, such as "foreigners," are concerned, social members will strategically try to realize both the aims of positive self-presentation and those of effective persuasion. Both aims, however, derive from the position of social members within their group. Positive self-presentation is not just a defense mechanism of individuals as persons, but also as respected, accepted, and integrated social members of ingroups. And the same holds for the persuasive

> nature of prejudiced talk; people do not merely lodge personal complaints or uneasiness about people of other groups, but intend to have their experiences, their evaluations, their opinions, their attitudes, and their actions shared by other members of the ingroup. (van Dijk, 1984, p. 154)

We all engage is prejudiced talk to some degree. It is inevitable when we communicate on automatic pilot. We can, however, reduce the degree to which we engage in prejudiced talk if we are mindful of our communication.

The "manner in which people talk to outgroup members reflects their lowered expectations for them" (Ruscher, 2001, p. 91). When communicating with strangers from other ethnic groups, for example, prejudiced communicators may use controlling talk (e.g., controlling the conversation by interrupting strangers), being impolite, or being pedantic. When communicating with elderly adults, prejudiced communicators may use "secondary baby talk" (e.g., use simple language). Controlling talk tends to be used when prejudiced communicators think that strangers want "equal status." To illustrate, prejudiced communicators speak to elderly adults using baby talk more than controlling talk when they think that the elderly do not "assert their independence" (Ruscher, 2001).

Prejudiced communication often occurs in the news media. "The news media's video and audio depictions of less powerful groups, namely, women and minorities, seem largely consistent with cultural stereotypes. Women subtly are portrayed as weak objects compared to their male counterparts; blacks often are portrayed as criminals" (Ruscher, 2001, p. 143). We often do not recognize the prejudice that is inherent in the news media's portrayals of strangers. We, therefore, not only need to be mindful when interacting with strangers, but also when watching stories about them in the news.

The more prejudiced we are, the less accurate our predictions of and explanations for strangers' behavior will be (Gudykunst, 1995). Also, the more prejudiced we are, the greater our anxiety when we interact with strangers (Stephan & Stephan, 1985). If we are moderately to highly prejudiced, we need to mindfully manage our prejudice when we interact with strangers if we want to communicate effectively with them.

Assessing Your Prejudice. Table 4.3 contains a questionnaire designed to assess your level of prejudice. Take a couple of minutes to complete it now. Answer the questions honestly.

Scores on the questionnaire range from 10 to 50. The higher your score on the questionnaire, the greater your level of prejudice. Everyone will be prejudiced to some degree. This is unavoidable. The important

TABLE 4.3 *Assessing Your Prejudice**

The purpose of this questionnaire is to assess your prejudice. Respond to each statement by indicating the degree to which the statement is true regarding the way you typically think about other groups. When you think about other groups, is the statement "Always False" (answer 1), "Mostly False" (answer 2), "Sometimes True and Sometimes False" (answer 3), "Mostly True" (answer 4), or "Always True" (answer 5)? Answer honestly, not how you think you should.

_____ 1. Affirmative action programs discriminate against whites.
_____ 2. Strangers have not received as much support as they deserve to make up for past discrimination.
_____ 3. Strangers have received more attention in the media than they deserve.
_____ 4. I understand why strangers are angry at my group.
_____ 5. Strangers should not go where they are not wanted.
_____ 6. Strangers are cooperative.
_____ 7. Strangers are too demanding in their push for equal rights.
_____ 8. Discrimination against strangers is a problem today.
_____ 9. Strangers are receiving unfair privileges in society today.
_____ 10. I have positive feelings about strangers.

To find your score, first reverse the responses for the even numbered items (i.e., if you wrote 1, make it 5; if you wrote 2, make it 4; if you wrote 3, leave it as 3; if you wrote 4, make it 2; if you wrote 5, make it 1). Next, add the numbers next to each statement. Scores range from 10 to 50. The higher your score, the greater your prejudice.

*Adapted in part from McConahay (1986).

thing to keep in mind is that we can manage how our prejudices influence our communication by being mindful when we communicate with strangers.

Before reading the next section, take a moment to answer the following questions about how you deal with people who make prejudiced remarks.

Assume that you are in a line at a department store. The European American standing in front of you says to the African American clerk, "I don't want you helping me." What would you do or say?

____

____

____

One of your relatives is visiting your house. You know this person always makes prejudiced comments about nonEuropean Americans and it bothers you. What would you say to your relative if you wanted the person to stop making prejudiced comments?

____

____

____

You are having a conversation with someone you do not know well, but a friend told you she or he is highly prejudiced. You are afraid this person might make prejudiced comments and you prefer that the person not do this. What might you do or say?

____

____

____

Your answers to these questions should provide some insight into how you view your role in stopping others from making prejudiced comments. Keep your answers to these questions in mind as you read the remainder of this section.

Responding to Others' Ethnocentrism and Prejudice

We can influence the amount of ethnocentric speech or prejudiced talk in which others engage. When we express culturally relative or antiprejudiced sentiments, others are less likely to make ethnocentric or prejudiced comments in our presence (Blanchard et al., 1991). When we are bystanders, we "can define the meaning of events and move others toward empathy and indifference. [We] can promote values and norms of caring, or by passivity or participation in the system [we] can affirm the perpetrators" (Staub, 1989, p. 87).

We can influence European Americans' prejudices and ethnocentrism by the nature of feedback we provide them (Stangor et al., 2001). The type of information they receive can inhibit or produce attitude change. If European Americans who hold prejudiced beliefs about African Americans are provided with information that other European Americans hold positive beliefs about African Americans, they tend to change their beliefs in a positive direction. If European Americans who hold prejudiced beliefs about African Americans receive information that other European Americans hold beliefs that are similar to theirs, in contrast, it bolsters their original prejudices.

If we find other people are making prejudiced remarks in our presence, we can point out that this type of speech is not acceptable to us (e.g., say something like "I would appreciate it if you would not talk like that when I am present"). If we do not, we are being morally exclusive. We could say something like "I'd prefer you did not put down other groups in my presence." By simply stating our opinion in this way, we decrease the likelihood that others will continue to make prejudiced remarks in our presence. It does not, however, mean that others will change their behavior when we are not present. **If we do not speak out when other people use ethnocentric speech or make prejudiced comments or behave in a discriminatory manner, we are partly responsible for the consequences of the remarks or behavior**.

Another way to respond to others' ethnocentric speech or expressions of prejudice is to create cognitive dissonance (see Shea, 1997, for a summary of work in this area). We want to see ourselves as holding a consistent set of views and behave in ways that are consistent with these views. When we recognize inconsistencies, we become uncomfortable and try to modify our thoughts or behavior to restore consistency. If we know others view themselves as "unprejudiced" and we hear them express prejudice, we can point out this inconsistency to them. If they recognize the inconsistency, they will probably strive to bring their behavior into consistency with their view of themselves (e.g., stop expressing prejudice).

Before reading further, take a few minutes to answer the following questions about your views on ethics and morality.

What does it mean to be ethical?

____

____

____

What ethical principles do you follow in your life?

____

____

____

Is hate speech (e.g., speech directed at groups that puts the groups down) moral? Why or why not?

____

____

____

Your answers to these questions should provide some insight into the role of ethics in your implicit theory of communication. Keep your answers in mind as you read the remainder of this section.

In order to be ethical, it is necessary to say something when others engage in prejudicial behavior or make prejudiced comments. Dignity and integrity play a large role in ethical behavior. *Dignity* involves a minimal level of self-respect (Pritchard, 1991). It refers to feeling worthy, honored, or respected as a person. Being moral involves maintaining our own sense of dignity, and maintaining others' sense of dignity as well.

Personal integrity reflects our view of what is important (Pritchard, 1991). Personal integrity is linked closely to moral integrity. Moral integrity requires "a somewhat unified moral stance. . . . Those with moral integrity can be expected to refuse to compromise moral standards for the sake of personal expediency" (Pritchard, 1991, p. 90). With respect to moral integrity, it is important to recognize that "when morality conflicts with other considerations, morality should prevail. Contemporary philosophers refer to this as the *overridingness* of morality. . . . The overridingness of morality need require only that one's conduct be limited to what is morally acceptable. That is, one should not choose immoral or morally objectionable courses of action over those that are morally acceptable" (Pritchard, 1991, pp. 225–226). The overridingness of morality must be a major concern anytime we communicate with strangers, see others communicate with strangers, or overhear others talk about strangers.

Behaving in a moral fashion requires that we respect strangers and their moral views (Gutmann, 1992). We do not have to agree with strangers' views of morality to respect them, we only have to see their views as based on a moral system. People who disregard strangers' views are not worthy of respect. This view has clear implications for what often is referred to as hate speech (i.e., speech that puts down strangers because of their membership in a group). There is "no virtue in misogyny, racial or ethnic hatred" (Gutmann, 1992, p. 22). **Racist and anti-Semitic remarks (hate speech) are not defensible on moral grounds**. "Hate speech violates the most elementary moral injunction, to respect the dignity of all human beings" (Gutmann, 1992, p. 23). It also is important to recognize that

> the language of rights is morally incomplete. To say that "I have a right to do X" [e.g., engage in hate speech] is not to conclude that "X is the right thing for me to do" . . . Rights give reasons to others not to interfere with me in the performance of the protected acts; however, they do not in and of themselves give me sufficient reason to perform the acts. There is a gap between rights and rightness that cannot be closed without a richer moral vocabulary—one that involves principles of decency, duty, responsibility, and the common good, among others. (Galston, 1991, p. 8)

Our rights are limited by the rights of strangers; we can do what we want only if it does not harm strangers (Etzioni, 1993).

We have a moral obligation to respond when we hear others engage in hate speech (Gutmann, 1992). "If we care about attaining a higher level of moral conduct than we now experience, we must be ready to express our moral sense" (Etzioni, 1993, p. 36, italics omitted). This does not mean that we should not disagree with strangers. We can and should articulate our disagreements with strangers in a respectful fashion.

Sexism

Sexism occurs when we assign characteristics to others based on their sex (Nilsen et al., 1977). While we can be sexist toward either males or females, sexism usually is viewed as prejudice against women. Sexism is manifested by viewing women as genetically inferior, support for discriminatory practices against women, engaging in hostility toward women who do not fulfill traditional sex roles, not supporting the women's movement, using derogatory names to refer to women or negatively stereotyping women, and treating women as sexual objects (Benson & Vincent, 1980). While both men and women are sexist, men tend to be more sexist than women. If we look at individual sex roles, however, it appears that masculine men and feminine women are more sexist than men and women who are androgynous or have an undifferentiated sex role (Faulkender, 1985).

Take a few minutes to answer the following questions designed to get you to think about the influence of sexism on communication before reading this section.

Why do men and women behave and communicate differently?

____

____

____

Do you try to use nonsexist language (e.g., using "he or she" and "her or his" instead of just using the masculine pronoun to refer to both sexes) when you speak and write? If yes, why? If no, why not?

____

____

____

We are all sexist to some extent. How does your sexism influence your communication?

___

___

___

Your answers to these questions should provide some insight into the role of sexism in your implicit theory of communication. Keep your answers in mind as you read the remainder of this section.

Sexism is manifested mainly through our language. There are three major forms of sexism in language: (1) ignoring women, (2) the way women are defined, and (3) deprecation of women (Henley et al., 1985). The first way that language usage is sexist is in how *women are ignored.* Probably the main way that our language usage ignores women is through the use of masculine words to include both males and females (Schmidt, 1991). There are many words in the English language, for example, that include the word "man" that traditionally have been meant to include women. Examples of these words include, but are not limited to chairman, mailman, spokesman, and mankind. Another way that women are ignored in language usage is through using "he" as a generic pronoun. Many of us learned that when we write or talk, pronouns for males can be used to refer to both males and females. This, however, is not how we actually process the information. When we use male pronouns, it elicits a vision of a male for the reader or listener (Schneider & Hacker, 1973).

The second way that our language usage can be sexist is in *how women are defined.* One way women are ignored is in our tendency to address women by their first names in situations where we would not address a man by his first name (McConnell-Ginet, 1978). Also, "women, much more than men, are addressed through terms of endearment such as honey, cutie, and sweetie, which function to devalue women by depriving them of their name while renaming them with trivial terms" (Schmidt, 1991, p. 30).

The third way that our language is sexist is in *deprecating women.* In English, for example, there are over 200 terms to call a woman sexually promiscuous, but fewer than 25 to call a man sexually promiscuous (Stanley, 1977). While there are more masculine terms (more than 350) in the English language than feminine (fewer than 150), there are more negative feminine terms than masculine (Nilsen, 1977).

College women, on average, experience one or two sexist incidents per week (Swim et al., 2001). These incidents involve demeaning or degrading comments or behavior, sexual objectification, and/or prejudice based on traditional sex-role stereotypes. Individuals "who attribute gender differences to primarily biological factors may be more likely to prescribe differences in behavior [e.g., endorse traditional sex-role stereotypes] than those who attribute the same gender differences to socialization or discrimination" (Swim & Campbell, 2001, pp. 223–234).

It appears that contemporary sexism involves a greater respect for men than women (Jackson et al., 2001). Both positive and negative attitudes toward women exist (Swim & Campbell, 2001). The coexistence of these attitudes may explain why some men like women but do not respect them.

The more sexist we are, the less accurate our predictions of and explanations for members of the opposite-sex's behavior will be. If we are moderately to highly sexist, we need to manage our sexism mindfully to communicate effectively with members of the opposite-sex.

The questionnaire in Table 4.4 is designed to help you assess your sexism. Take a few minutes to complete it now.

Scores on the questionnaire range from 10 to 50. The higher your score on the questionnaire, the more sexist you are. If your score is higher than you would like it to be, you need to keep in mind that you can choose to behave in a nonsexist fashion and to use nonsexist language when you are mindful of your communication.

Ageism

"Many, if not most, of the 'problems of aging' stem from or are exacerbated by prejudice and discrimination against the aged" (Palmore, 1982, p. 333). Typically, *ageism* is viewed as involving negative attitudes toward people who are older than we are (usually people we consider "old"). Teenagers, for example, may be prejudiced against people over 30, while a person who is middle-aged may be prejudiced against people who are retired. Ageism is based on "a deep-seated uneasiness on the part of the young and middle-aged—a personal revulsion to and distaste for growing older" (Butler, 1969, p. 243). It also can emerge from competition between the groups (young and old) over scarce resources and jobs (Levin & Levin, 1980). Overall, attitudes toward aging tend to be negative (Palmore, 1982). Even though ageism typically is viewed as young people being prejudiced against older people, older people also can be prejudiced against younger people (i.e., be ageist).

Take a few minutes to answer the following questions about your attitudes toward aging before reading this section.

What terms do you use to refer to "young" people? To refer to "old" people?

____

____

____

TABLE 4.4 *Assessing Your Sexism*

The purpose of this questionnaire is to assess your sexism. Respond to each statement by indicating the degree to which the statement is true regarding the way you typically think about men and women. When you think about women and men, is the statement "Always False" (answer 1), "Mostly False" (answer 2), "Sometimes True and Sometimes False" (answer 3), "Mostly True" (answer 4), or "Always True" (answer 5)? Answer honestly, not how you think you should.

_____ 1. Husbands should make decisions in the family.
_____ 2. Women and men are equal in all respects.
_____ 3. Men are more courageous than women.
_____ 4. Men and women can handle pressure equally well.
_____ 5. Women are more emotional than men.
_____ 6. Women can lead as effectively as men.
_____ 7. Men should be the dominant sex.
_____ 8. Women and men are equal in intelligence.
_____ 9. Women are influenced by others more than men.
_____ 10. Men and women should have the same rights.

To find your score, first reverse the responses for the even numbered items (i.e., if you wrote 1, make it 5; if you wrote 2, make it 4; if you wrote 3, leave it as 3; if you wrote 4, make it 2; if you wrote 5, make it 1). Next, add the numbers next to each statement. Scores range from 10 to 50. The higher your score, the greater your sexism.

Do you communicate as effectively with people your own age and people older than you? If yes, why? If no, why not?

____

____

____

We are all ageist to some extent. How does your ageism influence your communication?

____

____

____

Your answers to these questions should provide some insights into the role of ageism in your implicit theory of communication. Keep your answers in mind as you read this section.

Ageism is manifested in our language usage. While the term "old" has connotations of experience, skill, and wisdom, it also is used in derogatory terms used for others (e.g., "old hag," "old fogey"; Covey, 1988). There is a wide variety of terms in the English language referring to old people with negative overtones (e.g., "battle-ax," "geezer") and the attributes used to talk about the elderly (e.g., "cantankerous," "grumpy") often have negative connotations (Nuessel, 1984). More than one half of the jokes in English about aging reflect a negative view of old people, with a greater portion of jokes about women than men being negative. Terms such as aged and elderly are perceived to be negative, while terms such as senior citizen and retired person are evaluated more positively by people of all age-groups (Barbato & Feezel, 1987).

The more ageist we are, the less accurate our predictions of and explanations for members of other age categories will be. If we are moderately to highly ageist, we need to manage our ageism mindfully if we want to communicate effectively with members of other age-groups.

Table 4.5 contains a questionnaire designed to help you assess your ageism toward older people. Take a few minutes to complete it now.

Scores on the questionnaire range from 10 to 50. The higher your score, the greater your ageism. The higher your score, the greater the possibility of misunderstandings when you are communicating with someone older than you. If you have a high score, you can choose to stop your negative reaction to old people when you are mindful of your communication.

Changing Our Intergroup Expectations

Throughout this chapter, I have discussed our expectations for strangers. Our expectations are not static; they can and do change, either consciously or unconsciously. When we communicate with strangers there are five ways that we can change our attitudes toward strangers: (1) changing our attitudes toward the group as a whole, (2) increasing the complexity of our intergroup perceptions, (3) decategorizing outgroup members, (4) recategorizing outgroup members, and (5) mutually differentiating ingroup and outgroup members.

Changing Our Attitudes Toward the Group as a Whole

Many people assume that if we have contact with strangers, our attitudes toward their groups will become more positive. This, however, is not necessarily the case. Contact can promote better relations between groups or increase hostility between groups. The question that needs to be answered is when does contact lead to better relations between groups?

TABLE 4.5 *Assessing Your Ageism*

The purpose of this questionnaire is to assess your ageism toward older people. Respond to each statement by indicating the degree to which the statement is true regarding the way you typically think about others' age. When you think about someone's age, is the statement "Always False" (answer 1), "Mostly False" (answer 2), "Sometimes True and Sometimes False" (answer 3), "Mostly True" (answer 4), or "Always True" (answer 5)? Answer honestly, not how you think you should.

_____ 1. I find it more difficult to communicate with an old person than with a young person.
_____ 2. I am not afraid of growing old.
_____ 3. I see old people as cantankerous.
_____ 4. I learn a lot when I communicate with elderly people.
_____ 5. I prefer to interact with people my own age.
_____ 6. I do not see all old people as alike.
_____ 7. I see old people as individuals, not as a group.
_____ 8. My communication with people older than me is as effective as my communication with people my own age.
_____ 9. I have to speak loudly and slowly for old people to understand me.
_____ 10. I look forward to growing old.

To find your score, first reverse the responses for the even numbered items (i.e., if you wrote 1, make it 5; if you wrote 2, make it 4; if you wrote 3, leave it as 3; if you wrote 4, make it 2; if you wrote 5, make it 1). Next, add the numbers next to each statement. Scores range from 10 to 50. The higher your score, the greater your ageism.

There are at least 13 characteristics of contact situations that lead to positive attitude change toward a social group as a result of our contact with specific strangers:

1. Cooperation within groups should be maximized and competition between groups should be minimized.

2. Members of the in-group and the out-group should be of equal status both within and outside the contact situation.

3. Similarity of group members on nonstatus dimensions (beliefs, values, etc.) appears to be desirable.

4. Differences in competence should be avoided.

5. The outcomes should be positive.

6. Strong normative and institutional support for the contact should be provided.

7. The intergroup contact should have the potential to extend beyond the immediate situation.

8. Individuation of group members should be promoted.

9. Nonsuperficial contact (e.g., mutual disclosure of information) should be encouraged.

10. The contact should be voluntary.

11. Positive effects are likely to correlate with the duration of the contact.

12. The contact should occur in a variety of contexts with a variety of in-group and out-group members.

13. Equal numbers of in-group and out-group members should be used. (Stephan, 1985, p. 643)

While this list is long, it is incomplete. If we want to reduce our prejudice or ethnocentrism, we must make sure that our contact with strangers meets as many of these conditions as possible.

Increasing the Complexity of Our Intergroup Perceptions

Increasing the complexity of intergroup perceptions involves seeing the social category as heterogeneous, rather than homogeneous (Brewer & Miller, 1988). Stated differently, we can increase the complexity of our intergroup perceptions by recognizing how members of social categories are different. Think of the social groups males and females. Are all males and all females the same? Obviously, the answer is no. We see differences among males and females and place them in subcategories. Females, for example, may categorize males into "male chauvinists" and "feminists."

Increasing the complexity of our intergroup perceptions is consistent with mindfulness. As you may recall from Chapter 1, one aspect of becoming mindful of our communication is the creation of new categories (Langer, 1989). Creating new categories means differentiating among the individuals within the broad social categories we use. This means increasing the number of "discriminations" we make—using specific rather than global labels (e.g., a person with a lame leg, rather than a "cripple"). When we are mindful of differences among the members of the various outgroups with whom we communicate, our expectations are based on the subcategories, not the broader social category.

Decategorizing Outgroup Members

Decategorization occurs when we communicate with strangers based on their individual characteristics, rather than the categories in which we place them (i.e., communication is mainly interpersonal, not mainly intergroup) (Brewer & Miller, 1988).[19] In order to accomplish this, we must differentiate individual strangers from their groups. Differentiation alone, however, is not sufficient for decategorization or personalization to occur.

When we personalize or decategorize our interactions with strangers, personal identities take on more importance than social identities. "Consider the statement 'Janet is a nurse.' This description can be psychologically represented in one of two ways. It could mean that Janet is subordinate to (i.e., a specific instance of) the general category of nurses. Or it could mean that being a nurse is subordinate to (i.e., a particular characteristic of) the concept of Janet. The former interpretation is an example of category-based individuation, and the later is an example of personalization" (Brewer & Miller, 1988, p. 318). The difference lies in how we process the information. If we focus on the strangers' personal identities, we can decrease the degree to which their social identities affect our expectations.

Recategorizing Outgroup Members

The goal of recategorization is "to structure a definition of group categorization at a higher level of category inclusiveness in ways that reduce intergroup bias and conflict" (Brewer & Gaertner, 2001, p. 459). The common ingroup identity model (e.g., Dovidio et al., 2001; Gaertner & Dovidio, 2000), for example, suggests that the ingroup bias can be reduced when individuals' identities are transferred from two separate identities to a common, inclusive identity. To illustrate, members of two different ethnic groups might find that they share a common religious identity or start to think of themselves as "Americans" (Gaertner & Dovidio, 2000) or share a common organizational identity (Huo et al., 1996).

The cognitive processes that lead to ingroup favoritism when individuals perceive they are members of different groups is "redirected to benefit the former outgroup members" when a common identity is formed (Brewer & Gaertner, 2001, p. 459). When a common ingroup identity is discovered, "cooperative interaction, for example, enhances positive evaluations of outgroup members, at least in part, because cooperation transforms members' representations of the membership from 'Us' and 'Them' to a more inclusive 'We'" (p. 459). This changes the expectations for strangers' behavior.

Mutually Differentiating Ingroup and Outgroup Members

The ingroup bias also can be reduced when members of different ethnic groups engage in cooperative interactions without changing their original ingroup-outgroup differentiation (Hewstone & Brown, 1986). "This model favors encouraging groups working together to perceive complementarity by recognizing and valuing mutual superiorities and inferiorities within the context of an interdependent cooperative task or common superordinate goals" (Brewer & Gaertner, 2001, p. 461).

Contact situations can be structured in ways that allow members of different groups to have complementary roles that need to be performed to achieve a common goal (Hewstone & Brown, 1986). The cooperative interdependence between the groups overrides the ingroup bias and changes expectations.

To summarize, changing our attitudes toward outgroups, increasing the complexity of our intergroup perceptions, decategorizing outgroup members, recategorizing outgroup members, and mutually differentiating can all change our expectations for strangers. To create positive expectations and improve our relations with members of other groups, we need to use all five processes simultaneously. Changing our expectations of strangers is necessary for us to communicate effectively with them. To improve our communication effectiveness, we also need to understand how we make sense of strangers' behavior. This is the topic of the next chapter.

Study Questions

1. How are our expectations culturally based?
2. What factors lead to negative intergroup expectations?
3. How does ethnocentrism create expectations for strangers' behavior?
4. How are ethnocentrism and cultural relativism manifested in our speech?
5. How are our attitudes toward strangers both positive and negative?

6. How does integrated threat theory explain our prejudice?
7. How is aversive racism different from traditional racism?
8. How is our prejudice manifested in the ways that we communicate?
9. How can we respond if others talk in a prejudiced fashion in front of us?
10. Why is hate speech immoral?
11. What does the content of our stereotypes tell us about the relationships between groups in society?
12. How can we explain our tendency to engage in stereotype confirming behavior?
13. How can we change our expectations for strangers?

Applications

1. Over the next week, pay attention to how your prejudice and ethnocentrism influence your communication. When do you engage in prejudiced talk or ethnocentric communicative distances of disparagement, avoidance, or indifference? How can you decrease these tendencies in the future?

2. Over the next week, pay attention to how your sexism influences your communication. How are your sexist attitudes manifested in your communication? How can you decrease this in the future?

3. Over the next week, pay attention to how your stereotypes influence your communication. Which stereotypes are activated? How do these stereotypes influence your communication? How can you decrease their effect on your communication in the future?

Notes

1. Burgoon and Hale do not limit their statement to this group; I do.
2. See Stephan and Stephan (1989) for several citations to support this claim.
3. See Vassiliou et al. (1972) for a complete discussion of the complexity of stereotypes.

4. These conclusions are supported by Mullen and Johnson's (1993) research.

5. For a recent review of research on categorization and category representations, see Messick and Mackie (1989); for a current review of stereotypes and communication, see Hewstone and Brown (1986); see Jussim et al. (1987) for a summary of the major theories of stereotyping.

6. The studies that have been conducted are: Katz and Braly (1933), Gilbert (1951), Karlins et al. (1969), Dovidio and Gaertner (1986), Devine and Elliot (1995), and Madon et al. (2001). Madon et al.'s results (with comparison to other studies) are available at her web site at Iowa State University (she is in the psychology department).

7. Many of the ideas presented in this section were first brought to my attention in Kellermann (1993).

8. There is work on "passing" as a member of a different ethnic group (Winkler, 1997). See Browder (1998) for an example.

9. See Giles et al. (1987) for a review of research on accommodation.

10. This quote is from an afterword to a book for first grade teachers published in the early 1970s. Unfortunately, I lost the reference to the book in which it appeared.

11. Lukens isolated the first three distances discussed below. Gudykunst and Kim extended her work to include the last two distances.

12. See Mullen (2001) for a recent discussion of ethnophaulisms of immigrant ethnic groups.

13. There are other forms of covert racism including symbolic racism (e.g., Sears, 1988) and laissez-faire racism (e.g., Bobo & Smith, 1998).

14. The survey was conducted in October and November 1992 by Martilla & Kiley with a margin of error of plus or minus three percent. It was reported in the *Los Angeles Times,* June 12, 1993, p. A25.

15. European American racism toward African Americans is the most widely studied form of prejudice. The vast majority of research focuses on those who are prejudiced (i.e., European Americans; see Swim & Stangor, 1998, for an exception). The focus on African Americans made some sense when they were the largest "minority" group. This is no longer the case. Latino(a) Americans are now the largest "minority" group in the United States (e.g., Clemetson, 2003).

16. This statement may apply only in the presence of "educated" individuals. Spike Lee (1990) has said that "racism is fashionable today." I believe that both statements are "true" in specific contexts.

17. For excellent examples, see the *Frontline* video "Racism 101" or issues of newsmagazines that focused on this topic in the first six months of 1990.

18. These observations are drawn from comments by Jane Elliott in the *Frontline* video "A Class Divided."

19. Note that Brewer and Miller assume it is possible to stop categorizing. This position is different from Langer's (see Chapter 1). I believe that we can stop categorizing only when we are mindful of our behavior. We cannot stop when we communicate on automatic pilot.

CHAPTER 5

Attributing Meaning to Strangers' Behavior

In the previous chapter, I discussed how our expectations affect our communication behavior. In this chapter, I extend this analysis by looking at the way we make sense of our worlds—our perceptions and attributions. I begin by looking at the perception process. Next, I examine the individual and social attribution processes and isolate factors that lead us to make errors in attributions. I also discuss the role of cultural and personality factors in the attribution process. I conclude by looking at ways we can improve the accuracy of our perceptions and attributions.

The Perception Process

Our *perceptions* involve our awareness of what is taking place in the environment. Our perceptions take place unconsciously. Our unconscious involves "mental processes that are inaccessible to consciousness but that influence judgments, feelings, or behavior" (Wilson, 2002, p. 23, italics omitted). Take a moment to answer the following question, before proceeding.

On which aspects of members of other groups do you focus when you are interacting with them? Why do you focus on these aspects?

____

____

____

Keep your answer to this question in mind as you read the remainder of this section. There are three critical aspects of our perceptions that influence our communication with strangers: our perceptions are selective, our perceptions involve categorization, and having rigid categories inhibits effective communication.

Perceptions Are Selective

If we had to pay attention to *all* of the stimuli in our environments, we would experience information overload. One estimate is "that at any given moment our five senses are taking in more than 11,000,000 pieces of information" (Wilson, 2002, p. 24). In the interest of not overloading ourselves with too much information, we limit our attention to those aspects of strangers or the situation that are essential to understanding what we are doing (Bruner, 1958). We might, for example, perceive the color of strangers' skins, but not notice their skins' textures. "To notice is to select, to regard some bits of perception, or some features of the world, as more noteworthy, more significant than others. To these, we attend, and the rest we ignore—for which reason . . . attention is at the same time ignore-ance (i.e., ignorance) despite the fact that it gives us a vividly clear picture of what we choose to notice. Physically, we see, hear, smell, taste, and touch innumerable features that we never notice" (Watts, 1966, p. 29). Our perceptions of strangers, therefore, are highly selective. We tend to focus on aspects of strangers that are relevant to us in our interactions with them.

The process of selecting information from our environments and forming images takes place unconsciously (Bateson, 1979). We do not consciously decide on the things to which we pay attention. Our unconscious, however, is "more than just a gatekeeper, deciding what information to admit to consciousness. It also is a spin doctor that interprets information outside of awareness. One of the most important judgments we make is about motives, intentions, and dispositions of the people" with whom we are communicating (Wilson, 2002, p. 31). Our unconscious judgments of strangers' motives, intentions, and dispositions frequently are incorrect, especially when we are communicating with strangers from other cultures or ethnic groups.

We are conscious of what we see, but we need to keep in mind that what we see is manufactured in our brains. What we see does not really exist because "all experience is subjective" (Bateson, 1979, p. 31). Our presuppositions and expectations (e.g., our stereotypes and intergroup attitudes) influence the cues that we select from our environments and what we see. The information we unconsciously select from our environments also is influenced by its *accessibility*, "the activation potential of information in memory" (Wilson, 2002, p. 37). Accessibility is influenced by the relevance of the information to us and how recently we encountered the information. We are "creatures of habit, and the more [we] have used a particular way of judging the world in the past," the more likely we are to use this way of judging the world now and in the future (Wilson, 2002, p. 37).

Our perceptions are always a function of our interaction with specific strangers in specific situations (Ittelson & Cantril, 1954). We react to strangers based on the way we perceive them in interactions, *not* as entities independent of our interactions with them. The perceptions that each of us experience are unique; they are based on our cultures, our ethnicities, our sex, our background experiences, and our needs. Our perceptions overlap with strangers' to the extent that we share common experiences (e.g., culture). While our perceptions are based on our interactions with strangers, we tend to assume mistakenly that our perceptions are "real" and external to ourselves.

The problems for our communication with strangers arise because we mistakenly assume that we perceive and observe strangers in an unbiased fashion. This, however, is not the case. Our perceptions are highly selective and biased. Our past experiences are one source of bias in our perceptions. Our previous experiences with particular strangers also can bias our perception of their current behavior. Our emotional states also bias our perceptions. Our moods provide a lens through which we interpret our own and strangers' behavior. Other biases in our perceptions are a function of the categorization process and our expectations.

Our perceptions are biased, but we also have accurate social perceptions, even of people we meet for the first time (Zebrowitz & Collins, 1997). We pick up cues from strangers based on their faces, their nonverbal communication, and the way they speak. Based on these cues, we make judgments about their extroversion, agreeableness, emotional stability, and so forth. These judgments often are accurate. The accuracy, however, is not just a function of strangers' characteristics; rather, it emerges out of the task that is being completed and the interactions we have with strangers.

When our perceptions are biased, we may be highly confident in our predictions of and explanations for strangers' behavior. When our perceptions are biased, however, our predictions of and explanations for strangers' behavior are not accurate. When we are mindful, we can overcome the selection bias in our perceptions. When we are mindful, we "recognize that there is more than one perspective on the information given and we choose from among these" (Langer, 1997, p. 108).

Perceptions Involve Categorizations

When we select information from the environment we need to organize it in some way. We try to find meaningful patterns. We do this by putting strangers into categories. **Categorization is a fundamental aspect of thought**. It allows "us to structure and give coherence to our general knowledge about people and the social world, providing typical patterns of behavior and the range of likely variation between types of people and their characteristic actions and attributes" (Cantor et al., 1982, p. 34).

We "categorize along three dimensions: (1) categoric units to which self and others belong; (2) situations; and (3) levels of intimacy" (Turner, 2002, p. 155). These categories create expectations for what is going to occur in specific situations and for ourselves and strangers in these situations.

When we categorize strangers, we group them on aspects they have in common and ignore aspects they do not have in common. Our categorizations are based on selected aspects of the strangers with whom we interact. In categorizing, we have to ignore some aspects in order to classify strangers. Once we have created a category, we assume that strangers within the category are similar and that people in other categories are different. We might classify strangers as angry, but in so doing we ignore other qualities they have (e.g., they are friendly). Once formed, however, the category influences how we respond to strangers.

When we categorize strangers, we draw distinctions among them and ourselves, and create boundaries between us and them. "Things assume a distinctive identity only through being differentiated from other things, and their meaning is always a function of the particular mental compartment in which we place them" (Zerubavel, 1991, p. 3). Once the categories are formed, we tend to take them for granted and assume there are gaps between them. These gaps enhance our viewing the categories as separate and distinct. It is important to keep in mind that we created the categories in the first place and that the gaps between the categories are a function of the way we created the categories. If we are mindful, we can create new categories or make distinctions within the broad categories we already have created (Langer, 1997). Creating new categories for strangers will increase the effectiveness of our communication.

We categorize the situation in which we are interacting with strangers along "three dimensions: (1) *work/practical* where individuals are trying to complete a task; (2) *social* or where individuals are engaged in interaction for its own sake; and (3) *ceremonial* in which people are involved in stylized behaviors marking the significance of an occasion, honoring (or dishonoring) another or groups of others" (Turner, 2002, p. 155). Depending upon how we categorize the situation, we create expectations for how people in the situation should behave; that is, how we should behave and how strangers should behave.

We also categorize the level of intimacy involved in our interactions with strangers. We can, for example, define others "as *personages* of a given type (for example, cashier) toward whom little more than polite responses are owed; others can be defined as *persons* toward whom interpersonal responsiveness is required; or others can be seen as *intimates* whose biography, experiences, and feelings are known and are to be taken into consideration during the course of the interaction" (Turner, 2002, p. 155). The level of intimacy with which we categorize our interactions with strangers creates expectations for our interactions.

Rigid Categories Inhibit Accurate Perceptions

Creating gaps between the categories we form is a natural part of the perceptual process. What creates problems in communication is the rigidity with which we maintain the boundaries between categories. "The most distinctive characteristic of the rigid mind is its unyielding, obsessive commitment to the mutual exclusivity of mental entities. The foremost logical prerequisite of a rigid classification is that a mental item belong to no more than one category . . . the rigid mind cherishes sharp, clear-cut distinctions among mental entities" (Zerubavel, 1991, p. 34). People with rigid categories try to classify strangers into a single category. When strangers do not clearly fit one category, it threatens the cognitive structure of people with rigid categories. Forcing strangers into mutually exclusive categories biases our perceptions. People with rigid category systems experience anxiety or fear when confronted with strangers that cannot be categorized (Zerubavel, 1991).

If we hold our categories rigidly, we do not recognize individual variations within our categories or consider recategorizing strangers based on new information. If our categories are rigid, we may categorize strangers as disabled, for example, and then see *all* disabled people as alike. All disabled people, however, are not alike. To communicate effectively with strangers who are disabled, we must be able to recognize how they are like other disabled people *and* how they are different from other disabled people. Similarly, if our categories are rigid, we might categorize strangers as hostile and refuse to consider reclassifying them, even when confronted with consistent evidence that they are not hostile.

We draw boundaries and categorize strangers to make sense of the world. We draw a boundary between ourselves and strangers so that we will feel distinct. We not only have a need to be distinct, but we also have a need to feel connected. If we draw a rigid boundary between ourselves and strangers, we will be very lonely. If we do not draw a sufficient boundary between ourselves and strangers, on the other hand, we will have little sense of ourselves (e.g., who we are). Balancing our needs for distinction (autonomy) and connection requires that we have flexible categories. "Flexibility entails the ability to be both rigid and fuzzy. Flexible people notice structures yet feel comfortable destroying them from time to time" (Zerubavel, 1991, p. 120). If our mental structures are flexible and elastic, we can "break away from the mental cages in which we so often lock ourselves" (p. 122). Having rigid categories or mindsets about ourselves or strangers negatively affects our performance (Langer, 1997). **Having flexible categories or mindsets facilitates communicating effectively**. If we know we have rigid categories, we can choose to be more flexible when we are mindful of our communication.

When we are mindful, one thing we can do to overcome the biases in our perceptions is to look for exceptions or novelty. Once we recognize a single exception, it helps us to stop our cognitive distortions due to either/or thinking (Weiner-Davis, 1992). To illustrate, if we categorize strangers as hostile, we would try to think of times that they are not hostile. When we recognize that there are times that they are not hostile, we will not view them in exactly the same way. This change will lead to more accurate perceptions of strangers.

When we are mindful, we also can change the way we define strangers in categories (Langer, 1997). When we communicate on automatic pilot, we tend to think that strangers *are* something (e.g., hostile, dishonest). If we think that strangers *could be* something rather than *are* something when we are mindful, it increases our abilities to communicate effectively. "When we are told something 'could be,' we understand immediately that it also could not be or could be something else" (Langer, 1997, p. 81). When we think that strangers could be something, we open ourselves for the possibility of exceptions and we will not assume that our stereotypes apply to the strangers with whom we are communicating.

If we have rigid categories, we may have a high degree of confidence in our predictions of and explanations for strangers' behavior. Rigid categories, however, inevitably lead to inaccurate predictions of and explanations for strangers' behavior.

Perceptions of Strangers' Groups

Our implicit (i.e., unconscious) theories about human nature influence how we perceive strangers and strangers' groups (Levy et al., 2001). Answer the following question before proceeding.

To what extent is your behavior consistent across situations? Why?

____

____

____

Your answer should give you insight into whether you use static or dynamic implicit theories about human nature and groups. If we use *static implicit theories,* we believe that "personal characteristics are fixed entities despite a person's efforts or motivation to change them; that is, they are not under personal control" (p. 157). If we use *dynamic implicit theories,* we believe that "personal characteristics are malleable [changeable] and can be developed with time and effort" (p. 157). Using static implicit theories leads to viewing strangers' behavior as consistent across time and situations. Using dynamic implicit theories, in contrast, leads to viewing strangers' behavior as a function of the situations in which they are communicating.

The use of static or dynamic implicit theories influences the ways that we perceive strangers and their groups (Levy et al., 2001). Individuals who use static theories "express greater belief in social stereotypes" and endorse both negative and positive stereotypes more than individuals using dynamic implicit theories. Given the endorsement of stereotypes, individuals using static implicit theories perceive more homogeneity (similarity) in strangers' groups and exaggerate differences between their groups and strangers' groups more than individuals using dynamic implicit theories. Individuals using static implicit theories attribute "group traits more to innate factors and less to shared environment and experiences" than individuals using dynamic implicit theories (p. 160). Because of these differences, individuals using static implicit theories are more likely to be prejudiced against strangers' groups and to attribute strangers' negative behavior to their group memberships (i.e., commit the ultimate attribution error; see below) than individuals using dynamic implicit theories.

We have a general tendency to use either static or dynamic implicit theories when we communicate with strangers on automatic pilot. We can, however, choose to use a different implicit theory when we are mindful of our communication. Static and dynamic implicit theories appear to be related to how individuals adapt themselves to social organizations across cultures. In individualistic cultures, for example, individuals tend to believe that they have to "alter social organizations to meet their needs" (Levy et al., 2001, p. 164). This assumes that individuals are not highly malleable (changeable; e.g., static theories). In Asian collectivistic cultures, in contrast, individuals believe that "they have to shape themselves to fit into social organizations" (p. 164). This assumes that individuals are malleable (e.g., dynamic theories).

The Attribution Process

Attributions are our attempts to explain strangers' behavior. Answer the following questions before reading the remainder of this section.

How might you explain the behavior of a member of your ethnic group who refuses to give you a ride when your car is in the shop?

____

____

____

How might you explain the behavior of a member of another ethnic group who loans you a book you need to finish a class paper that is not available in the library?

____

____

____

How might you explain the behavior of a member of another ethnic group who refuses to loan you a book you need to finish a class paper that is not available in the library?

____

____

____

Your answers to these questions should provide some insight into the role of ethnicity in explaining people's behavior. Our attributions are based on strangers' individual and social characteristics. When we make attributions on automatic pilot, we make errors, especially when we communicate with strangers.

Individual Attributions

We act as naive or intuitive scientists when we are trying to make sense of the world (Heider, 1958). We are motivated by practical concerns such as our needs to simplify and comprehend our environments, and to predict strangers' behavior. In order to meet these needs, we try to get beneath external appearances to isolate stable underlying characteristics called dispositions (e.g., individual traits or group memberships). It is not our experiences per se, but our interpretations of our experiences that constitute our "realities."

When observing strangers' behavior we attempt to make attributions about the effect of the environment on their behavior by ruling out individual explanations for the behavior (Kelley, 1967). We organize our observations into a cube with three dimensions: person × object × situation. In the *person* dimension, we compare the person engaging in the behavior with others. Do other people engage in the same behavior as the person being observed? We are trying to find out the degree to which there is consensus on the behavior across people. In the *object* dimension, we compare the different objects of the person's behavior. Does the person behave the same way toward different people or objects? Here we are looking for whether the object of the person's behavior is distinctive. In the *situation* dimension, we vary the context in which the behavior occurs. Does the person behave the same in different situations? The focus here is on whether there is consistency across time and location of the behavior. We then use a covariation principle to assess the degree to which the behavior occurs in the presence and absence of the various causes.[1]

It may appear that the attributional process takes a long time, but in actuality we go through this analysis very quickly when we have complete information. In the presence of incomplete data, we infer meaning based on our preconceptions about how specific causes are associated with specific effects (Kelley, 1972). Our causal schemata permit "economical and fast attributional analysis, by providing a framework within which bits and pieces of information can be fitted in order to draw reasonably good inferences" (p. 152).

There are several biases that affect our attributional processes. First, we have a tendency to overestimate the influence of personal dispositions and underestimate the influence of situational factors when we make attributions about strangers' behavior. This is called the *fundamental attribution error* (Ross, 1977). This error is limited to individualistic cultures (Smith & Bond, 1993). Second, there is an *egocentric bias*—our tendency to see our own behavior as normal and appropriate (Kelley, 1967). We, therefore, explain strangers' behavior that is different from ours as a function of their personal dispositions. Third, we use an *ego-protective bias* when we tend to attribute our success to personal dispositions and our failures to situational factors (Kelley, 1967). Fourth, we tend to stop searching for interpretations of behavior once we have relevant and reasonable interpretations (*premature closure;* Taylor & Fiske, 1978). Fifth, we have a tendency to overemphasize negative information about strangers' behavior (*principle of negativity;* Kanouse & Hanson, 1972). We are more likely to make the fundamental attribution error when explaining behavior that we perceive to be negative than for behavior we perceive to be positive.

Social Attributions

Social attributions are concerned with how members of one social group explain the behavior of their own members and members of other social groups. There are three propositions regarding the social nature of attributions:

> 1. Attribution is social in origin (e.g., it may be created by, or strengthened through, social interaction, or it may be influenced by social information).
> 2. Attribution is social in its reference or object (e.g., an attribution may be demanded for the individual characterized as a member of a social group, rather than in purely individual terms; or for a social outcome, rather than any behavior as such).
> 3. Attribution is social in that it is common to the members of a society or group (e.g., the members of different groups may hold different attributions for the same event). (Hewstone & Jaspars, 1984, pp. 379-380)

We enhance our social identities when we make social attributions. Our social attributions usually are based on the social stereotypes we share with other members of our ingroups. Our social attributions, however, also can be based on our ethnocentrism or other intergroup attitudes.

When we perceive ourselves and strangers in individual terms (e.g., our personal identities generate our behavior) or we see strangers as atypical of their groups, we tend to make person-based attributions (Hewstone & Brown, 1986). Person-based attributions, in turn, lead us to look for personal similarities and differences between strangers and ourselves. When we perceive ourselves and strangers as members of groups (e.g., our social identities generate our behavior), we tend to make category-based attributions. Category-based attributions then lead us to look for differences between our ingroup and the strangers' groups.

The degree to which strangers' behavior is consistent with our stereotypes affects our attributions (Thomas & Meglino, 1997). When strangers' behavior is consistent with our stereotypes, we tend to attribute their behavior to strangers' group-based dispositions (e.g., their cultures, ethnicities). When strangers' behavior is inconsistent with our stereotypes (e.g., they adapt to our group), we tend to base our attributions on person-based characteristics (e.g., their personalities).

The natures of the attributions we make are important and influence our relations with strangers. When strangers are working with ingroup members and the group fails on its task, members of the ingroup usually blame the strangers for the failure. Attributions like this do not help to improve intergroup relations and can, in fact, have a negative influence. If ingroup members are somehow prevented from blaming strangers for the failure, cooperation that results in failure does not result in increased bias toward strangers (Worchel & Norwell, 1980).

The Ultimate Attribution Error

The *ultimate attribution error* is "a systematic patterning of intergroup misattributions shaped in part by prejudice" (Pettigrew, 1979, p. 464). Our tendency to attribute behavior to dispositional characteristics is enhanced when we perceive strangers to engage in negative behavior. When we perceive strangers to engage in positive behavior, in contrast, our tendencies are to treat them as "exceptions to the rule" and we discount dispositional explanations for their behavior. We, therefore, attribute strangers' behavior to situational factors.

When our expectations are confirmed by strangers' behavior, we rely on strangers' dispositions associated with our stereotypes of their groups and do not bother to consider other explanations for their behavior (Pyszczynski & Greenberg, 1981). When strangers do not confirm our expectations, we tend to attribute their behavior to external factors (Stephan & Rosenfield, 1982).

With respect to the ultimate attribution error, it can be argued that

> across-group perceptions are more likely than within-group perceptions to include the following:
>
> 1. For acts perceived as antisocial or undesirable, behavior will be attributed to personal, dispositional causes. Often these internal causes will be seen as innate characteristics, and role requirements will be overlooked. ("He shoved the white guy, because blacks are born violent like that.")
>
> 2. For acts perceived as prosocial or desirable, behavior will be attributed either: (a) to the situation—with role requirements receiving more attention ("Under the circumstances, what could the cheap Scot do, but pay the check?"); (b) to the motivational, as opposed to innate, dispositional

> qualities ("Jewish students make better grades, because they try so much harder"); or (c) to the exceptional, even exaggerated "special case" individual who is contrasted with his/her group—what Allport (1954) called "fence-mending" ("She is certainly bright and hardworking—not at all like other Chicanos" [*sic*]). (Pettigrew, 1978, p. 39)

We all make the ultimate attribution error when communicating on automatic pilot with strangers to some extent. The more prejudiced we are, the more likely we are to make the ultimate attribution error. To reduce the possibility of making this error when making attributions about strangers' behavior, we must be mindful of our interpretations of their behavior.

Culture and Attributions

Our cultures influence the attributions we make about our own and strangers' behavior. Our cultures also influence the type of mistakes we make in making attributions about strangers' behavior.

Cultural Differences in Attributions

Members of individualistic cultures in which low-context messages predominate are sensitive to dispositional characteristics and tend to attribute strangers' behavior to characteristics internal to the strangers (e.g., personalities, group memberships). Members of collectivistic cultures where high-context messages predominate, in contrast, are sensitive to situational features and explanations and tend to attribute strangers' behavior to the context, situation, or other factors external to the individual (Ehrenhaus, 1983). The collectivistic tendency to use situational information to explain others' behavior occurs especially when situational information is salient (Norenzayan et al., 2002; see Nisbett, 2003, for a review). To illustrate, people in India refer to the context more and to dispositional factors less than U.S. Americans when explaining others' behavior (Miller, 1984). Similarly, U.S. Americans make more internal attributions than Koreans (Cha & Nam, 1985).

One of the reasons collectivists tend to use factors external to the individual in explaining others' behavior is that they have different theories of agency (e.g., "notions of what kinds of entities act intentionally or autonomously"; Morris et al., 2001, p. 169) than individualists. U.S. Americans and members of other individualistic cultures tend to assume that only individuals have agency; that is, only individuals can form intentions. Members of collectivistic cultures, in contrast, assume that individuals are not the only entities that have agency. Collectivists view collectivities and groups as having agency. Collectivists, therefore, assume that organizations, political parties, and sports teams, to name only a few collectivities, can form intentions and act autonomously.

Culture and Misattributions

The cultural and ethnic rules for communication we learned as children often contribute to misunderstandings when we communicate with strangers. Understanding how individualism-collectivism and low- and high-context communication affect our attributions can help us to make appropriate attributions when we communicate with strangers.

Individualism-Collectivism. Members of collectivistic cultures are group-oriented and strongly identify with their ingroups. In individualistic cultures, emphasis is placed on the self. This influences the use of personal pronouns in individualistic and collectivistic cultures. A member of a collectivistic culture who identifies with the group, for example, may use the pronoun "we" when stating a personal opinion. A member of an individualistic culture would perceive such a statement as being something that the group may do or believe, but not necessarily interpret the statement as the speaker's opinion. This misinterpretation will result in misunderstanding if the cultural differences in use of personal pronouns are ignored.

Differences in individualism-collectivism can lead to misunderstanding involving how face is negotiated. *Face* involves our public self-images (Ting-Toomey, 1988; see Chapter 8 for more on face). Face can be based on our needs for inclusion or our needs for autonomy. Further, we can have a concern for our own faces or a concern for others' faces. Problems in communication may occur when there is a difference in interpretation of the face-concern being used. In collectivistic cultures, the concern for face is predominately other-oriented. In individualistic cultures, the concern is self-oriented.

Giving face, especially to people with higher status, is important in collectivistic cultures. When people from individualistic cultures violate this expectation, it can have major consequences for their relationship. Consider the following example of face in the context of business negotiations between individuals from Japan and the United States:

> Phil Downing . . . was involved in the setting up of a branch of his company that was merging with an existing Japanese counterpart. He seemed

> to get along very well with the executive colleagues assigned to work with him, one of whom had recently been elected chairman of the board when his grandfather retired. Over several weeks' discussion, they had generally laid out some working policies and agreed on strategies that would bring new directions needed for development. Several days later . . . the young chairman's grandfather happened to drop in. He began to comment on how the company had been formed and had been built up by the traditional practices, talking about some of the policies the young executives had recently discarded. Phil expected the new chairman to explain some of the new innovative and developmental policies they had both agreed upon. However, the young man said nothing; instead, he just nodded and agreed with his grandfather. Phil was bewildered and frustrated . . . and he started to protest. The atmosphere in the room became immediately tense. . . . A week later the Japanese company withdrew from the negotiations. (Brislin et al., 1986, pp. 155-156)

The young chairman of the Japanese company was giving his grandfather face by agreeing with him. This did not, however, negate any of the negotiations he had with Phil. Phil obviously did not understand this. By protesting and disagreeing with the grandfather, Phil not only failed to give face to the grandfather, he threatened the grandfather's face. The young chairman, therefore, decided not to do business with Phil.

Face issues also can lead to misunderstanding in interethnic encounters in the United States. In the European American, middle-class subculture, for example, refusing to comply with a directive given by a superior is considered as a face-threatening act. In the African American subculture, however, "stylin" includes refusing to comply as part of a verbal game. This can be a problem when European American teachers interact with African American students and neither understands the others' communication style: "The [European American] teachers, not realizing the play argument was a salient speech event in the children's speech community, took literally the child's refusal to comply, often with disastrous results for the child's reputation. Such children can be seen as recalcitrant and possibly emotionally disturbed" by European American teachers (Erickson, 1981, pp. 6-7). For effective communication to occur in situations like this at least one of the participants must be mindful and try to understand the other's styles of communication.

Low- and High-Context Communication. We use the type of information (e.g., personal dispositions, the situation) that we believe is useful in explaining strangers' behavior when interacting with them. Since our explanations are based on our own cultural presuppositions, there is a likelihood misattributions will occur. Members of cultures in which low-context messages predominate, for example, tend not to emphasize situational factors enough when explaining the behavior of members of cultures in which high-context messages predominate. Members of cultures in which high-context messages predominate, in comparison, tend not to emphasize factors internal to the individual enough when trying to explain the behavior of members of cultures in which low-context messages predominate.

Another area where misunderstandings may occur in communication between members of cultures in which low- and high-context cultures predominate is in the directness of speech used. As indicated in Chapter 2, members of cultures where low-context communication predominates tend to use a direct style of speech. Members of cultures in which high-context communication predominates, in contrast, tend to use an indirect style of speech. Greeks tend to employ an indirect style of speech and interpret others' behavior based on the assumption that they also are using the same style (Tannen, 1979). U.S. Americans, in contrast, use a direct style of speech and assume others are using the same style.

When Greeks and U.S. Americans communicate there often are misunderstandings due to these differences in style of speech. A conversation between a husband (nonnative speaker [NNS] of English who learned indirect rules) and a wife (native speaker [NS] using direct communication styles) illustrates these differences:

NS (wife): Bob's having a party. Wanna go?

NNS (husband): OK.

NS: (later) Are you sure you wanna go?

NNS: OK, let's not go. I'm tired anyway. (Tannen, 1975)

In this conversation the husband interpreted the wife's question "Are you sure you wanna go?" as an indirect indication that she did not want to go.

Overcoming misunderstandings due to direct-indirect style differences is difficult because "in seeking to clarify, each speaker continues to use the very strategy which confused the other in the first place" (Tannen, 1979, p. 5). To resolve the misunderstandings, obviously one of the people involved must recognize that the differences in styles are creating the problem, try to interpret the other person's messages accurately, and then shift her or his style of speech.

Misattributions also result from the way people try to reduce uncertainty using low- and high-context messages, particularly in initial interactions with strangers. To illustrate, consider how uncertainty is reduced in the United States and Japan. In the European American, middle-class subculture, individuals try to obtain information about others' attitudes, feelings, and beliefs to reduce their uncertainty. In Japan where high-context messages are emphasized, on the other hand, people must know others' status and background in order to reduce uncertainty[2] and know which version of the language to use (there are different ways to speak to people who are "superiors," "equals," and "inferiors"). This leads Japanese to introduce themselves saying things like "'I belong to Mitsubishi Bank.' and immediately asking . . . 'What is your job?,' 'How old are you?,' and 'What is the name of your company?'" (Loveday, 1982, pp. 4-5). These questions are designed to gather the information necessary for a Japanese to communicate with a stranger. They often are perceived, however, as "rude" and "nosey" by U.S. Americans.

Personality Factors Influencing Our Attributions

Our personalities influence the way we make attributions. Three personality characteristics—category width, uncertainty orientation, and cognitive complexity—affect the flexibility of our cognitive systems.

Category Width

"Category width refers to the range of instances included in a cognitive category" (Pettigrew, 1982, p. 200).[3] To illustrate, is a pane of glass in the wall that is one inch wide and 12 feet high a window? A narrow categorizer would probably say no, while a broad categorizer would probably say yes. Broad categorizers have more latitude in what they include in a category than narrow categorizers. *Category width* "is a term used to describe the amount of discrepancy tolerable among category members—how similar do things have to be to be called by the same name? A narrow categorizer might put only highly similar things in the same category, whereas a broad categorizer might put more discrepant things in the same category" (Detweiler, 1978, p. 263).

Individual differences in category width are related to more general information processing strategies people use (Pettigrew, 1982). Broad categorizers, for example, tend to perform better on tasks that require holistic, integrated information processing than narrow categorizers. Narrow categorizers, in comparison, tend to perform better on tasks that require detailed, analytic information processing than broad categorizers. Broad categorizers include concepts like Buddhism, Capitalism,

Christianity, Democracy, Judaism, and Socialism in the same category (e.g., beliefs or doctrines), but narrow categorizers do not (Rokeach, 1951). Narrow categorizers are more ethnocentric than broad categorizers. Narrow categorizers also "react more to change, seek less prior information, and are more confident of their performances" than broad categorizers (Pettigrew, 1982, p. 207).

Category width influences the attributions we make about people who are culturally similar and culturally dissimilar. Narrow categorizers

> assume that the effects of behavior of a person from another culture tell all about the person, even though he [or she] in fact knows nothing about the actor's [or actress'] cultural background. He [or she] seems to make strong judgments based on the positivity or negativity of the effects of the behavior as evaluated from his [or her] own cultural viewpoint. Contrarily, when making attributions to a person who is culturally similar, the narrow [categorizer] seems to view the similarity as overshadowing the behavior. Thus, positive effects are seen as intended, and negative effects are confidently seen as unintended. (Detweiler, 1975, p. 600)

Narrow categorizers, therefore, may have trouble making accurate attributions about messages from both people who are culturally similar and people who are culturally dissimilar.

When making attributions about culturally dissimilar people, a broad categorizer

> seems to assume that he [or she] in fact doesn't know enough to make "usual" attributions. Thus, behaviors with negative effect result in less confident and generally more neutral attributions when judgments are made about a person from a different culture. Conversely, the culturally similar person who causes a negative outcome is rated relatively more negatively with greater confidence by the [broad categorizer], since the behavior from one's own cultural background is meaningful. (Detweiler, 1975, p. 600)

Broad categorizers, therefore, are more likely to search for the appropriate interpretation of strangers' behavior than narrow categorizers.

Narrow categorizers tend to be highly anxious when communicating with strangers. Narrow categorizers also tend to have a high degree of confidence in their predictions of and explanations for strangers' behavior, but their predictions and explanations tend to be inaccurate. Broad categorizers tend to make more accurate predictions of and explanations for strangers' behavior than narrow categorizers.

Table 5.1 contains a questionnaire designed to help you assess your category width. Take a couple of minutes and complete it now.

TABLE 5.1 *Assessing Your Category Width**

The purpose of this questionnaire is to help you to assess your category width. Respond to each of the statements by indicating the degree to which the statement is true regarding how you typically think about yourself. When you think about yourself, is the statement "Always False" (answer 1), "Usually False" (answer 2), "Sometimes True and Sometimes False" (answer 3), "Usually True" (answer 4), or "Always True" (answer 5)?

_____ 1. I do well on tasks that require integrated information processing.
_____ 2. I do well on tasks that require detailed information processing.
_____ 3. Things can be very dissimilar and share a common quality and I will use the same label to describe them.
_____ 4. I make strong judgments about others.
_____ 5. I do well on tasks that require holistic information processing.
_____ 6. I am confident that I perform well in social situations.
_____ 7. I try to make sure I have sufficient information before judging others.
_____ 8. I do well on tasks that require analytic information processing.
_____ 9. I try to obtain a lot of information before making decisions.
_____ 10. I react strongly to change.

To find your score, first reverse the responses for the even numbered items (i.e., if you wrote 1, make it 5; if you wrote 2, make it 4; if you wrote 3, leave it as 3; if you wrote 4, make it 2; if you wrote 5, make it 1). Next, add the numbers in front of each statement. Scores range from 10 to 50. The higher your score, the broader your categories.

*Adapted from Pettigrew's (1982) description of category width.

Scores on the questionnaire range from 10 to 50. The higher your score, the broader your categories. The important thing to keep in mind is that lower scores suggest that you assume that you have sufficient information to make an attribution about strangers when you do not. This assumption, in turn, will lead you to make inaccurate attributions about strangers' behavior. These tendencies, however, can be managed cognitively by becoming mindful when narrow categorizers communicate with people who are different.

Uncertainty Orientation

Uncertainty orientation influences whether or not we try to gather information about strangers. Our orientations toward uncertainty are based on the degree to which we have an open or closed mind. People with an open mind "need to know and understand" themselves and others (Rokeach, 1960, p. 67). People with a closed mind, in contrast, "need to ward off threatening aspects of reality" (p. 67). This often is accomplished by ignoring new information made available.

We can differentiate people with an uncertainty orientation from those with a certainty orientation.

> There are many people who simply are not interested in finding out information about themselves or the world, who do not conduct causal searches, who could not care less about comparing themselves with others, and who "don't give a hoot" for resolving discrepancies or inconsistencies about the self. Indeed, such people (we call them certainty oriented) will go out of their way not to perform activities such as these (we call people who *do* go out of their way to do such things uncertainty oriented). (Sorrentino & Short, 1986, pp. 379-380)

Uncertainty oriented people are interested in reducing uncertainty, while certainty oriented people try to avoid looking at uncertainty when it is present.

Uncertainty oriented people integrate new and old ideas and change their belief systems accordingly (Sorrentino & Short, 1986).[4] They evaluate ideas and thoughts on their own merit and do not necessarily compare them with others. Uncertainty oriented people want to understand themselves and their environments. The more uncertainty oriented we are, the more likely we are willing to question our own behaviors and their appropriateness when communicating with strangers. Also, the more uncertainty oriented we are, the more we would try to gather information about strangers so we can communicate effectively with them. Certainty oriented people, in contrast, like to hold on to traditional beliefs and have a tendency to reject ideas that are different. Certainty oriented people maintain a sense of self by not examining themselves or their behavior.

Uncertainty oriented people tend to recall positive and negative events that occur in their interactions with strangers in an unbiased and accurate way (Huber & Sorrentino, 1996). Certainty oriented people, in contrast, tend to distort their recall of events that happened in their interactions with strangers in ways that are consistent with their stereotypes of strangers' groups. Certainty oriented people also "are more likely to think in terms of categories or stereotypes and see greater differentiation between categories" than uncertainty oriented people (p. 607).

Our certainty or uncertainty orientations influence our reliance on stereotypes when we communicate with strangers (Wilder & Simon, 1996). People with a certainty orientation rely on stereotypes more than people with an uncertainty orientation. One reason for this is that

TABLE 5.2 *Assessing Your Uncertainty Orientation**

The purpose of this questionnaire is to help you assess your orientation toward uncertainty. Respond to each statement indicating the degree to which it is true regarding the way to typically respond: "Always False" (answer 1), "Usually False" (answer 2), "Sometimes False and Sometimes True" (answer 3), "Usually True" (answer 4), or "Always True" (answer 5).

_____ 1. I do not compare myself with others.
_____ 2. If given a choice, I prefer to go somewhere new rather than somewhere I've been before.
_____ 3. I reject ideas that are different than mine.
_____ 4. I try to resolve inconsistencies in beliefs I hold.
_____ 5. I am not interested in finding out information about myself.
_____ 6. When I obtain new information, I try to integrate it with information I already have.
_____ 7. I hold traditional beliefs.
_____ 8. I evaluate people on their own merit without comparing them to others.
_____ 9. I hold inconsistent views of myself.
_____ 10. If someone suggests an opinion that is different than mine, I do not reject it before I consider it.

To find your score, first reverse the responses for the odd numbered items (i.e., if you wrote 1, make it 5; if you wrote 2, make it 4; if you wrote 3, leave it as 3; if you wrote 4, make it 2; if you wrote 5, make it 1). Next, add the numbers next to each statement. Scores range from 10 to 50. The higher your score, the greater your uncertainty orientation.

*Based on Sorrentino and Short's (1986) description of uncertainty orientation.

stereotypes simplify the world and allow certainty oriented people to maintain consistent views of the world. The differences between certainty and uncertainty oriented people will be larger when they are emotionally aroused than when they are not emotionally aroused.

Certainty oriented people will have a high degree of confidence in their predictions of and explanations for strangers' behavior, but their predictions and explanations may not be accurate. Uncertainty oriented people tend to make more accurate predictions of and explanations for strangers' behavior than certainty oriented people.

The questionnaire in Table 5.2 is designed to help you assess your certainty-uncertainty orientation. Take a few minutes and complete it now.

Scores on the questionnaire range from 10 to 50. The higher your score, the more uncertainty oriented you are. The less uncertainty oriented you are (or the more certainty oriented you are), the greater the potential misunderstandings you may have when you communicate with people who are different. If you are highly certainty oriented (i.e., you got a low score on the questionnaire), you may have a lot of misunderstandings and not know about them or care about them if you do recognize them. Uncertainty orientation tends to be viewed as a personality trait, but our orientations can be managed, at least in part, when we are mindful of our communication.

Cognitive Complexity

The complexity of our cognitive systems also affects the way we perceive strangers and interpret their messages (Applegate & Sypher, 1983). We use constructs to differentiate strangers when we communicate (Kelly, 1955). *Constructs* are perceptual categories used to organize our thoughts. When communicating with strangers, for example, we might use constructs such as similar-dissimilar, empathic-not empathic, extroverted-introverted, honest-dishonest, trustworthy-not trustworthy, and so forth in trying to understand their behavior.

Cognitively complex people use more constructs to understand strangers than cognitively simple people. It is not just the complexity of our cognitive system, however, that is important to how we communicate. The quality of the constructs we use in understanding strangers also is important (Clark & Delia, 1977). Determining quality is based on the relevance of the constructs to the situation in which we use them. If, for example, we are trying to improve the effectiveness of our communication with strangers, assessing whether they are generous-not generous will not be very useful and, therefore, the quality of our contrasts will be low. Assessing the degree to which strangers are trustworthy-not trustworthy, in contrast, will be useful in improving the quality of our communication because this construct is related directly to communication.

Take a few minutes to answer the following questions about your cognitive complexity before proceeding.

What constructs would you use to describe your best friend?

___

___

___

What constructs would you use to describe your worst enemy?

___

___

___

Look at the constructs you listed for each question. The first thing you want to consider is the number of constructs. Are there a large number of constructs you could have included to describe your best friend or worst enemy and did not? If you answered yes, your construct system is not as complex as it could be. Now look at whether the constructs you listed affect the way your best friend and worst enemy communicate with you. If a lot of the concepts are not related to their communication with you, you may want to reconsider how you think about others' communication with you (e.g., the quality of the constructs you use could be better).

Cognitively complex people form impressions of strangers that are more extensive and differentiated, and better represent the behavioral variability of strangers than cognitively simple people (O'Keefe & Sypher, 1981). Cognitively complex people seek out unique features of their environments more than cognitively simple people (Honess, 1976). Cognitively simple people tend to seek information that is consistent with their prior beliefs.

Cognitively complex individuals are likely to be more effective in intercultural interactions than cognitively simple individuals:

> a cognitively simple person has a single framework within which to evaluate the observed behavior of others in the target culture. Thus, when a behavior which he [or she] does not understand takes place, he [or she] is likely to evaluate it ethnocentrically. A complex person, on the other hand, has several frameworks for the perception of the same behavior. He [or she] might, for example, suspend judgment and obtain more information before evaluating the behavior. (Davidson, 1975, p. 80)

Cognitively complex individuals are more effective in intercultural interactions than cognitively simple individuals because cognitively complex individuals have the ability to take the perspective of the people with whom they are communicating (Detweiler, 1980).

Cognitive complexity is related directly to the management of uncertainty and anxiety when communicating with strangers (Gudykunst, 1995). The more complex our cognitions are, the greater our ability to manage our uncertainty and anxiety. If we tend to be cognitively simple when communicating on automatic pilot, we can choose to process information in a complex fashion when we are mindful of our communication.

Improving the Accuracy of Our Attributions

If we recognize that our perceptions of and attributions for strangers' behavior may be in error, we need to try to improve our accuracy. There are at least three communication skills that are useful in increasing our accuracy: perception checking, active listening, and feedback.

Perception Checking

If two people are communicating it is likely that they are perceiving what is going on differently. Much of the time when we communicate, small differences in perceptions are not problematic. At times, however, even small differences in perceptions can lead to ineffective communication. If strangers do not directly tell us what they are thinking or feeling, our perceptions can be inaccurate. When this occurs, perception checking is a valuable skill to have among our communication resources.

The purpose of perception checking is to send the relational message that we want to understand the strangers' thoughts or feelings. Perception checking provides us with an opportunity to make sure our interpretations of strangers' behavior is what they meant before we act. Perception checking helps reduce uncertainty for the person doing the perception checking. Checking perceptions also can reduce anxiety for both people involved because its helps each recognize that their need for a common shared view of the world is being met. Perception checking, therefore, increases the likelihood that we will communicate effectively.

Perception checking involves three processes. First, we have to describe the behavior we observe. Second, we tell what we perceive strangers' thoughts and/or feelings to be. In doing this, we *must* refrain from evaluating strangers' thoughts or feelings. Third, we need to ask strangers if our perceptions are accurate. An example of a perception check would be "You have a smile on your face. I assume you're happy. Are you?" This statement describes the behavior we observe, gives our perceptions of strangers' feelings without any evaluation, and asks if our perceptions are correct. If we are not sure what strangers feel, we can still check our perceptions. To illustrate, the statement "I'm not sure from the expression on your face whether you are hurt or angry. Which is it?" is a form of perception check.

Sometimes we may think we are checking our perceptions when we actually aren't. If we do not describe our perceptions without evaluation and ask if they are correct, we are not checking our perceptions. Only asking a question is not perception checking. "Are you angry with me?" and "Why are you mad at me?" are not perception checks. Speaking for strangers also is not checking our perceptions. If we said, "You're always depressed," we are not checking our perceptions. If we said "You are being very quiet and not saying much. I assume you are depressed. Are you?" we would be checking our perceptions. Also, if we express a judgment we are not checking our perceptions. If strangers expressed their feelings and we said, "Why on earth would you feel that way?," we would not be checking our perceptions. We would be judging strangers' feelings.

There are a few important things to keep in mind about perception checking. If the person doing the perception checking does not change his or her perceptions when strangers say "No. I'm not feeling . . . ," then the perception check will not improve the quality of communication. Rather, it will inhibit the possibility of effective communication. The reason for this is that strangers will interpret the relational message being transmitted as the person doing the perception checking not wanting to understand their feelings.

Strangers responding to the perception check also have a responsibility for the quality of the communication taking place. For communication to be effective, strangers responding to our perception checks need to tell the truth. If someone says to us, "You slammed the door. I assume you're angry. Are you?," we need to tell the truth. If we are angry and say "no," then our anger will still influence the way we communicate. If we say "no," then we have a responsibility to act as though we are not angry for communication to be effective.

Checking our perceptions is *not* something most of us do in our everyday communication. Using this skill in your everyday communication with strangers may feel awkward at first because we do not have scripts for perception checking. The more you use it, however, the more natural it will become. Also, the more you engage in perception checking, the more likely you will develop scripts for doing it, and the more likely that it will become one of your resources for communication when you are on automatic pilot.

As indicated earlier, most of us do not engage in perception checking on automatic pilot. Practicing perception checking will make it easier when we need to use it. Skill Exercise 5.1 is designed to help you practice perception checking. Take a few minutes to complete it now.

The first few times we use perception checking it will be unnatural. The more we practice perception checking in our everyday communication, the easier it becomes. Perception checking is one of the simplest and most powerful techniques we can use to improve the quality of our communication. I am not suggesting that you use perception checking all of the time. Use it when you think that there is a chance that your perceptions may not be accurate or when it is important that you base your behavior on accurate perceptions. Also, it is important to keep in mind that perception checking involves direct communication and, therefore, has an individualistic bias. If you are an individualist communicating with a collectivist, it is important to keep in mind that collectivists may

SKILL EXERCISE 5.1 *Perception Checking*

Perception checking involves telling others (1) what we perceived (i.e., describe the behavior), (2) how we interpreted the behavior, and (3) checking to see if our perception is correct. Take a few minutes to answer the following questions.

You are working in a class group and one person is from another culture. This person is always quiet when the group meets and does not contribute to the discussion. You interpret this person's behavior as indicating that he or she does not care about the group's work.

How would you typically respond?

____

____

How might you use perception checking to see if your interpretation is correct?

____

____

____

You are interacting with an African American who is an acquaintance. You ask him or her a question. When answering your question, she or he does not make eye contact. You interpret this as indicating that he or she is deceiving you.

How would you typically respond?

____

____

How might you use perception checking to see if your interpretation is correct?

____

____

____

not feel comfortable answering direct questions. In this case, you may have to ask your perception checking questions indirectly.

Listening Effectively

Often, we are not very good listeners. Take a few minutes to answer the following questions about your listening behavior before reading this section.

How do you know when someone is not listening to you?

___

___

___

How do you show others that you are listening to them?

___

___

___

What are some of the reasons you do not listen when others are speaking?

___

___

___

Your answers to these questions should provide some insight into the role of listening in your implicit theory of communication. Keep your answers in mind as you read this section.

Listening is not a natural activity, it is not a passive activity as most of us assume, and most of us are not very skilled listeners (Roach & Wyatt, 1988). Hearing is a natural, automatic process, while listening is the "process of discriminating and identifying which sounds are meaningful or important to us and which aren't" (p. 2). Effective listening, therefore, is a purposive activity (e.g., it requires that we are mindful). More specifically, "real listening involves taking in new information and checking it against what you already know, selecting important ideas from unimportant ideas, searching for categories to store the information in (or creating categories), and predicting what's coming next in order to be ready for it" (p. 4). Most of us need practice to accomplish this.

Table 5.3 contains an assessment designed to help you assess your typical listening behavior. Take a few minutes to complete it now.

Scores on this questionnaire range from 10 to 50. The higher your score, the better a listener you are. If your score is low, you can choose to listen more effectively when you are mindful of your communication behavior. When we are mindful, we need to try to engage in active listening.

Active listening is necessary to understand strangers.[5] We need to enter "the private perceptual world of the other and becom[e] thoroughly at home in it. It involves being sensitive, moment by moment, to the

TABLE 5.3 *Assessing Your Listening Behavior*

The purpose of this questionnaire is to assess your listening behavior with strangers. Respond to each statement indicating the degree to which it is true regarding the way you generally listen: "Always False" (answer 1), "Usually False" (answer 2), "Sometimes False and Sometimes True" (answer 3), "Usually True" (answer 4), and "Always True" (answer 5).

_____ 1. I have a difficult time separating important and unimportant ideas when I listen to strangers.
_____ 2. I check new information against what I already know when I listen to strangers.
_____ 3. I have an idea what strangers will say when I listen to them.
_____ 4. I am sensitive to strangers' feelings when I listen to them.
_____ 5. I think about what I am going to say next when I listen to strangers.
_____ 6. I focus on the process of communication that is occurring between me and strangers when I listen to them.
_____ 7. I cannot wait for strangers to finish talking so I can take my turn.
_____ 8. I try to understand the meanings that are being created when I communicate with strangers.
_____ 9. I focus on determining whether strangers understand what I said when they are talking.
_____ 10. I ask strangers to elaborate when I am not sure what they mean.

To find your score, first reverse your responses for the odd numbered items (i.e., if you wrote 1, make it 5; if you wrote 2, make it 4; if you wrote 3, leave it as 3; if you wrote 4, make it 2; if you wrote 5, make it 1). Next, add the numbers next to each statement. Scores range from 10 to 50. The higher your score, the better your listening behavior

changing felt needs which flow in this other person" (Rogers, 1980, p. 142). There are three sets of interrelated skills involved in active listening: attending skills, following skills, and comprehending skills.[6]

Attending skills involve the ways that we attend to strangers who are speaking. One thing we need to do is indicate to strangers that we are involved in the conversation. This is accomplished by our body postures. If we are leaning backward with our arms crossed, speakers will probably assume that we are not involved. If, in contrast, we lean forward and face strangers when they are talking, they will probably assume we are listening. Eye contact also is important. In the European American subculture "it involves focusing one's eyes softly on the speaker and occasionally shifting the gaze from his [or her] face to other parts of the body" (Bolton, 1990, p. 181). We need to keep in mind, however, that rules for eye contact vary across cultures (see the next chapter). Attending requires that we give strangers our undivided attention. To do this, the environment in which we are communicating should not distract us.

Following skills indicate to strangers that we are trying to understand their perspectives (Bolton, 1990). The first thing we need to do is give strangers time to speak. Strangers need time to decide whether they want to talk and to decide what to say. This often requires that we be silent more than we would like. We also need to indicate to strangers that we are interested in what they have to say. We could begin, for example, by checking our perceptions and then asking strangers to tell us more about their views. We can invite strangers to talk by saying "I'm interested in what you have to say" or "Would you like to talk about it?" When we are listening we need to let strangers know we are paying attention and encourage them to continue speaking. This can be accomplished by saying things like "mm-hmm," "oh," "I see," and so forth.

Comprehending skills involve ways that we can understand the strangers better (Bolton, 1990). Perception checking (discussed earlier) is one method that we can use to comprehend better what strangers are saying. Another way we can make sure we are understanding strangers is to *paraphrase* what they say in our own words. By restating what the other person says in our own words, we ensure that we have not misinterpreted the other person's position. This can easily be accomplished by saying something like "I want to make sure I understand what you're saying . . ." The other thing we can do to increase our understanding is to use *probing questions*—questions designed to find out who, what, when, where, why, and how. We need to be careful, however, when we ask questions. If we ask too many questions, we end up dealing with our own agenda, rather than trying to understand strangers.

Active listening can help us better understand strangers if we listen without presupposing any particular outcome, and focus on what is being said, as well as how it is being said in the conversation we are having. Stated differently, we must stop the internal monologue (e.g., thinking about what we are going to say next) that is going on in our heads (Howell, 1982).

Active listening obviously lengthens the amount of time it takes to have a conversation. There are other potential problems with the approach that stem from the fact that it is not the way we normally listen. Since most of us do not use active listening regularly, we do not have a script to guide us in active listening. Our initial attempts at active listening, therefore, may feel awkward. This is natural, and to be expected. The more we practice active listening, however, the more natural it will feel. When we use active listening, others may wonder what is happening when we ask them to "say more" or when we paraphrase what they said. Whether or not they cooperate will have a lot to do with our attitude. If we demonstrate that we really want to understand them and are not just playing some game, it will increase the likelihood they will cooperate.

Since active listening is not something most of us do on automatic pilot, practicing it can help us use the skill when it will help improve the quality of our communication. Skill Exercise 5.2 provides a chance for you to practice this skill. Take a few minutes to complete it now.

Active listening does not feel natural the first time we do it. The more we use the skill, however, the easier it becomes. Active listening is a simple way to increase the effectiveness of our communication. Using this skill with strangers can help us better understand how group differences affect our communication.

Feedback

We seek feedback from strangers and provide feedback on their communication when there is uncertainty present (Ashford & Cummings, 1983). *Feedback* refers to "the response listeners give to others about their behavior. . . . Feedback from others enables us to understand how our behavior affects them, and allows us to modify our behavior to achieve our desired goals" (Haslett & Ogilvie, 1988, p. 385). Feedback may be verbal or nonverbal. Affective or evaluative feedback tends to be given nonverbally, while cognitive or content feedback tends to be given verbally (Zajonc, 1980).

By paying attention to the feedback we receive and using it effectively, we engage in "a series of diminishing mistakes—a dwindling series of under-and-over corrections converging on the goal" (Deutsch, 1968, p. 390). To the extent that we use feedback effectively, we converge toward mutual understanding and shared meanings. If we do not receive feedback or use it effectively, however, we diverge from shared meanings and misunderstandings occur.

There are several concrete suggestions for giving effective feedback when communicating with strangers that are useful (Haslett & Ogilvie, 1988). First, feedback should be direct and specific, and be supported by evidence (e.g., a rationale needs to be given). Indirect and vague feedback generally is not effective with people in the United States (especially in the middle-class subculture). Second, the issue on which the feedback is given needs to be separated from the person. Avoid judging strangers being given feedback. Third, present the situation on which feedback is being given as a mutual problem (e.g., do not blame strangers for screwing up). Fourth, do not overload strangers with negative feedback;

SKILL EXERCISE 5.2 *Active Listening*

Active listening involves listening to understand what others are saying from their perspectives. Take a few minutes to answer the following questions.

An acquaintance of yours from another culture in one of your classes says "I'm really having trouble understanding our instructor."

How would you typically respond?

____

____

How would you respond to this person using active listening?

____

____

____

You see an acquaintance of yours from another ethnic group in a department store. Your acquaintance says "I think the clerk has been following me around the store."

How would you typically respond?

____

____

How would you respond to this person using active listening?

____

____

____

mix negative feedback with positive feedback. Fifth, provide the feedback at a time close to the occurrence, but at a time strangers will be receptive. If I am emotionally upset and unable to control my anger, for example, it will not do any good to give me feedback until I have calmed down. Sixth, deliver feedback in an assertive, dynamic, responsive, and relaxed style. Finally, be trustworthy, fair, credible, and preserve strangers' public images when giving feedback.

There are three other things to keep in mind when giving feedback. First, when we give feedback we need to use "I" statements. "I" statements are statements giving our own thoughts and feelings. Second, we should focus our feedback in the "here and now." If we bring up the past, it hinders the effectiveness of our feedback. Third, the feedback we give strangers must be our own. We need to avoid giving strangers feedback from third parties. We cannot use "I" statements to give third party feedback.

The suggestions for providing feedback outlined here are based on research with European Americans in the United States. Modifications are necessary when dealing with strangers. Feedback always has to be appropriate to the time, person, and our relationship with the strangers involved. When giving intergroup feedback, we also need to take into consideration the other person's group memberships. How would feedback be given in her or his group?

Assume that I (a European American male) want to present feedback to a Japanese male friend with whom I am communicating in Japan. If I am direct in the feedback that I give my friend, he may perceive my feedback as a threat to his public image (i.e., it may threaten his face). The reason for this is that Japanese try to preserve harmony in relations with friends. To accomplish this, they use an indirect style of communication. If I am direct and he perceives this as a threat, my feedback will be ineffective. To provide culturally sensitive feedback, I have to be indirect in the way I give it. If we are in the United States speaking English, I can be more direct than if we are in Japan speaking Japanese.

Giving effective feedback is not something most of us do naturally. Practicing the skill can make it easier to do when we need to use the skill. Skill Exercise 5.3 provides a chance for you to practice the skill. Take a few minutes to complete it now.

Being able to tell others our perceptions of their behavior can help us improve the quality of our communication. It is important to recognize that we may need to modify how we use the skill when the person to whom we are giving feedback is a collectivist.

Study Questions

1. Why are our perceptions selective?
2. How does categorization influence the perception process?
3. Why do rigid categories inhibit effective communication?
4. What are the differences between individual and social attributions?
5. What is the ultimate attribution error?

SKILL EXERCISE 5.3 *Giving Feedback*

Being able to give feedback is an important aspect of effective communication. Take a few minutes to answer the following questions.

An acquaintance of yours from another culture who is in one of your classes is always late when you get together to work on a joint paper. You want this person to be on time when you meet in the future.

How would you typically respond?

____

____

How could you give your acquaintance feedback to get the person to the meetings on time?

____

____

____

You are working on a group project in a class and one of the group members from a different ethnic group is not doing his or her fair share of the work. You think this person's performance will lower the group's grade and want the person to do what she or he is supposed to do.

How would you typically respond?

____

____

How could you give your acquaintance feedback to get the person to do his or her share of the work?

____

____

____

---

6. How does our culture influence the attribution process?
7. How does our category width influence the attribution process?
8. How does our certainty or uncertainty orientation influence the attribution process?

9. How does our cognitive complexity influence the attribution process?
10. How does performing perception checking improve the accuracy of our perceptions?
11. Why does active listening improve the accuracy of our perceptions?

Applications

1. Over the next week, pay attention to your perceptions of strangers. How are your perceptions biased? What factors lead to these biases? How can you decrease the biases in the future?

2. Sometime in the next week, check your perceptions of a stranger's behavior. Describe your conversation and make sure that you did the perception check correctly. What effect does this have on your understanding of the stranger and your communication with him or her?

3. Sometime in the next week, actively listen to a stranger when you are interacting. Try truly to understand the stranger's perspective on what is being discussed rather than just presenting your own view. What effect does this have on your encounter with the stranger?

Notes

1. Kelley uses an analysis of variance statistical analogy to explain this process.
2. For a complete discussion of the cultural differences in how uncertainty is reduced, see Gudykunst and Ting-Toomey (1988).
3. See Pettigrew (1982) for a summary of the findings from over 100 studies of category width.
4. This summary is drawn from Sorrentino and Short (1986).
5. See, for example, Roach and Wyatt (1988) and Rogers (1980).
6. My discussion is drawn is part from the work of Robert Bolton (1990).

CHAPTER 6

Exchanging Messages With Strangers

In the previous two chapters, I examined our expectations for strangers' behavior and how we make sense of strangers' behavior. The focus of these chapters was on how we interpret strangers' messages to us. The focus of this chapter is on the messages we exchange with strangers. I begin by examining the nature of language and nonverbal messages. Next, to place our intergroup messages in context, I look at cultural differences in language usage. Following this, I discuss cultural differences in nonverbal messages. I then look at language usage in intergroup contexts. I conclude this chapter by examining those things we can do to improve the quality of the messages we transmit to strangers.

The Nature of Language and Nonverbal Messages

Verbal and nonverbal aspects of communication are intertwined highly. They share some similarities and are different in some respects. Verbal and nonverbal behavior are discussed separately in this chapter, but it is important to keep in mind that verbal and nonverbal messages are exchanged at the same time, and both influence the meanings we attach to messages.

The Nature of Language

All languages contain elements that are universal and elements that are unique. Languages are all rule-governed. There are *phonological rules* that tell us how the sounds of our languages are combined to form words. *Grammatical rules* tell us how to order words (e.g., nouns, objects, verbs) to form sentences. *Semantic rules* tell us the relationship between words and the things to which they refer. *Pragmatic rules* tell us how to interpret the meaning of utterances. The rules of a language are a function of the speech community using the language. *Speech communities* are groups of people who use similar rules to guide how they use language and interpret others' use of language (Hymes, 1974).

The language spoken in a speech community serves at least three functions. First, the *informative* function of language is to provide others with information or knowledge. Second, the *expressive* function of language is to tell others our attitudes, feelings, and emotions. Third, the *directive* function of language is used to direct others (e.g., causing or preventing some action).

There are several characteristics of language important to understanding its role in communication (Hockett, 1958). First, the elements of languages can be combined in new meaningful utterances (*productivity*). Second, languages exhibit *discreteness* because we are able to perceive different sounds as discrete from one another. Third, languages are *self reflexive*, or they can be used to refer to themselves. Fourth, languages can be used to refer to things that are not present (*displacement*). Fifth, languages are *arbitrary*. Words are symbols and, therefore, there is not a direct connection between the words and the things they represent.

The Nature of Nonverbal Communication

Languages and nonverbal cues are similar in some ways and different in others. First, nonverbal cues are discrete like languages. Nonverbal cues can be separated from one another. Second, some nonverbal cues are created based on agreement among the members of a group using them and, therefore, they are arbitrary like symbols. To illustrate, "the finger" is an obscene gesture in the United States, but other cultures use different gestures to mean the same thing as the finger. Third, languages involve displacement (i.e., the ability to use language to refer to things that are not present), but nonverbal cues do not. Nonverbal cues are limited to referring to things that are present. Finally, language and nonverbal cues differ in terms of their relative weight in determining meaning. In general, "adults place more reliance on nonverbal cues than verbal ones in determining meaning" (Burgoon et al., 1989, p. 155). This is especially true when the verbal and nonverbal messages are inconsistent.

Nonverbal cues serve several functions in interaction (Ekman & Friesen, 1969). First, nonverbal cues may *repeat* verbal messages. Second, nonverbal cues may *contradict* verbal cues. In English, when people tell us they love us with a flat tone of voice, we are likely to interpret the flat tone of voice as contradicting the verbal message. Third, nonverbal cues can *substitute* for verbal cues. Fourth, nonverbal messages may *complement* verbal messages. Fifth, nonverbal cues can accent part of verbal messages. Sixth, nonverbal cues can regulate the flow of conversations.

Often nonverbal behavior is discussed as either universal or culture-bound. It, however, is not this simple. There are at least three layers of nonverbal behavior:

> The innermost core represents nonverbal behaviors considered to be universal and innate; facial expressions of some emotional states belong to this core. Next come the nonverbal behaviors that show both uniformity and diversity; members of all cultures display affect, express intimacy, and deal with status but the particular signs of so doing are variable. Finally, there are culture-bound nonverbal behaviors which manifest great dissimilarity across cultures—language-related acts such as emblems [nonverbal cues with a direct verbal translation; e.g., "V" for victory], illustrators [nonverbal cues which directly accompany speech; e.g., cues which illustrate what is being said—nodding our head to accompany verbal agreement in the United States], and regulators [cues which regulate the back and forth flow of speaking and listening; e.g., looking at speaker when listening and looking away when talking in European American culture] show diversity most clearly. (LaFrance & Mayo, 1978, p. 73)

Nonverbal behavior, therefore, varies from universal to dissimilarity across cultures.

Cultural Differences in Language Usage

Culture and language are interrelated highly. Our cultures influence the languages we speak, and how we use our languages influences our cultures.[1] In this section, I discuss how our cultures influence our use of language with an emphasis on selected aspects of low- and high-context communication: beliefs about talk, the use of direct and indirect messages, and the relationship between individualism-collectivism and low- and high-context communication. Next, I examine how topics are managed in conversations. I conclude this section with an overview of how culture influences the way we persuade others.

Beliefs About Talk

Beliefs about talk refers to our evaluations of the functions of talk and silence (Wiemann et al., 1986). There are many different beliefs about talk that we can hold. We can, for example, see talk as more important than silence. We also can hold different beliefs about the nature of the talk in which we engage. Take a few minutes to answer the following questions before reading the remainder of this section.

What is the role of talk (verbal messages) in communication?

____

____

____

What is the role of silence in communication?

____

____

____

To what extent should our communication be precise, involve exaggerations, or be animated? Why?

____

____

____

Your answers to these questions should provide some insight into the role of talk in your implicit theory of communication. Keep your answers in mind as you read the remainder of this section. To place these various beliefs in context, I begin with how culture influences the importance we place on talk.

Importance of Talk. European Americans see talk as more important and enjoyable than Chinese or Chinese Americans (Wiemann et al., 1986). European Americans are more likely than the other two groups to initiate conversations with others and to engage in conversations when opportunities present themselves. Chinese Americans are more likely to engage in these activities than Chinese. European Americans see talk as a means of social control, while Chinese see silence as a control strategy.

The differences in beliefs about talk between Chinese and European Americans can be explained by cultural differences in individualism-collectivism:

> Individualists have a choice among many groups . . . to which they do belong, and usually belong to these groups because they volunteer.

> Collectivists . . . are born into a few groups and are more or less stuck with them. So, the collectivists do not have to go out of their way and exert themselves to be accepted, while individualists have to work hard to be accepted. Hence, the individualists often speak more, try to control the situation verbally, and do not value silence [as much as collectivists]. (Triandis, cited in Giles, Coupland, & Wiemann, 1992, p. 11)

This should not be taken to suggest that collectivists do not engage in small talk or gossip, because they do. Collectivists, however, do not see talk as important in developing relationships as individualists.

Members of collectivistic Asian cultures (e.g., China, Japan, Korea) tend to have higher levels of communication apprehension (e.g., anxiety associated with verbal communication) than U.S. Americans (Kim et al., 2001; Klopf, 1984). Emphasizing the independent self construal is associated negatively with communication apprehension (Kim et al., 2001). Communication apprehension is problematic in individualistic cultures like the United States where verbal fluency is valued. Communication apprehension, however, is not necessarily problematic in collectivistic cultures. Koreans, for example, are attracted to individuals who do not engage in a lot of verbal communication more than those who do (Elliot et al., 1982). Japanese also value being constrained and reserved (Okabe, 1983).

Silence. One belief about talk that we can hold is that silence is an important part of communication. In individualistic cultures like the United States, silence often is viewed as the opposite of sound. Many people in individualistic cultures have a low tolerance for silence; it is something to be filled in conversations.

Silence is viewed differently in collectivistic cultures like Japan. It is viewed as an important part of communication. There are four meanings of what can be conveyed by silence in Japan: truthfulness, social discretion, embarrassment, and defiance (Lebra, 1987). Japanese view truth as occurring only in the inner realms. Activities regarding the outer self do not involve individuals' true feelings and, therefore, frequently involve distortion, deception, or "moral falsity." Japanese who speak little are trusted more than Japanese who speak a lot. Truthfulness emerges from silences, not words in Japan. Silence also allows Japanese to be socially discreet. "Social discretion refers to silence considered necessary or desirable in order to gain social acceptance or to avoid social penalty" (Lebra, 1987, p. 347). At times, talking may be dangerous and require that Japanese tell the truth. In these instances, silence allows Japanese to avoid social disapproval. Silence also saves Japanese from embarrassment.

Verbally expressing emotions to each other, for example, may cause a married couple to become embarrassed. Japanese also may indicate disagreement or anger with someone else by being silent.

Japanese have a more negative view of silence when communicating with strangers than with close friends, but there are no differences for U.S. Americans (Hasegawa & Gudykunst, 1998). One reason for this is that when strangers are silent, their behavior is not predictable in Japan. This is not the case for close friends. Japanese report using silence more than U.S. Americans, but U.S. Americans report using silence more strategically (to accomplish their goals) than Japanese.

There also are ethnic differences with respect to silence (Scollon & Wong-Scollon, 1990). Native Americans, for example, prefer silence more than European Americans. For European Americans, the primary function of talk is to bridge relational distances (e.g., to make themselves known to others). Silence is reserved for intimate relationships. For Native Americans, silence is used to protect themselves from people they do not know. Talk, in contrast, is used in intimate relationships.

Elaboration/Animation. Not valuing talk and valuing silence is one belief about talk that we can hold. We also can value using elaborate or animated forms of speech.

The forms of assertion and exaggeration used in the Arabic language clearly illustrate the use of elaboration in communication:

> The built-in mechanism of assertion in language affects the Arabs' communication behavior in at least two ways. First, an Arab feels compelled to overassert in almost all types of communication because others expect him [or her] to. If an Arab says exactly what he [or she] means without the expected assertion, other Arabs may still think that he [or she] means the opposite. For example, a simple "No" by a guest to the host's request to eat more or drink more will not suffice. To convey the meaning that he [or she] is actually full, the guest must keep repeating "No" several times, coupling it with an oath such as "By God" or "I swear to God." Second, an Arab often fails to realize that others, particularly foreigners, may mean exactly what they say even though their language is simple. To the Arabs, a simple "No" may mean the indirectly expressed consent and encouragement of a coquettish woman. On the other hand, a simple consent may mean the rejection of a hypocritical politician. (Almaney & Alwan, 1982, p. 84)

U.S. Americans might say "We miss you." The equivalent Arabic is "You made us desolate" (Patai, 1976). The Arab proclivity to use verbal exaggerations is probably responsible for more diplomatic misunderstandings between the United States and Arab countries than any other single factor (Cohen, 1987).

The French use an animated style in conversations with people close to them (Carroll, 1988). For the French, a conversation must be "engaged, sustained, fueled, and revived if it is 'dragging.' Once [the French] permit a conversation to begin, [they] owe it to [themselves] to keep it from dying, to care for it, to guide it, to nourish it, and to watch over its development as though it were a living creature" (p. 24). The animated style, however, is reserved for informal interaction in close relationships. In "serious" conversations, long, uninterrupted responses occur.

There also are ethnic differences in the use of animation. There are, for example, differences between European Americans and African Americans (Kochman, 1990). African Americans' verbal style tends to be emotionally animated and expressive. European Americans' style, in contrast, is more restrained and subdued than African Americans' style. African Americans often see European Americans as detached and distant, and European Americans often see African Americans as threatening and intimidating.

Assessing Your Beliefs About Talk. Table 6.1 contains a questionnaire designed to help you assess your beliefs about talk and silence. Take a few minutes to complete it now.

Scores on the questionnaire range from 10 to 50. The higher your score, the more important you see talk to be in expressing your identity. Neither high nor low scores on this questionnaire are the most desirable. It is important, however, to remember that if your score is high, you may have problems communicating with strangers who do not value talk as much as you do. Also, if your score is low, you may have problems communicating with strangers who value talk more than you do. Either way, to increase your effectiveness you must be mindful of your communication and recognize group-based differences in orientations toward talk and silence.

Direct Versus Indirect Language Usage

When individualists want to assert themselves as unique persons, they must be direct so that others will know where they stand. Individualists must be direct in order to tell others who they are. Indirect communication, however, often is used in intimate relationships (e.g., to express emotions). If collectivists' goals are to maintain harmony in their ingroups, they cannot be direct because they might offend other members of their ingroups. To maintain harmony, collectivists need to be cautious and indirect. Indirect communication, therefore, predominates in collectivistic

TABLE 6.1 *Assessing Your Beliefs About Talk*

The purpose of this questionnaire is to help you assess your beliefs about talk. Respond to each statement regarding the degree to which you agree or disagree with the statement. If you strongly disagree with the statement, answer 1; if you disagree, answer 2; if you neither agree nor disagree, answer 3; if you agree, answer 4; if you strongly agree, answer 5.

_____ 1. I enjoy talking when I find myself in social situations.
_____ 2. I do not enjoy small talk.
_____ 3. I try to break the ice by talking when I first meet others.
_____ 4. I view people who are reticent positively.
_____ 5. I could talk for hours at a time.
_____ 6. I do not enjoy talking with others.
_____ 7. I think that untalkative people are boring.
_____ 8. I do not trust the words people use when they talk.
_____ 9. I judge people by how well they speak.
_____ 10. I do not talk when I have nothing important to say.

To obtain your score, first reverse the answers you gave to the even numbered items (i.e., if you answered 1, make it a 5; if you answered 2, make it a 4; if you answered 3, leave it a 3; if you answered 4, make it a 2; if you answered 5, make it a 1). Once you have reversed the even numbered items, add the responses for the items. Your score will range from 10 to 50. The higher your score, the more you value talk as a way of communicating.

cultures whenever maintaining harmony is important. When maintaining harmony is not a primary concern, collectivists often use direct communication.

Before reading this section take a few minutes to answer the following questions regarding your beliefs about being direct or indirect in conversations.

You enter a room for a meeting with some co-workers and it is cold in the room because a window is open. You want someone to close the window. What would you say?

____

____

____

Under what circumstances do you think it is necessary or desirable to be direct when you communicate with others? Why?

____

____

____

Under what circumstances do you think it is necessary or desirable to be indirect when you communicate with others? Why?

____

____

____

Your answers to these questions should provide some insight into the role of being direct in your implicit theory of communication. Keep your answers in mind as you read the remainder of this section.

Cultural Differences in Direct and Indirect Language Usage. Analytic thinking tends to predominate in the United States, and synthetic thinking tends to predominate in Japan (Okabe, 1983). *Analytic thinking* involves looking at parts, rather than focusing on the whole. *Synthetic thinking,* in contrast, involves trying to grasp things in their totality. Constructing low-context messages requires analytic thinking, and constructing high-context messages involves synthetic thinking. Analytic thinking leads to the use of linear logic when talking or writing because it is necessary to specify how the parts are related to each other. Synthetic thinking leads to a more dotlike logic. "The speaker organizes his or her ideas in a stepping-stone mode: The listener is supposed to supply what is left unsaid" (Okabe, 1983, p. 29).

One way that languages can be direct or indirect is in their use of pronouns. In some languages pronouns indicating the subject or object of sentences can be dropped and in others they cannot. The cultures in which languages allow pronouns to be dropped are more collectivistic than those cultures that do not allow pronouns to be dropped (Kashima & Kashima, 1998). It is possible, for example, for two Japanese to speak for a long period of time without clearly expressing their opinions, in part, by dropping pronouns (Morsbach, 1976).

Speaking indirectly is not always ambiguous. Consider the example of a superior entering a room for a meeting with subordinates where the window is open and it is cold (drawn from Mizutani, 1981). The superior could say "Aren't you cold? Please close the window" (p. 31), but this does not take into consideration the relations between the superior and subordinates. The superior, therefore, could be tactful by saying "It's cold in here" (p. 31) and the subordinates would recognize that the superior wants the window closed.

Cultural differences in direct and indirect forms of communication can be illustrated further by comparing the United States and Japan:

> Reflecting the cultural value of precision, [U.S.] Americans' tendency to use explicit words is the most noteworthy in their communicative style. They

> prefer to employ such categorical words as "absolutely," "certainly," and "positively." . . . The English syntax dictates that the absolute "I" be placed at the beginning of the sentence in most cases, and that the subject-predicate relation be constructed in an ordinary sentence. . . . By contrast, the cultural assumptions of interdependence and harmony require that Japanese speakers limit themselves to implicit and even ambiguous use of words. In order to avoid leaving an assertive impression, they like to depend more frequently on qualifiers such as "maybe," "perhaps," "probably," and "somewhat." Since Japanese syntax does not require the use of a subject in a sentence, the qualifier-predicate is the predominant form of sentence construction. (Okabe, 1983, p. 36)

These differences often are manifested even when Japanese speak in English and U.S. Americans speak in Japanese.[2]

Indirection is used widely in other Asian cultures as well. Hindus in India, for example, tend to value "the unknown and undefined. . . . This attraction to the unknown resulted in a fondness for concealing even the obvious; their way of thinking tended to prefer the dark and obscure over that which was clear" (Nakamura, 1960, p. 31). In the gentry subculture in Java, being open and direct is perceived as being rude (Geertz, 1960). Etiquette in this group requires that Javanese use extensive forms of courteous expressions and complex forms of being indirect. Indirection also is used throughout Africa as well. In Somalia, for instance, "a message can be deliberately misinterpreted by the receiver, without his [or her] appearing to be stupid. Therefore, the person for whom the message was intended is never put in a position where he [or she] has to answer yes or no . . . He [or she] is able . . . to prevent direct confrontation" (Latin, 1977, p. 39).

Language use in Puerto Rico (a collectivistic, high-context culture) shares many commonalities with the Asian cultures:

> 1. In Puerto Rican society, one's place and one's sense of oneself depends on an even, disciplined, and unthreatening style of behavior . . .
>
> 2. In language one must take great care not to put oneself or others at risk, and one must reduce the risk of confrontation to the lowest degree possible. This implies a systematic blurring of meaning—that is, imprecision and indirectness . . .
>
> 3. This implies a constant problem of interpretation, testing, probing, second-guessing, and investigation, but conducted indirectly . . .
>
> 4. The personal value of the individual—and so the validity of his [or her] words—will be determined by what he [or she] actually *does*, not what he [or she] says . . .

5. Information does not come in discrete "bits," but as complex indicators of fluid human relationships, the "bits" being inextricable from the constant, implicit negotiation of meaning. (Morris, 1981, pp. 135–136)

As with other forms of indirect communication, what is not said may be as important as what is said in Puerto Rico.

There are two dimensions of indirectness in conversations (Holtgraves, 1997). The first dimension is that "people can differ in terms of the extent to which they look for, and find, indirect meanings in the remarks of others" (p. 626). The second dimension "refers to a person's tendency to speak indirectly (i.e., convey nonliteral meanings) or directly" (p. 626). Koreans (collectivists) score higher on both dimensions than U.S. Americans. Emphasizing interdependent self construals is associated positively with both dimensions of indirectness and emphasizing independent self construals is associated negatively with the tendency to speak indirectly (Hara & Kim, 2001).

Usually collectivists can make sense of others' indirect messages. There are times, however, that collectivists cannot figure out what others mean when they are indirect. Koreans, for example, "who decide not to express their meanings explicitly do not want the other to figure out their meanings, or do not necessarily assume that the other will be able to figure out their intentions" (Lim & Choi, 1996, p. 131). When others are indirect, Koreans use *noon-chi* to try to figure out what others mean. *Noon-chi* "makes use of all kinds of world knowledge, the knowledge of the other, knowledge of the context, the history of their interactions, and verbal and nonverbal messages" to try to figure out what others mean (p. 131).

Indirectness occurs in individualistic cultures like the United States. A professional interpreter in Japan says that

> [U.S.] Americans can be just as indirect as the Japanese, but they are indirect about different things, and being indirect carries a different meaning. [U.S.] Americans are usually indirect when something very sensitive is being discussed or when they are nervous about how the other person might react. Whenever [U.S.] Americans are indirect, I suspect that *something* is going on!
>
> Japanese indirectness is a part of our way of life. It is not because we are such kind and considerate people that we worry so about other's reactions. It is just that we know our own fates and fortunes are always bound up with others. I think you can value directness when you value individualism, or when you are with people you know and trust completely. (Condon, 1984, pp. 43–44)

U.S. Americans are indirect at times and Japanese also are direct (most frequently in close friendships or other situations in which what they say will not disturb ingroup harmony).

To conclude, direct and indirect forms of communication perform different communicative functions. "Univocal expressions [i.e., direct messages] enable, if not force, speakers and writers to communicate openly and clearly, and to hold back nothing of their intentions" (Levine, 1985, p. 32). Direct communication, therefore, focuses on clarity. Ambiguous expressions (e.g., extremely indirect messages) enable "their users to conceal, more or less deeply, what is really on their minds. Such concealment may be in the passive vein of withholding information for the sake of privacy or secrecy, or in the more active mode of seeking to deceive others for the sake of tact or some defensive strategy" (pp. 32–33). Extremely indirect messages (e.g., intentionally ambiguous messages) may not be easily interpreted by listeners, but other forms of indirect messages can be interpreted accurately, given knowledge of the context and the person transmitting the messages.

Assessing Your Direct and Indirect Tendencies. Table 6.2 contains a questionnaire designed to help you assess your tendency to use direct or indirect forms of communication. Take a few minutes to complete it now.

Scores on the questionnaire range from 10 to 50. The higher your score, the more direct your communication. As with beliefs about talk, neither high nor low scores are the most desirable. It is important to remember, however, that if your score is high or low you may have problems communicating with strangers who have the opposite tendency. If you find yourself in this situation, you need to be mindful of your communication and try to figure out how to adapt your communication to communicate more successfully (adapting communication is discussed in more detail in the next chapter).

Individualism-Collectivism and Low- and High-Context Communication

High-context communication can be characterized as being indirect, ambiguous, and understated with speakers being reserved and sensitive to listeners (Hall, 1976). Low-context communication, in contrast, can be characterized as being direct, explicit, open, precise, and being consistent with one's feelings. As indicated earlier, these patterns of communication predominate in collectivistic and individualistic cultures, respectively (Gudykunst & Ting-Toomey, 1988).

TABLE 6.2 *Assessing Your Direct and Indirect Communication Style*

The purpose of this questionnaire is to help you assess your tendency to be direct or indirect when you communicate. Respond to each statement regarding the degree to which you agree or disagree with the statement. If you strongly disagree with the statement, answer 1; if you disagree, answer 2; if you neither agree nor disagree, answer 3; if you agree, answer 4; if you strongly agree, answer 5.

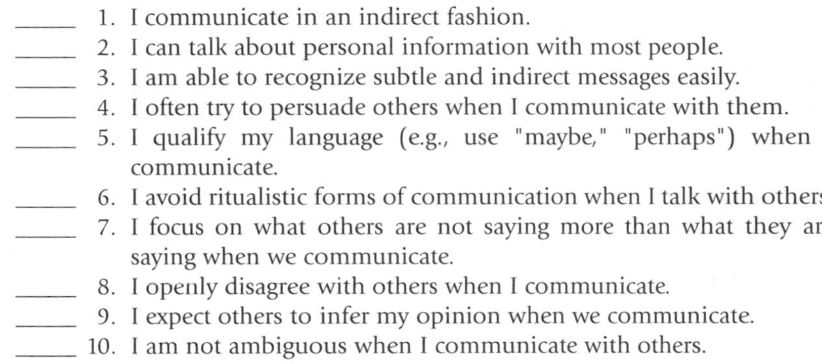

_____ 1. I communicate in an indirect fashion.
_____ 2. I can talk about personal information with most people.
_____ 3. I am able to recognize subtle and indirect messages easily.
_____ 4. I often try to persuade others when I communicate with them.
_____ 5. I qualify my language (e.g., use "maybe," "perhaps") when I communicate.
_____ 6. I avoid ritualistic forms of communication when I talk with others.
_____ 7. I focus on what others are not saying more than what they are saying when we communicate.
_____ 8. I openly disagree with others when I communicate.
_____ 9. I expect others to infer my opinion when we communicate.
_____ 10. I am not ambiguous when I communicate with others.

To obtain your score, first reverse the answers you gave to the odd numbered items (i.e., if you answered 1, make it a 5; if you answered 2, make it a 4; if you answered 3, leave it a 3; if you answered 4, make it a 2; if you answered 5, make it a 1). Once you have reversed the odd numbered items, add the responses for the items. Your score will range from 10 to 50. The higher your score, the more you are direct when you communicate; the lower your score, the more indirect you tend to be.

Individuals use low- and high-context messages depending upon their relationship with the person with whom they are communicating. To illustrate, people in the individualistic culture of the United States use low-context communication in the vast majority of their relationships (Hall, 1976). They may, however, use high-context messages when communicating with a twin or their spouse of 20 years. In these relationships, it is not necessary to be direct and precise to be clearly understood. People in Asian, African, and Latin collectivistic cultures, in contrast, tend to use high-context messages when harmony is important. They, nevertheless, also use low-context messages in some relationships (e.g., close friendships) or when harmony is not important.

Members of individualistic cultures are more affect oriented (i.e., base their behavior on their feelings; Frymier et al., 1990) and more inclined to talk (Gaetz et al., 1990) than members of collectivistic cultures. Members of individualistic cultures are motivated to communicate interpersonally to achieve affection, pleasure, and inclusion more than members of collectivistic cultures (Fernandez-Collado et al., 1991). Members of collectivistic cultures pay more attention to others' behavior and pay more attention to others' status characteristics than members of individualistic cultures (Gudykunst, Gao, Nishida et al., 1992).

Members of collectivistic cultures are more concerned with not hurting others or imposing on them than members of individualistic cultures (M. S. Kim, 1994). Members of individualistic cultures are concerned with clarity in conversations (M. S. Kim, 1994) and view clarity as necessary for effective communication (Kim & Wilson, 1994) more than members of collectivistic cultures. Members of individualistic cultures perceive direct requests as the most effective strategy for accomplishing their goals, and members of collective cultures perceive direct requests the least effective to accomplish goals (Kim & Wilson, 1994).

Individuals' communication styles are dependent upon the degree to which they have internalized the values of the cultures in which they are socialized, and the way their cultures socialize people to see themselves (e.g., as independent, unique individuals or individuals embedded in social groups). At the individual level, the independent self construal (one individual level aspect of individualism) is associated with being unique, expressing the self, realizing internal attributes, and being direct (Markus & Kitayama, 1991). The interdependent self construal (one individual level component of collectivism), in contrast, is associated with belonging (fitting in), occupying one's proper place, engaging in appropriate action, and being indirect. Individuals use independent and interdependent self construals in different situations, and depending on their cultures/ethnicities, they tend to use one more than the other.

"When a person's goal is to assert him or herself as a unique person (individualism), he or she must be direct so that others will know where he or she stands" (Gudykunst & Nishida, 1994, p. 40). Using interdependent self construals is associated with concern for others' feelings, and using independent self construals is associated with a concern for clarity in conversations (Kim et al., 1994). These patterns generalize across cultures (Kim et al., 1996). Interdependent self construals are related to using high-context communication styles, while independent self construals are not related to using high-context communication styles (Singelis & Brown, 1995). The more people emphasize independent self construals, the less embarrassment they feel (Singelis & Sharkey, 1995); and the more people emphasize interdependent self construals, the more they tend to feel embarrassment (Singelis et al., 1999).

Independent self construals and individualistic values influence the use of dramatic communication, the use of feelings to guide behavior, openness of communication, and preciseness of communication

(Gudykunst, Matsumoto et al., 1996). Interdependent self construals and collectivistic values influence the tendency to use indirect communication and being interpersonally sensitive.

Topic Management and Turn Taking in Conversations

In our conversations with others we have to coordinate our turn taking—who speaks and for how long. Conversations are constructed by the participants. We define our relationships with others by the way we converse with them. How we hold our initial conversations with others lays the foundation for our relationships with them.

The ways that we take turns and manage topics in conversations differ across cultures. Individualism-collectivism influences topic management and turn distribution in conversations.[3] Japanese (collective), for example, "take short turns, distribute their turns relatively evenly, and continue to distribute their turns evenly regardless of who initiates a topic" (Yamada, 1990, p. 291). U.S. Americans (individualists), in contrast, "take long monologic turns, distribute their turns unevenly, and the participant who initiates a topic characteristically takes the highest proportion of turns in that topic" (p. 291). **Collectivists organize topics interdependently, while individualists organize topics independently**.

The way we manage conversations also is affected by individualism-collectivism (Hayashi, 1990). Collectivists use verbal and nonverbal complementary expressions and repetition to support others when they speak and maintain negotiations. Individualists, in contrast, use less synchronizing behavior and repetition. Individualists tend to use feedback devices (e.g., questions, comments) to indicate they are attentive, while collectivists tend to use backchanneling (e.g., brief utterances that make conversation flow smoothly) to accomplish this purpose. To illustrate, when U.S. American "speakers orient attention, they focus on the specific topical content. Japanese speakers only value the emphatic interactional behavior and tend to consider the message exchange secondary" (p. 188).

Japanese speakers engage in simultaneous talk (i.e., two people speaking at once) more than U.S. Americans (Hayashi, 1996). Japanese's nonverbal behavior is synchronized when they talk more than U.S. Americans' nonverbal behavior. Japanese speakers often are so in sync when they talk that it is difficult to tell who the primary speaker is. The simultaneous talk that occurs in Japanese conversations does not lead to conflict as it often does when simultaneous talk occurs in U.S. Americans' conversations.

Collectivists send backchannel signals to the person with whom they are communicating more than individualists (e.g., White, 1989). Backchannel signals are the verbalizations we use to tell the other person that we are listening. To the extent that people are competent in using members of other cultures' backchanneling techniques when speaking their languages, effective communication is facilitated (LoCastro, 1987).

Persuasive Strategies

Another important aspect of verbal communication that varies across cultures is how we try to persuade others. Take a few minutes to answer the following questions before reading the remainder of this section.

Assume you are an assistant manager of a fast food restaurant. One of the employees is always late for work. The manager asked you to talk to the employee. How would you convince the employee to be on time in the future?

____

____

____

You want your romantic partner to go to your parents' house over the holidays. How would you convince him or her?

____

____

____

Your school club is holding a blood drive. You are talking to a student who has donated before and several of his or her friends have already agreed to donate. How would you convince her or him to donate this time?

____

____

____

Your answers to these questions should provide some insight into the role of persuasion in your implicit theory of communication. Keep your answers in mind as you read the remainder of this section.

Cultural individualism-collectivism appears to influence individuals' approaches to persuading and influencing others (Gudykunst &

Ting-Toomey, 1988). U.S. Americans, for example, are attuned to influencing others and remember situations based on influencing others more than Japanese (Morling et al., 2002). Japanese, in contrast, are attuned to adjusting to others and remember situations based on adjusting to others more than U.S. Americans. These patterns probably extend to individualistic and collectivistic cultures in general. Members of collectivistic cultures take the context into consideration and select persuasive strategies that are appropriate to the context. Members of individualistic cultures, in contrast, focus on the person they are trying to persuade and use persuasive strategies that may be perceived as socially inappropriate.

To illustrate the differences in persuasive strategy selection, consider comparisons of the strategies managers in corporations in the United States and Japan use to persuade their subordinates in two situations (Hirokawa & Miyahara, 1986). The first situation involves how managers try to persuade consistently tardy employees to change their behavior. Japanese managers indicate that they appeal to the employees' duty (e.g., "It is your duty as a responsible employee of this company to begin work on time."). U.S. American managers prefer to threaten the employees (e.g., "If you don't start reporting to work on time, I will have no choice but to dock your pay.") or to give an ultimatum (e.g., "If you can't come to work on time, go find yourself another job.").

A second situation involves how managers persuade employees to give their ideas and suggestions to managers (Hirokawa & Miyahara, 1986). Japanese managers prefer to use altruistic strategies (e.g., "For the sake of the company, please share your ideas and suggestions with us.") or appeal to employees' duty (e.g., "Remember that it is your duty as a good company employee to suggest how we can improve the overall performance of the company."). U.S. American managers prefer to make direct requests (e.g., "I want you to feel free to come to me with any ideas you have for improving the company."), to make promises (e.g., "Don't hesitate to offer ideas and suggestions because we always reward good suggestions."), or to ingratiate themselves to the employees (e.g., "You are one of our best people and I really value your judgment, so please feel free to come to me with ideas you have.").

Men and women in the United States use direct strategies (e.g., persistence) to persuade their romantic partners more than men and women in Mexico (Belk et al., 1988). Men and women in Mexico, in contrast, use bilateral, indirect strategies (e.g., positive affect) more than men and women in the United States. Mexican men also use indirect, unilateral strategies (e.g., negative affect) with romantic partners more than U.S. American men. These differences are compatible with cultural differences in individualism and collectivism.

Two social influence principles are used with different frequency in individualistic and collectivistic cultures (Cialdini et al., 1999). The *commitment/consistency principle* suggests that we comply with others' requests when we have engaged in the behavior in the past. We comply to be consistent with our past behavior. The *social proof principle* suggests that we comply with others' requests if people similar to us have complied. Both principles are used in all cultures. The commitment/consistency principle, however, is used in individualistic cultures more than in collectivistic cultures. The social proof principle, in contrast, is used in collectivistic cultures more than in individualistic cultures.

There also appear to be differences in upward influence tactics in organizations that are based on cultural power distance (Ralston et al., 2001). Subordinates in the United States and the Netherlands (both relatively low in cultural power distance) use "good soldier" tactics (e.g., "work overtime, if necessary, to get the job done," p. 729) and image management tactics (e.g., support superiors' views even if you disagree) more than subordinates in Germany and India (moderate power distance) who use these tactics more than subordinates in Hong Kong and Mexico (both relatively high power distance). Subordinates in Mexico and Hong Kong, in contrast, use information control tactics (e.g., "withhold information to make someone else look bad," p. 730) and strong-arm–coercion tactics (e.g., use negative information to "blackmail" people who can help) more than subordinates in India and Germany who use the tactics more than subordinates in the United States and the Netherlands.

Magazine advertisements also appear to vary across cultures as a function of individualism and collectivism. Advertisements in the United States, for example, emphasize benefits to individuals, personal success, and independence more than Korean advertisements (Han & Shavitt, 1994). Korean advertisements, in contrast, emphasize ingroup benefits, harmony, and family integrity more than those in the United States. Advertisements in the United States aimed at individual benefits are more effective than those aimed at group benefits, and the reverse is true in Korea. Advertisements in the United States also show people rebelling against social institutions more than advertisements in Asia, while advertisements in Asia show people following expectations to be in harmony with ingroup members more than advertisements in the United States (Kim & Markus, 1999). Similar results emerge when political advertisements are examined (Tak et al., 1997).

Cultural Differences in Nonverbal Communication

There are many aspects of nonverbal communication that vary across cultures. I focus here on three aspects of nonverbal communication that have relatively clear patterns across cultures: recognition and expression of emotions, contact, and the use of time.[4]

Emotion Expression and Recognition

People everywhere experience feelings such as happiness, sadness, and anger and exhibit a great deal of similarity in their expressions of these human emotions. Similarities in the expressive behavior of humans with different cultural backgrounds have been observed and interpreted as being due to characteristics inborn in all humans (Darwin, 1872). The innate view of emotional expression has been challenged repeatedly. Others argue that no expressive movement has a universal meaning and that all movements are a product of culture and not biologically inherited or inborn (e.g., Birdwhistell, 1963).

The innate and cultural variability views on human emotional expression have been integrated into a neuro-cultural theory of facial expressions of emotion (Ekman, 1972). In this theory, facial expressions of emotions are viewed as inherited, but cultural constraints play a very important role in shaping how emotions are expressed. Cultural *display rules* are learned within our culture, and these rules tell us when to express emotions and when not to express them. Cultural display rules lead us to intensify, deintensify, neutralize, or mask the facial displays to comply with the normative demands of specific situations in our cultures. There also are cultural *decoding rules* that tell us how to interpret emotions when they are displayed in specific situations.

There appears to be "universality" (e.g., the percentage of people recognizing the emotions across cultures is higher than would be expected by chance) in the recognition of seven emotions in facial expressions—anger, contempt, disgust, fear, happiness, sadness, and surprise (Matsumoto et al., 1989). There also may be "universal" recognition of embarrassment (Haidt & Keltner, 1999). People across cultures not only recognize the primary facial expression, but they also recognize the secondary emotion being expressed (Matsumoto et al., 1989). In addition to recognizing the emotion being expressed, people appear to agree on the relative intensity of the emotion being expressed across cultures.

While there is agreement in judging emotions across cultures that is better than would be expected by chance, there is variability in the levels of agreement. The accuracy of the judgments of facial expressions from one culture by members of other cultures is a function of the distance between the cultures (e.g., their cultural similarity or physical proximity; Elfenbein & Ambady, 2002a, 2002b). Cultural similarities in individualism-collectivism, uncertainty avoidance, and power distance are associated with the accuracy of judgments of emotions (Elfenbein & Ambady, 2003). Cultural similarity also explains the accuracy of recognizing other forms of nonverbal communication as well (Rosenthal et al., 1979).

Although there is consistency in the recognition of facial expressions across cultures,

> particular facial expressions may have appreciably different meanings in different cultures, notwithstanding the fact that their basic emotional message is similar. A smile may be an expression of pleasure or friendliness everywhere, but showing friendliness may be insolence in one culture, a reason for distrust in another, and a requirement for social interaction in a third. In other words, cross-cultural correspondence with regard to facial expression at one level in no way rules out the possibility of wide difference in the role and meaning of such processes at another level. (Mesquita et al., 1997, p. 285)

We, therefore, must understand the decoding rules to know the meaning of the various facial expressions in specific situations in specific cultures.

In addition to the recognition of emotions on the face, it appears that there may be agreement on the vocal expression of emotion. Interpreting anger, fear, joy, and sadness involve "similar inference rules from vocal expression across cultures" (Scherer et al., 2001, p. 76). The accuracy of inferring emotions from vocal cues, however, decreases as a function of language dissimilarity.

It also appears that there is consistency in antecedents for some emotions (Matsumoto et al., 1989). To illustrate, birth of new family members elicits joy; strangers, novel situations, and risky situations tend to elicit fear. Further, anger and disgust appear to occur most frequently and fear least frequently across cultures. Situations leading to sadness appear to be experienced most intensely, while situations eliciting shame and guilt are experienced least intensely.

People in masculine cultures tend to experience distress more than people in feminine cultures (Gudykunst & Ting-Toomey, 1988). Since masculine cultures emphasize achievement and excelling, people in the culture experience distress if they do not achieve or excel. Feminine cultures, in contrast, emphasize service and not trying to do better than others. Failure to accomplish these goals should not lead to distress. People in high uncertainty avoidance cultures experience less joy from relationships than people in low uncertainty avoidance cultures. This finding is consistent with relationships being guided by strict rules in high uncertainty avoidance cultures and by flexible rules in low uncertainty avoidance cultures.

Contact

We vary in terms of the amount of sensory exposure we want to others. Take a few minutes to answer the following questions before reading this section.

Assume that you are standing and holding a conversation with a friend of the same sex as you. How far away should your friend stand from you?

____

____

In the conversation with your same-sex friend, how much and where would you expect the person to touch you?

____

____

How much eye contact do you expect your friend to make and when should he or she make eye contact (e.g., when speaking or listening)?

____

____

Your answers to these questions should provide some insight into the role of nonverbal messages in your implicit theory of communication. Keep your answers in mind as you read the remainder of this section.

People regulate intimacy by controlling sensory exposure through the use of interpersonal distance and space (Hall, 1966). Cultures can be differentiated in terms of the degree of contact preferred by their members. Cultures in which the people tend to stand close and touch a lot are referred to as "high contact" cultures, and cultures in which people stand apart and tend not to touch are referred to as "low contact" cultures.

One area where there are differences between high and low contact cultures is in the distances people stand from each other when they are talking. In moderate contact cultures like the United States, people tend to stand an "arm's length" away from each other. In low contact cultures (e.g., Asian cultures), people tend to stand more than an "arm's length" away from each other. In high contact cultures (e.g., Latin, Arab cultures), people tend to stand less than an "arm's length" away from each other (and in some cases almost nose to nose). The language people speak influences how far away they stand or sit from each other (Sussman & Rosenfeld, 1982). When Japanese (low contact) speak English, for example, they stand or sit closer than when speaking Japanese. When Venezuelans (high contact) speak English, they stand or sit farther away than when speaking Spanish.

People in high contact cultures also prefer greater sensory involvement with the person with whom they are communicating than do people in low contact cultures. To illustrate, consider the role of smell in Arab cultures:

> To the Arab, to be able to smell a friend is reassuring. Smelling is a way of being involved with another, and to deny a friend his [or her] breath would be to act ashamed. In some rural Middle Eastern areas, when Arab intermediaries call to inspect a prospective bride for a relative, they sometimes ask to smell her. Their purpose is not to make sure she is freshly scrubbed; apparently what they look for is any lingering odor of anger or discontent. The Burmese [high contact] show their affection during greeting by pressing mouths and noses upon the cheek and inhaling the breath strongly. The Samoans [high contact] show affection by juxtaposing noses and smelling heartily. In contrast, [U.S.] Americans [moderate contact] seem to maintain their distance and suppress their sense of smell. (Almaney & Alwan, 1982, p. 17)

Differences in use of smell can create misunderstandings when people from different cultures communicate. When Arabs interact with U.S. Americans, they often feel sensory deprivation and become alienated because of the lack of sensory contact (Hall, 1983). U.S. Americans, in contrast, are anxious because of too much sensory contact.

Touch also is an aspect of sensory involvement. People in Latin American and Middle Eastern cultures engage in more tactile behavior than people in the United States and Northern Europe (e.g., Engebretson & Fullmer, 1970; Watson, 1970). People in Asian cultures, in contrast, tend to engage in less touching behavior than U.S. Americans and Northern Europeans (Barnlund, 1975). Asian cultures are low touch, the U.S. American culture is moderate touch, and Mediterranean cultures are high touch (Watson, 1970).

There is more touching behavior in high contact cultures than in low contact cultures. Other dimensions of cultural variability, however, will influence the type of touching that occurs. Masculinity, for example, should affect the amount of touching that occurs between males and females. People in highly masculine cultures tend to avoid opposite-sex touching more than people in low masculine (feminine) cultures. To illustrate, people in Asian cultures (low contact, high masculinity) avoid touching members of the opposite-sex the most, and members of the Mediterranean cultures (high contact, moderate masculinity) avoid opposite-sex touching less than people in the Asian cultures, but more than people in the United States (moderate contact, low masculinity) (Jones & Remland, 1982).

Distance, smell, and touch are not the only aspects of nonverbal communication that differ across cultures. There also are differences in eye contact. The differences have to do with the extent to which people engage in eye contact and when they engage in eye contact. Members of low contact cultures (e.g., Asian cultures) tend to avoid eye contact when speaking and listening. Members of moderate contact cultures (e.g., Australia, Northern Europe, United States), in contrast, engage in more eye contact than members of low contact cultures (e.g., Hall, 1966; Noesjirwan, 1978). Members of high contact cultures (e.g., Mediterranean cultures) engage in more eye contact than members of moderate contact cultures (e.g., Watson & Graves, 1966).

People in individualistic cultures tend to engage in eye contact when listening to others more than when speaking. The listeners' eye contact is interpreted as an indication that they are listening to the speaker. Members of other cultures (e.g., African cultures) learn to avoid eye contact when listening to others, especially when the person speaking is of higher status than the person listening (Byers & Byers, 1972). This pattern carries over to African Americans in the United States; that is, African Americans tend to look down (rather than engage in eye contact) to show respect when interacting with someone of higher status. European Americans often interpret this lack of eye contact as indicating that African Americans are inattentive or uninterested, or that they are lying (European Americans learn to look people in the eye to indicate they are telling the truth). European Americans' eye contact behavior, on the other hand, may be interpreted as aggressive by African Americans.

There is one final aspect of sensory involvement, how people use their voice. Members of high contact cultures tend to speak loudly (Hall, 1959; Watson & Graves, 1966). In Arab cultures, for example, loudness is viewed as indicating strength and sincerity, and softness is viewed as reflecting deviousness and weakness. Members of moderate contact cultures tend to speak more softly than members of high contact cultures, and members of low contact cultures tend to speak the softest.

Time

Another important form of nonverbal communication is the use of time. Take a few minutes to answer the following questions before reading the rest of this section.

Is it important for you to follow set daily schedules? If yes, why? If no, why not?

____

____

____

You have an appointment with a professor for 10:30 and she or he does not arrive until 10:45 and does not apologize for being "late." How do you react? Why?

____

____

____

A friend is visiting you at home. You get a phone call from your aunt. What do you do (e.g., talk to your aunt while your friend is there, say you'll call your aunt back)? Why?

____

____

____

Your answers to these questions should provide some insight into the role of time in your implicit theory of communication. Keep your answers in mind as you read the remainder of this section.

Two major patterns of the use of time can be distinguished: monochronic time and polychronic time (Hall, 1983). Monochronic and polychronic time are very different: "[Polychronic]-time stresses involvement of people and completion of transactions rather than adherence to preset schedules. Appointments are not taken as seriously and, as a consequence, are frequently broken. [Polychronic]-time is treated as less tangible than [monochronic]-time. For polychronic people, time is seldom experienced as 'wasted,' and is apt to be considered a point rather than a ribbon or a road, but that point is often sacred" (Hall, 1983, p. 46). Monochronic-time and polychronic-time patterns are different, "like oil and water," they "don't mix" (Hall, 1983, pp. 45–46).

TABLE 6.3 *Assessing Your Orientation Toward Time**

The purpose of this questionnaire is to help you assess your general orientation toward time. Respond to each statement by indicating the degree to which it is true about your behavior in general: "Always False" (answer 1), "Usually False" (answer 2), "Sometimes True, Sometimes False" (answer 3), "Usually True" (answer 4), and "Always True" (answer 5).

_____ 1. I do many things at the same time.
_____ 2. I stick to my daily schedule as much as possible.
_____ 3. I prefer to finish one meeting before starting another one.
_____ 4. I feel like I waste time.
_____ 5. I would take time out of a business meeting to talk with a relative or friend who called on the phone.
_____ 6. I separate work time and social time.
_____ 7. I break appointments with others.
_____ 8. It is important that events in my life occur in an orderly fashion.
_____ 9. I schedule more than one activity at a time.
_____ 10. Being on time for appointments is important to me.

To find your score, first reverse the responses for the odd numbered items (i.e., if you wrote 1, make it a 5; if you wrote 2, make it a 4; if you wrote 3, leave it as a 3; if you wrote 4, make it a 2; if you wrote 5, make it a 1). Next, add the numbers next to each statement. Scores range from 10 to 50. The higher your score, the more monochronic you are.

*Adapted from a scale I developed for Gudykunst et al. (1995).

People who use monochronic time usually engage in one activity at a time, compartmentalize time schedules, and separate task time from social time. People who use polychronic time tend to do multiple tasks at the same time and have fluid attitudes toward time schedules. People using polychronic time, for example, will stop a conversation with one person to take a phone call from another, especially a friend or relative. People who use monochronic time emphasize individual privacy, schedules, and appointments. People who use polychronic time, in contrast, emphasize the connection between people.

Table 6.3 provides an opportunity for you to determine your general time orientation. Take a few minutes to complete it.

Scores on Table 6.3 range from 10 to 50. The higher your score, the more monochronic you tend to be. The main thing to keep in mind is that whatever your orientation is, problems may arise in your interactions with other people who have the opposite orientation, especially when it involves making appointments.

Language Usage in Communicating With Strangers

Cross-cultural variations in languages and verbal communication styles influence how people from different cultures communicate. There also are language variations within cultures that influence the way we communicate. Each of us, for example, speaks a *dialect.* "Dialect refers to all the differences between varieties of a language, those in pronunciation, word usage, and syntax" (Chaika, 1982, p. 132). Sometimes the difference between language and dialect is not clear-cut.

> Political boundaries, in themselves, often determine whether two speech varieties will be considered different languages or not. For instance, some varieties of Swedish and Norwegian are mutually comprehensible, but they are considered different languages because they are separated by national borders. Conversely, the so-called dialects of Chinese are as different as French from Italian, but being spoken in one country they are not considered different languages. (Chaika, 1982, p. 133)

How we speak is tied closely to how we define ourselves. In highly mobile cultures like the United States, "speech is likely to be the most reliable determiner of social class or ethnic group" (Chaika, 1982, p. 139).

There are several aspects of language and dialect usage that are important in understanding our communication with strangers. Our attitudes toward other languages and dialects influence how we respond to strangers, whether we learn other languages, when we use other languages or dialects, and whether we accommodate to strangers with whom we are communicating. I begin the discussion of language usage in communicating with strangers by looking at attitudes toward language usage.

Language Attitudes

The language or dialect we speak influences how others judge us and whether they are willing to help us. Take a few minutes and answer the following questions before reading this section.

How do you speak when you visit a professor during office hours? Why?

____

____

____

How do you speak when you are at a party with your close friends from your ethnic groups? Why?

___

___

___

What impression do you have of business employees when you hear them speaking in an ethnic dialect to customers? Why?

___

___

___

Your answers to these questions should provide some insight into the role of dialects in your implicit theory of communication. Keep your answers in mind as you read the remainder of this section.

People speaking a standard dialect (e.g., like national newscasters speak on television) are more likely to receive help on the phone than people speaking an ethnic dialect (Gaertner & Bickman, 1971). People speaking a standard dialect also are perceived as competent, intelligent, industrious, and confident more than people speaking nonstandard dialects (see Bradac, 1990; Cargile & Bradac, 2001; for reviews). People speaking nonstandard dialects are rated higher on factors associated with ingroup solidarity (e.g., friendliness, likability) than people speaking a standard dialect.

Our language attitudes are influenced by our linguistic preferences, our expectations for others based on our stereotypes, our goals in the interaction, the amount of attention we pay to speakers, the depth to which we process what we hear, and the situation in which the language is used (Cargile & Bradac, 2001). Our social classes also influence language attitudes. Speaking properly "is a matter of great concern to the educated middle class, which above all wishes to be identified as educated. Its members' being recognized as those to be listened to hinges strongly on language. When people say they want to know the right way to speak, they do not mean the right way to communicate their ideas but rather the right way to announce that those ideas are to be respected, to be listened to" (Chaika, 1982, p. 239). Class differences in language usage were outlined in Chapter 2.

Our language attitudes can be characterized in terms of two interrelated dimensions, standardization and vitality:

> Standardization is the more static dimension, referring to the extent to which norms for correct usage . . . have been codified, adopted, and promoted for a particular variety. This might be accomplished through the compilation of dictionaries and grammars while the acceptance of a variety may be advanced by elites and government. . . . Vitality is the more dynamic dimension, reflecting the range and importance of functions served by language varieties . . . and the social pressures toward shift in language use. (Ryan et al., 1984, pp. 143–144)

Changes in our language attitudes are due mostly to changes in perceived vitality (Ryan et al., 1984). *Vitality* refers to the range and importance of the functions of our language or dialect for communication (Giles et al., 1977). The more vitality we perceive languages or dialects to have, the more positively we view the languages or dialects. Perceived vitality varies by location within a country. Spanish, for example, is more vital in Los Angeles than in Manning, Iowa.

Second Language Competence

There are numerous explanations of second language learning (see Gardner, 1985, for reviews of major theories), but only the intergroup model takes into consideration the intergroup factors relevant to second language learning. Second language learning cannot be explained unless the relations between the groups are taken into consideration (Giles & Byrne, 1982). There are five factors that contribute to members of a "minority" group learning the language of the "dominant" group (Garrett et al., 1989).

If members of minority groups identify weakly with their groups or do not view their languages as an important part of their identities, they tend to learn the dominant language (Garrett et al., 1989). If members of minority groups view their languages as important parts of their identities, they learn the dominant language if it does not threaten their identities. Further, if members of minority groups perceive few alternatives to their "subordinate" status and view the chance of it changing as small, they learn the dominant language. They also learn the dominant language if they perceive cognitive alternatives to their status and realize that these can be met by learning the dominant language.

Members of minority groups learn the dominant language if they perceive the boundaries between their groups and the dominant group to be soft and open (Garrett et al., 1989). If they believe that learning the dominant language will help them be accepted in the dominant group, they learn the language. Members of minority groups learn the dominant language if they are members of other social categories that provide them with satisfactory identities (e.g., occupations). If members of minority groups perceive the vitality of their group to be low, they learn the dominant group language. They also learn the dominant language if they believe learning it contributes to the vitality of their ingroups.

In addition to the intergroup factors, sociolinguistic factors contribute to second language learning (Garrett et al., 1989). First, the more similar the dominant language and the minority language, the more likely members of minorities are to learn the dominant language. Second, there must be exposure to the dominant language for it to be learned (e.g., members of minority groups must have contact with speakers of the dominant language). Third, members of minority groups need to have the opportunity to use the dominant language in a variety of contexts.

Communication Accommodation

We accommodate our behavior to others and others accommodate their behavior to us all of the time. Take a few minutes to answer the following questions before you read this section.

What do you think of members of your ingroups who talk like you when you interact? Why?

____

____

____

What do you think of members of your ingroups who do *not* talk like you when you interact? Why?

____

____

____

What do you think of members of other ethnic groups who talk like you when you interact? Why?

____

____

____

Your answers to these questions should provide some insight into the role of speech accommodation in your implicit theory of communication. Keep your answers in mind as you read the remainder of this section.

When we interact with strangers, we compare ourselves on a number of value dimensions with the strangers (Tajfel, 1978). Our intergroup social comparisons lead us to search for characteristics of our own groups that will enable us to differentiate ourselves favorably from outgroups. Such positive ingroup distinctiveness not only allows us personal satisfaction in our group memberships, but it also helps us form positive social identities. We also emphasize group differences in the ways we speak to strangers (Giles, 1973). The tendency to emphasize linguistic difference is *speech divergence*. We also may consciously or unconsciously modify our speech in the direction of the listeners' speech patterns, *speech convergence*.

When members of a subordinate group accept their inferior status, they attempt to converge into the dominant group socially and psychologically by means of speech convergence (Giles et al., 1977). If, on the other hand, members of subordinate groups consider their inferior status to be illegitimate and the intergroup situation to be unstable, they seek psychological distinctiveness by redefining their group attributes in a socially and psychologically more favorable direction. This can be accomplished linguistically by accentuating ingroup characteristics by means of speech divergence using the ingroup dialect, accent, jargon, or other form of speech variation.

We have a tendency to react favorably to strangers who linguistically converge toward us (Giles & Smith, 1979). This, however, is not always the case. As strangers begin to learn the speech style of our ingroup, we may diverge in some way to maintain our linguistic distinctiveness (Giles & Byrne, 1982). Our reaction to strangers' speech convergence depends on the intent we attribute to them. If we perceive their intent to be positive, we evaluate their convergence positively.

Our evaluation of strangers' language usage in conversations is based on situational norms in the initial stages of conversations and on interpersonal accommodation later in conversations (Genesse & Bourhis, 1982). Following situational norms is the strategy we use most frequently in early stages of hostile intergroup encounters (Bourhis, 1985). In later stages of conversations, however, we adopt strategies based on our goals, desire to assert our group identities, and our affective response to strangers.

Communication convergence is a function of speakers' desires for (1) social approval, (2) high communication efficiency, (3) shared self- or group-presentation, and (4) appropriate identity definition (Giles et al., 1987). For communication convergence to occur, there also needs to be a match between speakers' views of recipients' speech styles and the actual styles used, and that the specific speech styles used are appropriate for both speakers and recipients. Divergence, in contrast, is a function of speakers' desire (1) for a contrastive self-image, (2) to dissociate from the recipient, (3) to change the recipients' speech behavior, and (4) to define an encounter in intergroup terms. Divergence also occurs when recipients use speech styles that deviate from a norm that is valued and consistent with the speakers' expectations regarding the recipients' performances.

Individuals who are dependent on their groups and feel solidarity with them (intergroup oriented people) are more likely to perceive encounters with strangers in intergroup terms than individuals who are not dependent on their groups and feel little solidarity with them (interpersonal oriented people) (Gallois et al., 1995). Intergroup oriented individuals tend to perceive different rules for behavior with ingroup and outgroup members, and interpersonal oriented individuals tend to perceive similar norms for ingroup and outgroup encounters. When situations are defined in intergroup terms, individuals are likely to converge or diverge using social identities. When situations are defined in interpersonal terms, individuals tend to converge or diverge using behavior relevant to their personal identities.

The degree of convergence or divergence in which strangers engage influences the uncertainty and anxiety we experience interacting with them. When strangers diverge and assert their social identities, our uncertainty and anxiety will be high (e.g., above our maximum thresholds) if our behavior is based on our personal identities. If, however, our behavior is based on our social identities, our uncertainty and anxiety may be below our maximum thresholds. If strangers accommodate to our communication styles and we perceive their intent to be positive, it will reduce our uncertainty and anxiety in communicating with them.

It appears that there are cultural differences in how individuals respond to convergence by outgroup members.

> Individualists may react to convergence from outgroup interlocutors in a relatively positive manner, and converge toward the outgroup speaker reciprocally. With oftentimes softer group boundaries [than collectivists], thresholds for allowing linguistic penetration may be lower [than collectivists' thresholds]. Conversely, people from collectivistic cultures who perceive harder boundaries [between groups than individualists], may react to attempts at communication convergence more negatively [than individualists], and may diverge from them more if they perceive the convergence as overstepping of a valued cultural or national boundary [than individualists]. (Gallois et al., 1995, p. 131)

Members of collectivistic cultures, therefore, are more likely to diverge from outgroup members than members of individualistic cultures.

Code-Switching

The code (i.e., language or dialect) we use is, in part, a function of the vitality of the languages or dialects involved, and our desire to accommodate to strangers with whom we are communicating.[5] There are also normative factors that contribute to our code choice. Immigrants in the United States, for example, use English in public formal settings, while they use their native language in informal, nonpublic settings. Similarly, the topic of conversation affects the code used. Immigrants tend to use their native languages when discussing stressful or exciting topics and when discussing life in the native country. Using the first language to discuss life in the native country reinforces cultural heritage and fills a need to "identify with compatriots" (Chaika, 1982, p. 239).

In addition to the topic of conversation and the setting, people may switch languages to show warmth and group identifications (Gumperz & Hernandez-Chavez, 1972). Recall the discussion of the effect of speaking in Spanish on a Latino writer's feelings of being bonded to his family presented in the ethnic identity section of Chapter 3. We might also switch codes to increase the distance between ourselves and strangers (Scotton, 1993). We sometimes switch codes for emphasis or to see if strangers belong to our ingroups. "The switch from one language to another, in itself, has meaning. No matter what else a switch means, it reinforces bonds between speakers. Such switching can obviously only occur between those who speak the same language. It may be done in the presence of nonspeakers as a way of excluding them, just as jargon may" (Chaika, 1982, p. 238). The language or dialect we select, therefore, reinforces our social identities.

Code-switching performs several functions (Zentella, 1985). First, people may use code-switching to hide fluency or memory problems in the second language (but this accounts for about only 10 percent of code switches). Second, code-switching is used to mark switching from informal situations (using native languages) to formal situations (using second language). Third, code-switching is used to exert control, especially between parents and children. Fourth, code-switching is used to align speakers with others in specific situations (e.g., defining oneself as a member of an ethnic group). Code-switching also "functions to announce specific identities, create certain meanings, and facilitate particular interpersonal relationships" (Johnson, 2000, p. 184).

There are two maxims that tend to guide our choice of the code to speak in different situations when we speak two languages (Scotton, 1993). The *deference maxim* suggests that we use the code that others choose if we want something from them or have to negotiate face-threatening acts with them. The *virtuosity maxim* suggests that we base our choice of code on the abilities of the people with whom we are communicating (e.g., if they are not fluent in our language, we should speak their language).

Improving the Quality of Messages Exchanged With Strangers

There are several things we can do to improve the quality of the messages we exchange with strangers. We must, for example, adapt our messages to the strangers interpreting them (this is discussed in the next chapter). We also need to avoid being aggressive. Rather, we need to construct messages that are assertive, confirming, and inclusive.

Being Assertive, Not Aggressive

Verbal aggressiveness is "the tendency to attack the self-concepts of individuals instead of, or in addition to, their positions on topics of communication" (Infante, 1987, p. 164). All verbal aggressiveness involves a hostile response to strangers, but not all hostility involves attacking strangers' self-concepts. A verbally aggressive message is one designed to cause strangers pain or to have them think less favorably about themselves. We sometimes refer to these messages as put-downs. We are *not* necessarily conscious of our intention to put down strangers when we are verbally aggressive.

What is considered to be verbally aggressive depends on the individuals involved, who is observing the behavior, and the culture in which the interaction takes place (Infante, 1988). We may intend to be verbally aggressive, but strangers with whom we are communicating may not perceive our messages as aggressive. Alternatively, we may *not* intend to be verbally aggressive, but the strangers with whom we are communicating may perceive that they are being attacked.

There are several ways that we can be verbally aggressive: (1) character attacks, (2) competence attacks, (3) background attacks, (4) physical appearance attacks, (5) insults, (6) maledictions (speaking evil of others), (7) teasing, (8) ridicule, (9) profanity, (10) threats, and (11) nonverbal indicators (e.g., shaking a clenched fist, giving "the finger," rolling eyes, deep sigh) (Infante, 1988). We should not underestimate our use of verbal aggressiveness. We are much more verbally aggressive than we think we are when we communicate on automatic pilot. Engaging in verbal aggressiveness can lead to (1) damaged self-concepts, (2) hurt feelings, (3) anger, (4) irritation, (5) embarrassment, (6) relationship deterioration, (7) relationship termination, and (8) physical violence (Infante, 1988).

There are at least four causes of verbal aggression (Infante, 1988). First, verbal aggressiveness may be due to "mental disorders." Repressed hostility, for example, can lead to verbal aggressiveness. Second, feelings of disdain for strangers may cause us to be verbally aggressive. If we do not like strangers, we may be aggressive in our communication with them. Third, we may have been socialized to be aggressive. Males in the United States, for example, are taught "to be competitive, forceful, dominant, and aggressive. Females have been taught to be more submissive, less assertive, nice, and nonaggressive" (Infante, 1988, p. 26). Fourth, verbal aggressiveness may be due to a lack of skills for handling disagreements. This issue will be examined in more detail when I discuss managing conflict in Chapter 8.

While aggressive communicators usually achieve their goals, the strangers with whom they are aggressive do not and strangers frequently feel hurt, defensive, or humiliated (Alberti & Emmons, 1986). The alternative to aggressiveness is assertiveness. *Assertiveness* involves communicating in a way that indicates that we are standing up for our rights, but at the same time not trampling on the rights of strangers (Alberti & Emmons, 1986). Assertive communicators act in their own best interests, and they state their opinions and express their feelings directly and honestly. They express themselves in a way that is personally satisfying and socially effective.

Verbally, assertiveness involves (1) stating our wants, (2) honestly expressing our feelings, (3) using objective words (e.g., describing strangers' behavior, not interpreting it; this process is discussed in detail in the next chapter), (4) using direct statements of what we mean, and (5) using "I" messages (e.g., "I felt angry," not "You made me angry"; Bloom et al., 1975). Nonverbally, assertiveness involves active listening (discussed in Chapter 5 on listening) and communicating care for strangers.

When we are assertive we need to own our messages. One way to do this is speaking for ourselves using "I" messages. We speak for ourselves when we use personal pronouns like "I," "my," and "mine." When we indicate that "I think . . ." or "I feel . . . ," we are clearly owning our own thoughts and feelings. When we use the generic "you," or words like "some people" instead, it is not clear whose ideas are being expressed.

Skill Exercise 6.1 is designed to help you practice being assertive. Take a few minutes to complete the skill exercise now.

After completing this skill exercise you should understand the differences in being assertive, nonassertive, and aggressive. To illustrate, your response in the first example would be nonassertive if you did not ask the other person to return the book. Your response would be aggressive if you did not take the other person's feelings into consideration when asking for the book to be returned (e.g., you put the other person down by calling him or her irresponsible). Your response was assertive if you took both your rights and the other person's rights into consideration. You might have said, for example, "I need the book I loaned you. Would you please return it as soon as possible."

What constitutes assertive behavior is *"person-and-situation specific"* (Alberti & Emmons, 1986). How we perceive assertive behavior depends on the sex and the culture of the communicator. When males and females engage in exactly the same assertive behavior, males often are evaluated more positively (e.g., in terms of likability, attractiveness, and competence) than females (Stewart et al., 1990). In some collectivistic cultures (e.g., Japan, Korea), reticence (e.g., nonassertiveness) is prized.[6] What is perceived as assertive behavior in the United States might be perceived as aggressive behavior in some collectivistic cultures. This suggests that individualists need to adapt their assertive messages when communicating with collectivists to be effective. The adaptations necessary, however, depend on the specific individuals communicating. Individualists, for example, may have to use a more indirect, rather than direct, style of communication. They also would need to understand that when collectivists say "We think . . . ," they may really mean "I think." Similarly, collectivists need to adapt their behavior to communicate effectively with individualists. They need to be more assertive than they are when communicating with other collectivists.

Being Confirming

Confirmation is the most fundamental human need (Buber, 1958). *Confirmation* is "the process through which individuals are recognized, acknowledged, and endorsed" (Laing, 1961, p. 83). Confirming messages involves four components: (1) we recognize strangers, (2) we respond to strangers' messages to us, (3) we accept strangers' experiences as real, and (4) we indicate to strangers that we are willing to be involved with them (Sieburg, 1975). The relationship component of confirming

SKILL EXERCISE 6.1 *Being Assertive*

Being assertive requires that we assert our rights but not violate others' rights. Indicate below how you might respond in each of the following situations, and then consider whether this is assertive, nonassertive, or aggressive. If your typical response is not assertive, try to write an assertive response.

A classmate from another ethnic group borrowed one of your books. You need the book to complete a class paper and want her or him to return it.

How would you typically respond?

____

____

How would you respond assertively?

____

____

Why is this assertive and not nonassertive or aggressive?

____

____

A classmate from another culture is always late for your group's meetings. The group always has to wait for her or him. What would you say to this person?

How would you typically respond?

____

____

How might you respond assertively?

____

____

Why is this assertive and not nonassertive or aggressive?

____

____

messages implies three meanings: (1) "You exist," (2) "I acknowledge your way of experiencing," and (3) "We are relating" (pp. 4–10).

Disconfirmation occurs when strangers are denied, their experiences are denied, or their significance is denied (Cissna & Sieburg, 1981). Characteristics of disconfirming communication include (1) we do not recognize strangers, (2) we do not acknowledge that we have a relationship with strangers, (3) we do not accept strangers' experiences, and (4) we deny the validity of strangers' experiences (Cissna & Sieburg, 1981). The relationship component of disconfirming messages sends three relational meanings: (1) You do not exist, (2) I do not acknowledge your experiences, and (3) We are not relating.

Skill Exercise 6.2 is designed to help you practice being confirming. Take a few minutes to complete it now.

Compare your responses in Skill Exercise 6.2 to the characteristics of being confirming and disconfirming presented earlier. If the way you typically respond tends to be disconfirming, you can make confirming responses when you are mindful.

We confirm or disconfirm strangers by the words we choose to use when we talk to them and the way that we say what we do. Our relational messages define the relationship between us and strangers. We often are not aware of how strangers interpret our relational messages. We may not intend to send a disconfirming message, but strangers may interpret what or how we say something to be disconfirming. This can be especially problematic in our communication with strangers because they may interpret the relational component of our messages differently than we do. We need to make sure that our messages are interpreted as confirming by strangers. This requires that we be mindful of our communication and watch for signs that strangers may be interpreting our messages as disconfirming. To be confirming when communicating with collectivists, individualists need to remember to support collectivists' interdependent self construals. Similarly, collectivists need to remember to support individualists' independent self construals.

Creating Inclusive Messages

As indicated in the previous section, the words we use can disconfirm strangers. The words we use also influence how we think about strangers. If we consistently use male pronouns to refer to people in different occupations (e.g., the physician, he . . . ; policeman), for example, it affects the way we think about the occupations to which we refer.[7] To illustrate, if we use the term "mailman," for example, we will think of all people who deliver the mail as men. This obviously is not the case. Women

SKILL EXERCISE 6.2 *Being Confirming*

Being confirming involves acknowledging others when we interact. Indicate how you might typically respond to the following scenarios, and then if your typical response is not confirming, think of how you might give a confirming response.

A Japanese international student whom you know stops you after class one day and says, "The professor never calls on me in class when I raise my hand."

How would you typically respond?

____

____

How might you respond in a confirming way?

____

____

Why is this confirming, not disconfirming?

____

____

You meet an African American classmate coming out of the bookstore. The person says, "I'm really upset. The clerk followed me around the whole time I was in the bookstore."

How would you typically respond?

____

____

How might you respond in a confirming way?

____

____

Why is this confirming, not disconfirming?

____

____

deliver the mail too. The inclusive term we can use instead of mailman is "mailperson" or "mail carrier." By inclusive language, I am referring to language that makes everyone feel included. This may seem like a small thing, but our language usage clearly influences our attitudes toward and thoughts about particular groups, and strangers respond to the language we use.

Consistently using male pronouns disconfirms women. There also are many ethnic stereotypes we use in our everyday language (e.g., "Jew them down") that disconfirm members of the ethnic groups involved and idioms referring to disabilities (e.g., "the blind leading the blind") that disconfirm disabled people. To be confirming when we communicate with strangers we need to avoid the use of these terms and idioms. We all use noninclusive language in our everyday communication. To the extent that we can minimize our use of noninclusive language, we can be more confirming to strangers. To the extent that we use inclusive language, we can decrease the influence of our stereotypes on our communication.

Skill Exercise 6.3 gives you a chance to practice creating inclusive messages. Take a few minutes to complete it now.

Compare your responses in Skill Exercise 6.3 to the descriptions of inclusive messages presented earlier. If your responses are not as inclusive as you would like, keep in mind that you can generate inclusive messages when you are mindful.

Being inclusive also involves referring to strangers in a way that they want to be called. Sometimes we try to avoid the use of group labels when we talk about or to strangers. One reason for this is that we may want to downplay group differences. This strategy works well when we are interacting with strangers who do not identify strongly with their groups. Playing down group differences, however, does not work well when we are interacting with strangers who identify strongly with their groups. Another reason we may try to avoid the use of group labels is that we may want to try to focus on similarities rather than differences. This strategy never works well. To communicate effectively with strangers we must understand both the differences and the similarities. If we focus exclusively on the similarities, the differences become all the more problematic when they arise (I discuss the issue of similarities and differences in more detail in the next chapter).

Rather than ignoring group labels, it is important for us to understand how strangers want us to refer to them. I do *not* mean to suggest that we should use politically correct labels. We must, however, support strangers' self-concepts if we want to develop close relationships with them (this issue is discussed in more detail in Chapter 7). Calling

SKILL EXERCISE 6.3 *Creating Inclusive Messages*

Inclusive messages do not involve stereotyped language or ignore anyone. Indicate how you might create inclusive messages for the scenarios below. If your typical message is not inclusive, try creating an inclusive message.

You are in a group meeting for a class. The group is discussing the duties of the person to be elected to lead the group. It is your turn to turn to speak. What would you say?

____

____

Why is your response inclusive or not inclusive?

____

____

You are discussing how people who trace their heritage to Mexico are treated on campus with an acquaintance who mentions that he is a member of the Chicano Student Association. How would you refer to people who trace their heritage to Mexico while talking to this student?

____

Why is your response inclusive or not inclusive?

____

____

strangers what they want to be called and recognizing their group memberships is part of supporting their self-concepts.

Study Questions

1. How are languages and nonverbal messages similar and different?
2. Why is talk valued more in individualistic cultures than in collectivistic cultures?
3. How is silence used differently across cultures?
4. How are direct and indirect messages used differently across cultures?

5. How do low- and high-context messages vary as a function of cultural individualism-collectivism and individual self construals.
6. How does topic management differ across cultures?
7. How are persuasive messages used differently across cultures?
8. Why is there consistency in the recognition of emotions on the face across cultures?
9. How is nonverbal communication different in contact and noncontact cultures?
10. How are monochronic and polychronic approaches to time different?
11. How are evaluations of standard versus nonstandard dialects different?
12. How are linguistic convergence and divergence evaluated?
13. What are the functions of code-switching?

Applications

1. Over the next week, pay attention to how you talk to strangers. What are your beliefs about talk? Are your beliefs affected by the people with whom you communicate? How? When are you direct and indirect?

2. Over the next week, pay attention to your use of nonverbal communication. Is your behavior low, moderate, or high contact? How do you respond when others violate your nonverbal expectations?

3. Over the next week, pay attention to your verbal messages directed to and about strangers. To what extent are your messages inclusive? What can you do in the future to increase the inclusiveness of your messages?

Notes

1. Agar (1994) argues that language and culture are so intertwined that we should use the term "languaculture" instead of the two terms separately.

2. Miller (1994) reviewed studies comparing direct versus indirect communication in Japan and the United States and found that U.S. Americans are more direct and precise than Japanese.

3. The examples presented are drawn from Japanese-North American conversations, but I believe these patterns will generalize to other collectivistic and individualistic cultures.

4. A lot of nonverbal behavior does not appear to have consistent patterns across cultures, or at least there is not sufficient research for clear patterns to emerge.

5. See Gudykunst, Ting-Toomey, Hall, and Schmidt (1989) and Sachdev and Bourhis (1990) for sources for the arguments made here.

6. In some collectivistic cultures, aggressive behavior may be prized in some situations (e.g., *machismo* in Latin cultures leads to aggressive behavior toward females by males being acceptable).

7. See the references in Chapter 3 in my discussion of sexism.

CHAPTER 7

Being Perceived as Competent Communicators

In the previous chapter, I discussed exchanging messages with strangers. When we exchange messages with strangers, we may perceive them to be competent or incompetent communicators. Strangers also have perceptions about whether we are competent communicators. My purpose in this chapter is to look at what it means to be perceived as competent communicators in intergroup encounters. I begin by defining perceived communication competence. Following this, I examine the three components of perceived competence: motivation, knowledge, and skills.

Perceived Competence

In everyday usage, competence implies adequate, sufficient, and/or suitable (Wiemann & Bradac, 1989). Given this usage, we see people who get by and manage to avoid the pitfalls and traps of miscommunication as competent communicators. Misinterpreting strangers' messages is one of the major pitfalls or traps in the communication process. If we consistently misinterpret strangers' messages, our communication is not adequate or sufficient; that is, it is not effective (e.g., misunderstandings are not minimized).[1]

Saying that our communication is suitable implies that it is appropriate; we communicate in ways that meet the minimum requirements of the situations in which we find ourselves. There are at least three aspects of the context that are important in determining appropriateness:

"(1) The verbal context, that is, making sense in terms of wording, of statements, and of topic; (2) the relationship context, that is, the structuring, type and style of messages so that they are consonant with the particular relationship at hand; and (3) the environmental context, that is, the consideration of constraints imposed on message making by the symbolic and physical environments" (Wiemann & Backlund, 1980, p. 119). Our perceptions of competence vary across contexts. Former President Reagan, for example, was perceived as very competent when delivering canned speeches (i.e., he was called the "great" communicator). At the same time, President Reagan was not perceived as highly competent in answering questions extemporaneously at news conferences.

Competence as Impressions

Our view of our communication competence may not be the same as that of strangers with whom we are communicating. I, for example, might see myself as a very competent communicator, but when you and I interact you may perceive me as incompetent. Observers might have different perceptions of my competence. Understanding communication competence, therefore, minimally requires that we take into consideration our own and strangers' perspectives.

Since we can have different views of our competence than the strangers with whom we are communicating, **competence is an impression we have of ourselves and strangers**. Stated differently, "competence is not something intrinsic to a person's nature or behavior" (Spitzberg & Cupach, 1984, p. 115). There are several implications of this view of competence:

> First, competence does not actually reside in the performance; it is an *evaluation* of the performance by someone. . . . Second, the fact that *someone* is making the evaluation means that it is subject to error, bias, and judgment inferences; different judges using the same criteria may evaluate the performance differently. Third, since the evaluation always must be made with reference to some set of implicit or explicit *criteria*, the evaluation cannot be understood or validated without knowledge of the criteria being employed; thus, the same performance may be judged to be competent by one standard and incompetent by another. (McFall, 1982, pp. 13-14)

This view of competence suggests that the specific skills we have do not ensure that we will be perceived as competent in particular interactions. Our skills, however, do increase the likelihood that we are able to adapt our behavior so that strangers see us as competent (Wiemann & Bradac, 1989).

If strangers use the same criteria (e.g., appropriateness) as we do to judge our competence, they may still evaluate the same performance differently than we do. Consider the example at the end of Chapter 4 of the Japanese asking "How old are you?" during an initial interaction with a U.S. American. Another Japanese observing this interaction would likely evaluate the Japanese speaker's question as appropriate. The U.S. American who is asked the question, in contrast, is likely to see the question as inappropriate.

The standards people use to judge competence vary across cultures. The French, for example, value animated conversations that are fast-moving with frequent interruptions (Carroll, 1988). Often, the speakers ask questions and do not wait for answers. U.S. Americans, however, prefer fuller answers to questions, less interruptions, and more continuity in the conversation than the French. The French may interpret U.S. American conversation and readiness to discuss serious topics in social gatherings as inappropriate (and incompetent) because serious conversations occur in contexts other than social situations and they require a strong commitment between individuals. U.S. Americans may view the French style of frequent interruptions and short answers to their questions as inappropriate and, therefore, incompetent.

Components of Competence

There are three components of communication competence: motivation, knowledge, and skills (Spitzberg & Cupach, 1984). *Motivation* refers to our desire to communicate appropriately and effectively with strangers. *Knowledge* refers to our awareness or understanding of what needs to be done in order to communicate appropriately and effectively. *Skills* are our abilities to engage in the behavior necessary to communicate appropriately and effectively.

We may be highly motivated and lack the knowledge and/or the skills necessary to communicate appropriately and effectively. We also may be motivated and have the knowledge necessary, but not the skills. If we are motivated and have the knowledge and skills, this does not ensure that we will communicate appropriately or effectively. There are several factors that may intervene to affect our behavior. We may, for example, have strong emotional reactions to something that happens. Our emotional reactions, in turn, may cause us to "act out" a script we learned earlier in life that is dysfunctional in the situation in which we find ourselves. To illustrate, consider European Americans being served snake in another culture. They are likely to have strong negative reactions to eating this meat. If they are unable to control their emotional reactions cognitively, there is little chance that they will behave in ways that are perceived as competent by people in the other culture.

The environment in which we are communicating may influence our abilities to use the knowledge or skills we have. To illustrate, while I view myself as a person who can adjust to other cultures relatively easily, the environment in Calcutta, India, affected my ability to use my knowledge and skills. I had such a strong emotional reaction to the poverty I saw (e.g., people searching through garbage for food, large numbers of people sleeping in the street) that I was not able to use my knowledge or skills to adapt.

The strangers with whom we are communicating may also be a factor in our abilities to be perceived as competent. If strangers communicate with us in ways that suggest we are not competent, we will, in all likelihood, act in incompetent ways.[2] It is also possible that we may act appropriately and effectively without actually having the knowledge necessary to engage in the behavior by imitating the behavior of strangers. This can work when communicating with strangers when we do not have sufficient knowledge of their groups, but is not the best strategy. "Knowledge without skill is socially useless, and skill cannot be obtained without the cognitive ability to diagnose situational demands and constraints" (Wiemann & Kelly, 1981, p. 290).

Our motivation, knowledge, and skills interact with outcomes of our interactions with strangers to yield perceptions of competence. I have mentioned two outcomes—appropriateness and effectiveness—already. Other potential outcomes include, but are not limited to, interpersonal attraction, trust, satisfaction with our communication, the development of interpersonal relationships (i.e., intimacy), conflict management, adaptation to other cultures, and community building. The remainder of this chapter is devoted to the three components of competence. The final three chapters are devoted to applications of these ideas to managing conflict with strangers, developing intimate relationships with strangers, and building community with strangers.

Motivation

Our basic needs motivate us to interact with strangers (Turner, 1988). *Needs* are "fundamental states of being in humans which, if unsatisfied, generate feelings of deprivation" (p. 23). The needs that serve as motivating factors are: (1) our need for a sense of security as human beings, (2) our need for a sense of predictability (i.e., I trust you will behave as I think you will); (3) our need for a sense of group inclusion; (4) our need to avoid diffuse anxiety; (5) our need for a sense of a common shared world; (6) our need for symbolic/material gratification; and (7) our need to sustain our self-conceptions. We vary in the degree to which we are conscious of our various needs. We are the least conscious of the first three, moderately conscious of the fourth, and the most conscious of the last three.

Each of our needs, separately and in combination, influences how we want to present ourselves to strangers, the intentions we form, and the habits or scripts we follow.[3] The needs also can influence each other. Anxiety, for example, can result from not meeting our needs for group inclusion, predictability, security, and/or sustaining our self-concepts. Our overall level of motivational energy is a function of our level of anxiety produced by these four needs (Turner, 1988). Three of these needs are critical in our communication with strangers and warrant further discussion.

Need for Predictability

One of the major reasons that we are not motivated to communicate with strangers is that we often do not see their behavior as predictable. Take a few minutes to answer the following questions before reading this section.

What factors do you use to predict the behavior of members of your own groups (e.g., cultural, ethnic)?

____

____

____

What factors do you use to predict the behavior of members of other cultures or ethnic groups?

____

____

____

How does it affect your communication when you do not see others' behavior as predictable?

____

____

____

Your answers to these questions should provide some insight into the role of predictability in your implicit theory of communication. Keep your answers in mind as you read the rest of this section.

We "need to 'trust' others in the sense that, for the purposes of a given interaction, others are 'reliable' and their responses 'predictable'" (Turner, 1988, p. 56). When strangers' behavior is predictable, we feel that there is a rhythm to our interactions with them. **When strangers' behavior is not predictable, there is no rhythm to our interaction and we experience diffuse anxiety.**

If we do not feel a part of interaction taking place (i.e., our need for inclusion is not met), we will have difficulty seeing strangers' behavior as predictable. One reason we may not feel part of the interaction is that we have learned different communication rules than strangers and we often follow our own rules, even when communicating in strangers' languages. If Japanese follow their cultural norms regarding silence in conversations when speaking English, for example, U.S. Americans will feel that the rhythm of the conversation is off and they will not feel part of the conversation taking place.

If we do not recognize that predictability will be lower when we are getting to know strangers, the low level of predictability will decrease our motivation to communicate with them. One way that we can deal with this problem is to be mindful when we communicate with strangers. When we are mindful, we need to remind ourselves that the lack of predictability may not be due to the strangers; rather, there may be group differences influencing our communication. After recognizing this, we can try to gather information that will help us understand what is happening and, therefore, increase the predictability of strangers' behavior. In addition, we should recognize that "from a mindful perspective . . . uncertainty [lack of predictability] creates the freedom to create meaning. If there are meaningful choices, there is uncertainty" (Langer, 1997, p. 130).

Need to Avoid Diffuse Anxiety

Anxiety is a "generalized or unspecified sense of disequilibrium" (lack of balance) (Turner, 1988, p. 61). Take a few minutes to answer the following questions before reading this section.

What makes you anxious about communicating with members of your own groups?

____

____

____

What makes you anxious about communicating with members of other cultures or ethnic groups?

____

____

____

How does feeling anxious influence your communication?

____

____

____

Your answers to these questions should provide some insight into the role of anxiety in your implicit theory of communication. Keep your answers in mind as you read this section.

Anxiety stems from feeling uneasy, tense, worried, or apprehensive about what might happen (Stephan & Stephan, 1985). It is an emotional (affective) response to situations based on a fear of negative consequences (Stephan & Stephan, 1985). **Feelings of anxiety stem from deprivations in meeting our needs for security, predictability, group inclusion, and self-confirmation** (Turner, 1988). If we have not met our needs for security, predictability, and group inclusion, the focus of our behavior is on trying to deal with the anxiety associated with not meeting these needs. Because we are not highly aware of our needs for security, predictability, and group inclusion, however, we have a hard time pinpointing the source of the anxiety. The net result is that "considerable interpersonal energy can be devoted to meeting these needs as [we] grope around for a solution to [our] often vague feelings of discomfort" (Turner, 1988, p. 63).

Anxiety is an important motivating factor in intergroup encounters. If our anxiety is too high, we avoid communicating with strangers in order to lower our anxiety. To be motivated to communicate with strangers, we have to manage our anxiety if it is too high or if it is too low. This requires that we be mindful. When we are mindful, there are several things we can do to manage our anxiety. I discuss these techniques in the section on ability to manage anxiety later in this chapter.

Need to Sustain Our Self-Conceptions

Another consequence of high anxiety is that our need to sustain our self-conceptions becomes important (Turner, 1988). Sustaining our self-conceptions is much more difficult when we communicate with strangers than when we communicate with members of our ingroups. Our self-conceptions are made up of the various identities we have. They are our theories of ourselves: "Identity, like any theory, is both a *structure*, containing the organized contents of experience, and an active *process* that guides and regulates one's thoughts, feelings, and actions. . . . It influences how information is perceived, processed, and recalled . . . it acts as a script to guide behavior . . . and it contains the standards against which one's behavior can be compared and evaluated" (Schlenker, 1986, p. 24). Our self-conceptions, therefore, influence how we communicate with strangers and the choices (conscious and unconscious) of those with whom we form relationships.

We try to maintain our self-conceptions, even going to the point of using defense mechanisms (e.g., denial) to maintain our views of ourselves (Turner, 1988). Take a moment to answer the following questions before reading this section.

How do members of your own groups support your self-concept when you communicate with them?

____

____

____

How do members of other cultures and ethnic groups disconfirm your self-concept when you communicate?

____

____

____

How does lack of self-concept support influence your communication?

____

____

____

Your answers to these questions should provide some insight into the role of self-concept support in your implicit theory of communication. Keep your answers in mind as you read the remainder of this section.

Our need for self-concept support directly influences our communication. We are attracted to strangers who have the ability to support our self-concepts (Cushman et al., 1982). Perceiving that strangers support our self-concepts is necessary if we are going to form or maintain interpersonal relationships with them.

One of the problems in intergroup encounters is that one or both of the communicators perceives that the other person does not support his or her self-concept. If we are communicating on automatic pilot, we are likely to respond negatively in this situation. When we are mindful of our communication, however, we can recognize that strangers might emphasize different aspects of their self-concepts than we do. Individualists, for example, stress their personal identities and independent self construals, and collectivists emphasize their social identities and interdependent self construals. Failure to support each other's self-concepts, therefore, may not be due to lack of concern, but rather to a failure to understand group differences in what each considers to be important aspects of the self. To illustrate, Japanese are likely to ask questions about U.S. Americans' social identities when U.S. Americans expect questions about their personal identities. If U.S. Americans perceive this as lack of self-concept support, they will not be motivated to interact with Japanese. If U.S. Americans are mindful of their communication, however, they can recognize that this is just a cultural difference. This interpretation should not have a negative effect on U.S. Americans' motivation to communicate with Japanese.

Approach-Avoidance Tendencies

Most of us spend the vast majority of our time interacting with people who are relatively similar to us. Our actual contact with strangers is limited; it is a novel form of interaction (Rose, 1981). If our attempts to communicate with strangers are not successful and we cannot get out of the situations in which we find ourselves easily, then our unconscious need for group inclusion becomes unsatisfied. This leads to anxiety about ourselves and our standing in a group context (Turner, 1988). One way we deal with this anxiety is to retreat into known territory and limit our interactions to people who are similar. At the same time, most of us want to see ourselves as nonprejudiced and caring people. We may, therefore, want to interact with strangers to sustain our self-concepts. Holding both attitudes at the same time is not unusual. The combination of our need to avoid diffuse anxiety and our need to sustain our self-conceptions often leads us to an approach-avoidance orientation toward intergroup encounters.[4]

The questionnaire in Table 7.1 is designed to help you assess your tendency to approach or avoid interacting with strangers. Take a few minutes to complete it now.

Scores on the questionnaire range from 10 to 50. The higher your score, the greater your tendency to approach strangers. The important thing to remember is that if your score is low, you can consciously manage your anxiety and consciously decide to interact with strangers.

TABLE 7.1 *Assessing Your Approach-Avoidance Tendencies**

The purpose of this questionnaire is to help you assess your tendency to approach or avoid contact with strangers. Respond to each of the statements by indicating the degree to which the statement is true regarding how you typically think about yourself. When you think about yourself, is the statement "Always False" (answer 1), "Usually False" (answer 2), "Sometimes True and Sometimes False" (answer 3), "Usually True" (answer 4), or "Always True" (answer 5)?

_____ 1. I have the opportunity to meet strangers regularly.
_____ 2. I am highly anxious when I have to communicate with strangers.
_____ 3. I think close relations with strangers is desirable.
_____ 4. I avoid interacting with strangers when possible.
_____ 5. I enjoy interacting with strangers.
_____ 6. I would object if someone in my family married a stranger.
_____ 7. I try to encourage social relations with strangers.
_____ 8. I am never sure how to behave when I interact with strangers.
_____ 9. I have tried to develop friendships with strangers.
_____ 10. I do not feel secure when I interact with strangers.

To find your score, first reverse the responses for the even numbered items (i.e., if you wrote 1, make it 5; if you wrote 2, make it 4; if you wrote 3, leave it as 3; if you wrote 4, make it 2; if you wrote 5, make it 1). Next, add the numbers next to each statement. Scores will range from 10 to 50. The higher your score, the more willing you are to approach people who are different.

*Adapted in part from Hofman (1985).

Knowledge

Misunderstandings can occur for a variety of reasons when we communicate with strangers. We may not transmit our messages in ways that they can be understood by strangers, strangers may misinterpret what we say, or both can occur simultaneously. The problems that occur may be due to our or strangers' pronunciations, grammar, familiarity with the topic being discussed, familiarity with strangers, familiarity with strangers' native languages, fluency in strangers' languages, and/or social factors (Gass & Varonis, 1984). If we are familiar with and/or fluent in strangers' languages, for example, we can usually understand them better when they speak our languages than if we know nothing about their languages.

Generally speaking, the greater our cultural and linguistic knowledge, and the more our beliefs overlap with those of the strangers with whom we communicate, the less the likelihood there will be misunderstandings.

Lack of linguistic and cultural knowledge contributes to misunderstandings because we "listen to speech, form a hypothesis about what routine is being enacted, and then rely on social background knowledge and co-occurrence expectations to evaluate what is intended and attitudes being conveyed" (Gumperz, 1982, p. 171).

The knowledge component of communication competence refers to our awareness of what we need to do to communicate in an appropriate and effective way with strangers. This includes a specific awareness of the skills discussed in the next section and how they can be used when communicating with strangers. When communicating with strangers, we also need to have knowledge about strangers' groups. My focus is this section, therefore, is on how we can gather information about strangers and their groups so that we can interpret their messages accurately. While my focus is on gathering information about strangers, the processes outlined apply equally to gathering information about people who are similar.

Knowledge of How to Gather Information

"Because uncertainty so often arises from not knowing enough to predict what will happen, searching for more information or deeper understanding is one of the most powerful ways to contain it" (Marris, 1996, p. 10). There are three general types of strategies we can use to gather information about strangers and manage our uncertainty about them and the way they will interact with us: passive, active, and interactive strategies (Berger, 1979). To illustrate this process, assume that we want to find out about Atsuko, a Japanese to whom we have just been introduced. I am using an intercultural example, but the strategies discussed can be used to gather information about anyone.

When we use *passive strategies* we take the role of "unobtrusive observers" (i.e., we do not intervene in the situation we are observing) (Berger, 1979). Obviously, the type of situation in which we observe Atsuko influences the amount of information we gain about her. If we observe Atsuko in a situation where she does not have to interact with others, we will not gain much information about her. Situations in which she is interacting with several people at once, in contrast, allow us to make comparisons of how Atsuko interacts with the different people.

If we know any of the people with whom Atsuko is interacting, we can compare how Atsuko interacts with the people we know and how she might interact with us (Berger, 1979). It also should be noted that if other Japanese are present in the situation, we can compare Atsuko's behavior with theirs to try to determine how she is similar to and different from other Japanese.

There is one other aspect of the situation that will influence the amount of information we obtain about Atsuko's behavior (Berger, 1979). If the situation is a formal one, her behavior is likely to be a function of the role she is filling in the situation and we will not learn much about Atsuko as an individual. Informal situations where behavior is not guided by roles or social protocol, on the other hand, will provide useful information on Atsuko's behavior.

The preceding examples all involve our taking the role of an observer. The *active strategies* for reducing uncertainty require us to do something to acquire information about Atsuko without actually interacting with her (Berger, 1979). One thing we could do to get information about Atsuko is to ask questions of someone who knows her. When we ask others about someone we need to keep in mind that the information we receive may not be accurate. The other person may intentionally give us wrong information or the other person may not really know Atsuko well.

We can also gather information about other groups by asking people who have had contact with those groups or gathering information from the library. In this example, we could gather information on Japan by questioning someone we know who has lived in Japan, reading a book on Japanese culture, or completing a Japanese cultural assimilator (a programmed learning course that teaches the reader about the Japanese culture). This would give us information about Atsuko's cultural background and allow us to make cultural level predictions about her behavior. Again, we need to keep in mind that our informant may or may not have good information about Japan and that Atsuko may not be a typical Japanese.

This raises the issue of how we can select good informants to learn about other groups. People who have a lot of informal social contact with members of the other group, for example, are better informants than people who have little informal contact or even a lot of contact in formal settings. We also would be well off to select informants who have been successful in their interactions with members of other groups. To illustrate, if there are two members of our group who have frequent contact with the group in which we are interested, we would select the one who appears to be most successful in interacting with members of the other group (based on our observations of their interactions or their reports of their interactions).

When we use active strategies to gather information we do not actually interact with the people about whom we are trying to gather information. The *interactive strategies* of verbal interrogation (question asking) and self-disclosure, in contrast, are used when we interact with the other person (Berger, 1979).

One obvious way we can gather information about Atsuko is to use *interrogation;* that is, ask her questions. When we are interacting with someone from our own group, there are limitations to this strategy that have to be kept in mind. First, we can ask only so many questions. We may not be sure of what the exact number is, but we always know when we have asked too many. Second, our questions must be appropriate to the nature of the interaction we are having and the relationship we have with the other person.

When we are communicating with Atsuko, the same limitations on the questions we can ask are present, and there are others. The number and type of questions that Atsuko considers acceptable may not be the same as what we consider acceptable (recall the example of the questions the Japanese asked in the previous chapter). Atsuko also may not be able to answer our questions, especially if our questions deal with why she behaves the way she does (the ultimate answer to why questions is "because!" or "that is the way we do it here"). When interacting with Atsuko there is also the added problem of our not wanting to appear stupid or be rude. We, therefore, often avoid asking strangers questions to which we think we should know the answer.

If we can overcome our fear of looking stupid, asking questions is an excellent way to gather information about strangers. Generally speaking, strangers will probably respond in a positive way as long as they perceive that our intent is to learn about them personally or their group and *not* to judge them.[5]

The other way we can gather information about Atsuko when interacting with her is through *self-disclosure*—telling Atsuko unknown information about ourselves.[6] Self-disclosure works as an information gathering strategy because of the reciprocity norm.[7] Essentially, the reciprocity norm states that if we tell Atsuko something about ourselves, she will reciprocate and tell us similar things about herself. The reciprocity norm appears to be a cultural universal; it exists in all cultures.[8]

In conversations between people who are not close (i.e., people we meet for the first time, acquaintances), we tend to reciprocate and tell each other the same information about ourselves that the other person tells us. If I disclose my opinion on a topic when you and I are talking, you will probably tell me your opinion on the same topic. There will, however, be some differences when we communicate with strangers than when we communicate with people from our own group. The topics that are appropriate to be discussed, for example, vary from culture to culture and ethnic group to ethnic group. If we self-disclose on a topic with strangers and they do not reciprocate, there is a good chance we have found an inappropriate topic of conversation in the strangers' groups.

Since the timing and pacing of self-disclosure varies across cultures and ethnic groups, it is also possible that our timing is off or we have tried to self-disclose at an inappropriate pace.

Knowledge of Group Differences

Many people assume that to communicate effectively with strangers, we should focus only on similarities. This, however, is not the case. **If strangers strongly identify with their groups, they will feel that their self-concepts are not being confirmed if we focus only on similarities.** This is true whether strangers come from different cultures, ethnic groups, disability groups, age-groups, or social classes. To communicate effectively we must understand real differences between our groups and strangers' groups. We often are aware of differences based on our ethnocentrism, prejudice, sexism, ageism, and stereotypes. These differences, however, may not be real (e.g., our stereotypes may not be accurate or strangers may be atypical members of their groups).

Recognizing differences often facilitates effective communication. This is true for disabled-nondisabled communication. "[Nondisabled] people would rather work and socialize with disabled people who acknowledge their disability than with those who do not acknowledge it. . . . Although acknowledgement of the disability on the part of the disabled person does not always lead to acceptance . . . it does reduce uncertainty and tension and enhances the attractiveness of the disabled person. Interactions proceed less problematically when a disabled person 'appropriately' self-discloses about the disability" (Coleman & DePaulo, 1991, p. 82). A similar argument can be made for other group differences.

To communicate effectively, we need to have knowledge about the actual differences that exist between our groups and strangers' groups, and between ourselves and strangers. One way we can isolate these actual differences is to learn all we can about other groups (e.g., become an expert on another culture or ethnic group). This approach, however, is not practical. How can we be experts on all of the groups of which the strangers with whom we have contact are members? Obviously, we cannot.

When we are communicating with people from other cultures, we can use the dimensions of cultural variability discussed in Chapter 2 to develop a preliminary understanding of the real differences between our culture and another culture. To illustrate, there are several cultural differences that would help U.S. Americans better understand Japanese communication:

1. Japan is a collectivistic culture where people conceptualize themselves as interdependent with one another. This leads to an emphasis on *wa* [harmony] in the ingroup, as well as an emphasis on *enryo* [reticence] and *amae* [dependence] in interactions with others. The importance of *wa* also leads to drawing a distinction between *tatemae* [what is stated in public] and *honne* [what is truly believed].

2. High-context messages are used more frequently in Japan than low-context messages. This leads to an emphasis on indirect forms of communication, as opposed to an emphasis on direct forms of communication in the United States. *Sasshi* [the ability to guess] is necessary to understand indirect messages.

3. Japan is a high uncertainty avoidance culture. This leads to an emphasis on rituals and the specification of relatively clear rules in most communication situations. People who deviate from the rules are viewed as dangerous and, therefore, are avoided whenever possible.

4. Japan is a high power distance culture. This leads to an emphasis on status (e.g., position, age) in communication. Power distance also leads to an emphasis on *on* and *giri* [obligations] in relationships between individuals in Japan.

5. Japan is a highly masculine culture. This leads to an emphasis on communicating with members of the same-sex, and separation of the sexes in many social situations. (Gudykunst & Nishida, 1994, p. 112)

These five conclusions are not all-inclusive, but they summarize the way the major dimensions of cultural variability influence Japanese communication.

Broad generalizations like those isolated here can help us understand the differences between ourselves and strangers from another culture if the strangers are relatively typical members of their cultures. We have to remember, however, that strangers may not be typical members of their cultures or we may not actually understand their cultures. It is important that we maintain a mindful approach to understanding differences between our groups and strangers' groups (e.g., constantly being open to new information). The more we understand differences between our groups and strangers' groups, the more accurate our predictions of and explanations for strangers' behavior will be. To communicate effectively with a specific stranger, we also must go a step further and try to understand personal differences between us.

TABLE 7.2 *Assessing Your Knowledge of Another Group*

The purpose of this questionnaire is to help you assess your knowledge of another culture or ethnic group. The statements in this questionnaire contain a blank space. Think of a specific culture or ethnic group when you are reading the statements. Respond to each statement by indicating the degree to which the statement is true regarding your knowledge: "Always False" (answer 1), "Usually False" (answer 2), "Sometimes True and Sometimes False" (answer 3), "Usually True" (answer 4), or "Always True" (answer 5).

_____ 1. I understand the norms of ____________.
_____ 2. I do not understand how ______________ manage conflict.
_____ 3. I understand the customs of ____________.
_____ 4. I do not understand how ______________ support each other's self-concepts.
_____ 5. I understand the values of ____________.
_____ 6. I do not understand how ______________ persuade each other.
_____ 7. I understand the communication rules of __________.
_____ 8. I do not understand how ______________ comfort each other.
_____ 9. I understand the language (or dialect) of ______________.
_____ 10. I do not understand how ________________ joke with each other.

To find your score, first reverse your answers for the even numbered items (i.e., if you answered 1, make it a 5; if you answered 2, make it a 4; if you answered 3, leave it as 3; if you answered 4, make it a 2; if you answered 5, make it a 1). Once you have reversed the even numbered items, add the numbers you wrote next to each statement. Scores range from 10 to 50. The higher your score, the greater your knowledge of the group.

Table 7.2 contains a questionnaire designed to help you assess your knowledge about another group. To complete the questionnaire you need to think of a specific group (e.g., another culture or ethnic group). Take a couple of minutes to complete the questionnaire now.

Scores on the questionnaire range from 10 to 50. The higher your score, the greater your understanding of the other group. The thing to keep in mind is that the higher your score, the less likely you will misinterpret messages you receive from members of this group. If your score is relatively low, it suggests that you might want to try to understand the other group better to help you communicate more effectively with members of this group.

Knowledge of Personal Similarities

Understanding differences is important, but we also have to understand similarities if we are going to develop relationships with strangers.

Understanding similarities at the group level is important, but finding similarities at the individual level is critical if we want to develop a relationship with strangers (this issue is discussed in more detail in Chapter 9). Isolating similarities requires that we be mindful of our communication.

One way we can be mindful is by creating new categories. Creating new categories involves developing subcategories of a broader category (e.g., separating Chicanos and Chicanas from Mexican Americans in our stereotype of people from Mexico). The smaller our categories, the more effectively we can communicate with strangers in the categories. We create new categories when we consciously search for similarities we share with strangers rather than focusing only on differences. Do strangers, for example, have children who go to the same school as ours? Do strangers belong to the same social clubs we do? Do strangers experience similar frustrations in their professional and personal lives as we do? Do strangers have similar worries about their families as we do? The first two questions search for shared group memberships, while the second two focus on shared values, attitudes, or beliefs.

We need to seek out commonalities because "with a more explicit understanding of what we have in common and the goals we seek to attain together, the differences between us that remain would be less threatening" (Bellah et al., 1985, p. 287). Finding commonalities with strangers requires that we be mindful. "Because most of us grow up and spend our time with people like ourselves, we tend to assume uniformities and commonalities. When confronted with someone who is clearly different in one specific way, we drop that assumption and look for differences. . . . The mindful curiosity generated by an encounter with someone who is different, which can lead to exaggerated perceptions of strangeness, can also bring us closer to that person if channeled differently" (Langer, 1989, p. 156). Once we satisfy our curiosity about differences, understanding can occur.

What is needed is a way to make mindful curiosity about differences not taboo (Langer, 1989). Since most of us do not have a lot of contact with strangers, we are not comfortable with differences and we do not have much experience discussing them with strangers. We need to develop mindful curiosity about strangers and their groups. If strangers perceive our intent as involving satisfying our curiosity and not to put them down, they probably will not react negatively to our questions. One way that each of us can contribute to the acceptance of mindful curiosity is by accepting others' questions about us and our groups as "requests for information" until we are certain there is another motivation.

Knowledge of Alternative Interpretations

Effective communication requires that we minimize misunderstandings or maximize the similarity in the ways messages are interpreted when we interact with strangers. To accomplish this, we must recognize that there are many ways that messages can be interpreted, and often these interpretations involve evaluations of strangers' behavior. There are at least three interrelated cognitive processes involved in understanding strangers' perspectives: description, interpretation, and evaluation. To communicate effectively it is necessary to distinguish among these three processes.

By *description* I mean an actual report of what we have observed with the minimum of distortion and without attributing social significance to the behavior. Description includes what we see and hear and is accomplished by counting and/or recording observations. In order to clarify these processes, consider the following example:

Description

Kim did not look me in the eye when we talked.

This statement is descriptive in nature. It does not attribute social significance to Kim's behavior; it merely tells what the observer saw.

If we attribute social significance or make inferences about what we saw, we would be engaged in interpretation. *Interpretations* are what we think about what we see and hear. Multiple interpretations can be made for any particular description of behavior. Returning to our example, we have the following:

Description

Kim did not look me in the eye when we talked.

Possible Interpretations

Kim is lying.

Kim is shy.

Kim is evasive.

Each of these interpretations can have several different evaluations.

Evaluations are positive or negative judgments concerning the social significance we attribute to behavior; whether we like it or not. To illustrate this, we can use the second interpretation given above:

Interpretation

Kim is shy.

Evaluations

I like that; Kim is not aggressive.

I don't like that; Kim should stand up for herself.

Of course, several other evaluations could be made, but these two are sufficient to illustrate potential differences in evaluations that can be made regarding any one interpretation.

We do not distinguish among these three cognitive processes when we communicate on automatic pilot. On automatic pilot, we skip the descriptive process and jump immediately to either interpretation or evaluation when confronted with different patterns of behavior. This often leads to misattributions of meaning and, therefore, to ineffective communication when we interact with strangers. Being able to distinguish among the three processes, on the other hand, increases the likelihood that we are able to see alternative interpretations, thereby increasing our abilities to communicate effectively. Differentiating among the three processes also increases the likelihood of our making more accurate predictions of strangers' behavior. If we are able to describe strangers' behavior, we can make more accurate predictions because we are able to see alternative interpretations of behavior patterns.

Skill Exercise 7.1 provides an opportunity for you to practice separating descriptions, interpretations, and evaluations. Take a few minutes to complete it now.

If we do not separate descriptive and interpretive processes, misunderstandings are inevitable. When we communicate on automatic pilot we usually interpret strangers' behavior without describing it. Our interpretations are based on our cultural, ethnic, and social class upbringing. Our interpretations of strangers' behavior, however, may be very different from what they intended by the behavior. When we think there might have been misunderstandings, we need to stop and describe the behavior in question. Once we've described the behavior, we need to look for alternative interpretations. After we have thought of some alternative interpretations, we can ask strangers which interpretation is correct (using the perception checking skill discussed in Chapter 5). If we cannot ask strangers, we can make an educated guess as to what they meant based on our knowledge of them or their group memberships. Separating descriptions and interpretations, as I am suggesting here, requires that we be mindful.

SKILL EXERCISE 7.1 *Knowledge of Alternative Interpretations*

Descriptions of behavior involve reports of what is observed without attributing meaning. Interpretations attach meaning to what we see. Evaluations involve making judgments of like or dislike. Assume that you had a conversation with Kim, an Asian international student, earlier in the day. You left the conversation with a feeling that the student wasn't telling the truth. In thinking back, you realize that this was probably because the person didn't make eye contact when you were talking. This description is listed below with the one interpretation. Try to think of other possible interpretations of the behavior. Then look at alternative evaluations of two different interpretations.

Description
Kim did not make eye contact when we talked.

Possible Interpretations
Kim is not telling the truth.

____

____

____

Possible Evaluations
Interpretation: Kim is not telling the truth.

Alternative Evaluations
Its no big deal; we all avoid telling the truth sometimes.

____

____

Interpretation: ______________________
Alternative Evaluations

____

____

____

Often we need to differentiate among description, interpretation, and evaluation after our interactions with strangers are over. If we leave interactions with strangers with the feeling that they were lying to us, for example, we need to stop and recognize that "lying" was our interpretation of their behavior. We then need to ask ourselves which behavior led us to think that the strangers were lying. Once we have isolated the behavior we think leads us to our interpretations, we must ask ourselves if there are any other possible interpretations of that behavior. We can make an educated guess as to what strangers meant from the possible interpretations we isolate.

Skills

The skills necessary to communicate effectively and appropriately with strangers are those that are directly related to managing our uncertainty and anxiety.[9] Managing our anxiety requires at least three skills: ability to be mindful, ability to tolerate ambiguity, and ability to manage anxiety. Managing uncertainty minimally requires three skills: ability to empathize, ability to adapt our behavior, and ability to make accurate predictions of and explanations for strangers' behavior (the first two skills, however, are necessary to develop the third).

Ability to Be Mindful

By now it should be clear that I believe becoming mindful is the most important aspect of communicating effectively with strangers. We must be cognitively aware of our communication if we are to overcome our tendency to interpret strangers' behavior based on our own frames of reference. When we interact with strangers, we become mindful of our communication. Our focus, however, is usually on the outcome ("Will I make a fool of myself?" "Will strangers perceive me as prejudiced?"), rather than the process of communication. Focusing on the outcome, however, does not facilitate effective communication. For effective communication to occur, we must focus on the process of our communication with strangers.

Effective communication with strangers requires that we develop mindful ways of learning about strangers. With respect to learning,

> the concept of mindfulness revolves around certain psychological states that are really different versions of the same thing: (1) openness to novelty; (2) alertness to distinctions; (3) sensitivity to different contexts; (4) implicit, if not explicit, awareness of multiple perspectives; and (5) orientation in the present. Each leads to the others and back to itself. Learning a subject or skill with an openness to novelty and actively noticing differences, contexts, and perspectives—sideways learning—makes us receptive to changes in an ongoing situation. In such a state of mind, basic skills and information guide our behavior in the present, rather than run it like a computer program. (Langer, 1997, p. 23)

Engaging in this behavior will lead us to focus on the process of communication rather than getting hung-up on the potential outcomes of our communication with strangers.

When we are mindful, we do not want to be overly vigilant (Langer, 1997). If we become overly vigilant (e.g., concentrate with all of our will), we lock objects and strangers in our attention but our attention tends to be static and we become fatigued. If we engage in "soft vigilance," in contrast, we are open to novelty and take in new information. When we see the novelty in our interactions with strangers, our interactions will become enjoyable. Our enjoyment, in turn, will help us pay attention in our interactions with strangers.

When we are mindful, there are several things we can do to improve the effectiveness of our communication in conversations between native and nonnative speakers of a language. We can, for example, negotiate meanings. *Negotiating meanings* involves seeking clarification of meanings during conversations when we realize a misunderstanding has occurred (Varonis & Gass, 1985). Attempts to negotiate meanings usually are initiated by the person whose native language is being spoken when one person is not a native speaker. *Repairs* involve asking others to repeat what was said when one person does not understand (Gass & Varonis, 1985). Repairs usually are initiated by people not speaking their native language.

Being mindful is the single most important skill for improving the effectiveness of our communication. When we are mindful, we make conscious choices about what we need to do in specific situations to communicate effectively. Mindless behavior, no matter how well motivated or skillful, cannot substitute for mindful behavior (Langer, 1997).

The questionnaire in Table 7.3 is designed to help you assess how mindful you are when you communicate. This is a difficult idea to assess. To complete the questionnaire, you must think about your communication (i.e., become mindful of it). This will lead you to overestimate how mindful you actually are when you communicate. The questionnaire, nevertheless, will give you a rough idea of where you fall with respect to being mindful if you try to answer the questions based on your normal patterns of communication. Take a few minutes to complete it now.

Scores on the questionnaire range from 10 to 50. The higher your score, the more mindful you are when you communicate. Keep in mind that your score probably is inflated because you were mindful when you completed the questionnaire. Also remember that mindfulness is a skill that we can control. If your score is low, you can train yourself to be more mindful about your communication.

Being mindful is the single most important skill in communicating effectively with strangers. When we are mindful, we can make conscious

TABLE 7.3 *Assessing Your Mindfulness**

The purpose of this questionnaire is to help you assess your ability to be mindful when you communicate with strangers. Respond to each statement by indicating the degree to which it is true regarding the way you normally communicate: "Always False" (answer 1), "Usually False" (answer 2), "Sometimes False and Sometimes True" (answer 3), "Usually True" (answer 4), or "Always True" (answer 5).

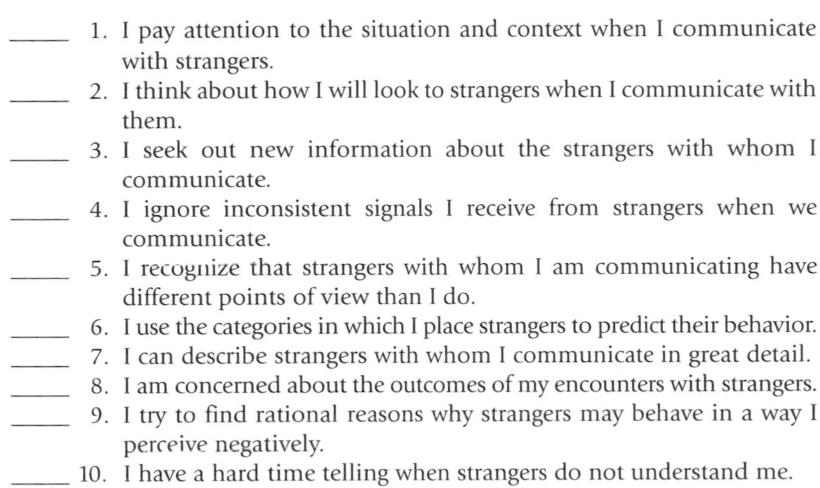

_____ 1. I pay attention to the situation and context when I communicate with strangers.
_____ 2. I think about how I will look to strangers when I communicate with them.
_____ 3. I seek out new information about the strangers with whom I communicate.
_____ 4. I ignore inconsistent signals I receive from strangers when we communicate.
_____ 5. I recognize that strangers with whom I am communicating have different points of view than I do.
_____ 6. I use the categories in which I place strangers to predict their behavior.
_____ 7. I can describe strangers with whom I communicate in great detail.
_____ 8. I am concerned about the outcomes of my encounters with strangers.
_____ 9. I try to find rational reasons why strangers may behave in a way I perceive negatively.
_____ 10. I have a hard time telling when strangers do not understand me.

To find your score, first reverse the responses for the even numbered items (i.e., if you wrote 1, make it 5; if you wrote 2, make it 4; if you wrote 3, leave it as 3; if you wrote 4, make it 2; if you wrote 5, make it 1). Next, add the numbers next to each statement. Scores range from 10 to 50. The higher your score, the more mindful you are when you communicate.

*Based on Langer's (1989) description of mindfulness.

choices as to what we need to do in the particular situation in order to communicate effectively. Unconscious behavior, no matter how well motivated or skillful, cannot substitute for mindful behavior. We always will be more effective when we are mindful than when we are on automatic pilot (Langer, 1997).

Ability to Tolerate Ambiguity

Tolerance for ambiguity implies the ability to deal successfully with situations, even when a lot of information needed to interact effectively is unknown (see Furnham & Ribchester, 1995, for a review). Lack of tolerance for ambiguity involves perceiving ambiguous situations as threatening and undesirable (Budner, 1962).

The greater our tolerance for ambiguity, the less anxiety we experience communicating with strangers. The greater our tolerance for ambiguity, the greater our effectiveness in communicating with strangers. Tolerance for ambiguity also influences our ability to work in new cultural environments.

> The ability to react to new and ambiguous situations with minimal discomfort has long been thought to be an important asset when adjusting to a new culture. . . . Excessive discomfort resulting from being placed in a new or different environment—or from finding the familiar environment altered in some critical ways—can lead to confusion, frustration and interpersonal hostility. Some people seem better able to adapt well in new environments and adjust quickly to the demands of the changing milieu. (Ruben & Kealey, 1979, p. 19)

The greater our tolerance for ambiguity, the more effective we are in completing task assignments in other cultures.

Our tolerance for ambiguity affects the type of information we try to find out about strangers. If we have a low tolerance for ambiguity, we tend to base our judgments of strangers on our first impressions (e.g., impressions made before all necessary information is available) (Smock, 1955). If we have a low tolerance for ambiguity, we try to gather information that supports our beliefs (McPherson, 1983). If we have a high tolerance for ambiguity, we tend to be open to new information about ourselves and strangers (Pilusuk, 1963). Also, if we have a high tolerance for ambiguity, we seek objective information about strangers (McPherson, 1983). Objective information is necessary to understand strangers and accurately predict and explain their behavior.

The questionnaire in Table 7.4 is designed to help you assess your tolerance for ambiguity. Take a couple of minutes and complete it now.

Scores on the questionnaire range from 10 to 50. The higher your score, the greater your tolerance for ambiguity. If your score is low, you can consciously choose not to panic in ambiguous situations when you are mindful.

Ability to Manage Anxiety

As indicated earlier, the amount of anxiety we experience when we communicate with strangers influences our motivation to communicate with them. If our anxiety is above our maximum thresholds or below our

TABLE 7.4 *Assessing Your Tolerance for Ambiguity*

The purpose of this questionnaire is to help you assess your orientations toward ambiguity. Respond to each statement indicating the degree to which it is true regarding the way you typically respond: "Always False" (answer 1), "Usually False" (answer 2), "Sometimes False and Sometimes True" (answer 3), "Usually True" (answer 4), or "Always True" (answer 5).

_____ 1. I am not comfortable in new situations.
_____ 2. I deal with unforeseen problems successfully.
_____ 3. I experience discomfort in ambiguous situations.
_____ 4. I am comfortable working on problems when I do not have all of the necessary information.
_____ 5. I am frustrated when things do not go the way I expected.
_____ 6. It is easy for me to adjust in new environments.
_____ 7. I become anxious when I find myself in situations where I am not sure what to do.
_____ 8. I am relaxed in unfamiliar situations.
_____ 9. I am not frustrated when my surroundings are changed without my knowledge.
_____ 10. I am comfortable in situations without clear norms to guide my behavior.

To find your score, first reverse the responses for the odd numbered items (i.e., if you wrote 1, make it 5; if you wrote 2, make it 4; if you wrote 3, leave it as 3; if you wrote 4, make it 2; if you wrote 5, make it 1). Next, add the numbers next to each statement. Scores range from 10 to 50. The higher your score, the greater your tolerance for ambiguity.

minimum thresholds, we will not be able to communicate effectively. If anxiety is too high, we are preoccupied with our anxiety to communicate effectively. If it is too low, we do not have enough adrenaline flowing to want to communicate with strangers.

There are two general issues in managing anxiety: (1) controlling our bodily symptoms, and (2) controlling our worrying thoughts or cognitive distortions (Kennerley, 1990). There are several physical symptoms associated with anxiety. When we are highly anxious we might experience respiratory problems (e.g., difficulty in breathing), palpitations of the heart, dry mouth, muscular tension, or a tension headache.

To manage our anxiety, the most important thing we can do is mindfully break away from the situation in which we feel anxious (Prather, 1986). This might mean excusing ourselves to leave the room, or mentally withdrawing for a short period of time. Once we have withdrawn, we need to calm ourselves and remember that our anxiety is not going to harm us. We can allow our anxious feelings to pass and then return to the situation.

If our anxiety does not dissipate quickly, we need to do something mindfully that will restore our calm. We can use various techniques to control the physical symptoms associated with our anxiety. These include, but are not limited to, yoga, hypnotism, meditation, and progressive muscular relaxation (i.e., relaxing the various muscle groups in our bodies in a systematic fashion). Respiratory control also can be used to manage the physical symptoms of anxiety. One way to practice controlled breathing is to sit up straight and concentrate on your breathing. Mindfully draw in a long breath and focus on your inhaling. Then let out the breath, focusing on your exhaling.

We can control our worrying thoughts by mindfully overcoming our cognitive distortions. When we interpret our own and strangers' behavior, our perceptions often are distorted because of the ways we think about our feelings and behavior. There are ten cognitive distortions that influence the ways we interpret behavior: all-or-nothing thinking; overgeneralizing; using mental filters; discounting the positive and focusing only on the negative; jumping to conclusions; magnification, or making problems bigger than they are; using emotional reasoning; using "should" statements (e.g., I should be a better person); labeling; and blaming ourselves or others (Burns, 1989).

All-or-nothing thinking involves seeing things based on dichotomies (it is sometimes also referred to as polarized thinking; Burns, 1989). If we are not perfect, for example, we think that we are a total failure. When we use this type of thought process, we do not see the possibility of alternative outcomes between being perfect and failing. This form of twisted thinking often leads us to see other people as either friends *or* enemies.

Overgeneralizing involves generalizing from one negative event to a "never ending pattern of defeat" (Burns, 1989). We tend to assume that negative events always happen to us and that positive events never occur. If a person turns us down for a date, for example, we would tend to think that we will *always* be turned down for dates if we are overgeneralizing. This form of twisted thinking also might lead us to believe that other people *never* understand us, if they misunderstood us once.

We use *mental filters* when we focus on specific negative details and the negative details affect the way we look at the world (Burns, 1989). Consider our boss telling us that we had one error in the report we wrote, but that generally the report was excellent. Our mental filter will cause us to focus on the error and this one negative comment will affect the remainder of our day.

When we ignore positive experiences, we are *discounting the positive* (Burns, 1989). Discounting the positive leads us to focus on negative aspects of our interactions with others. If we discount the positive and we have a positive interaction with another person, we would think that the experience does not count. Discounting the positive "takes the joy out of life" (Burns, 1989, p. 8) and leads to low self-esteem.

We *jump to conclusions* when we interpret events negatively even though the facts do not support our conclusion (Burns, 1989). There are two ways we jump to conclusions: *mind reading,* which involves concluding that others are reacting to us negatively without "checking it out," and *fortune-telling,* which involves predicting that things will turn out negatively. When communicating with our romantic partner, for example, we might predict that he or she will not tell us what we want to hear.

Magnification occurs when we exaggerate our negative qualities and minimize our positive qualities (Burns, 1989). We may, for example, assume that no one will like us because we are shy. When we magnify our problems, we let little problems that should not get in the way of our communication become major barriers to communication.

Emotional reasoning involves assuming that our negative emotions reflect who we really are. If we experience anger, for example, we would see ourselves as angry people. Alternatively, we might think "I feel guilty. I must be a rotten person" (Burns, 1989, p. 9).

When we assume that things "should" be the way we want them to be, we are using *should statements* (Burns, 1989). To illustrate, when communicating with others we want to speak fluently. If we use "you know" a few times when communicating with someone we want to impress, we might get very frustrated if we think we should always be fluent. When we direct should statements at ourselves and we do not live up to them, we get frustrated or feel guilty. When we direct should statements at others and they do not live up to them, we get frustrated or angry.

Labeling involves using a negative label for ourselves based on something we did. If we are not fluent when we communicate with someone, for example, we might label ourselves as an incompetent communicator. "Labeling is quite irrational because you are not the same as what you do" (Burns, 1989, p. 10). We can label ourselves or others. To illustrate, if someone does or says something we do not like, we might label the person a "jerk."

When we hold ourselves responsible for things that are not under our control, we are engaging in *personalization and blame* (Burns, 1989). If, for example, our romantic partner gets mad at us, we would assume that we are to blame. Blaming ourselves leads to feeling guilt, shame, and low levels of self-esteem. Instead of blaming ourselves, we may blame others. This also is problematic because if we blame others, they may turn around and blame us.

Skill Exercise 7.2 provides an opportunity for you to think about how you manage your anxiety. Take a few minutes to complete it now.

Cognitive distortions occur when we communicate on automatic pilot and when we are consciously thinking about the *outcomes* of our interactions with others. **To overcome our cognitive distortions, we must learn to replace our distorted automatic thoughts with rational responses**. This requires that we become mindful of the *process* of our communication and not focus on the outcome. Unless we stop distorting our thought processes, we will *not* be able to manage our anxiety consistently over long periods of time.

Ability to Empathize

The one skill that consistently emerges in discussions of effectively communicating with strangers is empathy. *Empathy* is multifaceted, involving cognitive (thinking), affective (feeling), and communication components:

"Cognitively, the empathic person takes the perspective of another person, and in so doing strives to see the world from the other's point of view. Affectively, the empathic person experiences the emotions of another; he or she *feels* the other's experiences. Communicatively, the empathic individual signals understanding and concern through verbal and nonverbal cues" (Bell, 1987, p. 204). The cognitive, affective, and communication components are interrelated and all must be present for strangers to perceive that we are being empathic.

Empathy involves (1) carefully listening to strangers, (2) understanding strangers' feelings, (3) being interested in what strangers say, (4) being sensitive to strangers' needs, and (5) understanding strangers' points of view (Hwang et al., 1980). While these indicators of empathy include verbal components, we tend to rely on nonverbal behavior more than verbal behavior when we interpret strangers' behavior as empathic (Bell, 1987).

When we are *empathic*, we imagine how strangers are feeling. Sympathy often is confused with empathy. When we are *sympathetic*, we imagine how we would feel in strangers' situations.[10] The "Golden Rule"—"Do unto others as you would have them do unto you"—that many people are taught as children involves a sympathetic response to strangers, not an empathic response (Bennett, 1979). The "Platinum Rule"—"Do unto others as they would have you do unto them"—involves an empathic

SKILL EXERCISE 7.2 *Managing Anxiety*

When our anxiety is above our maximum thresholds we need to manage it to communicate effectively. Think about how you might manage your anxiety in the situations described below.

You're working on a class project with a person from another ethnic group. You do not have much experience interacting with people from this group and you have a negative stereotype of people from this group (think of a specific group for which you have negative stereotypes). You are anxious about communicating with this person and your anxiety is above your maximum threshold. You have to meet this person in 15 minutes.

How could you manage your physical symptoms?

____

____

____

What worrying thoughts would you have? How might you manage them?

____

____

____

____

You've been invited to a party where there will be a lot of people from other ethnic groups and cultures. You think you may be the only person from your ethnic group there. You want to get to know some of the people, but you're afraid you won't fit in with the group attending the party. It's the night of the party and your anxiety is above your maximum threshold.

How could you manage your physical symptoms?

____

____

____

What worrying thoughts would you have? How might you manage them?

____

____

____

____

____

SKILL EXERCISE 7.3 *Being Empathic*

The purpose of this skill exercise is to help you differentiate responding to others using empathy and sympathy. Read the scenarios provided and answer the questions posed.

Kim meets Yuko, a Japanese international student acquaintance of Kim's, at the student union. While they are talking Yuko says that she got a call from her mother last night announcing that her parents are getting a divorce. Kim's parents have been divorced for years and she thinks it was a good thing for her family. Kim also knows that divorce is very rare in Japan.

How might Kim respond to Yuko using sympathy? Why is this sympathetic?

____

____

____

How might Kim respond to Yuko using empathy? Why is this empathic?

____

____

____

Chris is talking with his friend Chandra from India. Chandra tells Chris that his parents called the other night to tell him that they had arranged a marriage for him to a woman from a good family. Chris just recently asked his high school sweetheart to marry him, but he knows that arranged marriages are common in India.

How might Chris respond to Chandra using sympathy? Why is this sympathetic?

____

____

____

____

How might Chris respond to Chandra using empathy? Why is this empathic?

____

____

____

____

____

response. The Platinum Rule is reasonable as long as what strangers want done unto them does not violate our basic moral principles or universally accepted principles of human rights (ethical issues are discussed in Chapter 10).

Skill Exercise 7.3 provides an opportunity for you to practice thinking about how to respond empathically. Take a few minutes to complete it now.

Most of us are sympathetic, not empathic, when we communicate on automatic pilot. The reason for this is that we tend to assume that strangers look at the world same way we do when we communicate on automatic pilot. In order to respond to strangers with empathy, we must be mindful. It is only when we are mindful that we can imagine how strangers feel. The greater our empathy, the more accurate our predictions of and explanations for strangers' behavior will be.

"Empathy leads to prosocial behavior" (e.g., helping strangers, inhibiting aggression) (Stephan & Finlay, 1999, p. 732; also see Finlay & Stephan, 2000). Cognitive empathy may reduce perceptions of dissimilarities and feeling threatened by strangers, which, in turn, leads to reductions in prejudice. Emotional empathy with strangers may "arouse feelings of injustice" and this "counteracts prejudice" (p. 735). Empathizing with strangers without respecting them, however, can be problematic (e.g., it can lead to condescending behavior).

Feeling empathy for outgroup members not only leads to helping the specific stranger involved, it also can lead to helping the outgroup as a whole (Batson et al., 1997). There are three steps in this process. First, adopting the position of specific outgroup members (e.g., imagining how strangers are affected by the situations in which they find themselves) leads to empathy for the specific strangers. Second, feeling empathy for specific outgroup members leads to a concern for their welfare. Third, if ingroup members assume that the outgroup members' group memberships influence their "plight," the concern for the specific outgroup members generalizes to their groups as a whole and leads to positive attitudes toward the groups. These positive attitudes "provide the basis for increased motivation to help the group" (Batson et al., 2002, p. 1657).

Table 7.5 contains a questionnaire designed to help you assess your ability to display empathy. Take a few minutes to complete it now.

Scores on the questionnaire range from 10 to 50. The higher your score, the greater your empathy. If your score is on the low side, remember that you can increase your tendency to display empathy when you are mindful of your communication.

TABLE 7.5 *Assessing Your Empathy With Strangers*

The purpose of this questionnaire is to help you assess your ability to empathize with strangers. Respond to each statement by indicating the degree to which the statement is true regarding the way you typically communicate with others. When you think of your communication, is the statement "Always False" (answer 1), "Usually False" (answer 2), "Sometimes False and Sometimes True" (answer 3), "Usually True" (answer 4), or "Always True" (answer 5).

_____ 1. I try to understand strangers' experiences from their perspectives.
_____ 2. I follow the "Golden Rule" ("Do unto others as you would have them do unto you") when communicating with strangers.
_____ 3. I can "tune in" to the emotions strangers are experiencing when we communicate.
_____ 4. When trying to understand how strangers feel, I imagine how I would feel in their situation.
_____ 5. I am able to tell what strangers are feeling without being told.
_____ 6. Strangers experience the same feelings as I do in any given situation.
_____ 7. When strangers are having problems, I can imagine how they feel.
_____ 8. I find it hard to understand the emotions strangers experience.
_____ 9. I try to see strangers as they want me to.
_____ 10. I never seem to know what strangers are thinking when we communicate.

To find your score, first reverse the responses for the even numbered items (i.e., if you wrote 1, make it 5; if you wrote 2, make it 4; if you wrote 3, leave it as 3; if you wrote 4, make it 2; if you wrote 5, make it 1). Next, add the numbers next to each statement. Scores range from 10 to 50. The higher your score, the more you are able to empathize.

Ability to Adapt Our Communication

To gather information about and adapt our behavior to strangers requires that we be flexible in our behavior.[11] As suggested in the discussion of knowledge, we must be able to select strategies that are appropriate to gather the information we need about strangers in order to communicate effectively with them. This requires that we have different behavioral options for gathering information open to us. We also must be able to adapt and accommodate our behavior to strangers if we are going to be successful in our interactions with them. *Communication adaptability* involves: "1) The requirement of both cognitive (ability to perceive) and behavioral (ability to adapt) skills; 2) Adaptation not only of behavior but also interaction goals; 3) The ability to adapt to the requirements posed by different communication contexts; and 4) The assumption that perceptions of communicative competence reside in the dyad" (Duran, 1983, p. 320).

There are several suggestions for how individualists and collectivists might want to consider adapting their behavior and ways of thinking when communicating with each other (Triandis et al., 1988). *For individualists to communicate more effectively with collectivists,* individualists need to (1) recognize that collectivists pay attention to group memberships and use group memberships to predict collectivists' behavior; (2) recognize that when collectivists' group memberships change, their behavior changes; (3) recognize that collectivists are comfortable in vertical, unequal relationships; (4) recognize that collectivists see competition as threatening; (5) recognize that collectivists emphasize harmony and cooperation in the ingroup; (6) recognize that collectivists emphasize face (public self-image) and help them preserve their face in interactions; (7) recognize that collectivists do not separate criticism from the person being criticized and avoid confrontation whenever possible; (8) cultivate long-term relationships with collectivists; (9) be more formal than usual in initial interactions; and (10) follow collectivists' guide in disclosing personal information.

For collectivists to interact effectively with individualists, collectivists need to (1) recognize that individualists' behavior cannot be predicted accurately from group memberships; (2) recognize that individualists will be proud of their accomplishments and say negative things about others; (3) recognize that individualists are emotionally detached from their ingroups; (4) recognize that individualists prefer horizontal, equal relationships; (5) recognize that individualists do not see competition as threatening; (6) recognize that individualists are not persuaded by arguments emphasizing harmony and cooperation; (7) recognize that individualists do not form long-term relationships and that initial friendliness does not indicate an intimate relationship; (8) recognize that individualists maintain relationships when they receive more rewards than costs; (9) recognize that individualists do not respect others based on position, age, or sex as much as collectivists; and (10) recognize that outgroups are not viewed as highly different from the ingroup by individualists (Triandis et al., 1988). Suggestions also could be based on the other dimensions of cultural variability presented in Chapter 2.

It is not necessary to try to memorize these lists of how we can adapt our behavior when we communicate with strangers. Rather, what we need to do when we want to adapt our behavior is to become mindful and pay attention to the interactions in which we find ourselves. If we are mindful, we can determine which adaptations are useful in the specific situation. We cannot adapt successfully if we are on automatic pilot, even if we memorized these lists.

Often the adaptations we make when interacting with strangers do not improve the effectiveness of our communication (see, e.g., the discussion of communicative distance in Chapter 4). "Adjustments majority speakers make when speaking to minority members often give the impression that the speaker is patronizing and distant and, in turn, affect the recipients' behavior and conversational style" (Kraut & Higgins, 1984, p. 114). If strangers perceive we are patronizing they will become defensive. Communication cannot be effective when one of the individuals is defensive. To be more effective we must adapt our messages to the specific strangers with whom we are communicating. Strangers understand our messages better when they are constructed for them than when we do not adapt our messages.[12]

One important aspect of adapting our behavior is the ability to speak another language (or at least use phrases in another language). If we always expect strangers to speak our language, we cannot be effective in communicating with them. We "should become familiar with other languages and cultures so that [we] will be better able to live, with confidence, in an increasingly interdependent world" (Boyer, 1990, p. B4).

The importance of speaking another language depends, at least in part, on where we are:

> In some cultures foreigners are expected to know the local language. A Frenchman [or woman] who arrives in the United States without knowing a word of English, or an American who visits France with only a bit of French, is bound to find the locals rather unsympathetic. For example, I have found a discrepancy between my friends' and my own experience in Paris. Their accounts stress discourtesy of the French, while I have found the French to be quite courteous. I suspect the difference is that I speak better French than the majority of visitors and am therefore treated more courteously. In contrast, in other cultures the visitor is not expected to know the local language. In Greece, for example, one is not expected to know the language although a few words of Greek create delight, and increase by order of magnitude (a factor of ten) the normal hospitable tendencies of that population. (Triandis, 1983, p. 84)

Some attempt at using the local language is necessary to indicate an interest in the people and/or culture.

The need to adapt our behavior is not limited to speaking another language. If I (a European American male) am communicating with someone from another culture who wants to stand closer to me than I want him or her to stand (e.g., someone from a Latin or Arab culture), I have two options if I am mindful of my communication. First, I can choose to try to use my own interpersonal distance (e.g., the other person should stand at least at arm's length from me). If the other person keeps trying to use her or his distance, however, he or she will dance me around the room (i.e., the other person moves forward, I move back; to compensate and be at a distance that is comfortable for him or her, the other person moves closer). If I am not mindful of my communication, this is what is likely to occur. Alternatively, I can choose to use a different pattern of behavior. I can decide to stand closer to the other person than I would if I was communicating with someone from my own culture. This option will, in all likelihood, lead to more effective communication. When people are following different rules, at least one of the parties has to adapt for effective communication to occur.

You may be asking yourself, why do I have to adapt? Why don't strangers adapt, especially if they are foreigners in the United States? Strangers could adapt, and strangers visiting or living in the United States usually do to a large extent. As members of the human community, nevertheless, we have to make choices about whether to adapt and when to adapt to strangers. I believe that **if we know what can be done to improve the chances for effective communication, have the skills to do what needs to be done, and choose not to adapt our communication, we have to take responsibility for misunderstandings that occur as a result**. There are obviously situations where this principle may not hold. If the behavior required, for example, goes against our moral standards or violates another's human rights, some other option must be found.

The questionnaire in Table 7.6 is designed to help you to assess your ability to adapt your behavior. The questionnaire obviously does not tap all aspects of how we might adapt our behavior. It does, however, cover the major areas needed to communicate effectively with strangers. Take a few minutes to complete it now.

Scores on the questionnaire range from 10 to 50. The higher your score, the more flexible you are in your behavioral repertoire. The important thing to keep in mind if you do not have a high score is that you can increase your behavioral flexibility with practice. Once you understand what behavior is necessary in a particular situation (i.e., have the necessary knowledge), you can become mindful of your communication and decide to try out the behavior. Who knows, you may find that you like it. If you do not like the behavior or find it unethical, however, you will have to find an alternative way to respond.

TABLE 7.6 *Assessing Your Ability to Adapt Your Behavior**

The purpose of this questionnaire is to help you assess your ability to adapt your behavior to strangers. Respond to each statement by indicating the extent to which it is true of your normal patterns of communication: "Always False" (answer 1), "Usually False" (answer 2), "Sometimes False and Sometimes True" (answer 3), "Usually True" (answer 4), or "Always True" (answer 5).

_____ 1. I adapt my behavior to the strangers with whom I am communicating.
_____ 2. I use the same nonverbal communication with strangers I use with friends.
_____ 3. I am able to modify how I present myself to strangers.
_____ 4. I do not adapt my language to the way the strangers with whom I am communicating are speaking.
_____ 5. I adapt my behavior to the situation in which I find myself once I know what behavior is required.
_____ 6. I tend to use one communication style when I communicate with strangers.
_____ 7. I can modify the way I come across to strangers, depending on how I want them to see me.
_____ 8. I am not very flexible in the ways I communicate with strangers.
_____ 9. I communicate differently with strangers and members of my ingroups.
_____ 10. I insist that strangers communicate with me on my terms.

To find your score, first reverse your answers to the even numbered items (i.e., if you wrote 1, make it 5; if you wrote 2, make it 4; if you wrote 3, leave it as 3; if you wrote 4, make it 2; if you wrote 5, make it 1). Next, add the numbers you wrote next to each statement. Scores range from 10 to 50. The higher your score, the greater your ability to adapt your behavior.

*Ideas for some of the items are drawn from Lennox and Wolfe's (1984) ability to modify self-presentations scale.

Ability to Make Accurate Predictions and Explanations

The final skill is the ability to make accurate predictions of and explanations for strangers' behavior. If we can empathize, have the ability to adapt our communication, and are mindful, we can gather the information necessary to manage our uncertainty. Managing our uncertainty requires that we be able to describe strangers' behavior, select appropriate interpretations of their messages, accurately predict their behavior, and be able to explain their behavior accurately.

We tend to assume that strangers' thoughts, feelings, and behavior are rule governed (Karniol, 1990). If we do not make such an assumption we could not ever predict strangers' thoughts, feelings, or behavior. The problem with the accuracy of our predictions is that we know only a limited number of rules that we can use to understand strangers' thoughts, feelings, and behavior. Since we may not know the rules that strangers are using, we assume that they are the same as ours when we are on automatic pilot. To understand the rules that strangers are using to guide their thoughts, feelings, and behavior, we must be mindful. When we are mindful, we need to be empathic and use active listening in order to try to understand strangers' rules. Once we understand the rules strangers are using, we can make accurate predictions of and explanations for their behavior.

When we are on automatic pilot, our predictions of and explanations for strangers' behavior are based on our stereotypes, intergroup attitudes, and previous experiences with the strangers involved. (Note: My focus below is on strangers' behavior, but everything said also applies to their thoughts, attitudes, feelings, values, etc.). We may be highly confident of our predictions and explanations when we are on automatic pilot, but our predictions and explanations may *not* be accurate. If our predictions are based only on our stereotypes of strangers' groups, for example, our predictions will not be accurate if our stereotypes are inaccurate or strangers are not typical members of their groups. **Accurate predictions or explanations of strangers' behavior require that we mindfully use cultural, social, and personal information**.

To make accurate predictions of and explanations for strangers' behavior, we must be able to gather accurate information about strangers. When our anxiety is too high we are not able to gather accurate information about strangers (Wilder & Shapiro, 1989). If our anxiety is too low, we also will have problems gathering accurate information about strangers. To gather accurate information, we must mindfully manage our anxiety so that it is below our maximum thresholds and above our minimum thresholds. The accuracy of our predictions and explanations for strangers' behavior also is dependent upon our knowledge of group differences, our knowledge of similarities, and our knowledge of alternative interpretations. Our accuracy also is affected by our expectations. If we expect the interactions to be negative, for example, our anxiety will be high, probably above our maximum thresholds, and we will not be able to make accurate predictions or explanations. We also are better able to make accurate predictions and explanations if our needs (see Motivation section of this chapter) have been met.

Another factor that influences the accuracy of our predictions of and explanations for strangers' behavior is our view of our ingroups and outgroups. We tend to view our ingroups as being more differentiated than outgroups. The more familiar we are with outgroups, however, the greater our perceived differentiation of the outgroups (Linville et al., 1989). **The more variability we perceive in outgroups, the less our tendencies to treat all members in a similar negative fashion** (Johnstone & Hewstone, 1991). The variability we perceive in outgroups provides information about the strangers with whom we are communicating and, therefore, increases the accuracy of our predictions.

Our perceptions of strangers' intentions toward us also affects the accuracy of our predictions and explanations of their behavior. We tend to be more accurate, for example, in perceiving strangers' intentions when they are negative than when they are positive. "Intentions to convey hostility are perceived more accurately than intentions to convey positive feelings" (Bodenhausen et al., 1987, p. 159). Our accuracy in interpreting others' intentions also is lower if we have been dissatisfied with our previous interactions with them than if we have been satisfied with our previous interactions (Bodenhausen et al., 1987).

The questionnaire in Table 7.7 is designed to help you assess your ability to predict and explain strangers' behavior accurately when you communicate with them. Take a couple of minutes and complete the questionnaire now.

The scores on the questionnaire range from 10 to 50. The higher your score, the more accurate your predictions and explanations. The more accurate your predictions and explanations are, the more effective your communication will be. The questionnaire in Table 7.7 is designed to assess *either* your ability to predict and explain accurately the behavior of a group of people *or* your ability to predict and explain accurately the behavior of a specific person. When you first completed the questionnaire you focused on either a group or specific person. I suggest that before reading the next chapter you take the time to complete the questionnaire in Table 7.7 again focusing on a person, if you initially completed it for a group; or focusing on a group, if you initially thought of a specific person. Obviously, you can complete the questionnaire for many different groups or individuals.

To conclude, I have discussed the factors that contribute to our being perceived as competent communicators—our motivation, knowledge, and skills—in this chapter. In the next three chapters, I apply these ideas to managing conflict with strangers, developing relationships with strangers, and building community with strangers.

Study Questions

1. Why is communication competence an impression?
2. What provides rhythm to our interactions with others?

TABLE 7.7 *Assessing Your Ability to Predict/Explain Strangers' Behavior*

The purpose of this questionnaire is to help you assess your ability to accurately predict and explain the behavior of people from other groups. Respond to each statement by indicating the degree to which the statement is true with respect to your communication with either a particular group of people or a specific person from another group. When you communicate with people who are different, is the statement "Always False" (answer 1), "Usually False" (answer 2), "Sometimes True and Sometimes False" (answer 3), "Usually True" (answer 4), or "Always True" (answer 5).

_____ 1. I can make accurate predictions regarding the behavior of _______.
_____ 2. I cannot accurately predict how _______ will behave when we have a disagreement.
_____ 3. I can accurately explain the values of _______.
_____ 4. I do not understand how _______ see themselves when we communicate.
_____ 5. I can accurately explain the behavior of _______ to others.
_____ 6. I do not understand the attitudes _______ hold.
_____ 7. I can accurately interpret the messages I receive from _______.
_____ 8. I often make errors in attributions when I am trying to understand the behavior of _______.
_____ 9. I can accurately describe the behavior of _______.
_____ 10. I cannot tell when _______ misinterprets messages I transmit.

To find your score, first reverse your answers to the even numbered items (i.e., if you wrote 1, make it 5; if you wrote 2, make it 4; if you wrote 3, leave it as 3; if you wrote 4, make it 2; if you wrote 5, make it 1). Next, add the numbers you wrote next to each of the statements. Scores range from 10 to 50. The higher your score, the greater your understanding of people who are different.

3. Why is it important that we receive self-concept support in our interactions with strangers?
4. How does knowledge of group differences help us communicate effectively with strangers?
5. How does knowledge of alternative interpretations facilitate effective communication?
6. What do we need to do to be mindful? Why is being mindful the most important skill for improving the effectiveness of our communication?
7. How are tolerance for ambiguity and managing anxiety similar and different?
8. What is the difference between sympathy and empathy? Why is empathy without respect problematic?

9. How can individualists adapt their behavior to communicate effectively with collectivists? How can collectivists adapt their behavior to communicate more effectively with individualists?

Applications

1. Over the next week, pay attention to your motivation to communicate with strangers. When are you highly motivated? When is your motivation low? What influences the differences in your levels of motivation?

2. Over the next week, pay attention to your interpretations of strangers' behavior. When appropriate, use your knowledge of how to find alternative interpretations. How does this process help you understand strangers?

3. Over the next week, systematically apply one of the skills discussed in this chapter when you communicate with strangers. To illustrate, every time you communicate with strangers this week try to empathize with them. How does using this skill affect your communication? What can you do in the future to use this skill when you need it? Repeat this application till you have practiced all of the skills for one week. Then in the following week, try using all of the skills at the same time.

Notes

1. Spitzberg and Cupach (1984) use the term effectiveness to refer to task outcomes (e.g., goal achievement).

2. Watzlawick, Beavin, and Jackson (1967), for example, point out that the way members of a family communicate with each other can create mental illness.

3. J. H. Turner (1988) uses different labels for some of the terms (including the needs). He uses the ethnomethods, for example, to refer to what I call habits or scripts. I believe my terms capture the essence of his idea, but are not as full of academic jargon.

4. Spitzberg and Cupach (1984) also talk about approach avoidance as a factor in motivation. They, however, assume that it is a basic orientation to any encounter rather than deriving it from more basic needs as I am here.

5. Langer notes that there appear to be "taboo" questions. I believe, however, that most of the taboos are in our minds.

6. Berger (1979) actually isolates a third interactive strategy, deception detection, that I am not discussing.

7. See Gouldner (1960) for an extensive discussion of the reciprocity norm.

8. There are some differences in how the reciprocity norm is manifested in different cultures. See Gudykunst and Ting-Toomey (1988) for a detailed discussion.

9. The theory on which the book is based (Gudykunst, 1988, 1993, 1995) suggests that effectiveness and adaptation are a function of managing uncertainty and anxiety. Other variables (e.g., expectations) affect our level of uncertainty and anxiety and are not linked directly to effectiveness. Gao and Gudykunst (1990) tested this assumption in an adaptation context and it was supported. There are numerous other skills that could be discussed if I did not select the skills based on the theory. There is some overlap between those selected on the basis of the theory and atheoretically derived lists of skills. Ruben (1976), for example, listed seven skills: (1) empathy, (2) tolerance for ambiguity, (3) display of respect, (4) interaction posture, (5) orientation to knowledge, (6) role behavior, and (7) interaction management.

10. These differences also can be explained in terms of situational (sympathy) versus individual (empathy) role-taking. See Karniol (1990) for a discussion.

11. The way I am talking about behavioral flexibility is very similar to Lennox and Wolfe's (1984) notion of ability to modify self-presentations (which is a subscale in their revised self-monitoring scale). Spitzberg and Cupach (1984) included Snyder's (1974) notion of self-monitoring as a skill in communication competence. I have not called this self-monitoring or ability to modify self-presentations because I think the idea of behavioral flexibility is more general. The concepts, however, are interrelated.

12. See Kellermann (1993) for research to support this claim.

CHAPTER 8

Managing Conflict With Strangers

I examined the factors that contribute to perceptions of our competence in communicating with strangers in the preceding chapter. If we have the motivation, knowledge, and skills for effective communication discussed in the last chapter, it increases the likelihood we will be able to manage conflicts with strangers successfully. I begin this chapter by examining the nature of conflict, and cultural and ethnic differences in conflict. Next, I discuss cultural and ethnic differences in face (e.g., the image or "social value" we claim for ourselves in interactions; Goffman, 1955) and face-management. Face is included here because dealing with conflict is a face-threatening act. Following this, the characteristics of intergroup conflict are presented. I conclude this chapter by providing suggestions on how we can manage our conflicts with strangers constructively.

The Nature of Conflict

Conflict is inevitable in any ongoing relationship; it will happen whether we want it to or not. Many of us, nevertheless, view conflict negatively. Conflict itself, however, is not positive or negative. How we manage the conflicts we have, in contrast, can have positive or negative consequences for our relationships.

Dyadic *conflict* is "the process which begins when one party perceives that the other has frustrated, or is about to frustrate, some concern of his" or hers (Thomas, 1983, p. 891). This definition covers a broad range of phenomena (e.g., from minor disagreements to war). "The root causes of [intergroup] conflict are unfulfilled or threatened human needs . . . [including] security, identity, dignity, recognition, [and] justice" (Kelman, 2002, p. 34). Anytime we perceive that we have conflict with strangers, our anxiety tends to be high. Also, since we tend to feel agitated when we are engaged in conflicts with strangers, our predictions of and explanations for their behavior tend to be inaccurate.

Take a few minutes to answer the following questions before reading the remainder of this section.

What is your attitude toward conflict? Do you prefer to address it or avoid it? Why?

____

____

____

How do you typically deal with conflicts with members of your own groups (e.g., ethnic or cultural)?

____

____

____

How do you typically deal with conflicts with members of different ethnic groups or cultures?

____

____

____

Your answers to these questions should provide some insight into the role of conflict in your implicit theory of communication. Keep your answers in mind as you read the remainder of this chapter.

There are several sources of conflict with strangers (Roloff, 1987). First, conflict occurs when we misinterpret strangers' behavior. Second, conflict can arise from our perceptions of incompatibilities with strangers, such as perceiving that their personalities or group characteristics are not compatible with ours. Third, conflict arises when we disagree with strangers on the causes of their behavior or our behavior. As indicated in Chapter 5, we tend to explain our own positive behavior based on our personal characteristics, strangers' positive behavior, but attribute to situational demands. We tend to attribute our own negative behavior to situational demands, and strangers' negative behavior to their group memberships.

When a conflict occurs, neither of the parties, one of the parties, or both parties may recognize that a conflict exists. If neither of the parties recognizes that a conflict exists, the conflict may not create problems for the relationship. If only one of the parties recognizes that a conflict exists, it can create problems for the relationship, depending on the conflict and how the person handles it. To illustrate, if the person decides that the issue is not important, he or she could ignore the problem and it will not create problems in the relationship. If, however, she or he thinks the conflict is important and she or he ignores it, it will, in all likelihood, create problems in the relationship. If it does not come out in any other way, it will come out in how he or she reacts to the person with whom she or he has the conflict.

Communication is the medium through which conflict is created and managed. The way we communicate with strangers often creates conflict. The way we communicate with strangers reflects whether or not we are having conflicts with them. Conflict in relationships can be overt and out in the open (manifest conflict) or it can be out of sight (latent conflict). When conflict is out of sight, we easily can avoid addressing the conflict. In fact, avoidance is probably the most widely used strategy for dealing with conflict. It has been estimated that we avoid 50 percent of our conflicts with others (Sillars et al., 1982). We constructively or destructively manage our conflicts by the way we communicate.

Our conflicts with strangers often seem to get out of control without our realizing it. There are four aspects of conflict development that contribute to this happening (Donohue, 1993). First, once conflicts start, they tend to perpetuate themselves, especially if there are already problems between the people involved. "Conflict is often exacerbated as much by the process of the relationship as it is by the issues" (Kelman, 2002, p. 34). Conflict breeds conflict, unless it is managed successfully. Second, conflicts always take place within a context, but we often are not aware of how the context contributes to our conflicts with strangers. To manage conflicts we have to understand the contexts in which they occur. Third, our conflicts always have implications for our relationships with strangers. When conflicts are over, our relationships change in some way, but we often do not recognize that it is how we manage the conflict that is critical to how it will affect our relationships. Fourth, conflict gets out of control because we do not recognize that manifest conflict actually serves many positive functions in our lives. If two people have conflict with a common enemy, for example, it brings them closer together. Our conflict with strangers also helps define our roles, it helps us understand our feelings about strangers, and it helps make the conflict issues clearer. "Self-image is also very important. Each side sees itself as good and peaceful and the other side as evil and inherently hostile" (Kelman, 2002, p. 34).

Table 8.1 contains a questionnaire designed to assess your tendency to avoid conflicts with strangers. Take a few minutes to complete it now.

TABLE 8.1 *Assessing Your Tendency to Avoid Conflicts With Strangers*

The purpose of this questionnaire is to help you assess your tendency to avoid conflict with strangers. Respond to each statement by indicating the degree to which it is true regarding how you manage conflict with strangers: "Always False" (answer 1), "Usually False" (answer 2), "Sometimes True and Sometimes False" (answer 3), "Usually True" (answer 4), or "Always True" (answer 5).

_____ 1. When I think I have conflicts with strangers, I try to avoid them whenever possible.
_____ 2. When I think I have conflicts with strangers, I want to resolve them.
_____ 3. When I think I have conflicts with strangers, I do not confront them.
_____ 4. When I think I have conflicts with strangers, I make sure we discuss the problem.
_____ 5. When I think I have conflicts with strangers, I give in to what they want.
_____ 6. When I think I have conflicts with strangers, I try to control the situation.
_____ 7. When I think I have conflicts with strangers, I pretend there are no conflicts when we interact.
_____ 8. When I think I have conflicts with strangers, I try to get them to accept my solution.
_____ 9. When I think I have conflicts with strangers, I try to smooth over the problem.
_____ 10. When I think I have conflicts with strangers, I try to find a compromise with them.

To find your score, first reverse the responses for the even numbered items (i.e., if you wrote 1, make it 5; if you wrote 2, make it 4; if you wrote 3, leave it as 3; if you wrote 4, make it 2; if you wrote 5, make it 1). Next, add the numbers next to each statement. Scores range from 10 to 50. The higher your score, the greater your tendency to avoid conflicts with strangers.

Scores on the questionnaire range from 10 to 50. The higher your score, the greater your tendency to avoid conflicts with strangers. If your score is high (e.g., 30 or above), you need to recognize that you avoid conflicts with strangers. If this is the case, you can choose to act differently and use the material presented in this chapter to help manage conflicts with strangers when you are mindful.

Cultural and Ethnic Differences in Conflict

The way we deal with conflict is affected by many factors. Two of the important factors influencing how we manage conflict are our cultures and our ethnicities. All members of the same culture or ethnic group do not handle conflict in the same way, but there are relatively clear patterns across cultures and ethnic groups.

Cultural Differences in Conflict

The cultures in which we are raised influence our view of conflict. Our cultures influence the assumptions we make about conflict and the styles we use when we try to manage conflict.

Assumptions About Conflict. Conflicts arise from either instrumental or expressive sources (Olsen, 1978). *Expressive conflicts* arise from a desire to release tension, usually generated from hostile feelings. *Instrumental conflicts,* in contrast, stem from a difference in goals or practices. Members of individualistic cultures "are more likely to perceive conflict as instrumental rather than expressive in nature," and members of collectivistic cultures "are more likely to perceive conflict as expressive rather than instrumental in nature" (Ting-Toomey, 1985, p. 78).

Members of individualistic cultures often separate the issue on which they are having conflict from the person with whom they have the conflict (Ting-Toomey, 1985). Members of collectivistic cultures, in contrast, generally do not make this distinction. To illustrate, Japanese managers take criticism and objections to ideas they express as personal attacks (Nishiyama, 1971). U.S. American managers, on the other hand, do not necessarily take criticism of their ideas as personal attacks unless they are highly defensive.

In individualistic cultures, conflict is likely to occur when individuals' expectations of appropriate behavior are violated (Ting-Toomey, 1985). Conflict in collectivistic cultures, in contrast, is more likely to occur when the group's normative expectations for behavior are violated. The reason for this difference lies in the role of context in providing information in the two types of cultures. In collectivistic cultures, context plays a crucial role in providing meaning to communication messages, but in individualistic cultures, context plays a less crucial role because most information is provided in the message. The more important the context is, the more often violation of collective normative expectations leads to conflict. The less important the context is, the more often violation of individuals' expectations leads to conflict.

Members of individualistic cultures "are more likely to possess a confrontational, direct attitude toward conflicts" than members of collectivistic cultures (Ting-Toomey, 1985, p. 79). Members of collectivistic cultures, in contrast, "are more likely to possess a non-confrontational, indirect attitude toward conflicts" than members of individualistic cultures (p. 79). A direct approach to conflict in individualistic cultures stems from independent self construals and the use of linear logic. Members of collectivistic cultures have a strong desire for group harmony and tend to use indirect forms of communication and, therefore, tend to prefer a nonconfrontational approach to conflict.

Members of individualistic cultures tend to deal with conflict based on independent self construals, and members of collectivistic cultures tend to deal with conflict based on interdependent self construals (Ting-Toomey, 1994). In using independent self construals, members of individualistic cultures think only of themselves and the specific person with whom they have a conflict. Members of collectivistic cultures, in contrast, think about themselves and the members of their ingroups when their behavior is guided by an interdependent self construal. Since the self construal is interdependent, members of collectivistic cultures do not separate themselves from the ingroups of which they are members.

Members of individualistic cultures take a short-term view of managing conflict, and members of collectivistic cultures tend to take a long-term view of managing conflict (Ting-Toomey, 1994). Members of individualistic cultures are concerned with the immediate conflict situation. Members of collectivistic cultures, in contrast, focus on the long-term relationship with the other person. The immediate conflict is important, but the critical issue for collectivists is whether they can depend on the other person over the long term.

Members of collectivistic cultures prefer to use mediators to manage conflicts more than members of individualistic cultures (Ting-Toomey, 1994). The use of mediators allows conflicts to be managed without direct confrontation. If confrontation can be avoided, harmony in ingroup relationships can be maintained. Members of individualistic cultures generally do not use mediators to manage conflicts. When they do use mediators, members of individualistic cultures prefer formal mediators (e.g., lawyers) more than members of collectivistic cultures. Members of collectivistic cultures, in contrast, prefer informal mediators more than members of individualistic cultures.

Conflict Styles. Conflict styles are based on the degree of concern for self and concern for strangers inherent in the way we try to manage conflict (Rahim, 1983). An *integrating* style of managing conflict involves a high concern for ourselves and a high concern for strangers. When we use this style, we try to find solutions that are acceptable to us and strangers. A *compromising* style involves a moderate concern for ourselves and a moderate concern for strangers. When we use this style, we try to find an agreement that is acceptable to ourselves and strangers, but the agreement may not be either our first choice or strangers' first choice. Both integrating and compromising styles reflect a solution-orientation to conflict (Putnam & Wilson, 1982). A *dominating* style reflects a high concern for ourselves and a low concern for strangers. When we use this style, we try to control or dominate the conflict situation. An *obliging* style involves a low concern for ourselves and a high concern for strangers. When we use this style, we give in to what strangers want in conflict situations. Finally, an *avoiding* style involves a low concern for ourselves and low concern for strangers. When we use this style, we avoid the conflict topic or situation. This view has an individualistic bias. Avoiding can be seen as reflecting a high concern for strangers from a collectivistic perspective (see Gabrielidis et al., 1997). Obliging and avoiding styles of conflict involve nonconfrontation of conflict (Putnam & Wilson, 1982).

Members of individualistic cultures prefer direct styles of dealing with conflict such as integrating or compromising (Ting-Toomey, 1988). Members of collectivistic cultures, on the other hand, prefer indirect styles of dealing with conflict that allow all parties to preserve face. Collectivists tend to use obliging and avoiding styles of conflict resolution or avoid the conflict altogether. These patterns are consistent with descriptions of conflict strategies in Japan and the United States. U.S. Americans "prefer to defend themselves actively, employing or developing the rationale for positions they have taken. When pushed they may resort to still more aggressive forms that utilize humor, sarcasm, or denunciation. Among Japanese, the reactions are more varied, but defenses tend to be more passive, permit withdrawal, and allow greater concealment" (Barnlund, 1975, p. 423). U.S. Americans prefer solution-oriented strategies more than Japanese (Ting-Toomey et al., 1989).

Avoiding conflict in order to preserve face and maintain harmony is not limited to the Japanese culture. Chinese, for example, prefer bargaining and mediation more than U.S. Americans, and U.S. Americans prefer adjudicatory procedures more than Chinese (Leung, 1987). Chinese also would advise an executive to meet with an insulter and the target of the insult separately so that conflict between the two can be avoided (Bond et al., 1985). U.S. Americans, in contrast, would advise an executive to have a joint meeting so that the problem between the insulter and target of the insult can be resolved.

Members of collectivistic cultures tend to use indirect styles for dealing with conflict more than members of individualistic cultures. Chinese and Taiwanese, for example, use nonconfrontational styles for managing conflict more than U.S. Americans (Chiu & Kosinski, 1994; Knutson et al., 2000). Arabs also tend to use the avoiding style more than U.S. Americans, and U.S. Americans use the dominating style more than

Arabs (Elsayed-Ekhouly & Buda, 1996). Similarly, Mexicans tend to avoid or deny that conflict exists, and U.S. Americans tend to use direct strategies to deal with it (e.g., McGinn et al., 1973). Mexicans also emphasize others' outcomes more than U.S. Americans (Gabrielidis et al., 1997).

Whether conflict is with a member of the ingroup or a member of an outgroup affects how collectivists manage conflict. Chinese, for example, are less likely to pursue a conflict with an ingroup member and more likely to pursue a conflict with an outgroup member than U.S. Americans (Leung, 1988). European Americans tend to use integrating and obliging styles with members of ingroups more than with members of outgroups (Cole, 1990). Japanese, in contrast, tend to use an obliging style with members of ingroups more than with members of outgroups, and they tend to use a dominating style with members of outgroups more than with members of ingroups.

Collectivists are competitive with outgroup members more than individualists (Espinoza & Garza, 1985). Japanese, for example, are assertive with ingroup members more than outgroup members, but there is no difference between ingroup and outgroup assertiveness in the United States (Singhal & Nagao, 1993). Collectivistic Koreans draw a greater distinction between ingroups and outgroups when managing conflicts than individualistic Koreans (Han & Park, 1995).

The differences in how collectivists deal with ingroup and outgroup conflicts may be related to different concerns in the two situations (Leung, 1997). When conflicts are relatively intense (which usually happens with outgroup members), collectivists are concerned with reducing animosity. When there are conflicts with ingroup members or outgroup members with whom collectivists have ongoing relationships, in contrast, collectivists are concerned with avoiding the disintegration of the relationships. When collectivists are concerned with reducing animosity, they use problem-solving and compromising conflict strategies. When collectivists are concerned with avoiding the disintegration of the relationships, on the other hand, they use avoiding and yielding conflict strategies.

To understand fully how conflict operates with respect to ingroups in collectivistic cultures, it is necessary to take other dimensions of cultural variability into consideration. The level of power distance in a culture mediates how collectivists respond to someone who insults members of the ingroup (Bond et al., 1985). Chinese are less critical than U.S. Americans of people insulting ingroup members when they have higher status than the ingroup member compared with when the status is lower than the ingroup members' status. U.S. Americans make less of a distinction as a function of insulter's status or group membership.

Given the preceding discussion, readers may have the impression that conflicts do not occur in collectivistic cultures. This simply is not the case. Conflicts occur in collectivistic cultures in close ingroup relationships that do not require harmony or can survive the conflict (Maynard, 1997).

Ethnic Differences in Conflict

Most, if not all, of the cross-cultural studies comparing the United States with other cultures have focused on European Americans. There also are differences across ethnic groups in the United States.[1] African Americans, for example, prefer a controlling conflict resolution style, while European Americans prefer a solution-oriented style (Ting-Toomey, 1986). Members of collectivistic ethnic groups (e.g., African Americans, Arab Americans, Asian Americans, Latino[a] Americans) make more cooperative choices in dealing with conflicts than European Americans (Cox et al., 1991). Self construals, however, are sometimes better predictors of conflict styles than ethnicity (Oetzel, 1998). To illustrate, emphasizing the independent self construal is associated positively with using the dominating style, and emphasizing the interdependent self construal is associated positively with using the avoiding, obliging, and compromising conflict styles.

European Americans use the dominating style in romantic relationships more than Asian Americans (Kim & Kitani, 1998). Asian Americans, in contrast, use integrating, avoiding, obliging, and compromising styles more than European Americans. Emphasizing the independent self construal is associated positively with using the dominating style; emphasizing the interdependent self construal is related positively to using the integrating, obliging, avoiding, and compromising styles.

African American and European American styles of communication influence how they manage conflicts.[2] "Where [European Americans] use the relatively detached and unemotional *discussion* mode to engage an issue, [African Americans] use the more emotionally intense and involving mode of *argument.* Where [European Americans] tend to *underestimate* their exceptional talents and abilities, [African Americans] tend to *boast* about theirs" (Kochman, 1981, p. 106). African Americans favor forceful outputs (e.g., volume of voice), and European Americans prefer subdued outputs. African Americans interpret European Americans' subdued responses as lifeless and European Americans interpret African Americans' responses as in bad taste.

There are several other areas where European Americans' and African Americans' styles of communication may be problematic when they communicate with each other, particularly in a conflict situation (Kochman, 1981). One area of importance for dealing with conflict is how members of the two groups view their responsibilities for the others' sensibilities and feelings. Differences in this area can be illustrated by reactions to an assignment a professor gives in an interpersonal communication class. Students in the class are told to confront each other and comment on their perceptions of each other's style of communication. The student responses to the assignment divide basically along ethnic lines:

> Twelve of the fourteen [European American] students argued for the right of students *not* to hear what others might want to say about them—thus giving priority to the protection of individual sensibilities, those of others as well as their own, even if this might result in forfeiting their own chance to say what they felt. . . . The eight [African American] students and the remaining two [European American] students, on the other hand, argued for the rights of those students to express what they had to say about others even if the protection of all individual sensibilities would be forfeited in the process. On this last point, one [African American] woman said: "I don't know about others, but if someone has something to say to me, I want to hear it." (Kochman, 1981, pp. 122–123)

Withdrawing the protection of sensibilities is seen as insensitive or cruel by European Americans, and African Americans see European Americans failing to say what they think as lack of concern for their real selves.

"The greater capacity of [African Americans] to express themselves forcefully and to receive and manipulate the forceful assertions of others gives them greater leverage in interracial encounters" (Kochman, 1981, p. 126). When African Americans offend European Americans' social sensibilities, European Americans demand an apology. African Americans see this demand as weak and inappropriate. Part of the difference is in who is considered responsible when people are upset. When European Americans are upset, they tend to see the cause as the other person. African Americans, in contrast, see themselves as responsible for their feelings. African Americans "will commonly say to those who have become angry, '*Others* did not make you angry'; rather, 'You *let yourself* become angry'" (Kochman, 1981, p. 127).

Latino(a) Americans also tend to approach conflict differently than European Americans. The differences can be traced to Latino(a) Americans' communication styles.

> Whereas members of the dominant culture of the United States [i.e., European Americans] are taught to value openness, frankness, and

> directness, the traditional Mexican-American approach requires the use of much diplomacy and tact when communicating with another individual. Concern and respect for the feelings of others dictate that a screen be provided behind which an individual may preserve dignity. . . . The manner of expression is likely to be elaborate and indirect, since the aim is to make the personal relationship at least appear harmonious, to show respect to the other's individuality. To the Mexican-American, direct argument or contradiction appears rude and disrespectful. (Locke, 1992, p. 140)

Latino(a) Americans generally prefer to avoid conflict when possible (e.g., Kagan et al., 1982) and preserve harmony in the relationship (M. Collier, 1991).

The preceding examples are designed only to illustrate the cultural and ethnic differences in the approaches to conflict. It is important to keep in mind, however, that there are differences within ethnic groups. Responses to the class assignment discussed earlier, for example, illustrate that some European Americans share the approach of African American students. The differences should be due to the strength of the individuals' ethnic identities. In conflict situations, it is important to be aware of *potential* cultural or ethnic differences in the approach to conflict, but the focus in resolving the conflict has to be on being mindful of our communication and dealing with the other person as an individual.

One of the major factors that influences members of different ethnic groups' approach to managing conflict is the strength of their cultural and ethnic identities (Ting-Toomey et al., 2000). European Americans, Latino(a) Americans, and Asian Americans who strongly identify with the U.S. culture, for example, use an integrating style more than European Americans, Latino(a) Americans, and Asian Americans who weakly identify with the U.S. culture. Latino(a) Americans who strongly identify with their ethnic group tend to use an emotionally expressive conflict style more than Latino(a) Americans who weakly identify with their ethnic group. African Americans who identify strongly with the U.S. culture tend to use a compromising style more than African Americans who weakly identify with the U.S. culture. African Americans who strongly identify with their ethnic group tend to use an integrating style more than African Americans' who weakly identify with their ethnic group.

Face-Negotiation

Any conflict may threaten the face of one or more of the participants. The concept of face originated in China. Face in China involves "the respectability and/or deference which a person can claim for himself [or herself] from others, by virtue of the relative position he [or she] occupies in his [or her] social network and the degree to which he [or she] is judged to have functioned adequately in that position and acceptability in his [or her] general conduct" (Ho, 1976, p. 883). In China, face is not an "individual thing," but rather it is linked to others in individuals' social networks. In other words, it is based on the interdependent self construal.

Cultural Differences in Face-Concerns

Face in collectivistic cultures is based on the interdependent self construal (Morisaki & Gudykunst, 1994). Writers in the United States, however, often do not emphasize the interdependent basis of face when face is defined. One early conceptualization of face in the United States, for example, defines face as "the positive social value a person effectively claims for himself" or herself (Goffman, 1955, p. 213). This definition links face to the independent self construal (Morisaki & Gudykunst, 1994). Face can be lost, saved, and/or given (Goffman, 1955). Take a few minutes to answer the following questions before reading the remainder of this section.

Do you focus on your face or others' face when you communicate with acquaintances? Why?

____

____

____

What do you do when someone threatens your face? Why?

____

____

____

How do you give others face?

____

____

____

Your answers to these questions should provide some insight into the role of face in your implicit theory of communication. Keep your answers in mind when you read the remainder of this section.

Self-Face Versus Other-Face. A distinction can be drawn between self-face (e.g., our own face) and other-face (e.g., the face of the people with whom we are interacting) (Goffman, 1955). Members of individualistic cultures emphasize self-face maintenance more than members of collectivistic cultures (Ting-Toomey & Kurogi, 1998). Members of collectivistic cultures, in comparison, emphasize other-face maintenance more than members of individualistic cultures.

Chinese, Koreans, and Taiwanese have more other-face concerns than U.S. Americans and Japanese (Ting-Toomey et al., 1991). U.S. Americans, Chinese, Japanese, and Taiwanese, in contrast, have more self-face concerns than Koreans. Chinese have higher other-face concerns than Germans, Japanese, and U.S. Americans; and Japanese have more other-face concerns than Germans (Oetzel et al., 2001). Japanese have less self-face concerns than Chinese, Germans, and U.S. Americans. Japanese also have less self-face concerns than Germans, Mexicans, and U.S. Americans during conflicts with parents and siblings (Oetzel et al., 1999). Self construals, however, are better predictors of face-concerns than cultural individualism-collectivism. Emphasizing independent self construals is associated positively with self-face concern, and emphasizing interdependent self construals is associated positively with other-face and mutual-face concerns (Oetzel et al., 1999, 2000).

Face-concerns are reflected in all aspects of life, including the ways that journalists write about sporting events (Hallahan et al., 1997) and the ways that students deal with teachers in schools (Hwang et al., 2003). Sportswriters in the United States, for example, tend to focus on giving players face by explaining their successes using internal attributions (e.g., their abilities). Sportswriters in Hong Kong, in contrast, tend to focus on protecting players from loss of face by explaining their failures using external causes (e.g., things external to the players or coaches). Students in the United States also tend to try to gain face in their interactions with teachers more than students in Hong Kong or Singapore.

Individualists try to gain face by self-enhancement. Asian collectivists, in contrast, self-efface. Chinese, for example, indicate that they like self-effacing individuals more than self-enhancing individuals (Bond et al., 1982). Chinese self-efface more than they self-enhance, and they self-enhance at much lower rates than individualists (Yik et al., 1998). Given their focus on other-face, when Asians make self-effacing comments they are being modest and expect others to counter their self-effacing comments and give them face. Other-face concerns obligate communicators to give face to those with whom they are interacting. To illustrate, when a Japanese wife serves a guest dinner she might say, "This food is not very good but try it anyway." She really does not believe the food is bad (she would not serve it if she did). Rather, she is expecting the guest to give her face by saying the food is delicious.

U.S. Americans engage in self-enhancement more than Japanese (Kitayama et al., 1997), and more generally individualists engage in self-enhancement more than Asian collectivists (see Heine et al., 1999, for a review). Japanese may not engage in the same levels of self-enhancement as U.S. Americans because Japanese focus on other-face rather more than self-face. Japanese also value individual modesty (Takata, 1987). Modesty involves understating positive traits and abilities in public (Cialdini et al., 1998). Japanese learn to use modest self-presentations between the second and fifth grades (Yoshida et al., 1982). Modesty is associated negatively with self-enhancement (Kurman & Sriram, 2002). Individual modesty, however, would not stop Japanese from engaging in communal or group self-enhancement. Communal self-enhancement is associated positively with emphasizing interdependent self construals, and individual self-enhancement is associated positively with emphasizing independent self construals (Kurman, 2001).

Face in Asian Cultures. Face is particularly important in Asian cultures. There are two types of face in China (Hu, 1944). *Mien-tzu* refers to the social reputation, which is "achieved through getting on in life through success and ostentation" (p. 45). *Lien* "refers to the confidence of society in the integrity of ego's moral character" (p. 61). When individuals lose either type of face, the members of their ingroups also lose face. Similarly, there also are two types of face in Japan: *mentsu* (similar to Chinese *mien-tzu*) and *taimen* (e.g., the appearance we present to others) (Morisaki & Gudykunst, 1994). Both are based on the interdependent self construal.

There also is a distinction between personal and positional face in Korea (Lim & Choi, 1996). Personal face is similar to face in the United States (e.g., it is negotiated in interactions). Positional face, however, is different. Positional face is attached to the position a person fills in the social system (e.g., professor, physician), and people filling the positions are expected to behave in certain ways across situations. The amount of positional face is a function of how high the social position is in the social system. The amount of face attached to a position is static. Individual professors, for example, cannot increase their positional face. All they can do is to maintain or fail to maintain their positional face. They maintain their positional face if they behave in ways that meet the social expectations of professors in Korea (e.g., conducting their lives in a way professors are expected to act).

Engaging in appropriate behavior is important in China. If Chinese behavior is perceived as inappropriate by others, others will make negative remarks about the people engaging in the inappropriate behavior and they will lose face (Gao, 1996). Face need, therefore, is a major factor that regulates behavior in China. Face need also influences self-disclosure in China. To illustrate, Chinese will not expose family disgraces to outsiders because this would lead to loss of face for the family. Face also is reflected in Chinese conversations:

> A: Are you going to see that show on Saturday?
>
> B: I'm afraid not. Because I was invited to a piano recital.
>
> A: I thought you didn't like that kind of music.
>
> B: It's true, but I feel I need to show up to give my friend [face]. (Gao & Ting-Toomey, 1998, p. 56)

In this case, one person's actions (i.e., attending the recital) reflect on another's face (i.e., the person giving the recital). Chinese also employ face to make requests and gain others' compliance (e.g., Please give me face and help my friend).

Chinese students in Hong Kong are empathetic to fellow students (members of an ingroup) who do not perform well on mock presentations, and the students actively try to help the presenters save face (Bond & Lee, 1981). Chinese whose ingroups are insulted engage in rebuttal and retaliation more than Chinese who are insulted personally.

Face-Management. The way that individuals manage their face varies across cultures. U.S. Americans use antisocial, self-presentation, and self-attribution face-maintenance strategies more than Japanese, and Japanese use indirect face-maintenance strategies more than U.S. Americans (Cocroft & Ting-Toomey, 1994). U.S. Americans are more likely than Japanese to use humor and aggression to manage social predicaments, and Japanese are more likely than U.S. Americans to apologize (Cupach & Imahori, 1993). U.S. Americans use humor as a way to maintain face in embarrassing situations more than Japanese. Japanese, in contrast, use remediation (e.g., the correction of behavior) as a way to manage face more than U.S. Americans (Imahori & Cupach, 1994).

Facework tactics are the strategies used to threaten or support others' face and protect self-face when conflicts are managed (Oetzel et al., 1999). Germans and U.S. Americans use direct, confrontational facework tactics (e.g., problem-solving) in conflicts with parents and siblings. Japanese and Mexicans, in contrast, use facework tactics that suggest that the conflict does not exist. In conflicts in general, Chinese use avoiding, obliging, and aggression facework tactics; Germans use direct, confrontational tactics; Japanese use facework tactics that allow them to avoid direct confrontations; and U.S. Americans use respect and expression of feeling facework tactics (Oetzel et al., 2001). Self construals, however, are better predictors of facework tactics than cultural individualism-collectivism. Specifically, emphasizing the independent self construal is associated with using the defending and remaining calm facework tactics. Emphasizing the interdependent self construal is associated positively with using problem-solving, respect, apology, pretending, avoiding, giving in, and third-party facework tactics, and negatively with using the aggression facework tactic (Oetzel et al., 1999, 2001).

Face-concerns and facework tactics also are related (Oetzel et al., 2000). Self-face concerns are associated positively with using aggressive and defensive facework tactics. Other-face concerns, in contrast, are associated positively with using giving in, avoiding, pretending, and third-party facework tactics.

Face and Politeness. Face can be linked to politeness (Brown & Levinson, 1978). Politeness is required when our behavior may threaten someone else's face. There are three situational factors that influence our politeness: social distance, relative power, and how much of an imposition is being made on others. A large social distance between ourselves and the other person, large differences in power between ourselves and others, and/or making large impositions on others can be perceived as face-threatening and require polite behavior.

In determining when to be polite, Koreans are influenced by others' power and the relational distance between themselves and others more than U.S. Americans (Holtgraves & Yang, 1992). U.S. Americans, therefore, may assume a closer distance than Koreans when they interact and use less politeness behavior than Koreans expect. Koreans may interpret the lack of politeness as a claim to greater power in the relationship.

Apologies are one of the major strategies that individuals use to be polite and save face. Both Japanese and U.S. Americans use direct forms of apology. Japanese, however, use a wider variety of apologizing strategies than U.S. Americans, and Japanese adapt their strategies based on others' status more than U.S. Americans (Barnlund & Yoshioka, 1990). The most preferred Japanese strategy for apologizing is offering to do something for the offended person. U.S. Americans, in contrast, prefer to explain their actions when they apologize. Apologies restore relations between people to the way they were before the incident requiring the apology in Japan.

Japanese also use more elaborate apology strategies than U.S. Americans (Sugimoto, 1997). U.S. Americans and Japanese both give accounts to explain the transgression requiring the apology, but their accounts are different. U.S. Americans emphasize that they had no control over the situation or that the offense occurred because they were forgetful. Japanese, in contrast, emphasize that the offense occurred because of uncontrollable forces or that they did not intend to "wrong" the victim. Japanese also use statements of remorse, requests for forgiveness, reparation, compensation, and promise not to repeat the actions more than U.S. Americans.

Ethnic Differences in Face-Concerns

Mexican Americans emphasize other-face concerns less than European Americans when communicating with subordinates (Tata, 2000). When communicating with superiors, in contrast, Mexican Americans emphasize other-face concerns more than European Americans. These results appear to be due to differences in cultural power distance between Mexico and the United States.

The cultural differences in self-enhancement discussed earlier also are reflected in ethnic differences in the United States. European Americans engage in self-enhancement more than Asian Americans (Norasakkunkit & Kalick, 2002). Emphasizing the independent self construal is associated positively with self-enhancement for both groups. Emphasizing the interdependent self construal is not associated with self-enhancement.

Similar to the differences between Japanese and U.S. Americans, Japanese Americans self-efface more than European Americans (Akimoto & Sanbonmatsu, 1999). After completing a task and receiving the same feedback on their performance, Japanese Americans describe their performance "less favorably than European Americans in public but not in private" (p. 159). When the public descriptions of performance are evaluated by others, Japanese Americans are seen as "having performed less well," being "less competent, less likely to be hired, and less likeable" (p. 171). There are several possible explanations for these findings. Japanese Americans, for example, may follow the Japanese pattern of being modest in public. Japanese Americans also may "self-efface in public to gain acceptance by others" (p. 173). This does not appear to work, however, given the evaluations of their descriptions of their performance. Alternatively, Japanese Americans may emphasize other-face so that when they self-efface, they expect others to give them face.

Asian Americans have high face-concerns (Yeh & Huang, 1996). "Face includes the positive image, interpretations, or social attributes that one claims for oneself or perceives others to have accorded one. If one does not fulfill expectations of the self, then one loses face" (p. 651). Asian Americans with high face-concerns are likely to try to conform to interpersonal expectations that others have for them (Shon & Ja, 1982). When Asian Americans have high face-concerns, they tend to use shame to control their own and others' behavior. The fear of loss of face is related to ethnic identities for Chinese immigrants; the stronger their ethnic identities, the greater their face-concerns (Kwan & Sodowsky, 1997).

When individuals lose face, they feel shame or guilt (Morisaki & Gudykunst, 1994). "Guilt accompanies moral transgressions, acts that violate ethical standards" (Liem, 1997, p. 369). Shame, in contrast, "is provoked by exposure of the self to an audience, real or symbolic, in whose eyes the actor [or actress] experiences his or her total being as profoundly flawed" (p. 369). Guilt for European Americans emerges when they do something they know is wrong and no one knows about it. European Americans experience shame as being "embarrassed" or feeling "ashamed." Shame for European Americans emerges when something they do wrong becomes public. European Americans' shame is not shared with others; it is based on the independent self construal. Guilt for Asian Americans emerges from moral transgressions in hierarchical relationships. Asian Americans experience guilt when they feel they have not done their duty. Shame for Asian Americans emerges when the wrongdoing becomes public. Shame for Asian Americans is shared by ingroup members; it is based on the interdependent self construal.

Closely related to shame is embarrassment. Embarrassment involves threats to individuals' public images (e.g., their face). Emphasizing interdependent self construals is associated positively and emphasizing independent self construals is associated negatively with susceptibility to embarrassment across Asian American ethnic groups (Singelis & Sharkey, 1995). When self construals are held constant, European Americans perceive that they are susceptible to embarrassment less than Chinese Americans, Filipino Americans, Japanese Americans, and Korean Americans (there is no difference across Asian American ethnic groups). Self construals, however, are better predictors of susceptibility to embarrassment than ethnicity.

European Americans are less polite than Athapaskan Indians when members of the two groups interact. European Americans' politeness behavior is guided by how close they think they are to the other person. They often use less politeness than Athapaskan Indians expect. The Athapaskan Indians interpret the lack of politeness as being due to the European Americans' thinking they are culturally superior (Scollon & Scollon, 1981).

Face and Conflict

Face-concerns influence the ways that we deal with conflicts (Ting-Toomey & Kurogi, 1998). "In any conflict situation, conflict parties have to consider protecting self-interest conflict goals and honoring or attacking another person's conflict goals" (p. 188). This involves honoring or attacking the other's face.

Our orientation toward face-concerns (e.g., self-face concerns, other-face concerns) influences the conflict styles we tend to use. When our concern is with self-face maintenance, we tend to use dominating and competing conflict styles (Ting-Toomey et al., 1991) and confrontational facework tactics (Ting-Toomey & Kurogi, 1998). When our concern is with other-face maintenance, we tend to use avoiding, integrating, and compromising conflict styles (Ting-Toomey et al., 1991) and relational smoothing conflict tactics (Ting-Toomey & Kurogi, 1998).

Assessing Your Face-Concerns

The questionnaire in Table 8.2 is designed to help you assess your self-face and other-face concerns when managing conflicts. Take a few minutes to complete it now.

Scores for self-face concerns and other-face concerns range from 5 to 25. The higher your scores, the more you are concerned with self-face and other-face concerns when managing conflicts. If your scores are low on either scale, remember that you can focus on this face-concern when you are mindful. Individualists who score low on other-face concerns, for example, can pay attention to this type of face when they are mindful.

Characteristics of Intergroup Conflict

Intergroup conflict is occurring at alarming rates throughout the world today. Understanding why intergroup conflict occurs and the ways that members of different groups manage conflict is necessary if these conflicts are to be handled constructively. Some aspects of intergroup conflict are similar in kind to interpersonal conflict, but there are important differences: "Intergroup conflict is, by definition, a collective phenomenon, and requires a suitably collective 'model of [humans].' The psychological factors associated with intergroup hostility are best sought in *collective* social cognition and motivation. It is an important task . . . to examine the relationship between individual drives and cognition and those associated with the groups to which they belong" (Condor & Brown, 1988,

TABLE 8.2 *Assessing Your Face Concerns*

The purpose of this questionnaire is to assess your self-face concern and other-face concern when managing conflicts. Respond to each statement by indicating the degree to which it is true regarding how you think or behave when you manage conflict with strangers: "Always False" (answer 1), "Usually False" (answer 2), "Sometimes True and Sometimes False" (answer 3), "Usually True" (answer 4), or "Always True" (answer 5).

_____ 1. I support how the other person views him- or herself when I manage conflicts.
_____ 2. I am concerned about my reputation when I manage conflicts.
_____ 3. I protect the other person's self-image when I manage conflicts.
_____ 4. I work toward a solution that allows me to feel good about myself when I manage conflicts.
_____ 5. I make sure I do not insult the other person when I manage conflicts.
_____ 6. I worry about whether the other person respects me when I manage conflicts.
_____ 7. I work toward a solution that allows the other person to feel good about her- or himself when I manage conflicts.
_____ 8. I protect my self-image when I manage conflicts.
_____ 9. I demonstrate that I respect the other person when I manage conflicts.
_____ 10. I make sure the other person does not insult me when I manage conflicts.

To find your other-face concern score, add the numbers next to the odd numbered items. To find your self-face concern score, add the numbers next to the even numbered items. Both scores range from 5 to 25. The higher your score, the more you are concerned with self-face or other-face when managing conflicts.

p. 19). Intergroup conflicts, therefore, are different from interpersonal conflicts.

There are several characteristics of interethnic conflict that appear to apply to other forms of intergroup conflicts as well (Landis & Boucher, 1987). First, intergroup conflicts involve perceived (not necessarily real) group differences that lead to the activation of social identities and stereotypes. Second, intergroup conflicts often involve claims to a given territory. Third, intergroup conflicts tend to be based on group differences in power and resources. Fourth, intergroup conflicts may involve disagreements over language usage or language policies. Fifth, intergroup conflicts are affected by group differences in the process preferred for resolving conflicts (e.g., members of one culture may prefer to resolve conflicts through a third party, while members of another culture do not use third parties and prefer direct confrontation). Sixth, intergroup conflicts often are exacerbated by religious differences. Conflicts are intensified, for example, when religious differences are compounded with other group differences (e.g., in Sri Lanka the Tamil-Sinhalese conflict is intensified because Tamils are Hindu and Sinhalese are Buddhists).

Social categorization leads individuals to make evaluative judgments about members of the ingroups and outgroups (Lilli & Rehm, 1988). **When intergroup conflict occurs, social categorizations are particularly important and this heightens the ingroup bias.** Social categorizations lead to emphasizing social identities over personal identities. When social identities are enhanced by intergroup comparisons, the devaluation of outgroups can lead to conflict. The persistence of "being negatively categorized (labeled) may cause conflicts" (Lilli & Rehm, 1988, p. 35). Social categorizations also lead to deindividuation. Deindividuation can initiate conflicts or escalate conflicts that already exist. Social categorization also influences the way information about outgroups is processed; it is simplified (e.g., outgroups are seen as homogeneous and only stereotypical information about outgroups is obtained). Simplified information processing can lead to arguments that maintain and justify conflicts.

Conflict between groups is influenced by the attitudes members of one group have toward members of different groups (Sherif, 1966). "The attitudes of members of different groups towards one another are set by the functional relations between the groups" (p. 63). Competition for scarce resources leads to bias against outgroups (e.g., prejudice, negative stereotypes). The resources over which groups compete vary from concrete resources such as territory to abstract resources such as status. Competition does not emerge between groups when their goals are complementary (i.e., each group can reach its goals without help from the other groups). The more ingroup members perceive threats from outgroup members and have conflicts with outgroup members, the more hostility ingroup members have toward outgroup members. Intergroup cooperation emerges when the members of ingroups and outgroups work on superordinate goals (e.g., groups can achieve mutually desirable goals only by working together).

Threats to subgroup identities (e.g., ethnic identities, religious identities) are one of the largest obstacles to harmony between social groups (Hornsey & Hogg, 2000a). "Social arrangements that threaten social identity produce defensive reactions that result in conflict" (p. 143). Harmony between social groups is facilitated by "maintaining, not weakening, subgroup identities, and locating them in the context of a binding superordinate identity" (e.g., a cultural identity; p. 143).

We react more negatively to intergroup and international (e.g., between nations) conflicts than interpersonal conflicts (Derlega et al., 2002). Our interdependent self construals moderate our responses to different types of conflicts. People with strong interdependent self construals view threats as a more appropriate response to international conflicts than interpersonal conflicts. They also view accepting others' demands as a less appropriate response in international conflicts than in interpersonal conflicts. People with weak interdependent self construals, in contrast, respond to international and interpersonal conflicts similarly.

There are three general goals we might have in conflict situations: (1) resource goals, which involve conflict outcomes, (2) relational goals, which involve maintaining our relationships with people with whom we have conflicts, and (3) identity goals, which involve issues of self-esteem and face (Obuchi et al., 1996). Protecting face and maintaining relationships motivate us when we have relationships with the people with whom we have conflicts but not when we do not have relationships with the people with whom we have conflicts. We tend to be motivated by resource goals when we do not have relationships with the people with whom we have conflicts. This makes managing conflicts difficult (Leung & Chan, 1999).

One of the major differences between intragroup (e.g., ingroup, interpersonal) and intergroup (e.g., outgroup) conflict is the extent to which we are concerned with the quality of our relationship with the people with whom we have conflicts (e.g., treating strangers in a dignified manner, paying attention to their needs). We are concerned with our relationships in intragroup conflicts more than in intergroup conflicts (Tyler et al., 1998). This pattern appears to generalize across cultures.

Intergroup contact often is promoted as a way to manage intergroup conflicts. The contact hypothesis suggests that when contact takes place under favorable conditions (e.g., equal status, intimate contact, rewarding contact; see Chapter 4), contact leads to decreases in prejudice and discrimination. Contact under favorable conditions reduces intergroup hostilities across ethnic groups in the United States (Tzeng & Jackson, 1994).

Perceptions that the ingroup's norms have been violated lead members of ingroups to make negative attributions about outgroups (DeRidder & Tripathi, 1992). The negative attributions that ingroup members make lead outgroup members to make negative inferences about ingroup members. Norm violations, therefore, can lead to cycles of escalating conflict. Escalations are most likely when individuals strongly identify with their ingroups, when negative intergroup attitudes exist, when one group has feelings of relative deprivation, and when the group violating the norms has power over the group whose norms are violated.

Managing Intergroup Conflict

In many ways, managing conflict with members of other groups is similar to managing conflict with members of our own groups. To manage conflicts successfully with members of other groups, however, requires that we adapt our behavior in at least three ways. First, we must take strangers' group memberships into consideration. When managing interpersonal conflicts, we must focus on the other person as an individual. When managing conflicts with members of other groups, we must take the strangers' group memberships into consideration *and* understand the specific strangers with whom we have conflicts. Second, we must be aware of how our expectations for strangers' groups influence our communication. Our expectations (e.g., ethnocentrism, prejudice, stereotypes) influence how we interpret the strangers' messages when we are on automatic pilot. To manage conflict successfully, we must set our group-based expectations aside, understand real group differences, and focus on understanding strangers' perspectives on the conflict. To do this, we must be mindful. Third, we must adapt our style of communication. If strangers are collectivists, for example, they may prefer to avoid the conflict. If we are individualists and think it is important to address the conflict, we need to adapt our style of communication to accommodate to the collectivists (e.g., be more indirect than we usually are). We also must take strangers' group memberships into consideration in interpreting their messages.

Assessing How You Manage Conflict

Before discussing how to manage intergroup conflict, I want you to get a feel for how you typically manage conflict. The questionnaire in Table 8.3 is designed to help you assess how you manage conflict with strangers. Take a few minutes to complete it now.

Scores on the questionnaire range from 10 to 50. The higher your score, the greater your potential for successfully managing conflict with strangers. If your score is low, remember that managing conflict successfully requires that you be mindful of the *process* of your communication. When you are mindful, you may want to keep the material discussed in the remainder of this section in mind when you try to manage intergroup conflict.

Constructive Versus Destructive Conflict Management

When we try to manage conflict, our goals should be to "reach agreement" and, at the same time, "enhance the relationship" (Hocker & Wilmot,

TABLE 8.3 *Assessing Your Management of Conflict With Strangers**

The purpose of this questionnaire is to help you assess your ability to manage conflict with strangers successfully. Respond to each statement by indicating the degree to which it is true regarding how you manage conflict with strangers: "Always False" (answer 1), "Usually False" (answer 2), "Sometimes True and Sometimes False" (answer 3), "Usually True" (answer 4), or "Always True" (answer 5).

_____ 1. I respond emotionally when I have conflict with strangers.
_____ 2. I try to understand strangers with whom I am having a conflict.
_____ 3. If strangers reject my ideas during a conflict, I also reject theirs.
_____ 4. I act reliably (i.e., consistently) when trying to manage conflict with strangers.
_____ 5. I try to get strangers to agree with me when we have a conflict.
_____ 6. I balance emotion with reason when trying to manage conflicts with strangers.
_____ 7. I am not open to being persuaded when I have conflict with strangers.
_____ 8. I consult strangers before deciding on matters that affect them.
_____ 9. I am not as constructive as I could be when I have conflict with strangers.
_____ 10. I try to do what is best for the relationship, even if the strangers with whom I am having a conflict do not reciprocate.

To find your score, first reverse the responses for the odd numbered items (i.e., if you wrote 1, make it 5; if you wrote 2, make it 4; if you wrote 3, leave it as 3; if you wrote 4, make it 2; if you wrote 5, make it 1). Next, add the numbers next to each statement. Scores range from 10 to 50. The higher your score, the greater your potential to manage conflict with strangers successfully.

*Adapted from Fisher and Brown (1988).

1991, p. 64). These goals can be accomplished only if we manage conflict constructively. Conflicts can be classified as constructive or destructive based on the process used in managing them and the outcomes of the conflict (Johnson & Johnson, 1982). With respect to the *process,* our management of conflicts is *constructive* if we define conflicts as mutual problems, and we define them as "win-win" situations. We must express our ideas openly and honestly, and we must view ourselves and strangers as equals. Strangers' positions must be taken seriously, valued, and respected for conflict to be managed constructively. In constructive conflict management, we must use effective communication skills such as active listening and perception checking so that differences in our opinions and strangers' opinions can be clarified and understood. We must express our assumptions and perspectives on the problem and not take disagreements as rejection. Finally, similarities in our positions and strangers' positions on the conflict must be understood and integrated so that we work toward mutually satisfying solutions.

The *processes* involved in the *destructive* management of conflict are the opposite of those involved in the constructive management of conflict (Johnson & Johnson, 1982). Conflicts are *destructive* when we do *not* define them as mutual problems and we define them as "win-lose" situations. When we manage conflicts destructively, we are *not* open, or are deceitful, and we do not view strangers as our equals or respect strangers' ideas. In destructive conflict management, we do *not* use effective communication skills, and differences between our opinions and strangers' opinions are suppressed or ignored. We also do *not* clarify our assumptions or perspectives on the problem and we take disagreements as rejection in destructive conflict management. Finally, when we manage conflict destructively, we do *not* understand similarities in our positions and strangers' positions or try to integrate them, and we do *not* work toward mutually satisfying solutions.

With respect to *outcomes,* conflicts are *constructive* when we feel understood by strangers, we think we influenced strangers and they influenced us, we are committed to the solution, we are satisfied with the decision, we feel accepted by strangers, and our abilities to manage future conflicts are increased (Johnson & Johnson, 1982). Conflicts have *destructive outcomes* when we do *not* feel understood by strangers, we think we had little influence on strangers, we are *not* committed to the solution, we are *not* satisfied with the solution, we do *not* feel accepted, and our abilities to manage future conflicts are decreased. The outcomes have consequences beyond the immediate conflict situation. When members of different groups negotiate mutually satisfactory outcomes in an intergroup conflict situations, it leads to better relations between the groups (Thompson, 1993).

When we communicate on automatic pilot, many of us tend to manage conflict destructively. We can, however, change the way we manage conflict when we are mindful. One of the guiding principles we need to follow when we are mindful is to be unconditionally constructive.

Developing Supportive Climates

As indicated earlier, it is not conflict per se that is positive or negative. How we manage the conflict, however, can have positive or negative consequences for our relationships. Take a few minutes to answer the following questions about when you feel defensive and when you feel supported before you read the remainder of this section.

How do others communicate with you that makes you feel defensive?

____

____

____

How do others communicate with you that makes you feel supported?

____

____

____

How does feeling defensive or supported influence the way you communicate?

____

____

____

Your answers to these questions should provide some insight into the role of being supportive in your implicit theory of communication. Keep your answers in mind as you read the remainder of this section.

In managing conflict with strangers, or with people from our own groups, it is important that we establish supportive climates (Gibb, 1961). Supportive climates involve being descriptive, using a problem orientation, being spontaneous, being empathic, treating others as equals, and provisionalism. Defensive climates, in contrast, involve being evaluative, using a control orientation, being strategic, being neutral, acting superior to others, and certainty.

The first characteristic of supportive climates is *description* rather than evaluation (Gibb, 1961). We cannot understand strangers if we evaluate them before we understand their positions. Using evaluative speech brings up strangers' defenses. Descriptive speech, in contrast, does not make strangers uneasy and, in addition, it allows us to find out how strangers are interpreting what is happening.

Taking a *problem orientation* is the second characteristic of supportive climates (Gibb, 1961). Defining a mutual problem and expressing a willingness to collaborate in finding a solution implies that we have no predetermined outcome we want to see. If we have a predetermined outcome in mind and try to force this outcome on strangers, we are trying to control them. Attempts to control strangers are inevitably met with resistance.

SKILL EXERCISE 8.1 *Developing Supportive Climates*

Imagine that you are preparing to write a joint paper with a member of a different ethnic group in one of your intercultural communication classes (there is no choice, it must be a joint paper). The purpose of the paper is to analyze the interactions the two of you have had over the semester. You are beginning to discuss what to include in the paper. What could you say that presents this using a *problem orientation* rather than a control orientation?

____

____

____

Your partner suggests that you divide the paper into two parts and you each write your part. You do not think this is a good idea. How could you respond using a *descriptive* response rather than an evaluative one?

____

____

____

When discussing the outline for the paper, the two of you disagree on the importance of different aspects of your interaction. Your partner says that you've already made up your mind and are just trying to convince him or her what to discuss. What could you say that involves *being spontaneous* rather than strategic?

____

____

____

Your partner asks you to tell her or him your perception of what happened when you first met. You have a strong opinion that you should focus on the anxiety and uncertainty during this meeting, but also think that your partner may have different ideas. What might you say that reflects being *provisional* rather than showing a certainty orientation?

____

____

____

Your partner says that it is important to him or her that she or he gets an "A" on the paper. The grade is not that important to you; you just want to get it done. How might you respond to your partner showing *empathy* rather than neutrality?

____

____

____

Being spontaneous, as opposed to being strategic, is the third characteristic of supportive climates (Gibb, 1961). If we appear to have hidden motives and are acting in what appears to be a strategic way to strangers, they will become defensive. If we appear spontaneous and not strategic to strangers, on the other hand, they will not get defensive.

Empathy also is important in establishing supportive climates (Gibb, 1961). As indicated in the previous chapter, if we convey empathy in our communication with strangers, strangers will know that we are concerned with their welfare. If we appear neutral toward strangers, they will become defensive.

The fifth characteristic of a supportive climate is communicating that we are *equal* (Gibb, 1961). If we talk in a way that strangers perceive as sounding superior, they will become defensive. If we truly want to manage conflicts with strangers, we must avoid communicating at the distances of indifference, avoidance, and disparagement, and communicate at a distance of sensitivity or equality.

The final characteristic of a supportive climate is *provisionalism* (Gibb, 1961). If we communicate to strangers that we are open to their viewpoints and willing to experiment with our behavior (i.e., try to change it if needed), strangers will not become defensive. If, on the other hand, we communicate in such a way that indicates that we think we are right and certain of our attitudes and behavior, strangers will become defensive.

Skill Exercise 8.1 provides an opportunity to practice being supportive. Take a few minutes to complete it now.

Creating supportive climates is critical to managing conflict constructively. Most of us, however, do not tend to do this when we communicate on automatic pilot. Creating supportive climates requires that we are mindful of our communication.

Being Unconditionally Constructive

One participant can change a relationship (Fisher & Brown, 1988). If we change the way we react to strangers, they will change the way they react to us. The objective of change is developing "a relationship that can deal with differences" (p. 3). Achieving change requires that we separate relationship and substantive issues and pursue goals in each arena separately.

A prescriptive approach to effective negotiations suggests that we should always be unconditionally constructive (Fisher & Brown, 1988).

> Do only those things that are both good for the relationship and good for us, whether or not they reciprocate.

> 1. Rationality. Even if they are acting emotionally, balance emotion with reason.
>
> 2. Understanding. Even if they misunderstand us, try to understand them.
>
> 3. Communication. Even if they are not listening, consult them before deciding on matters that affect them.
>
> 4. Reliability. Even if they are trying to deceive us, neither trust nor deceive them; be reliable.
>
> 5. Noncoercive modes of influence. Even if they are trying to coerce us, neither yield to that coercion nor try to coerce them; be open to persuasion and try to persuade them.
>
> 6. Acceptance. Even if they reject us and our concerns as unworthy of their consideration, accept them as worthy of our consideration, care about them, and be open to learning from them. (Fisher & Brown, 1988, p. 38)

Few, if any, of us follow the six guidelines in our normal, everyday communication with strangers.

In order to apply these guidelines, we must be mindful. "What is unconscious is not within a person's control, but what is made conscious is available for human beings to understand, to change, or to reinforce" (Brodie, 1989, p. 16).

Communicating to Manage Conflict

The first step in managing conflicts is to *approach* strangers regarding the conflict (Johnson, 1986). The goal of approaching strangers is to clarify and explore the issues surrounding the conflict. We should approach strangers when we are sure that we are both available to discuss the conflict (e.g., neither is emotionally upset, both have time). When we approach strangers, we need to express our thoughts and feelings about the conflict and ask them to do the same. We should *not* try to manage the conflict when we approach strangers, but rather schedule a time when we can negotiate. We need to manage conflicts when both strangers and we are prepared and there is sufficient time. Strangers will not be ready to manage conflict with us when we approach them because it will probably be the first time they have heard about the conflict. To be effective, our approach needs to be done in a way that does *not* increase strangers' anxiety or defensiveness and allows them to maintain their self-concepts. This involves using the skills discussed throughout the book.

To manage intergroup conflict successfully we need to be *cooperative,* not competitive (Deutsch, 1973). This means that we need to define conflicts as *mutual problems* for both ourselves and strangers that need to be solved. When conflicts are defined as mutual problems to be solved, we can "win" and strangers can "win." In addition to defining conflicts as mutual problems, we need to look for a *common definition of the problem.* If we do not agree with strangers on the definition of problems, we cannot solve them. We also need to define problems in the most limited ways possible. If it is a big problem, we can break it down into smaller ones, and deal with each of them, one at a time.

In addition to cooperation, we need to try to communicate as effectively as possible. There are two sides to effective communication. We need to *adapt our messages* so that strangers can accurately interpret them. One of the major ways we can adapt our messages is to use concrete language rather than abstract language. Abstract language is open to interpretation, and strangers' interpretations often are different from ours. To illustrate, imagine your romantic partner says "You don't love me anymore." You respond "Yes, I love you." If you continue to use the abstract word "love," you will never agree. Obviously, there are differences in what "love" means to the two of you. To manage this situation, one of you must use concrete language to describe what you mean when you say "love."

Skill Exercise 8.2 provides an opportunity to practice using concrete language. Take a few minutes to complete it now.

The critical thing in adapting our messages is that we use language that is sufficiently concrete for others to attach similar meaning to the words that we do. This often does not occur with abstract language, especially when the participants have different native languages.

To communicate effectively, we also need to make sure that we *understand strangers'* positions and their messages. This requires that our perceptions be as accurate as possible. We can decrease the distortions and biases in our perceptions by using the perception checking and active listening skills discussed in Chapter 5, and the empathy skill discussed in Chapter 7. When our perceptions are distorted, we perceive that strangers have negative and hostile feelings toward us, and do not perceive the positive feelings they have. This can lead to a self-fulfilling prophecy, if we are not mindful.

Race and ethnicity "issues often pervade conflicts [with strangers], whether they are at the center of the dispute, an unacknowledged part of a specific conflict, or part of a general societal backdrop of unequal power and respect" (Stephan & Stephan, 2001, p. 203). We may have to directly address negative intergroup attitudes and stereotypes directly with strangers in order to minimize their influence on managing conflict with strangers (Craver, 1997).

To manage conflicts constructively we must *recognize differences* between our positions and strangers' positions. If we do not understand strangers' positions and they do not understand our positions, there is

SKILL EXERCISE 8.2 *Using Concrete Language*

Using abstract language can contribute to misunderstandings. Indicate concrete language that could be used in each of the situations below to increase the effectiveness of communication (using what the abstract words mean to you).

You are discussing a mutual friend, Pat, with a member of another ethnic group. The other person says "Pat is a very friendly person." You do not think Pat is friendly at all. How might you respond using concrete language?

____

____

____

An international student approaches you after class one day saying "The professor's grading system is very unfair." You think the instructor's grading system is "fair." How can you respond to the other student using concrete language to indicate that the instructor's grading is "fair" (use your concept of fair grading).

____

____

____

You are talking with an acquaintance from another ethnic group and you say that you think Kim, another acquaintance, is very aggressive. The other person says that he or she does not think that Kim is aggressive at all. How can you explain your position using concrete language?

____

____

____

no way we can find a solution acceptable to them and us. To manage conflict successfully we must be able to predict and explain strangers' behavior accurately. We also have to make it clear to strangers that we are interested in finding a solution that is fair to them and us.

Recognizing similarities and not just focusing on differences is necessary to manage conflict successfully. If we focus only on differences between our positions and strangers' positions, we will never be able to manage the conflict. Finding solutions that will work for them and us requires that we see similarities in our positions and then build on these similarities. In defining the problem, we need to understand how our behavior has helped create the problem, and make sure we understand strangers' positions. To manage conflicts successfully, both parties must understand and see similarities in each other's positions and feelings.

To manage conflicts successfully, we must be able to disagree with strangers and at the same time *confirm* them and their views of themselves. If we treat strangers as though they are not valued, they will become defensive and their anxiety will increase. Conflicts cannot be managed constructively when either party is defensive. Confirming strangers requires that we adapt our styles of communication.

Individualists and collectivists often need to adapt their behavior when they have a conflict (Ting-Toomey, 1994). Individualists can make several adaptations that will increase the likelihood of success in managing conflicts with collectivists. First, individualists need to remember that collectivists use interdependent self construals. Their actions reflect on their ingroup and they have to take their ingroups into consideration in managing conflicts. Second, individualists should try to deal with conflicts when they are small, rather than allow them to become large issues, and recognize that collectivists may want to use a third party to mediate the conflict. Third, individualists need to help the collectivists maintain face during the conflict. This means not humiliating or embarrassing collectivists in public. Fourth, individualists need to pay attention to collectivists' nonverbal behavior and pay attention to implicit messages. Fifth, individualists need to listen actively when collectivists talk. Sixth, individualists need to use indirect messages more than they typically do. This means using qualifier words (e.g., maybe, possibly), being more tentative, and avoiding bluntly saying no. Seventh, individualists need to let go of conflict if collectivists do not want to deal with it (recall that avoiding is the preferred collectivist strategy).

Collectivists also need to make adaptations when managing conflicts with individualists (Ting-Toomey, 1994). First, collectivists need to recognize that individualists often separate the conflict from the person with whom they are having conflict. Second, collectivists need to focus on the substantive issues involved in the conflict. Third, collectivists need to use an assertive, rather than nonassertive, style when dealing with conflict. Fourth, collectivists need to be more direct than they usually are. This involves using more "I" statements and directly stating opinions and feelings. Fifth, collectivists need to provide verbal feedback to individualists and focus on the verbal aspects of communication more than they typically do. Sixth, collectivists need to recognize that individualists do not value silence in conversations. Seventh, collectivists need to try to manage conflicts when they arise, rather than avoiding them.

Finally, we may have to coordinate our motivations to manage the conflict. We may be ready to manage the conflict today, but strangers are

SKILL EXERCISE 8.3 *Managing Conflict Constructively*

The purpose of this exercise is to give you an opportunity to think about how to manage conflict constructively. Read the following scenario and answer the questions posed.

You are working on a class project with Jasmine, a member of another ethnic group. Jasmine is always late for meetings, missed the last meeting entirely, and never has the work done that she has agreed to do. You think that Jasmine doesn't care about the class project. You are tired of doing all of the work and you decide to confront Jasmine about the problem.

How can you approach Jasmine about the conflict?

____

____

____

How can you define the conflict as a mutual problem?

____

____

____

How would you communicate your position and feelings to Jasmine?

____

____

____

How would you communicate your cooperative intentions to Jasmine?

____

____

____

How would you make sure you understand Jasmine's perspective?

____

____

____

not. Tomorrow strangers may be ready and we are not. We can, however, consciously change our own motivation if we choose. *Reaching an agreement* occurs when we have a joint solution. Our agreement should specify how each person will act differently in the future, including both new things that they will do in the future and things that will be avoided (e.g., criticism).

Skill Exercise 8.3 is designed to give you a chance to think about how to manage conflict constructively. Take a few minutes to complete it now.

Most of us have not been taught to manage conflict constructively. To manage conflict constructively we must learn new scripts and develop new attitudes toward conflicts (e.g., that both parties can "win"). We must find solutions that are acceptable to both parties. If we do not find solutions acceptable to both parties, the way we manage the conflict will cause problems in our relationships with others.

To conclude, most of us tend to avoid conflicts with strangers. Avoiding conflicts may not create any problems in our relationships with strangers if the conflicts are small and the issues involved are not important to us or strangers. If the conflicts are large or the issues involved are important to us or strangers, however, we need to try to manage the conflicts so they will not create problems in our relationships with strangers.

Study Questions

1. What are the major sources of conflicts with strangers?
2. How are the assumptions that individualists and collectivists make about conflict different?
3. How do the conflict styles used by individualists and collectivists differ?
4. How does ingroup and outgroup status influence conflict processes?
5. What are the general differences in how members of different ethnic groups manage conflicts?
6. How do face-concerns differ across cultures?
7. How do face-concerns influence the ways we manage conflict?
8. What are the characteristics of intergroup conflict?
9. How do our goals influence our approaches to conflict?

10. What are the characteristics of constructive and destructive approaches to conflict?
11. How can we develop supportive climates to manage conflict?
12. Why do we need to be unconditionally constructive when managing conflicts?
13. What do we want to do when we first approach others about a conflict?
14. What is the general process we can use to manage conflicts with strangers?
15. What adjustments do individualists and collectivists have to make to manage conflicts successfully with each other?

Applications

1. Over the next week, pay attention to your conflicts with others. How do you typically deal with these conflicts? Do you handle conflicts differently with different people? How does the way you handle conflicts affect your relationships with others?

2. Over the next week, try to construct a supportive climate when you communicate with a specific stranger. How does this influence your communication with this stranger? How does it influence the stranger's communication with you?

3. The next time you have a conflict apply the suggestions presented in this chapter. What effect does this have on your ability to manage the conflict? Why does the process work or why does it not work?

Notes

1. My focus below is on European American-African American differences. Japanese American, Chinese American, and Mexican American patterns are similar to the cultural differences cited above. For other examples, see Boucher et al. (1987), and Strobe et al. (1988).

2. Kochman's European American respondents may have been middle class and his African American respondents lower class. Social class, therefore, must be considered when interpreting the findings reported.

CHAPTER 9

Developing Relationships With Strangers

In the previous two chapters, I discussed how we can be perceived as competent communicators and manage conflict constructively when we communicate with strangers. If we have the motivation, knowledge, and skills to communicate effectively and appropriately, and we can manage conflicts with strangers, we have the basis for establishing ongoing relationships with strangers. In this chapter, I examine how we develop interpersonal and romantic relationships with strangers. To put this discussion in context, however, it is necessary to begin with a discussion of how communication in interpersonal relationships is similar and different across cultures and ethnic groups.

Similarities and Differences Across Groups

Before we can understand how we form relationships with strangers, we need to recognize how communication in relationships is similar and different across cultures and ethnic groups. In this section, I focus on similarities and differences in perceptions of the intimacy of our relationships, self-disclosure, and anxiety/uncertainty management, as well as how communication rules in relationships are similar and different.

Intimacy of Relationships

There are differences and similarities in how people communicate in interpersonal relationships across cultures. Japanese, for example, perceive ingroup relationships (e.g., co-worker and university classmate) to be more intimate than U.S. Americans (Gudykunst & Nishida, 1986b). The differences in perceived intimacy of relationships affect the way people communicate.[1] To illustrate, Japanese communicate more personally with members of their ingroups than with members of outgroups. U.S. Americans, in contrast, communicate with members of ingroups and outgroups relatively similarly, except when outgroup membership is determined by cultural background or ethnicity (Gudykunst & Hammer, 1988a).

In addition to the cultural differences in perceived intimacy, there are many similarities across cultures. People in Japan and the United States, for example, rate relationships with people they have never met as less intimate than relationships with acquaintances, relationships with acquaintances as less intimate than relationships with friends, and relationships with friends as less intimate than relationships with close friends (Gudykunst & Nishida, 1986a). The similarities in the perceived intimacy of relationships are manifested in our communication. Communication in both cultures becomes more personal as the perceived intimacy of the relationship increases (Gudykunst & Nishida, 1986a, 1986b). To illustrate, we talk about more intimate things about ourselves with friends than with acquaintances.

Elementary Forms of Social Relationships

There are four elementary forms of human relations: communal sharing, equality matching, authority ranking, and market pricing (Fiske, 1991). *Communal sharing* is "a relationship of equivalence in which people are merged (for the purpose at hand) so that the boundaries of individual selves are indistinct" (p. 13). *Equality matching* is an equal relationship between people who are distinct from each other and they are peers. *Authority ranking* is an asymmetrical relationship between two people who are not equals. *Market pricing* is a relationship mediated by the values of some "market system." The market system, for example, might be based on people's actions, services, or products. These four models provide the basic "grammars" for social relationships, and they give order to the way individuals think about their social interactions. The four elementary forms of social behavior are the basis for all other types of relationships, and are universal across cultures.

All forms of behavior can be used in any situation in any culture (Fiske, 1991). Members of cultures, however, learn preferences for particular forms of behavior in particular situations. People in collectivistic cultures learn to use communal sharing and authority ranking more than equality matching and market pricing (Triandis, 1994). Members of individualistic cultures, in contrast, learn to use equality matching and market pricing more than the other two. Authority ranking also can be seen to vary as a function of power distance (Triandis, 1994). Market pricing appears to be related to a masculine orientation, and equality matching is related to a feminine orientation (Smith & Bond, 1993).

Anxiety/Uncertainty Management

Effective interpersonal and intergroup communication is a function of how individuals manage the anxiety and uncertainty they experience when communicating with others (Gudykunst, 1995). As indicated in Chapter 1, *uncertainty* involves individuals' abilities to predict and/or explain others' feelings, attitudes, and behavior (Berger & Calabrese, 1975). Managing uncertainty is a cognitive process. The reduction of uncertainty leads to changes in the nature of the communication that takes place; for example, it brings about increases in the amount of communication and increases in the amount of interpersonal attraction (Berger & Calabrese, 1975). If the amount of uncertainty present in initial interactions is not reduced, further communication between the people will, in all likelihood, not take place.

Anxiety is the affective equivalent of uncertainty. It stems from feeling uneasy, tense, worried, or apprehensive about what might happen and is based on a fear of potential negative consequences (Stephan & Stephan, 1985). Members of high uncertainty avoidance cultures experience higher anxiety in communicating with strangers than do members of low uncertainty avoidance cultures (Gudykunst, 1995). You might want to look back at the factors you said caused you anxiety and uncertainty in Chapter 1 before reading the remainder of this section.

Cultural Differences in Uncertainty. Typical patterns of initial interactions used in the individualistic culture of the United States may not generalize to collectivistic cultures (Gudykunst, 1983c). Members of collectivistic cultures reduce uncertainty in initial interactions, but the nature of the information they seek is different from the information sought when two people meet for the first time in the United States. Since much of the information necessary for communication in collectivistic cultures resides in the context or is internalized in the individual (as opposed to being mostly in the message in individualistic cultures), members of collectivistic cultures are cautious concerning what they talk about with people they do not know more than members of individualistic cultures.

Members of collectivistic cultures make assumptions about others based on cultural background more than members of individualistic cultures (Gudykunst, 1983c). Members of collectivistic cultures ask questions about others' backgrounds more than members of individualistic cultures. It is the background information that allows members of collectivistic cultures to determine whether or not a person is indeed unknown or a member of an ingroup who has not been met before (Nakane, 1974).

Members of individualistic cultures seek out person-based information to reduce uncertainty about people they have not met more than members of collectivistic cultures (Gudykunst & Nishida, 1986a). The *person-based* information used to reduce uncertainty involves knowing others' attitudes, beliefs, feelings, values, and past behavior. **Members of collectivistic cultures seek out group-based and situation-based information to reduce uncertainty more than members of individualistic cultures** (Gudykunst & Nishida, 1986a). The *group-based* information used to reduce uncertainty involves knowing others' ages, statuses, schools, hometown, and group memberships. The focus on person-based information leads members of individualistic cultures to search for personal similarities when communicating with outgroup members more than members of collectivistic cultures (Gudykunst, 1995). The focus on group-based information, in contrast, leads members of collectivistic cultures to search for group similarities when communicating with outgroup members more than members of individualistic cultures.

U.S. Americans find that individuating information (e.g., individuals' beliefs and accomplishments) is more useful than relational information (e.g., group memberships and social status) in "predicting how others will behave and their degree of trustworthiness" (Gelfand et al., 2000, p. 509). The Chinese, in contrast, find relational information more useful than individuating information in predicting others' behavior.

There also are differences in how members of individualistic and collectivistic cultures explain others' behavior. **Members of collectivistic cultures emphasize the importance of context in explaining others' behavior more than members of individualistic cultures** (e.g., Kashima et al., 1992). Members of collectivistic cultures use situation-based information to make social inferences more than members of individualistic cultures when situational information is salient (Norenzayan et al., 2002). The emphasis on context in collectivistic cultures affects other aspects of communication as well. To illustrate, adapting and accommodating to the context in which they are communicating are important parts of the high-context communication patterns used in collectivistic cultures (Hall, 1976).

Cultural individualism-collectivism also influences differences in ingroup and outgroup communication (Gudykunst, Gao, Schmidt et al., 1992). Recall from Chapter 2 that members of collectivistic cultures draw a sharper ingroup-outgroup distinction than members of individualistic cultures. This leads to greater differences in the ability to predict the behavior of members of ingroups and outgroups in collectivistic cultures than in individualistic cultures.

To illustrate collectivistic uncertainty reduction consider a story told by a professor at the University of Tokyo (Nakane, 1974). The professor was invited to give a talk at another university in Japan. She did not know the male professor who invited her. Prior to her arrival she was apprehensive about interacting with the person meeting her. When she arrived at the lecture hall a man approached her and bowed. Before he said anything else, the man said, "I am from the University of Tokyo," indicating to the professor that he had attended the University of Tokyo and that he shared an ingroup membership with her. The man then went on to give his name and present his business card. Once the professor knew that she shared an ingroup membership (the University of Tokyo) with the other professor, she relaxed because she knew that his behavior was predictable. There is not one piece of information in individualistic cultures that would provide the same degree of predictability.

There also are cultural differences in the factors that are related to reducing uncertainty. Frequency of communication predicts uncertainty reduction in individualistic cultures, but not in collectivistic cultures (Gudykunst & Nishida, 1986b). Self-disclosure does not predict uncertainty reduction in collectivistic cultures, but it does in individualistic cultures (Sanders et al., 1991).

Cultural Differences in Perceptions of Effective Communication. Anxiety and uncertainty predict perceived effective communication in ingroup and outgroup relationships in individualistic and collectivistic cultures (Gudykunst & Nishida, 2001). What is perceived as effective communication, however, differs in individualistic and collectivistic cultures. U.S. Americans perceive effective communication to involve (from most to least frequent): (1) understanding, (2) compatibility, (3) displaying positive behavior, (4) smoothness of communication, (5) positive outcomes, (6) positive nonverbal communication, and (7) adapting messages (Tominaga et al., 2003). Japanese, in contrast, perceive effective communication to involve: (1) compatibility between communicators, (2) appropriate behavior, (3) good relations between communicators, (4) positive outcomes, (5) smoothness of communication, (6) displaying positive behavior, (7) understanding, (8) positive nonverbal communication, and (9) clear messages.

Clearly, there are similarities and differences in what U.S. Americans and Japanese perceive as effective communication (Tominaga et al., 2003). The labels for many themes are similar, but the content of the themes is different. The largest group of U.S. Americans, for example, associate effective communication with cognitive understanding. Only a small percentage of the Japanese, in contrast, view effective communication as involving cognitive understanding. Rather, their focus is on understanding others' feelings. Japanese tend to associate compatibility, appropriate behavior, and good relations with effective communication. These factors all have an emotional component. It, therefore, appears that U.S. Americans emphasize cognitive understanding and Japanese emphasize good emotional relations between communicators when they want to communicate effectively. Perceptions of effective communication in the United States appear to be outcome-based and individual-focused, and perceptions of effective communication in Japan appear to be process-based and relationship-focused.

Ethnic Differences. There are no differences in the amount of uncertainty European Americans and African Americans experience when communicating with strangers from their own ethnic groups (Gudykunst & Hammer, 1987). There are, however, differences in what influences uncertainty reduction. Asking questions leads to uncertainty reduction for European Americans, but not for African Americans. Reducing uncertainty leads to attraction to others for European Americans, but not for African Americans.

The amount of information others disclose predicts uncertainty reduction across ethnic groups (Sanders & Wiseman, 1991). Positive nonverbal expressiveness predicts uncertainty reduction for European Americans, Latino(a) Americans, and Asian Americans, but not for African Americans. Self-disclosure predicts uncertainty reduction for European Americans and Latino(a) Americans, but not the other two groups. Finally, asking questions of the other person reduces uncertainty for European Americans, but not the other three groups.

Self-Disclosure

Self-disclosure involves individuals telling information about themselves to others that the other people do not know (Altman & Taylor, 1973). Closely related to self-disclosure is social penetration. As relationships become more intimate, there is an increase in social penetration;

that is, participants engage in self-disclosure on a larger variety of topics and with more intimacy. Take a few minutes to answer the following questions before reading the remainder of this section.

What type of information do you generally self-disclose the first time you meet someone?

To whom do you usually self-disclose the most information about yourself? The least information?

How is what you self-disclose to members of your own groups and to members of other groups similar and different?

Your answers to these questions should provide some insight into the role of self-disclosure in your implicit theory of communication. Keep your answers in mind as you read the remainder of this section.

Cultural Differences. There are similarities between Japanese and U.S. Americans in terms of what they consider appropriate topics for self-disclosure. Tastes and opinions are seen as the most appropriate by members of both cultures, and physical attributes and personality traits are least preferred (Barnlund, 1975). Further, the hierarchy of preferences for targets of self-disclosure is the same in the United States and Japan: same-sex friend, opposite-sex friend, mother, father, stranger, and untrusted acquaintance. The level of self-disclosure, however, is higher for U.S. Americans than for Japanese. This pattern is consistent across all six topics of conversation and all six target persons. "Interpersonal distance, as estimated by self-disclosure, was substantially greater among Japanese than Americans" (Barnlund, 1975, p. 79).

Generally, self-disclosure is associated with direct communication styles that predominate in individualistic cultures, rather than the indirect communication styles that predominate in collectivistic cultures (Gudykunst & Ting-Toomey, 1988). Intuitively, it appears that individualists engage in self-disclosure more than collectivists. Japanese, for example, prefer an interpersonal style in which little information about the self is made accessible to others in everyday interactions (i.e., the public self is relatively small), while the majority of information one knows about oneself is kept private (i.e., the private self is relatively large) (Barnlund, 1975). The preferred interpersonal style in the United States, in contrast, is one in which large portions of information about the self are made available to others (i.e., the public self is relatively large), while little of such information is kept to oneself (i.e., the private self is relatively small). Self-disclosure in Korea is similar to that in Japan. Koreans, for example, self-disclose less in opposite-sex relationships than U.S. Americans (Won-Doornink, 1985).

Not all research indicates that individualists self-disclose more than collectivists. Chinese in Hong Kong, for example, engage in self-disclosure in everyday communication more than U.S. Americans (Wheeler et al., 1989). On the surface, this appears inconsistent with the claim that self-disclosure is associated with direct communication, but this is not necessarily the case. Most of the Chinese respondents' contacts are with members of their ingroups, and communication in ingroups in collectivistic cultures tends to be intimate (e.g., involves self-disclosure). Most of the U.S. American respondents' contacts, in contrast, are with superficial acquaintances where self-disclosure is not expected.

Koreans and Japanese engage in greater personalization (e.g., knowing personal information), synchronization (e.g., coordination), and have less difficulty of communication with ingroup members (e.g., classmates) than with outgroup members (e.g., strangers). The difference between ingroup and outgroup communication is greater for Koreans than Japanese (Koreans are more collectivistic than Japanese; Hofstede, 2001) There are, however, few differences in communication between ingroups and outgroups for U.S. Americans (Gudykunst, Yoon, & Nishida, 1987). These results suggest that the more collectivistic the culture, the greater the difference in ingroup and outgroup communication.

Ethnic Differences. African Americans tend to self-disclose more than Mexican Americans (Littlefield, 1974). European Americans tend to disclose more than African Americans (Diamond & Hellcamp, 1969). This may be due to social class rather than race, because there are no differences between lower-class African Americans and lower-class European Americans (Jaffee & Polanski, 1962).

European Americans self-disclose with people they do not know more than African Americans when social class is controlled (Gudykunst & Hammer, 1987). By the time close friendships are formed, however, the pattern reverses. African Americans self-disclose with friends more than European Americans (Gudykunst, 1986). African Americans self-disclose on a wider variety of topics and in more depth with their best friends than European Americans (Hammer & Gudykunst, 1987). These patterns are consistent with the view that "[African Americans] seem to require deeper, more intimate topical involvement than [European Americans]. This intimacy must be seen as intrinsic to the relationship, therapeutic, and involving trust" (Hecht & Ribeau, 1984, p. 147).

Communication Rules

Similar to cultural norms, communication rules provide guidelines for our behavior. The major difference between norms and rules is that norms are based on morals, communication rules are not (Olsen, 1978). We will be perceived as "immoral" if we violate a norm, but not if we violate a communication rule. There are cultural rules and ethnic rules for communication. We often are not aware of the rules guiding our communication. Take a few minutes to answer the following questions before reading the remainder of this section.

What are the rules for greeting people in your ethnic group?

____

____

____

What are the rules for interacting with acquaintances in your ethnic group?

____

____

____

What are the rules for interacting with potential romantic partners in your ethnic group?

____

____

____

Your answers to these questions should provide some insight into the role of communication rules in your implicit theory of communication. Keep your responses in mind as you read the rest of this section.

Cultural Rules. There are different rules for dealing with other people in waiting rooms and at bus stops in individualistic and collectivistic cultures (Noesjirwan, 1978). The rule in both situations in Indonesia (collectivistic) requires one to talk to any other person present. The rule for Australians (individualistic) in both situations, in contrast, requires one to ignore any other person present. Similarly, there are rules for how children are expected to interact with others that are consistent in individualistic and collectivistic cultures (Kroonenberg & Kashima, 1997). Japanese children, for example, are expected to greet and share undesirable secrets with ingroup adults (e.g., mother, father) more respectfully than with other people, and they do this more than Australian children.

There are six universal rules in personal relationships: (1) we should respect others' privacy, (2) we should look the other person in the eye during conversations, (3) we should or should not discuss that which is said in confidence with the other person, (4) we should or should not indulge in sexual activity with the other person, (5) we should not criticize the other person in public, and (6) we should repay debts, favors, or compliments no matter how small (Argyle & Henderson, 1984). The respect privacy rule receives the strongest endorsement across cultures (Argyle et al., 1986). The keeping confidence rule receives strong support in Britain, Italy, and Hong Kong, but not in Japan. The public criticism rule is endorsed more strongly in Japan and Hong Kong than in Italy and Britain. This finding is to be expected given that Japan and Hong Kong are collectivistic cultures and Italy and Britain are individualistic cultures. Harmony is maintained in collectivistic cultures by avoiding criticism of ingroup members.

Ethnic Rules. In addition to differences in communication rules across cultures, there are differences among ethnic groups within cultures. The rules for Mexican Americans are: "Be polite and show verbal and nonverbal concern for the other, acknowledge your cultural identity, conform to your sexual and professional role, be friendly, support your point of view, offer relevant comments and constructive criticism, be open-minded and direct" (Collier et al., 1986, p. 452). These rules include some aspects that are derived from the collectivistic culture of Mexico (e.g., show concern for others), and some from the individualistic culture of the United States (e.g., be direct).

African Americans' rules for communication are similar in some ways to Mexican Americans' rules, but they also are different. The rules for

African Americans are: "Conform to societal and individual norms by acting verbally and nonverbally polite, support your position and stay on the topic, follow professional role prescriptions, but modify these to individual needs, be assertive yet open-minded, and be friendly" (Collier et al., 1986, p. 453). Similar to Mexican Americans' rules, African Americans' rules require politeness and supporting positions. African Americans' rules, in contrast, emphasize assertiveness and Mexican Americans' rules do not.

European American rules also share some similarities with Mexican Americans and African Americans, but there also are some differences. The rules for European American conversations are: "Be socially polite and show concern for the individual, especially through verbal behavior; follow professional, sexual, and personal role prescriptions; use relevant arguments and support them; be open-minded and friendly" (Collier et al., 1986, p. 453). The similarities across the three groups' communication rules are a function of them all being subcultures of the U.S. American culture. The differences are due to ethnic socialization.

Intergroup Relationships

Most of our close interpersonal relationships are with people who are relatively similar to us. We tend to develop close relationships with members of our own cultures and members of our ethnic groups (Pogrebin, 1987). We also tend to develop relationships with people who are like us in terms of disabilities, class, and age. "There is considerable evidence that very often [nondisabled] people do not want to enter unpredictable, and therefore, stressful interactions with visibly disabled people, and they avoid doing so by extending only 'fictional acceptance' which does not go beyond a polite, inhibited, and overcontrolled interaction" (Safilios-Rothchild, 1982, p. 44). Class differences similarly hinder members of different social classes from developing close relationships (Fussell, 1983). With respect to intergenerational interactions, age segregation in society "has hampered the opportunity for young and old to come to know one another. Hence, when they do come into contact, well-worn and often detrimental stereotypes may persist, and participants must make an active effort to dispel these preconceptions for a healthy dialogue to take place" (Tamir, 1984, p. 39).

One reason why we do not have close relationships with strangers is that we do not have a lot of contact with them.[2] Another reason is that our initial interactions and superficial contacts with strangers often result in ineffective communication. Since our communication with strangers is not as effective and satisfying as we would like, we generally do not *try* to develop intimate relationships with strangers. If we understand the process of relationship development, however, we can make an informed conscious decision as to whether or not we want to have intimate relationships with strangers. In making such a decision, it is important to keep in mind that the more we know about strangers, the more accurately we can predict their behavior (Honeycutt et al., 1983).

Expectations

Since proximity is one of the major factors involved in interpersonal attraction (Berscheid & Walster, 1969), strangers may be attracted to us simply because we are nearer to them than members of their own groups. In interacting with us, strangers may expect that they have nothing to lose. "The costs of pursuing a dissimilar relation are negligible relative to the rewards" for strangers (Knapp, cited in Crockett & Friedman, 1980, p. 91). We may, however, expect that we have something to lose when interacting with strangers since the rewards may be negligible and the costs high. Specifically, we may expect that if we interact with strangers, we may be looked down on by members of our ingroups. Regardless of any actual or potential sanctions, however, some of us expect positive interactions with strangers.

We expect our interpersonal encounters (i.e., interactions with ingroup members) to be more agreeable and less abrasive than our intergroup encounters (Hoyle et al., 1989). These expectations generalize to Japan (Gudykunst et al., 1999) and Greece (Broome, 1990). In Greece, for example, ingroup members are expected to be cooperative, polite, reliable, and warm, and outgroup members are expected to be competitive, deceitful, hostile, and untrustworthy. Expectations, however, become more positive as relationships with strangers become more intimate (Gudykunst & Shapiro, 1996). Expectations also become more positive over time in intergroup encounters simply as a function of their communication (Hubbert et al., 1999).

Violations of expectations can be problematic in intercultural interactions. Status, for example, influences the ways Japanese respond to requests and invitations (Beebe et al., 1990). To illustrate, Japanese use direct strategies to refuse requests and invitations from lower status individuals, but they use polite, indirect strategies with higher status individuals. U.S. Americans, in contrast, use indirect strategies to refuse requests and invitations, irregardless of the person's status. Japanese tend to be cautious when others' statuses are unknown (Knowner, 2002). Japanese expectations regarding foreigners taking their status into consideration tend to be violated in their intercultural interactions. These violations of expectations cause Japanese "alarm and distress" (Knowner, 2002, p. 357).

Our expectations for interactions with strangers can create self-fulfilling prophecies. Negative expectations can lead us to want to avoid interacting with strangers or keep our interactions as short as possible. Positive expectations, in contrast, can lead us to look for positive aspects of our interactions with strangers. If we find positive aspects of the interaction, we want to interact more. Positive expectations for strangers' behavior reduces our uncertainty and anxiety about interacting with them (Hubbert et al., 1999).

Interaction Involvement

Communicators in initial intercultural encounters are less perceptive (e.g., understanding meanings others attribute to messages) and less responsive (e.g., knowing what to say and when to say it) than communicators in initial intracultural encounters (Chen, 1995). Communicators use alignment talk (e.g., telling partners how to interpret messages) more in intercultural encounters than in intracultural encounters (Chen, 1997). Alignment talk is used to increase clarity and understanding. We tend to take clarity and understanding for granted in intracultural encounters.

U.S. Americans discuss explicit and accessible topics and engage in information exchange more in intercultural interactions than in intracultural interactions (Chen & Cegala, 1994). Topic sharing is associated positively with interaction involvement and the perception of intercultural accommodation (e.g., that others adjust to us). Perceived accommodation and interaction involvement in initial interactions may be factors that lead communicators to have future interactions.

Communication Satisfaction

Satisfaction is an affective (i.e., emotional) reaction to communication that meets or fails to meet our expectations (Hecht, 1978). Take a few minutes to answer the following questions before you read the remainder of this section.

How do other members of your ethnic group communicate when you are satisfied with your communication with them?

____

____

____

How do other members of your ethnic group communicate when you are dissatisfied with your communication with them?

____

____

____

How do members of other ethnic groups communicate when you are satisfied with your communication with them? Dissatisfied?

____

____

____

Your answers to these questions should provide some insight into the role of satisfaction in your implicit theory of communication. Keep your answers in mind as you read the remainder of this section.

The more communication in a relationship is personalized and synchronized, and the less difficulty people experience in communicating with strangers, the more satisfied they are with the communication in their relationships (Gudykunst et al., 1986). The more communication is synchronized, the more common ground is discovered, and the less difficulty experienced, the more satisfied we are with our initial interactions with strangers (Chen, 2002). Also, the more partners self-disclose to each other, the more they are attracted to each other, the more similarities they perceive, and the more uncertainty they reduce about each other, the more satisfied they are (Gudykunst et al., 1986). Further, the more effective the partners judge each other's communication to be, the more satisfied they are.

There are several factors that contribute to African Americans' satisfaction with their conversations with European Americans (Hecht et al., 1989). The first factor necessary for satisfaction is acceptance. To be satisfied, African Americans need to feel that they are respected, confirmed, and accepted by the European Americans with whom they communicate. Satisfying conversations with European Americans also include emotional expression and the European Americans being authentic (i.e., European Americans in satisfying conversations are perceived as genuine; European Americans in dissatisfying conversations are perceived as evasive). African Americans also perceive that there is understanding (e.g., shared meanings) and goal attainment in satisfying conversations. They perceive negative stereotyping and feel powerless (e.g., manipulated or controlled) in dissatisfying conversations.

Similarly, there are several factors associated with Mexican Americans having satisfying and dissatisfying conversations with European Americans (Hecht et al., 1990). Similar to African Americans, Mexican Americans see acceptance as an important aspect of satisfying conversations. Satisfying conversations with European Americans also include the expression of feelings and behaving rationally. The presence of self-expression and relational solidarity also contribute to satisfaction in conversations. Negative stereotyping and failure to discover a shared worldview (i.e., absence of perceived similarities) emerge as important factors in dissatisfying conversations.

European Americans need to communicate acceptance, express emotions, and avoid negative stereotyping in order for nonEuropean Americans to be satisfied with interethnic conversations. Communicating acceptance and avoiding negative stereotyping are important in developing relationships across class, age, and disability lines as well (Pogrebin, 1987).

Satisfaction is higher in intragroup encounters than in intergroup encounters, and satisfaction increases as relationships become more intimate (Gudykunst & Shapiro, 1996). Satisfaction increases over time in intergroup encounters for nonEuropeans, but it remains relatively constant over time for European Americans (Hubbert et al., 1999). The greater our satisfaction with our communication with strangers, the less our uncertainty and anxiety.

The questionnaire in Table 9.1 is designed to help you assess your satisfaction with your communication with strangers. Take a couple of minutes to complete the questionnaire now.

Scores on the questionnaire range from 10 to 50. The higher your score, the greater your satisfaction with communicating with strangers. Even though your perceptions of your communication with strangers is different than the strangers' perceptions, you also can "reverse" the statements in Table 9.1 and assess your perceptions of strangers' satisfaction with your communication with them. Remember, however, that how you think you are coming across to strangers may not be the same as how they perceive your communication with them.

Perceived Similarity

The extent to which we perceive similarity of self-concepts with strangers influences our attraction to them. Actual similarities in our self-concepts and strangers are *not* related to our attraction to them (Wylie, 1979). Rather, we are attracted to strangers we perceive to be similar to

TABLE 9.1 *Assessing Your Communication Satisfaction in Different Relationships**

The purpose of this questionnaire is to help you assess your satisfaction with your communication in different relationships. Respond to each statement by indicating the degree to which it is true of your communication with strangers: "Always False" (answer 1), "Usually False" (answer 2), "Sometimes True and Sometimes False" (answer 3), "Usually True" (answer 4), or "Always True" (answer 5). Answer all of the questions regarding your communication with a stranger (i.e., member of outgroup). Then answer all of the questions again thinking about a member of your ingroup. Think of your communication with specific people when you answer the questions.

OTHER GROUP	OWN GROUP	
______	______	1. I am satisfied with my communication with ______.
______	______	2. ______ is evasive when we communicate.
______	______	3. I enjoy communicating with _____.
______	______	4. I do not feel confirmed when I communicate with ______.
______	______	5. I feel accepted when I communicate with _____.
______	______	6. I do not get to say what I want to say when I communicate with ______.
______	______	7. I am able to present myself as I want to when I communicate with ______.
______	______	8. ______ does not understand me when we communicate.
______	______	9. Conversations flow smoothly when I communicate with ______.
______	______	10. I do not accomplish my goals when I communicate with _____.

To find your score, first reverse the responses for the even numbered items (i.e., if you wrote 1, make it 5; if you wrote 2, make it 4; if you wrote 3, leave it as 3; if you wrote 4, make it 2; if you wrote 5, make it 1). Next, add the numbers next to each statement. Scores range from 10 to 50. The higher your score, the greater your satisfaction in communicating with these people.

*Adapted from Hecht (1978).

us. Take a few minutes to answer the following questions before reading the remainder of this section.

What similarities with members of your ethnic group lead you to want to form relationships with them?

____

____

____

What similarities with members of other ethnic groups lead you to want to form relationships with them?

____

____

____

How does lack of perceived similarity with others influence your communication with them?

____

____

____

Your answers to these questions should provide some insight into the role of similarity in your implicit theory of communication. Keep your answers in mind as you read the remainder of this section.

We are attracted to strangers if we perceive similarities in attitudes, values, and communication styles. If we perceive that our attitudes are similar to strangers', we are attracted to them because the similarity in attitudes validates our view of the world (Byrne, 1971). We filter potential relational partners on the extent to which we perceive that they are similar to us (Duck, 1977). In the initial stages of getting to know strangers, we tend to focus on general attitudes and opinions that we hold. As we get to know strangers, we search for similarities in central aspects of our worldviews (e.g., our core values).

Probably one of the most important similarities we search for in potential relational partners is similarity in our orientations toward interpersonal interactions (Sunnafrank, 1991). That is, if we perceive similarities in our orientations toward communication, we are likely to form close relationships with strangers. Close friends have similar orientations toward five specific communication activities: conflict management, ways to comfort each other, ways to persuade each other, ways to support each other's self-concepts, and ways to tell stories and jokes (Burlson et al., 1992). Perceived similarity in communication styles is a strong predictor of attraction in early interethnic interactions (Lee & Gudykunst, 2001).

When we meet strangers, one of the main factors inhibiting the development of close relationships is the differences in cultures and ethnic groups. While it is important to recognize genuine differences, it also is important to go beyond looking at differences. In order to go beyond recognizing differences and develop close relationships with strangers, we must talk with them in order to discover that we are similar in other areas.[3] Perceived similarities in attitudes, lifestyles, and worldviews are necessary for close relationships to develop with strangers (Sudweeks et al., 1990). The more we perceive similarities between ourselves and strangers, the less our uncertainty and anxiety about communicating with them (Hubbert et al., 1999).

Table 9.2 contains an assessment designed to help you assess the degree of perceived similarity in different relationships. Take a few minutes to complete it now.

Scores on the two scales range from 10 to 50. The higher your score, the more similarities you perceive in the relationship. In general, you probably perceive more similarities with your acquaintance from your own group than with the acquaintance from another group.

Uncertainty and Anxiety Management

Our major concern during the initial stages of interaction with strangers is the management of uncertainty and anxiety. Managing uncertainty is necessary if we are to arrive at a basis for predicting strangers' responses to our communication behavior and accurately interpret strangers' behavior. **Managing anxiety is necessary to decrease our tendencies to avoid interacting with strangers and to motivate us to want to communicate with them.**

Uncertainty. There are differences in uncertainty reduction processes when we communicate with strangers and people who are familiar. U.S. Americans make assumptions based on cultural background in initial interactions with strangers more than in initial interactions with members of their groups (Gudykunst, 1983a). U.S. Americans also prefer to talk in initial encounters with members of their groups, while they prefer to ask questions in initial encounters with strangers. U.S. Americans perceive strangers from other cultures as less attractive than people from their own cultures, and have less confidence in predicting the behavior of strangers in initial interactions than members of their own cultures (Lee & Boster, 1991). Individuals ask for intimate information from members of their own groups more than from strangers.

There is greater uncertainty in intergroup encounters (interethnic and intercultural) than in intragroup encounters (Gudykunst & Shapiro, 1996). Uncertainty is associated negatively with positive expectations, communication satisfaction, and quality of communication. Uncertainty is associated positively with the degree to which social identities are activated in the interaction, and with the amount of anxiety experienced.

TABLE 9.2 *Assessing Perceived Similarity in Different Relationships*

The purpose of this questionnaire is to help you assess the amount of similarity you perceive when you communicate in different relationships. Respond to each statement by indicating the frequency that the statement applies in the particular relationship. If you "Never" have the experience, answer 1 in the space provided; if you "Almost Never" have the experience, answer 2; if you "Sometimes" have the experiences and sometimes do not, answer 3; if you "Almost Always" have the experience, answer 4; if you "Always" have the experience, answer 5. Answer all questions for the amount of similarity you perceive an initial interaction with a person from a different group. Then answer all of the questions again thinking of an initial interaction with a person from your own group. Think of specific individuals when you answer the questions.

OTHER GROUP	OWN GROUP	
______	______	1. I perceive that ______ and I have similar opinions.
______	______	2. I do not think that ______ and I have similar values.
______	______	3. I think that ______ and I have similar attitudes.
______	______	4. I do not think that _____ and I have similar beliefs.
______	______	5. I perceive that _____ and I have similar lifestyles.
______	______	6. I do not think that _____ and I have similar ways of telling stories and jokes.
______	______	7. I think that ______ and I have similar ways of managing conflict.
______	______	8. I do not think that _____ and I have similar ways of comforting each other.
______	______	9. I perceive that _____ and I have similar ways of persuading each other.
______	______	10. I do not think that _____ and I have similar ways of supporting each other's self-concepts.

To find your scores, first reverse the responses for the even numbered items (i.e., if you wrote 1, make it 5; if you wrote 2, make it 4; if you wrote 3, leave it as 3; if you wrote 4, make it 2; if you wrote 5, make it 1). Next, add the numbers next to each of the items. Scores range from 10 to 50. The higher your scores, the more similarity you perceive when interacting in the different relationships.

Uncertainty decreases over time in intergroup encounters (Guerrero & Gudykunst, 1997; Hubbert et al., 1999). Uncertainty decreases as the intimacy of intercultural relationships increases (Gudykunst et al., 1986). Similarly, there is less uncertainty in intercultural friendships than in intercultural acquaintance relationships (Gudykunst, 1985b).

Our social identities affect the reduction of uncertainty when we communicate with strangers (Gudykunst & Hammer, 1988a; Gudykunst, Sodetani, & Sonoda, 1987). The more positive individuals' relevant social identities (e.g., ethnic identity when interacting with someone from a different ethnic group) are, for example, the more they are able to reduce uncertainty when communicating with strangers (Gudykunst & Hammer, 1988a). This only holds, however, when they see strangers as typical members of their groups and when they recognize group differences. If individuals view strangers as atypical members of their groups and/or they do not recognize group differences, their personal identities, not social identities, influence their interaction with strangers.

The cultural differences in the types of information needed to reduce uncertainty can lead to interesting exchanges when individualists and collectivists meet for the first time. Individualists inevitably tell others personal information about themselves and seek this type of information from others, while collectivists tell others information about their group memberships and seek the same type of information from others. If we ask individualists what they do for a living, they will probably tell us their occupations. If we ask collectivists the same question, they will probably tell us the companies for which they work. Collectivists might ask individualists their age so that they can determine who is older. Many individualists will take offense in being asked their age by strangers. Individualists, in contrast, might ask collectivists about their feelings or attitudes when they first meet. The collectivists would probably answer questions about their feelings or attitudes indirectly and avoid directly answering the individualists' questions because they see these questions as too personal. Both parties will be frustrated—the collectivists because the individualists asked personal questions, the individualists because the collectivists did not answer their questions. U.S. Americans perceive the behavior of people from other cultures as less predictable than the behavior of people from their own culture (e.g., Gudykunst, 1983a; Lee & Boster, 1991).

Table 9.3 contains a questionnaire designed to help you assess the degree to which you experience uncertainty in your initial interaction with members of other groups and with members of your own group. Take a few minutes to complete it now.

Scores on the questionnaire in Table 9.3 range from 10 to 50. Most people will experience more uncertainty in their initial interactions with members of other groups than with members of their own group.

Anxiety. Actual or anticipated interaction with strangers leads to anxiety. As indicated in Chapter 1, we fear four types of negative consequences in

TABLE 9.3 *Assessing Your Uncertainty in Different Relationships*

The purpose of this questionnaire is to help you assess the amount of uncertainty you experience when you communicate in different relationships. Respond to each statement by indicating the frequency that the statements occur when you communicate in different relationships. If you "Never" have the experience, answer 1 in the space provided; if you "Almost Never" have the experience, answer 2; if you "Sometimes" have the experiences and sometimes do not, answer 3; if you "Almost Always" have the experience, answer 4; if you "Always" have the experience, answer 5. Answer all questions for strangers from other groups first. Next, answer the questions again for your initial interactions with members of your own group.

OTHER GROUP	OWN GROUP	
______	______	1. I am not confident when I communicate with _____.
______	______	2. I can interpret _____'s behavior when we communicate.
______	______	3. I am indecisive when I communicate with ______.
______	______	4. I can explain _____'s behavior when we communicate.
______	______	5. I am not able to understand _____ when we communicate.
______	______	6. I know what to do when I communicate with _____.
______	______	7. I am uncertain how to behave when I communicate with ______.
______	______	8. I can comprehend _____'s behavior when we communicate.
______	______	9. I am not able to predict _____'s behavior when we communicate.
______	______	10. I can describe _____'s behavior when we communicate.

To find your scores, first reverse the responses for the even numbered items (i.e., if you wrote 1, make it 5; if you wrote 2, make it 4; if you wrote 3, leave it as 3; if you wrote 4, make it 2; if you wrote 5, make it 1). Next, add the numbers next to each of the items. Scores range from 10 to 50. The higher your scores, the more uncertainty you experience when interacting in the different relationships.

our interactions with strangers: negative psychological consequences (e.g., frustration), negative behavioral consequences (e.g., exploitation), negative evaluations by members of outgroups (e.g., negative stereotyping), and negative evaluations by members of our ingroups (e.g., disapproval) (Stephan & Stephan, 1985).

The amount of anxiety we experience interacting with strangers is, in part, a function of our intergroup attitudes (Stephan & Stephan, 1985,

1989, 1992). The greater our prejudice and ethnocentrism, for example, the greater our anxiety about interacting with strangers. Contact with strangers, however, also leads to decreases in anxiety (Islam & Hewstone, 1993; Stephan & Stephan, 1992).

Greater anxiety is experienced in intergroup encounters (interethnic and intercultural) than in intragroup encounters (Gudykunst & Shapiro, 1996). Anxiety is associated negatively with positive expectations, communication satisfaction, and quality of communication. Anxiety is associated positively with the degree to which social identities are activated in the interaction, and the amount of uncertainty experienced. Anxiety decreases over time in intergroup encounters with strangers as a function of the communication that takes place (Hubbert et al., 1999).

Managing anxiety is associated closely with developing trust. *Trust* is "confidence that one will find what is desired from another, rather than what is feared" (Deutsch, 1973, p. 149). When we trust others, we expect positive outcomes from our interactions with them; when we have anxiety about interacting with others we fear negative outcomes from our interactions with them. When we first meet someone, "trust is often little more than a naive expression of hope" (Holmes & Rempel, 1989, p. 192). For us to have hope about the relationship, our anxiety must be below our maximum thresholds. For relationships to become close, "most people need to act *as if* a sense of [trust] were justified, and set their doubts aside. To do so requires a 'leap of faith' in the face of evidence that can never be conclusive. Thus trust becomes . . . an emotionally charged sense of closure. It permits an illusion of control . . . where one can plan ahead without anxiety" (Holmes & Rempel, 1989, p. 204). Without some minimal degree of trust, our relationships with strangers cannot become close.

Table 9.4 contains a questionnaire designed to help you assess the amount of anxiety you experience when communicating with members of other groups and with members of your own group. Take a few minutes to complete it now.

Scores on the questionnaire in Table 9.4 range from 10 to 50. The higher your score, the more anxiety you experience. Most people will experience more anxiety in interacting with members of other groups than in interacting with members of their own group.

Quality and Effectiveness of Communication. *Quality of communication* refers to the extent *to which* our communication is relaxed, smooth, involves understanding, and communication breakdowns are minimized (Duck et al., 1991). Perceptions of the quality of communication are higher in intragroup relationships than in intergroup relationships (Gudykunst & Shapiro, 1996). The perceived quality of our communication with

TABLE 9.4 *Assessing Your Anxiety in Different Relationships**

The purpose of this questionnaire is to help you assess the amount of anxiety you experience when you communicate in different relationships. Respond to each statement by indicating the frequency that the statement applies in the particular relationship. If you "Never" have the experience, answer 1 in the space provided; if you "Almost Never" have the experience, answer 2; if you "Sometimes" have the experience and sometimes do not, answer 3; if you "Almost Always" have the experience, answer 4; if you "Always" have the experience, answer 5. Answer all questions for the amount of anxiety you experience when communicating with strangers from other groups for the first time. Next, answer the questions again regarding the amount of anxiety you experience interacting with people from your own group for the first time.

OTHER GROUP	OWN GROUP	
______	______	1. I feel calm when I communicate with _____.
______	______	2. I get frustrated when I communicate with _____.
______	______	3. I do not get ruffled when I communicate with _____.
______	______	4. I am insecure when I communicate with _____.
______	______	5. I feel composed when I communicate with _____.
______	______	6. I feel anxious when I communicate with _____.
______	______	7. I do not get excited when I have to communicate with _____.
______	______	8. I feel stress when I communicate with _____.
______	______	9. I feel relaxed when I communicate with _____.
______	______	10. I am worried when I communicate with _____.

To find your scores, first reverse the responses for the odd numbered items (i.e., if you wrote 1, make it 5; if you wrote 2, make it 4; if you wrote 3, leave it as 3; if you wrote 4, make it 2; if you wrote 5, make it 1). Next, add the numbers next to each of the items. Scores range from 10 to 50. The higher your scores, the more anxiety you experience when interacting in the different relationships.

*Adapted from Stephan and Stephan (1985).

strangers increases over time as a function of the interaction (Guerrero & Gudykunst, 1997; Hubbert et al., 1999). The perceived quality of our communication with strangers increases as our intergroup relationships become more intimate (Gudykunst & Shapiro, 1996).

The effectiveness of our communication with strangers is a function of our abilities to manage our anxiety and uncertainty (Gudykunst, 1995). Perceived quality and perceived effectiveness of communication are affected by the amount of uncertainty and anxiety present in our interactions with strangers (Hubbert et al., 1999). The less uncertainty and anxiety we have, the greater the perceived quality and effectiveness of our communication with strangers. The perceived quality and effectiveness of our communication at one point in time influences the amount of uncertainty and anxiety we will have the next time we communicate with strangers (unreported data from Hubbert et al., 1999). If we perceive our communication is effective when we interact with strangers today, we will have less uncertainty and anxiety when we interact with the same strangers tomorrow than we had today.

One factor that affects the quality or effectiveness of our communication is the information that is exchanged when we interact. More information is exchanged in intracultural interactions than in intercultural interactions (Li, 1999a).[4] This may be due to individuals being less involved in the process of communication in intercultural interactions than in intracultural interactions (Li, 2001). The more Canadians engage in grounding activities when listening, the more they communicate effectively in intracultural interactions with other Canadians and intercultural interactions with Chinese. The same, however, does not occur when Chinese are listening to Canadians. *Grounding* refers to updating "common understanding of what is exchanged in the ongoing conversation" (Li, 1999b, p. 196). It is possible that Chinese see listeners' roles as building rapport with speakers and Canadian's view listeners' roles as understanding speaker's content (Li, 1999b). These differences are consistent with the cultural differences in effective communication discussed earlier in the chapter.

Situational factors play a major role in the success of intercultural interactions.

> In general, the factors that appear to contribute most to lack of success were: a topic that aroused strongly held but conflicting cultural beliefs, tasks that did not clearly depend on cooperation to achieve completion, and one participant with a voluble, fluent style of interacting with others who were unable or unwilling to match this style. Conversely, the factors that contributed to success of interactions were: tasks requiring or encouraging collaboration and inclusivity, non-controversial topics, and participants whose styles were equally matched in terms of fluency and volubility. (FitzGerald, 2003, pp. 205–206)

These findings suggest that the task, the topic, and the match of communication styles contribute to the effectiveness of our communication with strangers.

Self-Disclosure

One of the major factors that contributes to the development of personal relationships with strangers is self-disclosure. There is a greater intention to disclose information in initial intercultural encounters than in initial encounters with people from the same culture (Gudykunst & Nishida, 1984). This pattern, however, does not hold when self-disclosure in intracultural and intercultural acquaintances and friendships are compared; there are no differences between the amount of self-disclosure in intercultural and intracultural acquaintances and/or friendships (Gudykunst, 1985b). There is, nevertheless, more self-disclosure in both intracultural and intercultural friendships than in intracultural or intercultural acquaintances.

Nondisabled people react more positively to disabled people who self-disclose than to those who do not self-disclose, especially when the self-disclosure is about the disability (Thompson, 1982). It must be recognized, however, that self-disclosure does not necessarily reduce tension, but it does increase the nondisabled people's acceptance of disabled people (Thompson & Seibold, 1978). Disabled people tend to disclose about their disability in response to nondisabled people's questions about their disabilities if they perceive that the disclosure is appropriate to the relationship and the context in which they are communicating (Braithwaite, 1991). Disabled people, however, prefer to have nondisabled people get to know them as individuals before answering questions about their disabilities. To accomplish this, disabled people may try to direct the conversation and suggest topics for conversation other than their disabilities. If disabled people perceive that a nondisabled person with whom they are communicating is experiencing great discomfort, they may choose to disclose about their disabilities to make the other person comfortable (Braithwaite, 1991).

The age of the communicators also affects self-disclosure. Older people, for example, tend to disclose more than younger people, especially with respect to negative feelings (Dickson-Markman, 1986). Self-disclosure in intergenerational encounters does not necessarily follow the same patterns as it does in encounters with members of the same generation (Giles, Coupland, Coupland, et al., 1992). When older people interact with younger people, they tend to self-disclose more than younger people, especially about painful information such as accidents, deaths in the family, and medical problems. When older people self-disclose to younger people they do not know, the younger people do not necessarily reciprocate self-disclosures at the same rate they do when communicating with other younger people. When young people self-disclose, in contrast, older people tend to reciprocate.

Strangers' self-disclosures affect our uncertainty about communicating with them. Strangers' self-disclosures provide information we can use to predict and explain their behavior. The more strangers self-disclose, the greater our confidence in predicting their behavior (Gudykunst et al., 1986). The more intimate strangers' self-disclosure, the more accurate our predictions of and explanations for their behavior. If members of "minority" groups self-disclose about their experiences with prejudice and discrimination, it can help members of the "majority" group have feelings of "injustice" (Stephan & Finlay, 1999). This can lead to decreases in "majority" group members' tendencies to "blame the victim."

Intergroup Relationship Development

As our relationships with strangers become more intimate (e.g., move from initial interactions to close friend), our communication becomes more personal; for example, there are increases in self-disclosure, interpersonal attraction, perceived similarities, and uncertainty reduction (Gudykunst, Nishida, & Chua, 1986, 1987). Group similarities appear to have a major influence on our communication in the early stages of relationship development (e.g., initial interactions and acquaintance relationships), but not in the final stages (e.g., close friend; Gudykunst, Chua, & Gray, 1987).[5]

I do not want to imply here that group differences are not problems in close relationships. Group differences can be sources of misunderstandings in intimate relationships, particularly in marital relationships. How to raise children, for example, is a central issue in intercultural or interethnic marriages. Group differences can be major problems if the partners are not mindful of their communication around core issues like this.

There may be problems in close relationships due to group differences, but group differences have less of an effect on communication in close friendships than in acquaintance relationships.[6] The nature of the relationship development process itself appears to offer a reasonable explanation as to why group dissimilarities do not influence communication in close friendships as much as in earlier stages of relationships.[7] In early stages of relationship development, we must rely on cultural and social information to predict strangers' behavior because we do not have sufficient information to use personal information in making predictions. As the relationship develops and we gather information about strangers, we begin to use personal information about them to predict their behavior. When we use personal information, we are differentiating how strangers are similar to and different from other members of their groups. In other words, we no longer rely on our stereotypes to predict strangers' behavior.

What is it about our initial interactions and our communication with acquaintances who are from other groups that allows the relationship to develop into a "friendship"? As indicated earlier, we must communicate in a way that signals we accept strangers, we must express our feelings, and we must avoid negative stereotyping. The contact also must involve equal status between the "majority" and "minority" group members. If the interaction does not involve equal status, then negative stereotypes will not be dispelled (Pettigrew & Tropp, 2000). All of these factors combined suggest that our communication with strangers helps them have positive personal and social identities and they do not feel threats to their identities. Stated differently, we must support strangers' self-concepts.[8]

We must perceive some degree of similarity between ourselves and strangers if an intimate relationship is to develop (Gudykunst et al., 1991; Sudweeks et al., 1990).[9] The display of empathy and mutual accommodation regarding differences in communication styles (e.g., adapting our styles to the other person's) also appears to be critical.[10] It is also important that at least one person has some competency in the other's language or dialect and that both parties demonstrate some interest in the other's group memberships. Other factors that appear to be important are similar to those in developing relationships with people from our own groups. We must, for example, make time available to interact with strangers and consciously or unconsciously attempt to increase the intimacy of our communication (e.g., talk about things that are important to us).[11]

When we communicate on automatic pilot, we often filter out strangers as potential friends simply because they are different and our communication with them is not as effective as our communication with people from our own group. Whether or not we want to act differently depends on our motivation. Pluralistic friendships celebrate

> *genuine* differences arising out of life experiences and culture but reject *socially constructed* differences resulting from stereotypes or discrimination . . .
>
> Ethnicity is friendship-enhancing when it does not make another group into an "Other" group.
>
> Ethnicity is friendship-enhancing when we make it an "and" not a "but." The difference is palpable: "She's my friend *and* she's Jewish" allows me the pride of difference that a "but" would destroy.
>
> Group pride spawns both pride *and* prejudice. What makes a group special also makes it different. For some people, "different" must mean "better" or it is experienced as "worse." But people who do not need ethnic supremacy to feel ethnic pride find comfort and attitudinal regeneration among their "own kind" and also are able to make friends across racial and ethnic boundaries. (Pogrebin, 1987, pp. 187–188)

These comments on ethnicity apply to other group differences (e.g., disability, age, social class) that affect relationship development as well.

Do we want to approach strangers or continue to avoid them? I believe that relationships with strangers provide a chance for us to grow as individuals. The choice about developing these relationships, however, is an individual one. I encourage you to make a conscious (i.e., mindful) choice about whether or not you want to communicate effectively and develop relationships with strangers rather than relying on unconscious, mindless decisions. If you choose to approach strangers and are mindful of your communication, you will recognize real differences and eventually discover similarities between yourselves and the strangers with whom you communicate. The similarities you discover provide the foundation for developing intimate relationships.

Romantic Relationships

Romantic relationships are similar to and different from other forms of interpersonal relationships. Because of the differences, they are being discussed separately. I begin by looking at cultural differences in romantic relationships. Following this I look at intergroup romantic relationships.

Cultural Differences in Romantic Relationships

Individualism-collectivism is the major dimension of cultural variability that influences similarities and differences in romantic relationships across cultures (Dion & Dion, 1996). In individualistic cultures like the United States, the idea of being dependent on someone else either is viewed negatively or receives a neutral response. This, however, is not the case in collectivistic cultures. Japanese, for example, relate the concept of *amae* to love (Doi, 1973). *Amae* refers to the tendency to depend on another person and/or presume upon that person's benevolence. "*Amae*, generally speaking, is an inseparable concomitant of love" (p. 118).

Romantic love is less likely to be considered an important reason for marriage in collectivistic cultures than it is in individualistic cultures (Dion & Dion, 1993; Levine et al., 1995). In individualistic cultures, romantic love is considered the main reason for marriage. In collectivistic cultures, however, having a family tends to be the main reason for marriage. If having a family is the most important consideration, the acceptability of the potential mate to the family is critical. This explains the emphasis on arranged marriages in collectivistic cultures. There is, however, a tendency in many collectivistic cultures for young people to marry on the basis of love today. Psychological intimacy is more important to marital satisfaction in individualistic cultures than in collectivistic cultures.

Individualism-collectivism influences the stereotyping of members of the opposite-sex based on physical attractiveness (Dion et al., 1990). Collectivism leads individuals to stereotype members of the opposite sex on group-related attributes (e.g., the other person's position in a social network and family memberships) rather than individual attributes such as physical attractiveness.

Individualism-collectivism influences love and intimacy in romantic relationships. There is more love and self-disclosure in romantic relationships in France and the United States than in Japan (Ting-Toomey, 1991). U.S. Americans emphasize romantic love, passionate love, and love based on friendship more than Japanese or Russians (Sprecher et al., 1994). U.S. Americans also rate physical appearance, similarity, personality, affection, and mystery as more important factors in romantic relationships than Japanese or Russians. Partners in romantic relationships in the United States report more passion than partners in romantic relationships in China (Gao, 2001). Partners in Chinese romantic relationships, in contrast, report more intellectual intimacy than partners in U.S. American relationships.

There is greater high-context attributional confidence (e.g., reducing uncertainty indirectly) in Chinese romantic relationships than in European American romantic relationships (Gao & Gudykunst, 1995). Perceived attitude similarity is higher among European American romantic partners than among Chinese romantic partners. Finally, others socially react to European American romantic partners as a couple more than others react to Chinese romantic partners.

Intergroup Romantic Relationships

The major motivation for interethnic dating in the United States is the same as that for intraethnic dating, namely, personal liking for the other person (Lampe, 1982). There are no consistent reasons against interethnic dating; "the most commonly cited reason given by both males and females was a lack of desire" (p. 118). The most common reasons against interethnic dating given by European Americans are "no desire," "don't know any well enough," and "no chance." The most common reasons given by African Americans are "no desire," "hadn't thought of it," and "no chance." Mexican Americans give "don't know any well enough," "no desire," and "no chance" as the most common reasons against interethnic dating.

One of the major factors that influence Asian Americans' interethnic dating is their generation in the United States (e.g., immigrants are the first generation, their children the second, etc.; Spickard, 1989). Interethnic dating with European Americans is prevalent among third-generation Asian Americans who do not live in ethnic enclaves and those who live outside the western part of the United States (e.g., away from large groups of Asian Americans). California *Sansei* (third-generation Japanese Americans) are more likely to have dated another Japanese American than *Sansei* living in other parts of the country probably because of the higher concentration of Japanese Americans in California than in other parts of the country (Nagata, 1993). Asian Americans from higher socioeconomic groups also are more likely to date out of their ethnic groups than those from lower socioeconomic groups (Johnson & Ogasawara, 1984).

Asian American women who date European Americans come from families that have lived in the United States longer than the families of those who do not date European Americans (Fujino, 1997). Only 41 percent of the first-generation Asian American women have had "significant" dating relationships with European Americans, 65 percent of the second-generation Asian American women have had "significant" dating relationships with European Americans, and 77 percent of the third-generation Asian American women have had "significant" dating relationships with European Americans.

Our stereotypes influence our attraction to members of other ethnic groups as potential romantic partners. Answer the following questions before reading the remainder of this section.

What are your stereotypes of males or females in your ethnic group (whichever is a potential romantic partner)?

____

____

____

What are your stereotypes of males or females (whichever is a potential romantic partner) from another ethnic group (think of a specific ethnic group)?

____

____

____

Keep your answers to these questions in mind as you read the remainder of this section.

Asian American women date outside their ethnic groups more than Asian American men (e.g., Kitano et al., 1984). One reason Asian American women may date out of their ethnic groups more than Asian American men has to do with gender stereotypes. European American men, for example, have positive stereotypes of Chinese American women (e.g., "sexy," "quiet," "subservient") (Weiss, 1970). Chinese American women, in turn, have negative stereotypes of Chinese American men (e.g., "weak," "traditional," "old-fashioned") and positive stereotypes of European American men (e.g., "suave," "cool," "sophisticated," "sexy"). When asked why they date Chinese American men, Chinese American women say things like "parental coercion," "respect for tradition," and "race consciousness." When asked about dating European American men, Chinese American women say things like they are "more fun on dates" and "more considerate" than Chinese American men, and have "easygoing personalities." The combination of stereotypes and preconceptions facilitates Chinese American women dating European American men.

The influence of stereotyping on interethnic dating also may involve Asian American women not fitting Asian American men's stereotypes. One Japanese American woman who is married to a European American says:

> [European Americans] were the only guys I was attracted to, felt more comfortable with. I always would feel that Japanese guys [pause] I just wasn't what they were looking for, and they weren't what I was looking for either because I didn't fit into that conforming mold. I never kept up with all the things that were important to Japanese girls so I don't think I was desirable to them [Japanese guys], that I was ever on the list. And all the guys liked the same girls. There'd really be like a list of who was not desirable. I'm too outspoken and too intimidating. (Tuan, 1998, p. 121)

This woman's preference may be a function of both her stereotypes of Japanese American men and Japanese American men's stereotypes of Japanese American women.

Another potential explanation for Asian American women engaging in interethnic dating more than Asian American men involves issues of racism (Fujino, 1997). Asian American men, for example, are expected to initiate dates. Since they are expected to initiate dates, Asian American men who perceive that they are subject to racism may not tend to initiate dates with European American women. Asian American women, in contrast, can determine whether European American men who approach them are highly racist and choose not to date those who are. Asian

American women's dating patterns, therefore, are not as influenced by racism as Asian American men's dating patterns.

Over half the African Americans, Latino(a) Americans, and European Americans in one survey conducted in southern California date members of other ethnic groups (Tucker & Mitchell-Kernan, 1995). Interethnic dating is associated with being a young male who is highly educated, and perceiving the possibility of marrying members of other ethnic groups. African Americans and Latino(a) Americans are more likely to engage in interethnic dating than European Americans. This is partly a function of the size of the group. The smaller the group, the more likely members are to date outside the group.[12]

The strength of individuals' ethnic identities is related to their out-group dating and marriage (Alba, 1976). Specifically, those with weak ethnic identities have a greater tendency to date and/or marry out of their groups than those with strong ethnic identities. Another factor that influences the decision to date strangers is the degree to which they are perceived to be typical members of their cultures. Individuals in intercultural romantic relationships see their partners as atypical of their cultures (Gudykunst et al., 1991). The Japanese respondents, for example, view their U.S. American partners as different from other U.S. Americans and as possessing some Japanese characteristics.

Perceptions of same ethnicity and mixed ethnicity relationships are different (Garcia & Rivera, 1999). Same ethnicity opposite-sex friendships and romantic relationships are perceived more positively than mixed ethnicity relationships. Mixed ethnicity relationships are perceived as more likely to dissolve and receive less support from members of their social networks than same ethnicity relationships. Partners in mixed ethnicity relationships also are viewed as less compatible than partners in same ethnicity relationships. Mixed ethnicity engaged couples are viewed as more likely to argue and break up than mixed ethnicity opposite-sex friendships.

Interracial marriages have always been legal in some states, but 38 states had antimiscegenation laws at one time. Some southern colonies made interracial marriages illegal in the 1690s (Kennedy, 2003). Wyoming was the last state to pass a law against interracial marriages in 1913. Whom it was illegal to marry varied by state. California, for example, passed a law prohibiting marriages between people of European descent and "Negroes," "Mulattos," "Indians," "Mongolians," and people of "mixed-blood" in 1880. The law was amended in 1934 to include "Malays." The California law was found unconstitutional in 1948. Like California, 21 other state laws were overturned or repealed, but it was not until 1967 that the last 16 state laws were declared unconstitutional (U.S. Supreme Court, *Loving v.*

Virginia). Between 1960 and 1997, the percentage of all marriages that are interethnic marriages increased almost five-fold (1960 = 0.49 percent; 1997 = 2.3 percent; U.S. Census Bureau, 1997). In 1998, 0.6 percent (300,000) of all marriages (55.3 million) involved African Americans and European Americans (Kennedy, 2003).

Individuals' social dominance orientation (e.g., viewing it natural that some ethnic groups have more status than others) influences their attitudes toward interracial marriages (Fang et al., 1998). Specifically, there is a moderately strong positive association between social dominance orientation and antimiscegenation for members of high status ethnic groups (i.e., European Americans) regarding marriage with members of low status ethnic groups (i.e., African Americans, Asian Americans, Latino[a] Americans). The association between social dominance orientation and antimiscegenation for members of low status ethnic groups' marriage with members of high status ethnic groups, in contrast, is relatively weak.

The decision to date or become friends with strangers is not the same as the decision to marry strangers. A marriage with strangers requires a lifelong commitment to live with someone who is culturally or ethnically different. Any marriage calls for adjustments, but marriages to strangers generally demand more adjustments on the part of both partners than do marriages to members of ingroups. One of the adjustments necessary is adjusting to the ingroup's reaction to intergroup couples. European Americans in the United States, however, are becoming more tolerant of interethnic marriages (National Opinion Research Center, 1991).

Generation is the best predictor of interethnic marriage across Asian American ethnic groups (Kitano et al., 1998). The later the generation in the United States, the greater the interethnic marriage rate. Second-generation Asian Americans are three times more likely to marry outside their ethnic groups than first-generation Asian Americans. Third-generation Asian Americans are five times more likely to marry outside their ethnic groups than first-generation Asian Americans.

To conclude, as intergroup romantic relationships become more intimate, the individuals' group memberships (e.g., culture, ethnicity) influence their communication less (e.g., like close friendships, close romantic relationships are person-specific; this is not to say group memberships play no role, only that it decreases). There are, however, two times when group memberships come back to influence romantic partners communication: when they marry and when they have children. When a couple from different cultures gets married, for example, the cultural expectations for being a husband or wife are activated and the newly married couple usually is not aware that these expectations are influencing their behavior. To illustrate, the romantic partners may have developed a relationship where they were equals when they were courting. One of the cultures, nevertheless, may require that the wife be subservient to the husband. Similarly, when children are born, cultural expectations for being parents are activated. Mindfulness is required to negotiate these culturally prescribed role expectations in intergroup romantic relationships.

Study Questions

1. How is the perceived intimacy of relationships similar and different across cultures?
2. How is the management of uncertainty different in individualistic and collectivistic cultures?
3. How are perceptions of effective communication similar and different across cultures?
4. How does self-disclosure differ across cultures?
5. How do our expectations for strangers change over time in intergroup relationships?
6. What factors lead to nonEuropean Americans' satisfaction with their communication with European Americans?
7. What types of similarity lead to attraction in intergroup interactions?
8. How are uncertainty and anxiety related to effective communication in intergroup interactions?
9. How does communication change as intergroup relationships become more intimate?
10. How is communication in romantic relationships different in individualistic and collectivistic cultures?
11. What factors explain the development of intergroup romantic relationships?

Applications

1. Over the next week, pay attention to how you manage your uncertainty when you communicate with strangers. When do you use passive,

active, and interactive strategies to manage your uncertainty? What do you do when your uncertainty is above your maximum threshold?

2. Over the next week, pay attention to how you manage your anxiety when you communicate with strangers. What do you do when your anxiety is above your maximum threshold? How can you bring your anxiety down below your maximum threshold in future interactions with strangers?

3. Think about a relationship you have with a stranger. How intimate is your relationship with this person (e.g., are you strangers, acquaintances, friends, close friends)? How did your relationship reach this stage of intimacy and/or why has it not progressed to higher levels of intimacy?

Notes

1. This research was an extension of Knapp et al.'s (1980) research in the United States.

2. The amount of contact that occurs between members of different groups should increase as the size of the nonEuropean groups grow. There is, nevertheless, less intergroup interaction taking place in public schools because of the resegregation that is occurring. See a summary of the Harvard Civil Rights Project in Winter (2003).

3. Sunnafrank and Miller's (1981) research clearly indicates that communication can lead to perceptions of similarity when we initially thought there was only dissimilarity.

4. The studies discussed in this paragraph used simulated physician-patient interactions (with the person playing the physician serving as "listener," and the patient as "speaker"). It is possible that the results do not generalize to everyday interactions.

5. There are differences in the relationship labels used in the various studies. I have used the labels isolated above for illustrative purposes.

6. There obviously will be exceptions here. A man may want an "Oriental" wife, for example, because he thinks she will be passive and serve him.

7. Much of the argument I make in this section is drawn from Gudykunst (1989).

8. Self-concept support has been found to be critical in relationship development. See Cushman and Cahn (1985) for a summary of this research. These factors also are related to Bell and Daly's (1984) "concern and caring" affinity-seeking strategy.

9. See Gudykunst (1989) for a summary of this research. Similarity is part of Bell and Daly's (1984) "commonalities" affinity-seeking strategy.

10. This is related to Bell and Daly's (1984) "politeness" affinity-seeking strategy.

11. These issues are related to Bell and Daly's "other involvement" affinity-seeking strategy.

12. See Kennedy (2003) for a historical overview of European American-African American romantic relationships.

CHAPTER 10

Building Community With Strangers

As indicated in Chapter 1, the late Mother Teresa saw spiritual deprivation (i.e., a feeling of emptiness associated with separation from our fellow humans) as the major problem facing the world today (Jampolsky, 1989). Over the years, the social code in the United States has changed from one of self-restraint to self-gratification (J. Collier, 1991). The focus on self-gratification has led to a rise in selfishness and disconnection from others. One way to deal with spiritual deprivation, selfishness, and disconnection from others is to build community in our lives.

I begin this chapter with a discussion of the nature of community. Next, I examine the characteristics of community, community in public life, civic engagement, and diversity and community. Following this, I isolate ethical issues in developing community with strangers. I conclude this chapter and the book with a set of principles for building community with strangers.

The Nature of Community

The term community is derived from the Latin *communitas,* which has two related, but distinct interpretations: (1) the quality of "common interest and hence the quality of fellowship," and (2) "a body of people having in common an external bond" (Rosenthal, 1984, p. 219). Community evokes the "feeling that 'Here is where I belong, these are my people, I care for them, they care for me, I am part of them' . . . its absence is experienced as an achy loss, a void . . . feelings of isolation, falseness, instability, and impoverishment of spirit" (Yankelovich, 1981, p. 227).

Community is a choice around a common center; the voluntary coming together of people in a direct relationship that involves a concern for the self, others, and the group (Buber, 1958, 1965). A community is *not* a group of like-minded people; rather, it is a group of individuals with complementary natures who have differing minds. We can draw a distinction between a community of otherness and a community of affinity (Friedman, 1983). A *community of affinity* is a group of like-minded people who have come together for security. People feel safe because they use a similar language and the same slogans, but they do not have close relations with one another. A *community of otherness*, on the other hand, begins from the assumption that each member has a different point of view that contributes to the group. Members are not alike, but they share common concerns. Throughout this chapter, I focus on communities of otherness. Building communities of otherness must begin in small groups, and it cannot be forced on organizations or nations (Buber, 1958, 1965). At the same time, some form of **community is necessary to make life worth living.**[1]

Take a few minutes to answer the following questions before reading the next section.

What do you do when you are interacting with strangers and they are speaking? Thinking about what you're going to say? Listening carefully to strangers? Why?

____

____

____

____

Do you try to convince strangers of your point of view or try to understand them when you communicate with them? Why?

____

____

____

____

Are you concerned primarily with yourself, primarily with strangers, or both when you communicate with them? Why?

____

____

____

____

Keep you answers to these questions in mind as you read the next few sections of this chapter.

Openness and Community

Openness, *not* intimacy, is the key to developing community (Buber, 1958, 1965). "A real community need not consist of people who are perpetually together; but it must consist of people who, precisely because they are comrades, have mutual access to one another and are ready for one another" (Buber, quoted by Friedman, 1986, p. xiii). The importance of openness becomes clear when we look at the distinctions among three forms of communication: monologue, technical dialogue, and dialogue.

Monologues are self-centered conversations (Buber, 1958). When we engage in monologues, we are *not* guided by a need to communicate something to strangers nor a need to learn something, nor a need to make connections with strangers. If we are thinking about what we will say next when strangers are talking rather than listening to what they are saying, we are engaged in monologue. Also, when we engage in monologues, we say things that are designed (intentionally or unintentionally) to hurt strangers or put them down. We do not think of strangers as persons, but rather strangers are treated as objects. When we engage in monologues we do not see strangers as unique human beings and we do not take their needs into consideration. Monologues, in and of themselves, are not negative. When monologues become the regular form of communication, however, people become disconnected, and community cannot develop.

Technical dialogues are information centered conversations. In technical dialogues, our goal is to exchange information with strangers, not establish a contact with them (Buber, 1958). Technical dialogues are a necessary part of modern experience. Technical dialogues are necessary and appropriate at times, but problems emerge when they are used too frequently (e.g., there is a lack of connection between the participants), and community, therefore, cannot develop.

For community to develop, dialogue is necessary (Buber, 1958). *Dialogue* involves communication between individuals. **The goal of a dialogue is not to change strangers, but to understand them**. In a dialogue, there is a search for mutuality. The focus is on what is happening between the two people in the present. When we engage in dialogue, we present our points of view and listen to what strangers have to say. When we listen to strangers, we try to understand their points of view and respond to what they say, not pursue our own agenda. In a dialogue, each participant's feeling of control and ownership is minimized; each participant confirms the other, even when conflict occurs. It is the mutual confirmation that occurs in dialogues that allows us to feel human.

When we communicate on automatic pilot, most of our conversations are monologues or technical dialogues. Engaging in these types of conversations exclusively does not allow us to make contact with strangers. For most of us, engaging in dialogue requires that we be mindful of our communication. When we are mindful, we need to focus on the process of communication, not worry about outcomes. If we focus on what is happening between ourselves and strangers and we do not think about our goals, we can engage in dialogue with strangers.

Developing community requires engaging in dialogue with others, and it also requires a commitment to values higher than our own (Arnett, 1986). The values of civility and tolerance of plurality and diversity are necessary for community (Tinder, 1980). Holding these values requires that we accept that our own needs will not always be met in our interactions with strangers (Arnett, 1986).

Walking a Narrow Ridge

The key to building community is for us to walk a narrow ridge (Buber, 1958). The concept of *narrow ridge* involves taking both our own and strangers' viewpoints into consideration in our dealings with them. The metaphor of tightrope walkers illustrates the narrow ridge concept (Arnett, 1986). If tightrope walkers lean too much in one direction they will begin to loose their balance. To regain their balance, tightrope walkers must compensate by leaning in the other direction. The same is true of walking the narrow ridge in our dealings with strangers. If we give our own opinions too much weight in a conversation, we must compensate by giving the strangers' opinions equal weight if we are going to walk a narrow ridge.

In walking the narrow ridge, we must try to understand the strangers' points of view. We should *not*, however, take a nonjudgmental or relativistic attitude toward strangers (Buber, 1958). Rather, we should openly listen to strangers, but if we are not persuaded by their arguments, we should maintain our original positions; if we are persuaded, we should modify our opinions. There is a subtle difference between listening openly and not changing our minds, or being close-minded. The difference depends on our intentions. If our intentions are to consider strangers' opinions seriously, we are walking the narrow ridge; if our intentions are not to consider strangers' opinions, then we are close-minded. It is the dual concern for ourselves and strangers in walking the narrow ridge that stops polarized communication and allows community to develop (Arnett, 1986).

We should avoid giving in and accepting strangers' opinions just for the sake of peace (Buber, 1958). Rather, we should accept strangers' opinions or compromise if it is the way to the best solution. Our commitment must be to principles (e.g., civility, tolerance), not false peace. It is also important to note that we should not accept everything strangers say unquestioningly. Suspicion is sometimes warranted, but problems occur when suspicion becomes a norm of communication. When suspicion is always present, however, existential mistrust exists.

One factor that contributes to mistrust in individualistic cultures like the United States that value direct communication is looking for hidden meanings. Suspicion and looking for hidden meanings are only two of the factors that lead to mistrust. No matter how mistrust comes about, it always polarizes communication. Understanding strangers requires "a willing suspension of disbelief" (Trilling, 1968, p. 106). Developing superordinate goals and developing community require trust (Staub, 1989).

Table 10.1 contains a questionnaire designed to help you assess your general tendency to walk a narrow ridge when you communicate with strangers. Take a few minutes to complete it now.

Scores on the questionnaire range from 10 to 50. The higher your score, the more you tend to walk a narrow ridge when you communicate with strangers. If your score is low (e.g., 30 or below), you tend to be more concerned with yourself than strangers. If this is the case, you can consciously choose to balance your concern for yourself and strangers if you are mindful.

Characteristics of Community

Community is critical to peace and intergroup harmony in our individual lives and in the world. "In and through community lies the salvation of the world. Nothing is more important. Yet it is virtually impossible to describe community meaningfully to someone who has never experienced it—and most of us have never had an experience of true community. The problem is analogous to an attempt to describe the taste of artichokes to someone who has never eaten one" (Peck, 1987, p. 17). Community, in this view, is "a group of individuals who have learned how to communicate honestly with each other, whose relationships go deeper than their masks of composure, and who have developed some significant commitment to 'rejoice together, mourn together' and to 'delight in each other, make others' conditions our own'" (p. 59).[2]

TABLE 10.1 *Assessing Your Tendency to Walk a Narrow Ridge With Strangers**

The purpose of this questionnaire is to assess the degree to which you walk a narrow ridge when you communicate with strangers. Respond to each statement indicating the degree to which you agree or disagree: "Strongly Disagree" (answer 1), "Disagree" (answer 2), "Sometimes Disagree and Sometimes Agree" (answer 3), "Agree" (answer 4), and "Strongly Agree" (answer 5).

_____ 1. I do not need to be connected to strangers when we communicate.
_____ 2. I do not try to change strangers when we communicate,
_____ 3. I pursue my own agenda when I communicate with strangers.
_____ 4. I always take strangers needs into consideration when we communicate.
_____ 5. I do not try to learn anything from strangers when we communicate.
_____ 6. I view strangers as individuals when I communicate with them.
_____ 7. I say things that hurt strangers when we communicate.
_____ 8. I try to understand strangers when we communicate.
_____ 9. I put strangers down when we communicate.
_____ 10. I balance my concern for myself and my concern for strangers when we communicate.

To find your score, first reverse your responses for the odd numbered items (i.e., if you wrote 1, make it 5; if you wrote 2, make it 4; if you wrote 3, leave it as 3; if you wrote 4, make it 2; if you wrote 5, make it 1). Next, add the numbers next to each statement. Scores range from 10 to 50. The higher your score, the more you walk a narrow ridge when you communicate with strangers.

*Based on Buber's (1958, 1965) discussion of walking a narrow ridge.

Communities are inclusive (Peck, 1987). Communities are *not* made up of the like-minded; different types of people, ideas, and emotions must be present in a community. Exclusivity is the enemy of community. When individuals are excluded, cliques are formed, and cliques are defensive bastions against community.

Commitment is necessary for community to develop (Peck, 1987). *Commitment* involves "a willingness to coexist together and hang in there when the going gets rough" (p. 62). It is commitment to the community that allows the differences among the individuals in the group to be absorbed. If people are not committed to each other, community cannot develop.

Once communities are developed, members perceive them as "safe places" (Peck, 1987). It is rare for any of us to feel completely safe; we spend most of our lives feeling only partly safe. Members of communities feel like they are accepted and their identities are not threatened. Members of communities can speak from their hearts because they feel safe. Feeling safe allows them to be vulnerable.

Communities seek agreement among all of the members (Peck, 1987). Developing a consensus requires that differences be confronted and discussed. A consensus cannot emerge if differences are ignored or if conflict is suppressed. In a community, differences are transcended, *not* obliterated or demolished. "Perhaps the most necessary key to transcendence is the appreciation of differences. In community, instead of being ignored, denied, hidden, or changed, human differences are celebrated as gifts" (p. 62).

Members of a community examine it (Peck, 1987). "The essential goal of contemplation is increased awareness of the world outside oneself, the world inside oneself, and the relationship between the two" (p. 66). The need for contemplation is consistent with Socrates' claim that "the life which is unexamined is not worth living." By examining the interaction that occurs within a group, the members can improve the quality of their interaction and increase the likelihood they can build community.

For community to develop, members must drop their mask of composure (Peck, 1987). The development of community requires that we be open and expose our inner selves to strangers. We also have to allow ourselves to be affected by strangers when they expose their inner selves to us.

A community cannot exist without conflict (Peck, 1987). The management of the conflict that occurs, however, must be based on a real desire to listen and understand each other's opinions, not being right. People tend to believe the fantasy that "If we can resolve our conflicts, then someday we will be able to live together in a community" (p. 72). This fantasy, however, has the relationship between conflict and community backwards. The goal should be: "If we can live together in community, then someday we shall be able to resolve our conflicts" (p. 72).

Community and Public Life

Without community, "there may be very little future to think about at all" (Bellah et al., 1985, p. 286). Community is an inclusive group of people who share their public and private lives, or more specifically, "a group of people who are socially interdependent, who participate together in discussion and decision-making and who share certain practices that both define the community and nurture it" (p. 333). A genuine community (e.g., a marriage, a university, a whole society) is defined by its practices.

Practices refer to "shared activities that are not undertaken as a means to an end but are ethically good in themselves" (Bellah et al., 1985, p. 335). This definition is similar to Aristotle's use of the term *praxis*.

Genuine practices virtually always involve commitment because they involve activities that are ethically good.

Communities consist of different types of people, even though we have a tendency to want to be with people who are similar to us. "The [U.S.] American search for spontaneous community with the likeminded is made urgent for fear that there may be no way at all to relate to those who are different. . . . the public realm still survives, even though with difficulty, as an enduring association of the different" (Bellah et al., 1985, p. 251). At times, the associations in the public realm may approach community. The Civil Rights Movement and the response to Martin Luther King, Jr. is an example of community in public life: "The powerful response King elicited, transcending simple utilitarian calculations, came from the reawakened recognition by many [U.S.] Americans that their own sense of self was rooted in companionship with others who, though not necessarily like themselves, nevertheless shared with them a common history and whose appeals to justice and solidarity made powerful claims on their loyalty" (p. 252). Developing community, therefore, requires that we value justice and loyalty, and recognize the commonalities we share.

There are two sources of moral integration that serve as the foundation for community: civility and piety (Selznick, 1992). *Civility* involves being "guided by the distinctive virtues of public life. These include, especially, moderation in pursuit of one's own interests, and concern for the common good. More particularly, civility signals the community's commitment to dialogue as the preferred means of social decision" (p. 391). Civility "presumes diversity, autonomy, and potential conflict" and that "norms of civility are predicated on a regard for the integrity and independence of individuals and groups" (p. 391). Civility emerges out of being conscious of our behavior (i.e., mindful) and is based on ethical behavior toward strangers (Peck, 1993). *Piety* involves a "reflection of the need for coherence and attachment. The distinctive virtues of piety are humility and loyalty" (Selznick, 1992, p. 387).

"Individuals need the nurture of groups that carry a moral tradition reinforcing their own aspirations" (Bellah et al., 1985, p. 286). We need to develop a conception of the common good because "with a more explicit understanding of what we have in common and the goals we seek to attain together, the differences between us that remain would be less threatening" (p. 287). Finding commonalities requires that we be mindful of our prejudices. "Racism and sexism and homophobia and religious and cultural intolerance . . . are all ways of denying that other people are the same kind as ourselves" (Brodie, 1989, p. 16).

Learning to deal with cultural and/or ethnic differences is necessary

> because most of us grow up and spend our time with people like ourselves, we tend to assume uniformities and commonalities. When confronted with someone who is clearly different in one specific way, we drop that assumption and look for differences. . . . The mindful curiosity generated by an encounter with someone who is different, which can lead to exaggerated perceptions of strangeness, can also bring us closer to that person if channeled differently. (Langer, 1989, p. 156)

Once we satisfy our curiosity about differences, understanding can occur.

Civic Engagement

Individuals in the United States today feel disconnected from others (Putnam, 2000). To understand why this is happening, civic engagement (e.g., involvement in community organizations) over the last several decades can be examined. There have been ups and downs in civic engagement in the United States over its history, especially in the last 100 years: "For the first two-thirds of the twentieth century a powerful tide bore [U.S.] Americans into ever deeper engagement in the life of their communities, but a few decades ago—silently, without warning—that tide reversed and we were overtaken by a treacherous rip current. Without at first noticing, we have been pulled apart from one another and from our communities over the last third of the century" (p. 27). These changes affect all aspects of society in the United States (e.g., how well schools work, democracy in the country, the health and happiness of people living in the United States).

Three-quarters of the U.S. workforce view "the breakdown of community" and "selfishness" as "serious" or "very serious" problems (Putnam, 2000). Two-thirds of U.S. Americans say that "civic life has weakened in recent years" and that there is more emphasis on the individual than on the community. Further, "more than 80 percent said that there should be more emphasis on community, even if that put more demands on individuals" (p. 25).

Civic engagement builds social capital. *Social capital* "refers to connections among individuals—social networks and the norm of reciprocity and trustworthiness that arise from them" (Putnam, 2000, p. 19). There are both public and private components of social capital. The connections we form with others benefit each of us individually (e.g., help us find jobs, provide social support; the private good). The connections we form with others also provide benefits to society (e.g., if neighbors are connected to each other, they watch each other's houses, and this leads to decreases in the crime rate in the neighborhood; the public good). The "touchstone" of social capital "is the principle of generalized reciprocity—I'll do this for you now, without expecting anything immediately in return and perhaps without even knowing you, confident that down the road you or someone else will return the favor" (p. 134). Generalized reciprocity leads to trustworthiness among members of society and provides benefits to individuals.

There are several things that we can do to increase civic engagement, social capital, generalized reciprocity, and community in the United States (Putnam, 2000). First, we need to develop programs that will increase the civic engagement of U.S. Americans over what it is today. One way to do this is through community service programs in schools. Volunteering in our youth is one of the best ways to establish lifelong volunteering patterns. Second, workplaces need to become more "family-friendly and community-oriented" than they are today. This will allow workers to help "replenish our stocks of social capital both within and outside the workplace" (p. 406, italics omitted). Third, U.S. Americans need to become more involved with their neighbors than they are today and develop spaces in public areas that encourage "casual socializing." Fourth, U.S. Americans need to become more involved in spiritual communities, and be more tolerant of other spiritual communities than they are today. Fifth, U.S. Americans need to "spend less leisure time sitting passively alone in front of glowing screens and more time in active connection with fellow citizens" than they do today (p. 410, italics omitted). New forms of electronic entertainment that foster community need to be developed. Sixth, U.S. Americans need to engage in more cultural activities (e.g., artistic activities such as community theater) than they do today. Seventh, U.S. Americans need to be more involved in public life than they are today (e.g., serving on community committees, attending public meetings).

Each of these activities will increase civic engagement and social capital in the country. Increasing social capital will increase generalized reciprocity and trustworthiness among members of the society. These changes will, in turn, improve intergroup relations in the country and facilitate community building.

Diversity and Community

Diversity has been part of life in the United States since the founding of the nation (de Tocqueville, 1876/1835). U.S. Americans have "an ambivalent relationship to difference" (Sarat, 2002, p. 397). Many U.S. Americans "harbor suspicions that difference may be our national undoing, that differences can never be bridged, and that without assimilation, disorder lurks just below the surface of our national life" (p. 397).

Models of Diversity

U.S. Americans have different implicit models of diversity. Their models of diversity influence their everyday interactions with strangers and may inhibit the development of community. Take a few minutes to answer the following questions before reading the remainder of this section.

To what extent should racial and ethnic differences influence the way people are treated? Why?

____

____

____

____

To what extent should we give up our identification with our ethnic groups and focus on our identification with our culture? Why?

____

____

____

____

To what extent should we accommodate cultural, ethnic, gender, and gender orientation differences in the ways that organizations are managed? Why?

____

____

____

____

Your answers to these questions should help you figure out the model of diversity that you prefer. Keep your answers in mind as you read the remainder of this section.

Models of diversity provide "shared understanding and practices of how groups come together or should come together, relate to one another, and include and accommodate one another in light of the differences associated with group identity" (Plaut, 2002, p. 368). Models of diversity are reflected in our interactions with strangers, as well as in institutional policies and practices (e.g., government and organizational policies and practices). Four models can be identified: sameness model, common identity creation model, value-added model, and mutual accommodation model.

The *sameness model* "is characterized by the notion that differences among people are superficial and mostly irrelevant" (Plaut, 2002, p. 372). U.S. Americans using this model struggle with the idea of diversity. They value "difference, uniqueness, and nonconformity," but at the same time, they also value individualism, which requires "treating everyone the same" (p. 372). U.S. Americans using this model view everyone as being equal and often advocate a colorblind approach to dealing with differences. In other words, race and ethnicity are supposed to be "irrelevant to how individuals are treated" (p. 373). The sameness model of diversity tends to be used by a majority of European Americans who assume that differences across groups (e.g., ethnic, cultural groups) are superficial (Plaut & Markus, 2002; cited by Plaut, 2002). NonEuropean Americans and members of the lower social classes, in contrast, tend to view differences among people as significant.

The *common identity creation model* "holds that perceived differences among people and groups are substantial and should be minimized, and that a common, overarching identity should be created" (Plaut, 2002, p. 377). As indicated in Chapter 4, the common ingroup identity approach to intergroup relations (e.g., Gaertner & Dovidio, 2000) suggests that prejudice and bias are reduced when members of different groups form common identities (e.g., rather than "us" vs. "them," there is a "we"). This model presupposes that we can create an overarching identity with which members of different groups can identify. If people share a common identity and have a common purpose, they can work together and this should lead to them liking each other. This model is used by the military and by sports teams.

The *value-added model* of diversity suggests that "differences among people and groups are substantial, and some should be utilized to add value" (Plaut, 2002, p. 381). In this view, "individuals should be distinguished by the experience and expertise they bring to the situation" (p. 382). There is, however, little research on the "value" added by different types of diversity. Frequently when this model is used, people emphasize different ways of thinking and different ideas. When organizations use this type of model, they often have not incorporated different perspectives in their practices. In practice, this model runs the risk of "pigeonholing people into niches according to identity group memberships" (p. 383).

The *mutual accommodation model* "focuses on the notion that differences among people and groups are substantial and must be accommodated whether or not they are perceived to add value" (Plaut, 2002, pp. 383-384). This model assumes that "individuals need to feel safe, valued, and respected in order to contribute their full potential" (p. 384). If African American college students, for example, perceive that their identities are safe and not threatened, they perform better and do not stereotype as much as when they feel that they are being treated in a colorblind way (Purdie et al., 2000, cited by Plaut, 2002). In other words, **individuals perform their best when they feel identity safety** (e.g., their identities are not threatened). The mutual accommodation model allows us to recognize the importance of group memberships without leading to competition between the groups.

We all use one of these models of diversity (or some other) when we interact with members of other groups. The sameness model clearly inhibits the development of community among members of diverse groups of people. NonEuropean Americans who strongly identify with their ethnic groups do not feel supported when their ethnic identities are ignored. The common identity creation model might provide the basis for developing community, but creating common ingroup identities does not always eliminate bias against outgroup members (e.g., Hornsey & Hogg, 2000b). The value-added model also presents potential problems for developing community because the differences that are not perceived to "add value" may not be respected or tolerated. The mutual accommodation model provides the soundest basis for developing community with strangers. If we interact with strangers using this model, we do not threaten their group identities and they feel identity safety. We must, nevertheless, also recognize that people are more than their group identities. We also must recognize that strangers are individuals as well, if this is an important aspect of who they are. In other words, we must take both personal and social identities into consideration when developing community with strangers.

Power and Intergroup Interactions

The ways that strangers choose to interact with ingroup members influence whether community can be developed. One of the factors that complicates communication between ingroup members and strangers' groups is that one group often has power over the others. Usually the ingroups have power over strangers' groups. The power that ingroups have over strangers' groups influences the ways that strangers choose to communicate with ingroup members. In this section, I overview ways that strangers might chose to interact with ingroup members and then discuss their influence on community development.

Social hierarchies in society privilege some groups over others ("muted group theory"; Ardener, 1975; Kramarae, 1981), and some groups hold dominant positions in society (e.g., the groups have power over other groups) and other groups are in nondominant positions (e.g., the groups do not have power). The specific positions that individuals' groups hold in society provide subjective ways in which they look at the world ("standpoint theory"; Smith, 1987). Nondominant groups include, but are not limited to, non-whites, women, people with disabilities, homosexuals, and those in the lower social classes (Orbe, 1998).[3] The ways members of these groups choose to interact with members of the dominant groups affect the possibility of developing community.

Nondominant "group members negotiate attempts by others to render their voices muted within dominant societal structures" (Orbe, 1998, p. 4). Members of nondominant groups are marginalized in society, and they generally have one of three goals when interacting with members of dominant groups: assimilation (e.g., becoming part of the mainstream culture; emphasizing cultural identities over ethnic identities or other social identities), separation (e.g., rejecting the possibility of common bonds with members of dominant groups; emphasizing ethnic identities or other social identities over cultural identities), and accommodation (e.g., trying to get members of the dominant groups to accept members of nondominant groups; equally emphasizing cultural identities and ethnic identities or other social identities). Members of nondominant groups also tend to use one of three general communication styles to achieve success when confronting the "oppressive dominant structures": nonassertive (e.g., not standing up for the rights of members of nondominant groups), aggressive (e.g., focusing on the rights of members of nondominant groups and not protecting the rights of members of dominant groups), or assertive (e.g., standing up for rights of members of nondominant groups, but also protecting the rights of members of dominant groups).

Members of nondominant groups' communication with dominant group members is influenced by their past experiences with dominant group members, individuals' abilities to enact different ways to negotiate with dominant group members, where are they communicating with dominant group members, the pros and cons of certain of the different ways of negotiating with dominant group members, and their "communication approach" (i.e., being aggressive, assertive, or nonassertive) (Orbe, 1998). The ways members of nondominant groups "negotiate their muted group status" in their interactions with dominant group members are called practices (Orbe, 1998b, p. 8).

The practices used are a function of the individuals' goals (i.e., assimilation, separation, accommodation) and communication approaches (i.e., nonassertive, aggressive, assertive) (Orbe, 1998). The combination of these yield nine communication orientations in which different practices tend to be used: (1) nonassertive separation, (2) nonassertive accommodation, (3) nonassertive assimilation, (4) assertive separation, (5) assertive accommodation, (6) assertive assimilation, (7) aggressive separation, (8) aggressive accommodation, and (9) aggressive assimilation.

Nonassertive assimilation involves members of nondominant groups using practices "such as emphasizing commonalities [with the dominant group], developing positive face [e.g., being polite, respectful], censoring self [e.g., monitoring negative responses], and averting controversy, to blend unobtrusively into dominant society" (Orbe, 1998, pp. 110-111). Nondominant group members' goals are to fit into the dominant society and avoid conflict, even if it means not standing up for themselves. Using this approach reinforces the dominant groups' power in society.

Aggressive assimilation involves using practices such as "dissociating" (e.g., negating group identity), "mirroring" (e.g., recognize but downplay differences), "strategic distancing" (e.g., from other members of nondominant groups), and "ridiculing self" (e.g., making demeaning comments about their own groups) (Orbe, 1998). Nondominant group members using this approach take "a determined, sometimes belligerent," approach to being seen as members of the dominant groups.

Assertive assimilation uses practices such as "extensive preparation," "overcompensating" (e.g., being an "exemplary team player"), "manipulating stereotypes" (e.g., changing stereotypes of nondominant groups), and "bargaining" (Orbe, 1998). Bargaining, for example, involves members of the dominant and nondominant groups negotiating "an arrangement by which neither party will make an issue of [group] differences" (p. 111). The goal of this approach is for nondominant group members to become part of the mainstream but not to privilege the needs of either the dominant or nondominant groups.

Nonassertive separation involves using practices such as "avoiding" or "maintaining interpersonal barriers" (e.g., do not make eye contact). "Our society is one that is typically segregated regarding where we live, work, learn, pray, and play," especially with respect to ethnicity and social class (Orbe, 1998, p. 115). When members of nondominant groups want separation, they tend to avoid contact with members of the dominant groups. If they are forced to engage in interactions, members of nondominant groups may "find themselves fulfilling existing expectations placed on them by the dominant society" (p. 116).

Aggressive separation involves using practices such as "attacking" or "sabotaging" members of the dominant groups (Orbe, 1998). Members of nondominant groups may use "whatever means necessary" to achieve separation between their groups and members of the dominant groups. This may include strongly criticizing other members of nondominant groups who choose to assimilate or accommodate with the dominant groups. They also may confront the "evils" of the dominant society. Their aggressive stance, however, often leads to them not being heard by members of the dominant groups.

Assertive separation involves practices such as "communicating self" (e.g., trying to dispel stereotypes by being themselves), "intragroup networking" (e.g., networking with other members of nondominant groups), "exemplifying strengths" of members of nondominant groups, and "embracing stereotypes" viewed as positive (Orbe, 1998). This approach promotes "unity and self-determination" among nondominant groups (p. 117). Their outsider position, however, does not allow them to influence decisions in the dominant society, "including many decisions that directly or indirectly affect their livelihood" (p. 117).

Nonassertive accommodation involves practices such as "increasing visibility" of members of nondominant groups and "dispelling stereotypes" perceived as negative (Orbe, 1998). Members of nondominant groups using this approach try to change the dominant society to reflect their experiences in a "constrained and nonconfrontational manner" (p. 113). This should not lead to members of dominant groups becoming defensive in their interactions with members of nondominant groups. This stance "can subtly influence certain issues," but it cannot "promote major change" (p. 114).

Aggressive accommodation involves using practices such as "confronting" and "gaining advantage" over members of the dominant group (Orbe, 1998). The focus of individuals using this orientation "is on becoming a part of the dominant structures and then working from within to promote significant change despite personal costs" (p. 114). The aggressive practices used by individuals using this approach inhibit their ability to promote major changes.

Assertive accommodation involves using practices such as "communicating self," "intragroup networking," "using liaisons" (e.g., members of dominant groups who provide support), and "educating others" about nondominant groups (Orbe, 1998). The goal of individuals using this approach is "to create a cooperative balance" between the dominant and nondominant groups (p. 114). Since being assertive recognizes the rights of members of both groups, nondominant group members using this approach tend to be perceived more positively than those using aggressive accommodation (which focuses on the rights of members of nondominant groups). Nondominant group members' assertiveness, however, may be perceived as aggressive by members of dominant groups (e.g., women using the same communication assertive behaviors as men in organizations often are perceived as aggressive).

Clearly, nondominant group members using an assertive accommodation approach to interacting with members of the dominant groups provides the soundest foundation for developing community. True communities respect differences among members of the community, which does not occur with either an assimilation or separation approach to intergroup relations. Also, members of true communities walk a narrow ridge in their concern for themselves and others. This requires assertiveness, not nonassertiveness or aggressiveness.

Ethical Issues in Building Community With Strangers

In Chapter 4, I indicated that our expectations for strangers have a "should" component. The "should" aspect of our expectations is derived from our ethical systems. Take a moment to answer the following question before reading further.

Should we make moral judgments about strangers' behavior? Why or why not?

____

____

____

____

Keep your answer to this question in mind when you read the rest of this section.

We cannot develop community if we do not treat each other in an ethical fashion. I, therefore, include ethical issues in communicating with strangers in this chapter. There are two issues that are critical in developing community: taking an ethical stand and being morally inclusive.

Taking an Ethical Stand

We are living in a time of "moral skepticism." Many of us today are *not* sure that it is valid to make moral judgments (Taylor, 1992). This creates moral uncertainty (Marris, 1996). Moral uncertainty is highly stressful. One way we deal with our moral uncertainty is "by accepting that a moral choice is simply what feels right, and so, if what feels right to me does not sit well with you, I should respect rather than argue with your different feelings" (Marris, 1996, p. 157).[4] This position, however, leaves us no way to judge our own or strangers' behavior.

One reason we may have trouble making ethical judgments is that we have extended the idea of cultural relativity to the domain of ethics. The theory of cultural relativism asserts that the behavior of people in different groups can be *understood* only in the context of those groups. Stated differently, if we want to understand strangers' behavior, we have to do it from their frames of reference. There is no question that this is true; we cannot understand members of other groups using our frames of reference. The idea of tolerance was incorporated into some discussions of cultural relativism. Cultural relativism, for example, is "a philosophy which, in recognizing the values set up by every society to guide its own life, lays stress on the dignity in every body of custom, and on the need for tolerance of conventions though they may differ from one's own" (Herskovits, 1950, p. 76).

Incorporating tolerance in the theory of cultural relativity was due to the time in which the theory was developed; "cultural relativism was introduced in part to combat . . . racist, Eurocentric notions of progress" (Renteln, 1988, p. 37); for example, viewing people from the Third World as savages or primitive. It is necessary, however, to draw a distinction between the evaluative and descriptive aspects of ethical relativity: "[Cultural] relativism . . . asserts the factual diversity of customs, of moral beliefs and practices. . . . The thesis itself, however, is purely a factual one. . . . Ethical relativism proper, on the other hand, is an evaluative thesis, affirming that the value of actions and the validity of moral judgments are dependent upon their sociocultural context. The two theses are logically distinct, though not unrelated" (Barnsley, 1972, pp. 326-327). In other words, saying that ethics develop out of culture and vary across cultures (cultural relativism) is different from saying that valid moral judgments can only be made within a particular cultural context (ethical relativism).

Cultural relativity "does not, of course, free the individual from finding his [or her] own way morally. That would be another instance of 'bad faith,' with the objective fact of relativity being taken as an alibi for the subjective necessity of finding those single decisive points at which one engages one's whole being" (Berger, cited by Barnsley, 1972, p. 355). Even if we accept cultural diversity, we must still make ethical judgments in our interactions with people from other groups. Cultural relativism "does not force its adherents to foreswear moral criticism" (Renteln, 1988, p. 63).

We cannot avoid making ethical judgments. We must deal with our own moral uncertainty. There is "no escape from the need to find a moral understanding of the entire world of social relationships of which we are a part" (Marris, 1996, p. 170). We can find a morality to guide our behavior in the "fundamental, universal qualities of our common humanity" (Marris, 1996, p. 171). There appear to be cultural universals that can be used. There may, for example, be universals regarding prohibitions against activities such as treason, murder, rape, and incest because "in all cultures the perpetuation of society takes precedence over the life of the individual" (Bidney, 1968, p. 545). The Aspen Declaration on Character Education also isolates six core values that constitute a unified moral stance that may be universal: (1) respect, (2) responsibility, (3) trustworthiness, (4) caring, (5) justice and fairness, and (6) civic virtue and citizenship.

The four moral constraints necessary to establish peace also may be cultural universals in ethical behavior:

> Of the four, two are the widely acknowledged curbs on violence and deceit. . . . To cement agreement about how and to who those curbs apply, and to keep them from being ignored or violated at will, a third constraint—on breaches of valid promises, contracts, laws, and treaties—is needed.
>
> Whether expressed in religious or secular form, these three values are shared by every civilization, past and present. Any community, no matter how small or disorganized, no matter how hostile toward outsiders, no matter how cramped its perception of what constitutes, say, torture, has to impose at least *some* internal curbs on violence, deceit, and betrayal in order to survive. But because persons acting clandestinely easily bypass or ignore these constraints, a fourth is necessary on excessive secrecy. (Bok, 1989, pp. 81-82)

This list of moral constraints is not the only possible basis for making ethical judgments, but the list of moral constraints provides the basis for the development of a set of ethical principles that we can use in our own lives (see Gandhi, 1948; King, 1958; for discussions of the importance of nonviolence).

In making moral judgments we have to balance individual and community needs (Taylor, 1992). Individuals have a right to define themselves however they want, but they must do this in dialogue (discussed earlier in this chapter) with others. To make moral judgments of strangers, we must first seriously study strangers so that we understand them and their morality before we judge them. One way we can do this is by engaging in moral dialogues. "*Moral Dialogues* occur when a group of people engage in a process of sorting the values that guide their lives" (Etzioni, 2001, p. 240). **Shared views of what is "good" emerge from moral dialogues**. "Moral dialogues are not merely a matter of reasonable people coming to terms, but of people of divergent convictions finding a common normative ground" (p. 241).

Moral dialogues generally take place within nations but they can occur across national boundaries as well (Etzioni, 2001). When members of different cultures engage in moral dialogues, there is a possibility of a "global moral base" being negotiated. Engaging in moral dialogues across cultures, however, does not legitimize berating people from other cultures. "The moral voice is most compelling when it is firm but not screeching, judging not judgmental, critical but not self-righteous" (p. 244).

Before reading the next section, take a few minutes to answer the following questions.

Are there people you think do not have to be treated in a "moral" way? If yes, who? If no, why not?

____

____

____

____

Are there situations where you do not think about the morality of your behavior? If yes, what situations? If no, why not?

____

____

____

____

How does your behavior differ when you are aware of the need to behave morally and when you are not?

____

____

____

____

Your answers to these questions should provide some insights into the role of moral inclusion in your implicit theory of communication. Keep your answers in mind as you read the next section.

Moral Inclusion-Exclusion

As indicated in Chapter 1, "moral exclusion occurs when individuals or groups are perceived as *outside the boundary in which moral values, rules, and considerations of fairness apply*. Those who are morally excluded are perceived as nonentities, expendable, or undeserving; consequently, harming them appears acceptable, appropriate, or just" (Optow, 1990, p. 1). There are three attitudes associated with being morally inclusive (Optow, 1990). First, we are morally inclusive if we assume that considerations of fairness apply to strangers. Second, we are morally inclusive if we are willing to provide a share of community resources to strangers who need them. Third, we are morally inclusive if we are willing to make sacrifices to help strangers.

Many moral philosophers (e.g., Nozick, 1974) suggest that our considerations of fairness and principles of morality should be applied to only members of the human species. Others (e.g., Regan, 1983) believe that our boundaries for moral behavior should be animals that have cognitive awareness. This criterion extends our boundaries of moral behavior to many mammals (e.g., dolphins, whales, dogs). Still others (e.g., Stone, 1974) suggest that our boundaries of moral behavior should extend to inanimate objects (e.g., the planet, plants).

There are two major factors that lead us to behave in a morally exclusive fashion (Optow, 1990). When we are engaged in group *conflict*, for example, ingroup cohesiveness is high, but at the same time concern for fairness for strangers is low. Another factor that contributes to moral exclusiveness is *feeling unconnected* to strangers. When we feel connected to strangers in any way, we feel attraction, empathy, and engage in helpful behavior toward them. These behaviors are morally inclusive. When we see strangers within our moral communities harmed, we perceive an injustice to have taken place. If we harm strangers in our moral communities, we will feel shame, guilt, remorse, or self-blame. When we see strangers as outside our moral communities and they are harmed, we may not perceive that their rights are violated and we may not be concerned. When this occurs, we are being morally exclusive.

A Protestant minister who was imprisoned in Dachau, a concentration camp in Germany, in 1938, illustrates one of the problems with being morally exclusive:

> In Germany, the Nazis first came for the communists, and I didn't speak up because I wasn't a communist. Then they came for the Jews, and I didn't speak up because I wasn't a Jew. Then they came for the trade unionists, and I didn't speak up because I wasn't a trade unionist. Then they came for the Catholics, but I didn't speak up because I was a Protestant.

TABLE 10.2 *Assessing Your Moral Inclusiveness With Strangers**

The purpose of this questionnaire is to assess your moral inclusiveness. Respond to each statement indicating the degree to which you agree or disagree: "Strongly Disagree" (answer 1), "Disagree" (answer 2), "Sometimes Disagree and Sometimes Agree" (answer 3), "Agree" (answer 4), and "Strongly Agree" (answer 5).

_____ 1. Strangers should be treated fairly.
_____ 2. There are strangers who do not deserve my respect.
_____ 3. Strangers have a right to be treated with dignity.
_____ 4. I do not make sacrifices to foster strangers' well-being.
_____ 5. Moral values apply equally to strangers.
_____ 6. I am not morally obligated to treat strangers with respect.
_____ 7. I apply the same rules to my friends and strangers.
_____ 8. It is not my responsibility to help strangers who need assistance.
_____ 9. All forms of life should be treated with reverence.
_____ 10. There are conditions (other than in a declared war) under which it is acceptable to harm strangers.

To find your score, first reverse your responses for the even numbered items (i.e., if you wrote 1, make it 5; if you wrote 2, make it 4; if you wrote 3, leave it as 3; if you wrote 4, make it 2; if you wrote 5, make it 1). Next, add the numbers next to each statement. Scores range from 10 to 50. The higher your score, the more morally inclusive you are.

*Based on Optow's (1990) discussion of moral exclusion.

> Then they came for me, and by that time there was no one left to speak for me. (Reverend Martin Niemoeller; from a wall at the Holocaust Museum in Washington, D.C.)

Clearly, if we are morally exclusive toward strangers, they will be morally exclusive toward us.

Moral exclusion can take many forms. It can range from slavery, genocide, political repression, and violations of human rights to failing to recognize strangers' undeserved suffering.[5] The Holocaust during World War II and the My Lai massacre during the Vietnam War are examples of severe moral exclusion. Moral exclusion, however, occurs in our everyday interactions too. **If we distance ourselves from strangers psychologically, ignore our responsibility to strangers, or glorify violence, we are being morally exclusive**.

Table 10.2 contains a questionnaire designed to help you determine how morally inclusive you are. Take a few minutes to complete it before you continue reading.

Scores on the questionnaire range from 10 to 50. The higher your score on the assessment in Table 10.2, the more morally inclusive you are. If we score low, we can choose to increase our moral inclusiveness if we are mindful when we make judgments of strangers.

Principles of Community Building

To review, a community consists of diverse individuals who are honest and open with each other, trust each other, engage in ethical behavior, and are committed to living together. Members of a community are civil to each other, and they value diversity while, at the same time, they search for the commonalities humans share. Community makes life worth living and the existence of community makes peace and intergroup harmony possible. While community occurs in groups, individuals must take the responsibility for building community in their marriages, workplaces, schools, cities, nations, and the world. Finally, members of a community behave ethically.

Assumptions

To conclude the book, I synthesize the information presented in this chapter into a set of principles for community building. The principles presented are based on several *assumptions*.

Assumption 1: Community Is Necessary in Our Lives. Most of us do not experience much community in our lives. Community, however, is necessary to make life worth living. "People who fully develop and harmoniously integrate their capabilities, values, and goals will be connected to others. The full evolution of the self . . . requires relationships and the development of deep connections and community—as well as the capacity for separateness" (Staub, 1989, p. 269). Being part of a community does not mean giving up our individuality. "Individuals without community are without substance; while communities without individuals are blind" (Kegley, 1997, p. 37).

The more we develop community, the greater the potential for peace in the world. **Peace is not possible without community**. "Our experience of connection and community shape who we are, how we experience other people, and how we bear the stresses of both ordinary and extraordinary events" (Staub, 1989, p. 269). We must build social capital in our communities (e.g., connections with others; Putnam, 2000).

Assumption 2: We Have a Responsibility to Develop Community. Each of us has a responsibility for developing community in our lives. Most of us, however, do not try to build community in our lives.

The major reason we do not try to develop community in our lives is that we engage in most of our interactions on automatic pilot. If we are mindful, we are mindful of the outcome, not the process of our communication with strangers. To build community in our lives we must be mindful of the processes occurring in our interactions with strangers. Building community requires a conscious effort. Without mindful attention, we will not be able to build community in our lives.

Assumption 3: Diversity Is Necessary for Community. Cultural and ethnic diversity (and all other forms of diversity, as well) are necessary resources for building community. When we interact with strangers on automatic pilot, we assume that diversity inhibits the development of community. This, however, is not the case. Being exclusive and not allowing strangers to be part of our communities inhibits the development of true community. Variety and diversity are the basis for excellence (see Gould, 1996).

We need to work toward developing communities that respect and encourage diversity (Lippmann, 1937). A true community (i.e., a community of otherness) cannot exist without diversity. It is necessary to recognize, however, that "to prevent the wholeness from smothering diversity, there must be a philosophy of pluralism, an open climate for dissent, and an opportunity for subcommunities to retain their identity and share in the setting of larger goals" (Gardner, 1991, p. 11).

Assumption 4: Communities Can Be Big or Small. Communities can be any size (e.g., a marriage, social organization, university, town, country, or even the world). We often mistakenly assume that community exists only in large groups. The feeling of community, however, can exist in any relationship we have.

We must start building community in the smaller groups of which we are members (e.g., interpersonal relationships, families) and work toward developing community in the larger groups (e.g., universities, societies). If we have not built community in the small groups of which we are members, we cannot build community in the large groups of which we are members. The important thing is that we try to build community in the groups to which we belong.

Assumption 5: We Are What We Think. "Everything in life depends on the thoughts we choose to hold in our minds and our willingness to change our belief systems" (Jampolsky, 1989, p. 31). Similarly, in *The*

Dhammapada, Buddha said that "our life is shaped by our minds; we become what we think." The way we think about strangers influences the way we act toward them.

If we think community is important and think strangers are as important as we are, we will treat strangers differently than if we do not think strangers are important or that we are more important than they are. If we think about the negative things in our lives, they become our central focus. If we think about the positive things in our lives, they become the central focus. The same is true of our relationships with strangers.

Assumption 6: Community Cannot Exist Without Conflict. We should expect "ineliminable and acceptable conflicts, and . . . rationally controlled hostilities, as the normal condition" (Hampshire, 1989, p. 189). We need to be able to manage the conflicts that occur, especially the conflicts that emerge from the diversity of our community (Lippmann, 1937).

As indicated earlier, we tend to assume that "if we can resolve our conflicts, then someday we will be able to live together in community" (Peck, 1987, p. 72). This assumption is mistaken. Actually, "if we can live together in community, then someday we shall be able to resolve our conflicts" (p. 72). To develop community, therefore, we must engage in graceful fighting; try to persuade each other, but not coerce each other.

Assumption 7: One Person Can Begin a Community. One person can change a relationship and/or start the development of community within the relationship (Fisher & Brown, 1988). All relationships involve some degree of interdependence, even our relationships with strangers. The way we act influences the way that strangers act toward us. We can change our relationships with strangers when there are problems by changing the way we behave.

If we change our behavior, strangers cannot continue to engage in the same old behavior. Eventually, strangers will change the way they act toward us. Rather than waiting for strangers to change their behavior, we can take the first step and try to develop community in our relationships with them. If we follow the principles suggested below, strangers with whom we come in contact eventually will change the way they interact with us.

Principles

Given these assumptions and the material summarized throughout the book, I present seven *community building principles.* The principles are not presented in any order of priority. All are necessary for community to develop.

Principle 1: Be Committed. We must be committed to the principle of building community in our lives, as well as to the strangers with whom we are trying to develop a community (Peck, 1987). Commitment to strangers is a prerequisite for community to exist. We must be committed to "welcoming" strangers. We must convey that "we know that racism, sexism, homophobia and other forms of discrimination exist on our campuses, as everywhere, and that we are actively seeking to discover how they are intertwined in what we do" (Cullen, 2002, p. B13). Being committed means being willing to "stick in there when the going gets tough." Stated differently, if we are committed, we will not abandon our relationships with strangers just because there are problems in the relationships. If we are not committed, strangers will sense this and it will affect the quality of our relationships with them.

We also need to be committed to dialogue as a way of solving problems (Selznick, 1992). Without commitment to our relationships with strangers and to dialogue, we cannot constructively manage our conflicts with them. It is the commitment present in a community that allows the differences inherent in its diversity to be absorbed (Peck, 1987). We need to be committed to our collective (social) identities associated with our communities and to a participatory mode of politics within the community (Taylor, 1991). We must be committed to cooperating with strangers on our shared goals. We also need to be committed to principles (e.g., respect, tolerance, civility), not being right (Buber, 1958).

Principle 2: Be Mindful. We must pay attention to what we do and say. When we communicate with strangers, we need to pay attention to the process of communication that is occurring between us and them rather than worrying about the outcome of our interactions. If we worry about the outcome, we will not be able to communicate effectively. "When we are giving our full attention to something, when we are really attending, we are calling on all of our resources of intelligence, feeling, and moral sensitivity. . . . We are not thinking about ourselves, because we are completely absorbed in what we are doing" (Bellah et al., 1991, p. 254). "A good society is one in which attention takes precedence over distraction" (p. 273). **Mindfulness facilitates excellence and ethical behavior** (Gardner et al., 2001).

If we communicate on automatic pilot, we will interpret strangers' behavior using our own frames of reference and evaluate them, rather than try to understand them. If we are not mindful of our communication, we will be more concerned for ourselves than for strangers. This makes it impossible to develop community. Our emphasis should be on adapting our messages so that strangers can understand them the ways we meant them, and interpreting strangers' messages using their frames of reference.

Principle 3: Be Unconditionally Accepting. For community to develop, we must accept strangers as they are, and not try to change or control them (Fisher & Brown, 1988). If we try to change strangers, they will become defensive and building community will not be possible. If we accept strangers, they will sense this. **Feeling accepted allows strangers to be open with us and be concerned with our welfare.**

We must accept strangers' diversity and not judge them based only on their group memberships. We need to recognize and support the personal and social identities strangers claim for themselves. Identity safety allows individuals to perform their best. If we do not support strangers' self-concepts, we cannot develop satisfying relationships or develop community with them. We need to minimize our expectations, prejudices, suspicion, and mistrust (Peck, 1987). Trusting strangers is necessary for community to develop (Bellah et al., 1991). This can only be accomplished when we are mindful.

Principle 4: Be Concerned for Both Ourselves and Others. Communities are inclusive; they are *not* groups of like-minded people. If we think we are better than strangers or try to exclude them from our lives, we are being exclusive. If we are morally exclusive, we accept harming strangers (physically or psychologically) as moral behavior. We must walk a narrow ridge in our interactions with strangers whenever practical (Buber, 1958). This means that we avoid polarizing our communication (Arnett, 1986), actively listen to strangers when they speak, and engage in dialogue whenever possible (Buber, 1958, 1965).

Our survival depends on the survival of the communities of which we are members (Loewry, 1993). Being authentic (e.g., self-fulfilled, empowered) and identifying with strangers and our communities are *not* incompatible (Taylor, 1991). We need to be concerned with our own and strangers' personal and social identities. We must consult strangers on issues that affect them, and be open to their ideas (Fisher & Brown, 1988). We must take strangers into consideration when there is a conflict, and fight gracefully (Peck, 1987). We also need to be contemplative in examining our own behavior and that of the communities of which we are members (Peck, 1987).

Principle 5: Be Understanding. **We need to understand strangers as completely as possible.** "Shallow understanding from people of good will is more frustrating than absolute misunderstanding from people of ill will" (King, 1963, p. 88). To be understanding, we must determine how strangers' interpretations of events and/or behavior are different from and similar to our own.

To be understanding, we also must recognize how culture, ethnicity, and other forms of diversity affect the way we think and behave. We must understand real differences between our groups and strangers' groups, not base our interpretations of differences on our stereotypes and prejudices. Building community requires "the appreciation of differences. In community, instead of being ignored, denied, hidden, or changed, human differences are celebrated as gifts" (Peck, 1987, p. 62). We also need to search for commonalities with strangers on which community can be built (Bellah et al., 1985). In our communication, we must balance emotion, anxiety, and fear with reason (Fisher & Brown, 1988).

Principle 6: Be Ethical. **We must engage in behavior that is not a means to an end, but behavior which is morally right in and of itself** (Bellah et al., 1985). We have to be reliable in what we say and do (Fisher & Brown, 1988). We need to recognize that being moral takes precedence over all other concerns (Pritchard, 1991). Behaving morally toward strangers requires that we allow them to maintain their dignity.

We must be morally inclusive (Optow, 1990) and engage in service to others (Lynberg, 1989). "Starting with common everyday acts and moving on to acts requiring greater sacrifice . . . can lead to genuine concern and a feeling of responsibility for people" (Staub, 1989, p. 276). This is not to say that we should not make moral judgments. We cannot avoid making moral judgments, but we need to understand strangers' behavior in their frames of reference before we make judgments. A community is based on its moral principles (Etzioni, 1993).

Principle 7: Be Peaceful. We need to work toward developing peace in all of our thoughts, words, and actions. If peace is the goal of our interactions with strangers, our communication with strangers will be effective. Developing peace requires that we are *not* violent, we are *not* deceitful, we do *not* breach valid promises, and we are *not* secretive (Bok, 1989). Even if strangers engage in these behaviors toward us we are not justified in engaging in these behaviors toward them (Fisher & Brown, 1988). As Socrates pointed out, retaliation is never justified (Vlastos, 1991).

We must strive for internal harmony (Prather, 1986) and harmony in our relations with strangers. "Practicing mindfulness in each moment of our daily lives, we can cultivate our own peace. With clarity, determination, and patience . . . we can sustain a life of action and be real instruments of peace" (Hanh, 1991, p. 99). If we are peaceful, strangers with whom we come into contact will benefit from our peace.

Conclusion

These seven principles are ideals for which we can strive. The more we are able to put them into practice individually, the greater the chance for community and peace in the world. We must not, however, punish ourselves when we fail to achieve the ideal. Achieving these ideals is a lifetime's work and requires extensive practice.

If we are to tolerate strangers, we must begin by accepting our own mistakes. When we find that we are not engaging in behavior we want to practice (e.g., building community), we must forgive ourselves and start anew at practicing the behavior (Prather, 1986). For most of us, this will occur numerous times a day initially. The behaviors suggested in the ideals are different from those we have learned from birth. To engage in these behaviors consistently, we must unlearn many of our normal behaviors (e.g., behaviors that occur at low levels of awareness such as reacting defensively and looking out only for ourselves). The critical thing is *not* the outcome, but the process. If we behave in a way consistent with these ideals (the process), community (the desirable outcome) will occur.

Study Questions

1. Why is dialogue necessary for community to develop?
2. How can we walk a narrow ridge when communicating with strangers?
3. What are the characteristics of community?
4. What does it mean to say that "a community is defined by its practices"?
5. How is social capital related to understanding community?
6. Why must we take an ethical stand when we communicate with strangers?
7. Why is moral inclusion necessary for community to develop?
8. Why is diversity necessary for community?
9. What are the principles of community development?

Applications

1. Over the next week, pay attention to when you engage in monologues, technical dialogues, and dialogues. Under what conditions do you engage in each of these forms of communication? How does the type of communication you have with others influence your relationship with them?

2. Over the next week, pay attention to your moral inclusion. When are you morally exclusive? When are you morally inclusive? What can you do in the future to be more morally inclusive?

3. Over the next week, apply the principles of community building in a specific relationship. Keep track of how you apply the various principles. What effect does applying the principles have on your relationship?

Notes

1. See Arnett (1986) for an application of Buber's philosophy to communication and community.
2. Peck (1987) provides suggestions on how we can develop community in the groups of which we are members.
3. Orbe refers to these groups as "co-cultures." I have used nondominant because it makes the comparison to "dominant" groups direct.
4. This position was taken by several people in Bellah et al.'s (1985) study.
5. See Ignatieff (2001) for a discussion of human rights, including the arguments for and against.

REFERENCES

Abelson, R. (1976). Script processing in attitude formation and decision making. In J. Carroll & J. Payne (Eds.), *Cognition and social behavior.* Hillsdale, NJ: Lawrence Erlbaum.

Aboud, F. (1988). *Children and prejudice.* Oxford, UK: Blackwell.

Agar, M. (1994). *Language shock.* New York: William Morrow.

Akimoto, S., & Sanbonmatsu, D. (1999). Differences in self-effacing behavior between European Americans and Japanese Americans. *Journal of Cross-Cultural Psychology, 30,* 159-177.

Alba, R. (1976). Social assimilation among American Catholic national origin groups. *American Sociological Review, 41,* 1030-1046.

Alba, R. (1990). *Ethnic identity: The transformation of white America.* New Haven, CT: Yale University Press.

Alberti, R., & Emmons, M. (1986). *Your perfect right* (5th ed.). San Louis Obispo, CA: Impact.

Allport, G. (1954). *The nature of prejudice.* New York: Macmillan.

Almaney, A., & Alwan, A. (1982). *Communicating with the Arabs.* Prospect Heights, IL: Waveland.

Altman, I., & Taylor, D. (1973). *Social penetration.* New York: Holt, Reinhart & Winston.

Ang, I. (1993). Migrations of Chineseness. In D. Bennett (Ed.), *Cultural studies.* Melbourne, Australia: University of Melbourne Press.

Applegate, J., & Sypher, H. (1983). The constructivist approach. In W. Gudykunst (Ed.), *Intercultural communication theory.* Beverly Hills, CA: Sage.

Ardener, S. (1975). *Perceiving women.* London: Malaby.

Argyle, M., & Henderson, M. (1984). The rules of relationships. In S. Duck & D. Perlman (Eds.), *Understanding personal relationships.* Beverly Hills, CA: Sage.

Argyle, M., Henderson, M., Bond, M., Iizuka, Y., & Contarelo, A. (1986). Cross-cultural variations in relationship rules. *International Journal of Psychology, 21,* 287-315.

Armour, J. (1997). *Negrophobia and reasonable racism.* New York: New York University Press.

Arnett, R. C. (1986). *Communication and community.* Carbondale: Southern Illinois University Press.

Arnoff, C. (1974). Old age in prime time. *Journal of Communication, 24,* 86-87.

Ashford, S., & Cummings, L. (1983). Feedback as an individual resource. *Organizational Behavior and Human Performance, 32,* 370-398.

Ball-Rokeach, S. (1973). From pervasive ambiguity to definition of the situation. *Sociometry, 36,* 378-389.

Ball-Rokeach, S., Rokeach, M., & Grube, J. (1984). *The great American values test.* New York: Free Press.

Banks, S., Gao, G., & Baker, J. (1991). Intercultural encounters and miscommunication. In N. Coupland, H. Giles, & J. Wiemann (Eds.), *"Miscommunication" and problematic talk.* Newbury Park, CA: Sage.

Barbato, C., & Feezel, J. (1987). The language of aging in different age-groups. *Gerontological Society of America, 27,* 527-531.

Barnlund, D. (1962). Toward a meaning centered philosophy of communication. *Journal of Communication, 2,* 197-211.

Barnlund, D. (1975). *Public and private self in Japan and the United States.* Tokyo: Simul.

Barnlund, D., & Yoshioka, M. (1990). Apologies: Japanese and American styles. *International Journal of Intercultural Relations, 14,* 193-206.

Barnsley, J. (1972). *The social reality of ethics.* London: Routledge.

Barringer, F. (1993, May 16). Pride in a soundless world. *New York Times,* pp. 1, 14.

Barth, F. (1969). *Ethnic groups and boundaries.* London: Allen and Unwin.

Bartlett, T. (2001, November 30). An ugly tradition persists at southern fraternity parties. *The Chronicle of Higher Education,* pp. A33-34.

Bateson, G. (1979). *Mind and nature.* New York: E. P. Dutton.

Batson, C., Chang, J., Orr, R., & Rowland, J. (2002). Empathy, abilities, and action. *Personality and Social Psychology Bulletin, 28,* 1656-1666.

Batson, C., Polycarpon, M., Harmon-Jones, E., Inhoff, H., Mitchner, E., Bednar, L., Klein, T., & Highberger, L. (1997). Empathy and attitudes. *Journal of Personality and Social Psychology, 72,* 105-118.

Beck, A. (1988). *Love is never enough.* New York: Harper & Row.

Beebe, L., Takahashi, T., & Uliss-Wetz, R. (1990). Pragmatic transfer in ESL refusals. In R. Scarcella, E. Anderson, & S. Krashen (Eds.), *Developing communication competence in a second language.* New York: Newbury House.

Belk, S., Snell, W., Garcia-Falconi, R., Hernandez-Falconi, J., Hargrove, L., & Holtzman, W. (1988). Power strategy use in the intimate relationships of women and men from Mexico and the United States. *Personality and Social Psychology Bulletin, 14,* 439-447.

Bell, R. (1987). Social involvement. In J. McCroskey & J. Daly (Eds.), *Personality and interpersonal communication.* Newbury Park, CA: Sage.

Bell, R., & Daly, J. (1984). The affinity-seeking function of communication. *Communication Monographs, 51,* 91-115.

Bellah, R. N., Madsen, R., Sullivan, W. M., Swidler, A., & Tipton, S. M. (1985). *Habits of the heart: Individualism and commitment in American life.* Berkeley: University of California Press.

Bellah, R. N., Madsen, R., Sullivan, W. M., Swidler, A., & Tipton, S. M. (1991). *The good society.* New York: Knopf.

Bem, S. (1974). The measurement of psychological androgyny. *Journal of Consulting and Clinical Psychology, 42,* 155-162.

Bem, S. (1993). *The lens of gender.* New Haven, CT: Yale University Press.

Bennett, M. (1979). Overcoming the Golden Rule: Sympathy and empathy. In D. Nimmo (Ed.), *Communication yearbook 3.* New Brunswick, NJ: Transaction Books.

Benson, P., & Vincent, S. (1980). Development and validation of the Sexist Attitude Toward Women Scale. *Psychology of Women Quarterly, 5,* 276-291.

Berger, C. R. (1979). Beyond initial interactions. In H. Giles & R. St. Clair (Eds.), *Language and social psychology.* Oxford, UK: Blackwell.

Berger, C. R., & Bradac, J. (1982). *Language and social knowledge.* London: Edward Arnold.

Berger, C. R., & Calabrese, R. (1975). Some explorations in initial interactions and beyond: Toward a developmental theory of interpersonal communication. *Human Communication Research, 1,* 99-112.

Berger, C. R., & Douglas, W. (1982). Thought and talk. In F. Dance (Ed.), *Human communication theory.* New York: Harper & Row.

Berlo, D. (1960). *The process of communication.* New York: Holt.

Bernstein, B. (1973). *Class, codes, and control* (Vol. 1). London: Routledge and Kegan Paul.

Berscheid, E., & Walster, E. (1969). *Interpersonal attraction.* Reading, MA: Addison-Wesley.

Bidney, D. (1968). Cultural relativism. In D. Sills (Ed.), *International encyclopedia of the social sciences* (Vol. 3). New York: Free Press.

Birdwhistell, R. (1963). The kinesics level in the investigation of emotions. In P. Knapp (Ed.), *Expressions of emotions in man.* New York: International University Press.

Blair, I. (2002). The malleability of autonomic stereotypes and prejudice. *Personality and Social Psychology Review, 6,* 242-260.

Blanchard, F., Lilly, T., & Vaughn, L. (1991). Reducing the expression of racial prejudice. *Psychological Science, 2,* 101-105.

Bloom, L., Coburn, K., & Pearlman, J. (1975). *The new assertive woman.* New York: Dell.

Bobo, L., & Smith, R. (1998). From Jim Crow racism to laissez faire racism. In W. Katkin, N. Landsman, & A. Tyree (Eds.), *Beyond pluralism.* Urbana: University of Illinois Press.

Bodenhausen, G., Gaelick, L., & Wyer, R. (1987). Affective and cognitive factors in intragroup and intergroup communication. In C. Hendrick (Ed.), *Group processes and intergroup relations.* Newbury Park, CA: Sage.

Bodenhausen, G., & Macrae, C. (1996). The self-regulation of intergroup perception. In C. Macrae, C. Stagnor, & M. Hewstone (Eds.), *Stereotypes and stereotyping.* New York: Guilford.

Bok, S. (1989). *A strategy for peace: Human values and the threat of war.* New York: Pantheon.

Bolton, R. (1990). Listening is more than merely hearing. In J. Stewart (Ed.), *Bridges not walls.* New York: McGraw-Hill.

Bond, M. H., & Lee, P. (1981). Face-saving in Chinese culture. In A. King & R. Lee (Eds.), *Social life and development in Hong Kong.* Hong Kong: Chinese University Press.

Bond, M. H., Leung, K., & Wan, K. (1982). The social impact of self-effacing attributions: The Chinese. *Journal of Social Psychology, 118,* 157-166.

Bond, M. H., Wan, K., Leung, K., & Giacalone, R. (1985). How are the responses to verbal insults related to cultural collectivism and power distance? *Journal of Cross-Cultural Psychology, 16,* 111-127.

Bonus, E. (1997). Marking and marketing "difference." *Positions, 5,* 643-670.

Boucher, K., Landis, D., & Clark, K. (Eds.). (1987). *Ethnic conflict.* Newbury Park, CA: Sage.

Boulding, E. (1988). *Building a global civic culture.* Syracuse, NY: Syracuse University Press.

Bourhis, R. (1985). The sequential nature of language choices in cross-cultural communication. In R. Street & J. Cappella (Eds.), *Sequence and pattern in communicative behavior.* London: Edward Arnold.

Boyer, E. (1990, June 20). Letter to the editor. *Chronicle of Higher Education,* p. B4.

Bradac, J. (1990). Language attitudes and impression formation. In H. Giles & P. Robinson (Eds.), *Handbook of language and social psychology.* London: Wiley.

Braithwaite, D. (1991). "Just how much did that wheelchair cost?" *Western Journal of Speech Communication, 55,* 254-274.

Branscombe, N., & Wann, D. (1994). Collective self-esteem consequences of outgroup derogation when a valued social identity is on trial. *European Journal of Social Psychology, 24,* 641-657.

Brewer, M. (1981). Ethnocentrism and its role in interpersonal trust. In M. Brewer & B. Collins (Eds.), *Scientific inquiry and the social sciences.* San Francisco: Jossey-Bass.

Brewer, M. (1991). The social self. *Personality and Social Psychology Bulletin, 17,* 475-482.

Brewer, M. (2002). Ingroup identification and intergroup conflict. In R. Ashmore, L. Jussim, & D. Wilder (Eds.), *Social identity, intergroup conflict, and conflict reduction.* New York: Oxford University Press.

Brewer, M., & Brown, R. (1998). Intergroup relations. In D. Gilbert, S. Fiske, & G. Lindzey (Eds.), *Handbook of social psychology* (4th ed., Vol. 2). New York: McGraw-Hill.

Brewer, M., & Campbell, D. (1976). *Ethnocentrism and intergroup attitudes.* New York: John Wiley.

Brewer, M., & Gaertner, S. (2001). Toward reduction of prejudice. In R. Brown & S. Gaertner (Eds.), *Intergroup processes.* Oxford, UK: Blackwell.

Brewer, M., & Miller, N. (1988). Contact and cooperation: When do they work? In P. Katz & D. Taylor (Eds.), *Eliminating racism.* New York: Plenum.

Brewer, M., & Roccas, S. (2001). Individual values, social identity, and optimal distinctiveness. In C. Sedikides & M. Brewer (Eds.), *Individual self, relational self, and collective self.* Mahwah, NJ: Lawrence Erlbaum.

Brislin, R. W., Cushner, K., Cherrie, C., & Yong, M. (1986). *Intercultural interactions: A practical guide.* Beverly Hills, CA: Sage

Britt, T., Boniecki, K., Vescio, T., Biernat, M., & Brown, L. (1996). Intergroup anxiety: A person X situation approach. *Personality and Social Psychology Bulletin, 22,* 1177-1188.

Brodie, H. K. (1989, September 9). No we're not taught to hate, but we can overcome instinct to fear "the other." *Los Angeles Times,* Part II, p. 16.

Broome, B. (1990). "Palevome": Foundations of struggle and conflict in Greek interpersonal communication. *Southern Journal of Communication, 55,* 260-275.

Browder, L. (1998). *Ethnic performance and American identities.* Chapel Hill: University of North Carolina Press.

Brown, L. (1998). Ethnic stigma as a contextual experience. *Personality and Social Psychology Bulletin, 24,* 163-172.

Brown, P., & Levinson, S. (1978). Universals in language usage. In E. Goody (Ed.), *Questions and politeness.* Cambridge, UK: Cambridge University Press.

Bruner, J. (1958). Social psychology and perception. In E. Maccoby, T. Newcomb, & E. Hartley (Eds.), *Readings in social psychology* (3rd ed.). New York: Holt, Rinehart & Winston.

Buber, M. (1958). *I and thou.* New York: Scribner.

Buber, M. (1965). *Between man and man.* New York: Macmillan.

Budner, S. (1962). Intolerance of ambiguity as a personality variable. *Journal of Personality, 30,* 29-50.

Burgoon, J., Buller, D., & Woodall, W. (1989). *Nonverbal communication.* New York: Harper & Row.

Burgoon, J., & Hale, J. (1988). Nonverbal expectancy violations. *Communication Monographs, 55,* 58-79.

Burlson, B., Samter, W., & Lucchetti, A. (1992). Similarity in communication values as predictors of friendship choices. *The Southern Communication Journal, 57,* 260-276.

Burns, D. (1989). *The feeling good handbook.* New York: William Morrow.

Butler, R. (1969). Age-ism: Another form of bigotry. *Gerontologist, 9,* 243-246.

Byers, P., & Byers, H. (1972). Nonverbal communication and the education of children. In C. Cozden et al. (Eds.), *Functions of language in the classroom.* New York: Teachers College Press.

Byrne, D. (1971). *The attraction paradigm.* New York: Academic Press.

Cameron, J., Alvarrez, J., Ruble, D., & Fuligini, A. (2001). Children's lay theories about ingroups and outgroups. *Personality and Social Psychology Review, 5,* 118-128.

Cantor, N., Mischel, W., & Schwartz, J. (1982). Social knowledge. In A. Isen & A. Hastorf (Eds.), *Cognitive social psychology.* New York: Elsevier.

Cargile, A., & Bradac, J. (2001). Attitudes toward language. In W. Gudykunst (Ed.), *Communication yearbook 25.* Mahwah, NJ: Lawrence Erlbaum.

Carroll, R. (1988). *Cultural misunderstandings: The French-American experience.* Chicago: University of Chicago Press.

Cegala, D., & Waldron, V. (1992). A study of the relationship between communicative performance and conversational participants' thoughts. *Communication Studies, 43,* 105-123.

Cha, J., & Nam, K. (1985). A test of Kelly's cube of attribution. *Korean Social Science Journal, 12,* 151-180.

Chaika, E. (1982). *Language: The social mirror.* Rowley, MA: Newbury House.

Charles, C., & Massey, D. (2003). *The source of the river: The social origins of freshmen at American selective colleges and universities.* Princeton, NJ: Princeton University Press.

Chen, L. (1995). Interaction involvement and patterns of topical talk. *International Journal of Intercultural Relations, 19,* 463-482.

Chen, L. (1997). Verbal adaptive strategies in U.S. American dyads with U.S. Americans or East-Asian partners. *Communication Monographs, 64,* 302-323.

Chen, L. (2002). Perceptions of intercultural interactions and communication satisfaction. *Communication Reports, 15,* 133-147.

Chen, L., & Cegala, D. (1994). Topic management, shared knowledge, and accommodation. *Research in Language and Social Interaction, 27,* 389-417.

Chin, J. (1983). Diagnostic considerations in working with Asian Americans. *American Journal of Orthopsychiatry, 53,* 100-109.

Chinese Culture Connection. (1987). Chinese values and the search for culture-free dimensions of culture. *Journal of Cross-Cultural Psychology, 18,* 143-164.

Chiu, R., & Kosinski, F. (1994). Is Chinese conflict-handling behavior influenced by Chinese values? *Social Behavior and Personality, 22,* 81-90.

Cialdini, R., Wosinska, W., Barret, D., Butner, J., & Gornick-Durose, M. (1999). Compliance with a request in two cultures. *Personality and Social Psychology Bulletin, 25,* 1242-1253.

Cialdini, R., Wosinska, W., Dabul, A., Whestone-Dion, R., & Heszen, I. (1998). When role salience leads to social role rejection. *Personality and Social Psychology Bulletin, 24,* 473-481.

Cissna, K., & Sieburg, E. (1981). Patterns of interactional confirmation and disconfirmation. In C. Wilder-Mott & J. Weakland (Eds.), *Rigor and imagination.* New York: Praeger.

Clark, H. (1996). *Using language.* New York: Cambridge University Press.

Clark, H., & Marshall, C. (1981). Definite reference and mutual knowledge. In A. Joshi, B. Webber, & I. Sag (Eds.), *Elements of discourse understanding.* New York: Cambridge University Press.

Clark, R., & Delia, J. (1977). Cognitive complexity, social perspective-taking, and functional persuasive skills in second- to ninth-graders. *Human Communication Research, 3,* 128-134.

Clemetson, L. (2003, January 22). Hispanics now largest minority, census shows. *New York Times,* pp. A1, A19.

Cocroft, B., & Ting-Toomey, S. (1994). Facework in Japan and the United States. *International Journal of Intercultural Relations, 18,* 469-506.

Cohen, R. (1987). Problems in intercultural communication in Egyptian-American diplomatic relations. *International Journal of Intercultural Relations, 11,* 29-47.

Cohen, R., & Kennedy, P. (2000). *Global sociology.* London: Macmillan.

Cole, M. (1990). *Relational distances and personality influences on conflict communication.* Paper presented at the Speech Communication Association convention.

Coleman, L., & DePaulo, B. (1991). Uncovering the human spirit: Moving beyond disability and "missed" communication. In N. Coupland, H. Giles, & J. Wiemann (Eds.), *"Miscommunication" and problematic talk.* Newbury Park, CA: Sage.

Collier, J. (1991). *The rise of selfishness in America.* New York: Oxford University Press.

Collier, M. (1991). Conflict competence within African, Mexican, and Anglo American friendships. In S. Ting-Toomey & F. Korzenny (Eds.), *Cross-cultural interpersonal communication.* Newbury Park, CA: Sage.

Collier, M., Ribeau, S., & Hecht, M. (1986). Intracultural communication rules and outcomes within three domestic cultures. *International Journal of Intercultural Relations, 10,* 439-458.

Condon, J. (1984). *With respect to the Japanese.* Yarmouth, ME: Intercultural Press.

Condor, S., & Brown, R. (1988). Psychological processes in intergroup conflict. In W. Strobe, A. Kruglanski, B. Bar-Tal, & M. Hewstone (Eds.), *The social psychology of intergroup conflict.* New York: Springer.

Coupland, J., Nussbaum, J., & Coupland, N. (1991). The reproduction of aging and ageism in intergenerational talk. In N. Coupland, H. Giles, & J. Wisemann (Eds.), *"Miscommunication" and problematic talk.* Newbury Park, CA: Sage.

Coupland, N., Coupland, J., Giles, H., & Henwood, K. (1988). Accommodating the elderly. *Language in Society, 17,* 1-42.

Covey, H. (1988). Historical terminology used to represent older people. *Gerontologist, 28,* 291-297.

Cox, T., Lobel, S., & Mcleod, P. (1991). Effects of ethnic group cultural differences on cooperative and competitive behavior on a group task. *Academy of Management Journal, 34,* 827-847.

Craver, C. (1997). *Effective legal negotiation and settlement* (3rd ed.). Charlottesville, VA: Michie Law.

Crisp, R., Hewstone, M., & Rubin, M. (2001). Does multiple categorization reduce intergroup bias? *Personality and Social Psychology Bulletin, 27,* 76-89.

Crocker, J., & Luhtanen, R. (1990). Collective self-esteem and ingroup bias. *Journal of Personality and Social Psychology, 58,* 60-67.

Crocker, J., Major, B., & Steele, C. (1998). Social stigma. In D. Gilbert, S. Fiske, & G. Lindzey (Eds.), *Handbook of social psychology* (4th ed., Vol. 2). New York: McGraw-Hill.

Crockett, W., & Friedman, P. (1980). Theoretical explorations in the process of initial interactions. *Western Journal of Speech Communication, 44,* 86-92.

Csikszentmihalyi, M. (1990). *Flow: The psychology of optimal experience.* New York: Harper & Row.

Cullen, C. (2002, May 31). Finding racism where you least expect it. *The Chronicle of Higher Education,* p. B13.

Cupach, W., & Imahori, T. (1993). Managing social predicaments created by others. *Western Journal of Communication, 57,* 431-444.

Current Population Reports. (1999). *Profile of the foreign-born population in the United States.* Washington, DC: U.S. Bureau of the Census.

Cushman, D. P., & Cahn, D. (1985). *Interpersonal communication.* Albany: State University of New York Press.

Cushman, D. P., Valentinsen, B., & Dietrich, D. (1982). A rules theory of interpersonal relationships. In F. Dance (Ed.), *Human communication theory.* New York: Harper & Row.

Dahnke, G. (1983). Communication between handicapped and nonhandicapped. In M. McLaughlin (Ed.), *Communication yearbook 6.* Beverly Hills, CA: Sage.

Darwin, C. (1872). *Journal of researches into the natural history and geology of the countries visited during the voyage of H.M.S. "Beagle" round the world, under the command of Capt. Fitzroy, R.N.* London: Ward, Lock, and Bowden.

Davidson, A. (1975). Cognitive differentiation and culture training. In R. Brislin, S. Bochner, & W. Lonner (Eds.), *Cross-cultural perspectives on learning.* Beverly Hills, CA: Sage.

Davidson, A., & Thompson, E. (1980). Cross-cultural studies of attitudes and beliefs. In H. Triandis & R. Brislin (Eds.), *Handbook of cross-cultural psychology* (Vol. 5). Boston: Allyn & Bacon.

Davis, F. (1977). Deviance disavowal. In J. Stubbins (Ed.), *Social and psychological aspects of disability.* Baltimore: University Park Press.

Deaux, K. (1993). Reconstructing social identity. *Personality and Social Psychology Bulletin, 19,* 4-12.

DeRidder, R., & Tripathi, R. (1992). *Rules to live by.* Oxford, UK: Clarendon.

Derlega, V., Cukan, C., Kuang, J., & Forsyth, D. (2002). Interdependent construal of self and the endorsement of conflict resolution strategies in interpersonal, intergroup, and international conflicts. *Journal of Cross-Cultural Psychology, 33,* 610-625.

Derricotte, T. (1997, November 17). Racism: Invisible thoughts and the twisted heart. *The Chronicle of Higher Education,* p. B11. (Excerpt from *The black notebooks.* New York: Norton, 1997)

de Tocqueville, A. (1876/1835). *Democracy in America.* Boston: John Allyn.

Detweiler, R. (1975). On inferring the intentions of a person from another culture. *Journal of Personality, 43,* 591-611.

Detweiler, R. (1978). Culture, category width, and attributions. *Journal of Cross-Cultural Psychology, 11,* 101-124.

Detweiler, R. (1980). Intercultural interaction and the categorization process. *International Journal of Intercultural Relations, 4,* 275-293.

Deutsch, K. (1968). Toward a cybernetic model of man and society. In W. Buckley (Ed.), *Modern systems theory for the behavioral scientist.* Chicago: Aldine.

Deutsch, M. (1973). *The resolution of conflict.* New Haven, CT: Yale University Press.

Devine, P. (1989). Stereotypes and prejudice. *Journal of Personality and Social Psychology, 56,* 5-18.

Devine, P., & Elliott, A. (1995). Are racial stereotypes really fading? *Personality and Social Psychology Bulletin, 21,* 1139-1150.

Devine, P., Evett, S., & Vasquez-Suson, K. (1996). Exploring the interpersonal dynamics of intergroup contact. In R. Sorrentino & E. Higgins (Eds.), *Handbook of motivation and cognition* (Vol. 3). New York: Guilford.

DeVos, G. (1975). Ethnic pluralism. In G. DeVos & L. Romanucci-Ross (Eds.), *Ethnic identity.* Palo Alto, CA: Mayfield.

Diamond, R., & Hellcamp, D. (1969). Race, sex, ordinal position of both and self-disclosure in high school students. *Psychological Report, 25,* 235-238.

Dickson-Markman, F. (1986). Self-disclosure with friends across the life cycle. *Journal of Social and Personal Relationships, 3,* 259-264.

Dion, K. K., & Dion, K. L. (1993). Individualistic and collectivistic perspectives on gender and the cultural context of love and intimacy. *Journal of Social Issues, 49*(3), 53-69.

Dion, K. K., & Dion, K. L. (1996). Cultural perspectives on romantic love. *Personal Relationships, 3*, 5-17.

Dion, K. K., Pak, A., & Dion, K. L. (1990). Stereotyping and physical attractiveness. *Journal of Cross-Cultural Psychology, 21*, 378-398.

Doi, T. (1973). *The anatomy of dependence.* Tokyo: Kodansha.

Donohue, W., with Kolt, R. (1993). *Managing interpersonal conflict.* Newbury Park, CA: Sage.

Dovidio, J. (1997, July 25). "Aversive" racism and the need for affirmative action. *The Chronicle of Higher Education*, p. A60.

Dovidio, J., & Gaertner, S. (1986). Prejudice, discrimination, and racism. In J. Dovidio & S. Gaertner (Eds.), *Prejudice, discrimination, and racism.* Orlando, FL: Academic Press.

Dovidio, J., Gaertner, S., Niemamn, Y., & Snidre, K. (2001). Racial, ethnic, and cultural differences in responding to distinctiveness and discrimination on campus. *Journal of Social Issues, 57*, 167-188.

Downs, J. (1971). *Cultures in crisis.* Chicago: Glencoe.

Duck, S. (1977). *The study of acquaintance.* Farnborough, UK: Saxon House.

Duck, S., Rutt, D., Hurst, M., & Strejc, H. (1991). Some evident truths about conversations in everyday relationships. *Human Communication Research, 18*, 228-267.

Duran, R. L. (1983). Communicative adaptability. *Communication Quarterly, 31*, 320-326.

The Economist. (2003, January 4). Special report: American values, pp. 18-20.

Edwards, J. (1985). *Language, society, and identity.* Oxford, UK: Blackwell.

Ehrenhaus, P. (1983). Culture and the attribution process. In W. Gudykunst (Ed.), *Intercultural communication theory.* Beverly Hills, CA: Sage.

Ekman, P. (1972). Universals and cultural differences in facial expressions of emotions. In J. Cole (Ed.), *Nebraska Symposium on Motivation* (Vol. 19). Lincoln: University of Nebraska Press.

Ekman, P., & Friesen, W. (1969). The repertoire of nonverbal behavior. *Semiotica, 1*, 49-98.

Elfenbein, H., & Ambady, N. (2002a). Is there an ingroup advantage in emotion recognition. *Psychological Bulletin, 128*, 243-249.

Elfenbein, H., & Ambady, N. (2002b). On the universality and cultural specificity of emotion recognition: A meta-analysis. *Psychological Bulletin, 128*, 203-235.

Elfenbein, H., & Ambady, N. (2003). Cultural similarity's consequences: A distance perspective on cross-cultural differences in emotions. *Journal of Cross-Cultural Psychology, 34*, 92-110.

Elliot, S., Scott, M., Jensen, A., & McDonald, M. (1982). Perceptions of reticence. In M. Burgoon (Ed.), *Communication yearbook 5.* New Brunswick, NJ: Transaction Books.

Elsayed-Ekhouly, S., & Buda, R. (1996). Organizational conflict. *International Journal of Conflict Management, 7,* 71-81.

Engebretson, D., & Fullmer, D. (1970). Cross-cultural differences in territoriality. *Journal of Cross-Cultural Psychology, 1,* 261-269.

Erickson, F. (1981). *Anecdote, rhapsody, and rhetoric.* Paper presented at the Georgetown University Roundtable on Language and Linguistics, Washington, DC.

Espinoza, J., & Garza, R. (1985). Social group salience and interethnic cooperation. *Journal of Experimental Social Psychology, 21,* 697-715.

Essed, P. (1991). *Understanding everyday racism.* Newbury Park, CA: Sage.

Etzioni, A. (1993). *The spirit of community.* New York: Crown.

Etzioni, A. (2001). *The monochrome society.* Princeton, NJ: Princeton University Press.

Fang, C., Sidanius, J., & Pratto, F. (1998). Romance across the social status continuum. *Journal of Cross-Cultural Psychology, 29,* 290-305.

Faulkender, P. (1985). Relationships between Bem sex-role inventory and attitudes of sexism. *Psychological Reports, 57,* 227-235.

Feather, N. (1990). Bridging the gap between values and action. In E. Higgins & R. Sorrentino (Eds.), *Handbook of motivation and cognition* (Vol. 2). New York: Guilford.

Feather, N. (1995). Values, valences, and choices. *Journal of Personality and Social Psychology, 68,* 1135-1151.

Fernandez-Collado, C., Rubin, R., & Hernandez-Sampieri, R. (1991). *A cross-cultural examination of interpersonal motives in Mexico and the United States.* Paper presented at the International Communication Association convention.

Finlay, K., & Stephan, W. (2000). Reducing prejudice: The effect of empathy on intergroup attitudes. *Journal of Applied Social Psychology, 30,* 1720-1737.

Fisher, B. A. (1978). *Perspectives on human communication.* New York: Macmillan.

Fisher, R., & Brown, S. (1988). *Getting together: Building relationships as we negotiate.* New York: Houghton Mifflin.

Fiske, A. (1991). *Structures of social life: The four elementary forms of human relations.* New York: Free Press.

Fiske, A., Kitayama, S., Markus, H., & Nisbett, R. (1998). The cultural matrix of social psychology. In D. Gilbert, S. Fiske, & G. Lindzey (Eds.), *Handbook of social psychology* (4th ed., Vol. 2). New York: McGraw-Hill.

Fiske, S., & Morling, B. (1996). Stereotyping as a function of personal control motives and capacity constraints. In R. Sorrentino & E. Higgins (Eds.), *Handbook of motivation and cognition* (Vol. 3). New York: Guilford.

Fiske, S., Morling, B., & Stevens, L. (1996). Controlling self and others: A theory of anxiety, mental control, and social control. *Personality and Social Psychology Bulletin, 22,* 115-123.

Fiske, S., Xu, J., Cuddy, A., & Glick, P. (1999). (Dis)respecting versus (dis)liking. *Journal of Social Issues, 55*(3), 473-489.

FitzGerald, H. (2003). *How different are we?* Clevendon, UK: Multilingual Matters.

Fitzgerald, T. (1993). *Metaphors of identity.* Albany: State University of New York Press.

Flores, J. (1997). Que assimilated, brother, yo say asimilas. In M. Romero, P. Hondagneu-Satelo, & V. Ortiz (Eds.), *Challenging fronteras: Structuring Latina and Latino lives in the U.S.* London: Routledge.

Frable, D., Blackstone, T., & Scherbaum, C. (1990). Marginal and mindful. *Journal of Personality and Social Psychology, 59,* 140-149.

Friedman, M. (1983). *The confirmation of otherness: In family, community and society.* New York: Pilgrim Press.

Friedman, M. (1986). Foreword. In R. Arnett, *Communication and community.* Carbondale: Southern Illinois University Press.

Frymier, A., Klopf, D., & Ishii, S. (1990). Japanese and Americans compared on the affect orientation instrument. *Psychological Reports, 66,* 985-986.

Fuentes, C. (1992). *The buried mirror.* Boston: Houghton Mifflin.

Fujino, D. (1997). The rates, time patterns and reasons for forming heterosexual interracial dating relationships among Asian Americans. *Journal of Social and Personal Relationships, 14,* 809-828.

Furnham, A., & Ribchester, T. (1995). Tolerance for ambiguity. *Current Psychology, 14,* 179-199.

Fussell, P. (1983). *Class.* New York: Summit Books.

Gabrielidis, C., Stephan, W., Ybarra, O., Pearson, V., & Villareal, L. (1997). Preferred styles of conflict resolution: Mexico and the United States. *Journal of Cross-Cultural Psychology, 28,* 661-677.

Gaertner, S., & Bickman, L. (1971). Effects of race on the elicitation of helping behavior. *Journal of Personality and Social Psychology, 20,* 218-222.

Gaertner, S., & Dovidio, J. (1986). The aversive form of racism. In J. Dovidio & S. Gaertner (Eds.), *Prejudice, discrimination, and racism.* Orlando, FL: Academic Press.

Gaertner, S., & Dovidio, J. (2000). *Reducing intergroup bias.* Philadelphia: Psychology Press.

Gaetz, L., Klopf, D., & Ishii, S. (1990). *Predispositions toward verbal behavior of Japanese and Americans.* Paper presented at the Communication Association of Japan conference.

Gallois, C., Giles, H., Jones, F., Cargile, A., & Ota, H. (1995). Accommodating intercultural encounters. In R. Wiseman (Ed.), *Intercultural communication theory.* Newbury Park, CA: Sage.

Galston, W. (1991). Rights do not equal rightness. *Responsive Community, 1,* 7-8.

Gandhi, M. K. (1948). *Nonviolence in peace and war.* Ahmedabad, India: Garland.

Gans, H. (1979). Symbolic ethnicity. *Ethnic and Racial Studies, 2,* 1-20.

Gao, G. (1996). Self and OTHER: A Chinese perspective on interpersonal relationships. In W. Gudykunst, S. Ting-Toomey, & T. Nishida (Eds.), *Communication in interpersonal relationships across cultures.* Newbury Park, CA: Sage.

Gao, G. (2001). Intimacy, passion, and commitment in Chinese and U.S. American relationships. *International Journal of Intercultural Relations, 25,* 329-342.

Gao, G., & Gudykunst, W. B. (1990). Uncertainty, anxiety, and adaptation. *International Journal of Intercultural Relations, 14,* 301-317.

Gao, G., & Gudykunst, W. B. (1995). Attributional confidence, perceived similarity, and network involvement in Chinese and European American romantic relationships. *Communication Quarterly, 43,* 431-445.

Gao, G., & Ting-Toomey, S. (1998). *Communicating effectively with the Chinese.* Thousand Oaks, CA: Sage.

Garcia, S., & Rivera, S. (1999). Perceptions of Hispanic and African-American couples at the friendship and engagement stage of a relationship. *Journal of Social and Personal Relationships, 16,* 65-86.

Gardner, H., Csikszentmihalyi, M., & Damon, W. (2001). *Good work: When excellence and ethics meet.* New York: Basic Books.

Gardner, J. (1991). *Building community.* Washington, DC: Independent Sector.

Gardner, R. (1985). *Social psychology and second language learning.* London: Edward Arnold.

Gardner, W., Gabriel, S., & Lee, A. (1999). "I" value freedom but "we" value relationships. *Psychological Science, 10,* 321-326.

Garreau, J. (1981). *The nine nations of North America.* New York: Houghton Mifflin.

Garrett, P., Giles, H., & Coupland, N. (1989). The contexts of language learning. In S. Ting-Toomey & F. Korzenny (Eds.), *Language, communication, and culture.* Newbury Park, CA: Sage.

Gass, S., & Varonis, E. (1984). The effect of familiarity on the comprehensibility of nonnative speech. *Language Learning, 34,* 65-89.

Gass, S., & Varonis, E. (1985). Variations in native speaker speech modification on nonnative speakers. *Studies in Second Language Acquisition, 7,* 37-58.

Gass, S., & Varonis, E. (1991). Miscommunication in nonnative speaker discourse. In N. Coupland, H. Giles, & J. Wiemann (Eds.), *"Miscommunication" and problematic talk.* Newbury Park, CA: Sage.

Geertz, C. (1960). *The religion of Java.* Glencoe, IL: Free Press.

Geertz, C. (1973). *The interpretation of cultures.* New York: Basic books.

Gelfand, M., Spurlock, D., Sniezel, J., & Shao, L. (2000). Culture and social prediction. *Journal of Cross-Cultural Psychology, 31,* 498-516.

Genesse, F., & Bourhis, R. (1982). The social psychological significance of code switching in cross-cultural communication. *Journal of Language and Social Psychology, 1,* 1-28.

Gerbner, G. (1978). The dynamics of cultural resistance. In G. Tuchman et al. (Eds.), *Health and home.* New York: Oxford University Press.

Gerbner, G., Gross, L., Morgan, M., & Signorielli, N. (1980). The "mainstreaming" of America. *Journal of Communication, 30,* 10-29.

Gibb, J. (1961). Defensive communication. *Journal of Communication, 11,* 141-148.

Gilbert, G. (1951). Stereotype persistence and change among college students. *Journal of Abnormal and Social Psychology, 46,* 245-254.

Giles, H. (1973). Accent mobility. *Anthropological Linguistics, 15,* 87-105.

Giles, H., Bourhis, R., & Taylor, D. (1977). Towards a theory of language in ethnic group relations. In H. Giles (Ed.), *Language, ethnicity, and intergroup relations.* London: Academic Press.

Giles, H., & Byrne, J. (1982). The intergroup theory of second language acquisition. *Journal of Multilingual and Multicultural Development, 3,* 17-40.

Giles, H., & Coupland, N. (1991). *Language: Contexts and consequences.* Pacific Grove, CA: Brooks/Cole.

Giles, H., Coupland, N., Coupland, J., Williams, A., & Nussbaum, J. (1992). Intergenerational talk and communication with older people. *International Journal of Aging and Human Development, 34,* 271-297.

Giles, H., Coupland, N., & Wiemann, J. (1992). "Talk is cheap . . ." but "my word is my bond." In R. Bolton & H. Kwok (Eds.), *Sociolinguistics today.* London: Routledge.

Giles, H., & Johnson, P. (1981). The role of language in ethnic group relations. In J. Turner & H. Giles (Eds.), *Intergroup behavior.* Chicago: University of Chicago Press.

Giles, H., Mulac, A., Bradac, J., & Johnson, P. (1987). Speech accommodation theory. In M. McLaughlin (Ed.), *Communication yearbook 10.* Newbury Park, CA: Sage.

Giles, H., & Smith, P. (1979). Accommodation theory. In H. Giles & R. St Clair (Eds.), *Language and social psychology.* Oxford: Blackwell.

Gilligan, C. (1982). *In a different voice.* Cambridge, MA: Harvard University Press.

Glazer, N. (1993). Is assimilation dead? *Annals of the American Academy of Political and Social Science, 530,* 122-136.

Glazer, N., & Moynihan, D. (1975). *Ethnicity.* Cambridge, MA: Harvard University Press.

Goffman, E. (1955). On face-work. *Psychiatry, 18,* 213-231.

Goffman, E. (1963). *Stigma.* Englewood Cliffs, NJ: Prentice Hall.

Gonzalez, D. (1992, November 15). What's the problem with Hispanic? Just ask a Latino. *Los Angeles Times,* p. E 6.

Gorden, M. (1964). *Assimilation in American life.* Oxford, UK: Oxford University Press.

Gotanda, P. K. (1991). Interview with Philip Kan Gotanda. *Los Angeles Performing Arts, 25(1),* p-10, p-11.

Gould, S. J. (1996). *Full house: The spread of excellence from Plato to Darwin.* New York: Three Rivers Press.

Gouldner, A. (1960). The norm of reciprocity. *American Sociological Review, 25,* 161-179.

Greeley, A. (1989). Protestant and Catholic: Is the analogical imagination extinct? *American Sociological Review, 54,* 485-502.

Greenland, K., & Brown, R. (1999). Categorization and intergroup anxiety in contact between British and Japanese nationals. *British Journal of Social Psychology, 29,* 503-521.

Greenland, K., & Brown, R. (2000). Categorization and intergroup anxiety in intergroup contact. In D. Capozza & R. Brown (Eds.), *Social identity processes.* London: Sage.

Greenwald, A., McGhee, D., & Schwartz, J. (1998). Measuring individual differences in implicit cognition. *Journal of Personality and Social Psychology, 74,* 1464-1480.

Grieve, P., & Hogg, M. (1999). Subjective uncertainty an intergroup discrimination in the minimal group situation. *Personality and Social Psychology Bulletin, 25,* 926-940.

Grove, T., & Werkman, D. (1991). Communication with able-bodied and visually disabled strangers. *Human Communication Research, 17,* 507-534.

Gudykunst, W. B. (1983a). Similarities and differences in perceptions of initial intracultural and intercultural encounters. *The Southern Speech Communication Journal, 49,* 49-65.

Gudykunst, W. B. (1983b). Toward a typology of stranger-host relationships. *International Journal of Intercultural Relations, 7,* 401-415.

Gudykunst, W. B. (1983c). Uncertainty reduction and predictability of behavior in low and high context cultures. *Communication Quarterly, 31,* 49-55.

Gudykunst, W. B. (1985a). An exploratory comparison of close intracultural and intercultural friendships. *Communication Quarterly, 33,* 236-251.

Gudykunst, W. B. (1985b). The influence of cultural similarity, type of relationship, and self-monitoring on uncertainty reduction processes. *Communication Monographs, 52,* 203-217.

Gudykunst, W. B. (1985c). A model of uncertainty reduction in intercultural encounters. *Journal of Language and Social Psychology, 4,* 79-98.

Gudykunst, W. B. (1986). Toward a theory of intergroup communication. In W. B. Gudykunst (Ed.), *Intergroup communication.* London: Edward Arnold.

Gudykunst, W. B. (1987). Cross-cultural comparisons. In C. Berger & S. Chaffee (Eds.), *Handbook of communication science.* Newbury Park, CA: Sage.

Gudykunst, W. B. (1988). Uncertainty and anxiety. In Y. Kim & W. Gudykunst (Eds.), *Theories in intercultural communication.* Newbury Park, CA: Sage.

Gudykunst, W. B. (1989). Culture and communication in interpersonal relationships. In J. Anderson (Ed.), *Communication yearbook 12.* Newbury Park, CA: Sage.

Gudykunst, W. B. (1993). Toward a theory of interpersonal and intergroup communication: An anxiety/uncertainty management (AUM) perspective. In R. Wiseman & J. Koester (Eds.), *Intercultural communication competence.* Newbury Park, CA: Sage.

Gudykunst, W. B. (1995). Anxiety/uncertainty management theory. In R. Wiseman (Ed.), *Intercultural communication theory.* Thousand Oaks, CA: Sage.

Gudykunst, W. B. (2001). *Asian American ethnicity and communication.* Thousand Oaks, CA: Sage.

Gudykunst, W. B. (in press). Anxiety/uncertainty management (AUM) theory: Making the mesh of the net finer. In W. Gudykunst (Ed.), *Theorizing about culture and communication* [tentative title]. Thousand Oaks, CA: Sage.

Gudykunst, W. B., Chua, E., & Gray, A. (1987). Cultural dissimilarities and uncertainty reduction processes. In M. McLaughlin (Ed.), *Communication yearbook 10.* Newbury Park, CA: Sage.

Gudykunst, W. B., Gao, G., & Franklyn-Stokes, A. (1996). Self-monitoring in China and England. In J. Pandy, D. Sinha, & D. Bhawuk (Eds.), *Asian contributions to cross-cultural psychology.* New Delhi: Sage.

Gudykunst, W. B., Gao, G., Nishida, T., Nadamitsu, Y., & Sakai, J. (1992). Self-monitoring in Japan and the United States. In S. Iwaki, Y. Kashima, & K. Leung (Eds.), *Innovations in cross-cultural psychology.* The Hague: Swets & Zeitlinger.

Gudykunst, W. B., Gao, G., Schmidt, K., Nishida, T., Bond, M. H., Leung, K., Wang, G., & Barraclough, R. A. (1992). The influence of individualism-collectivism on communication in ingroup and outgroup relationships. *Journal of Cross-Cultural Psychology, 23*, 196-213.

Gudykunst, W. B., Gao, G., Sudweeks, S., Ting-Toomey, S., & Nishida, T. (1991). Themes in opposite-sex Japanese-North American relationships. In S. Ting-Toomey & F. Korzenny (Eds.), *Cross-cultural interpersonal communication*. Newbury Park, CA: Sage.

Gudykunst, W. B., & Hammer, M. R. (1987). The influence of ethnicity, gender, and dyadic composition on uncertainty reduction in initial interactions. *Journal of Black Studies, 18*, 191-214.

Gudykunst, W. B., & Hammer, M. R. (1988a). The influence of social identity and intimacy of interethnic relationships on uncertainty reduction processes. *Human Communication Research, 14*, 569-601.

Gudykunst, W. B., & Hammer, M. R. (1988b). Strangers and hosts. In Y. Kim & W. Gudykunst (Eds.), *Cross-cultural adaptation*. Newbury Park, CA: Sage.

Gudykunst, W. B., & Kim, Y. Y. (1984). *Communicating with strangers: An approach to intercultural communication*. New York: McGraw-Hill.

Gudykunst, W. B., & Kim, Y. Y. (1992). *Communicating with strangers: An approach to intercultural communication* (2nd ed.). New York: McGraw-Hill.

Gudykunst, W. B., & Kim, Y. Y. (2003). *Communicating with strangers: An approach to intercultural communication* (4th ed.). New York: McGraw-Hill.

Gudykunst, W. B., & Lee, C. M. (2003). Assessing the validity of self construal scales: A response to Levine et al. *Human Communication Research, 29*, 253-274.

Gudykunst, W. B., & Lim, T. S. (1985). Ethnicity, sex, and self-perceptions of communicator style. *Communication Research Reports, 2*(1), 68-75.

Gudykunst, W. B., Matsumoto, Y., Ting-Toomey, S., Nishida, T., Kim, K., & Heyman, S. (1996). The influence of individualism-collectivism, self construals, and individual values on communication styles across cultures. *Human Communication Research, 22*, 510-543.

Gudykunst, W. B., & Nishida, T. (1984). Individual and cultural influences on uncertainty reduction. *Communication Monographs, 51*, 23-36.

Gudykunst, W. B., & Nishida, T. (1986a). Attributional confidence in low- and high-context cultures. *Human Communication Research, 12*, 525-549.

Gudykunst, W. B., & Nishida, T. (1986b). The influence of cultural variability on perceptions of communication behavior associated with relationship terms. *Human Communication Research, 13*, 147-166.

Gudykunst, W. B., & Nishida, T. (1994). *Bridging differences between Japan and the United States*. Thousand Oaks, CA: Sage.

Gudykunst, W. B., & Nishida, T. (1999). The influence of culture and strength of cultural identity on individual values in Japan and the United States. *Intercultural Communication Studies, IX*(1), 1-18.

Gudykunst, W. B., Nishida, T., & Chua, E. (1986). Uncertainty reduction processes in Japanese-North American relationships. *Communication Research Reports, 3*, 39-46.

Gudykunst, W. B., Nishida, T., & Chua, E. (1987). Perceptions of social penetration in Japanese-North American relationships. *International Journal of Intercultural Relations, 11,* 171-190.

Gudykunst, W. B., Nishida, T., Morisaki, S., & Ogawa, N. (1999). The influence of students' personal and social identities on their perceptions of interpersonal and intergroup encounters in Japan and the United States. *Japanese Journal of Social Psychology, 15,* 47-58.

Gudykunst, W. B., & Shapiro, R. (1996). Communication in everyday interpersonal and intergroup encounters. *International Journal of Intercultural Relations, 20,* 19-45.

Gudykunst, W. B., Sodetani, L., & Sonoda, K. (1987). Uncertainty reduction in Japanese-American/Caucasian relationships in Hawaii. *Western Journal of Speech Communication, 51,* 13-29.

Gudykunst, W. B., & Ting-Toomey, S., with Chua, E. (1988). *Culture and interpersonal communication.* Newbury Park, CA: Sage.

Gudykunst, W. B., Ting-Toomey, S., Hall, B. J., & Schmidt, K. L. (1989). Language and intergroup communication. In M. K. Asante & W. B. Gudykunst (Eds.), *Handbook of international and intercultural communication.* Newbury Park, CA: Sage.

Gudykunst, W. B., Ting-Toomey, S., Sudweeks, S., & Stewart, L. (1995). *Building bridges.* Boston: Houghton-Mifflin.

Gudykunst, W. B., Yoon, Y., & Nishida, T. (1987). The influence of individualism-collectivism on perceptions of communication in ingroup and outgroup relationships. *Communication Monographs, 54,* 295-306.

Guerrero, S., & Gudykunst, W. B. (1997). A thematic analysis of intergroup communication. *Intercultural Communication Studies, VI*(2), 43-76.

Gumperz, J. (1982). *Discourse strategies.* Cambridge, UK: Cambridge University Press.

Gumperz, J., & Hernandez-Chavez, E. (1972). Bilingualism, bidialectism and classroom interaction. In C. Cazden, V. John, & D. Hymes (Eds.), *Functions of language in the classroom.* New York: Teachers College Press.

Gutmann, A. (1992). Introduction. In A. Gutmann (Ed.), *Multiculturalism and the politics of recognition.* Princeton, NJ: Princeton University Press.

Haidt, J., & Keltner, D. (1999). Culture and facial expression. *Cognition and Emotion, 13,* 225-266.

Hall, E. T. (1959). *The silent language.* New York: Doubleday.

Hall, E. T. (1966). *The hidden dimension.* New York: Doubleday.

Hall, E. T. (1976). *Beyond culture.* New York: Doubleday.

Hall, E. T. (1983). *The dance of life.* New York: Doubleday.

Hallahan, M., Lee, F., & Herzog, T. (1997). It's not whether you win or lose, it's also how you play the game. *Journal of Cross-Cultural Psychology, 28,* 768-778.

Hamaguchi, E. (1985). A contextual model of the Japanese. *Journal of Japanese Studies, 11*(2), 289-321.

Hamilton, D., Sherman, S., & Ruvolo, C. (1992). Stereotyped based expectancies. In W. B. Gudykunst & Y. Y. Kim (Eds.), *Readings on communicating with strangers.* New York: McGraw-Hill. (Originally published in *Journal of Social Issues,* 1990, *46*(2), 35-60)

Hammer, M., & Gudykunst, W. (1987). The influence of ethnicity, sex, and dyadic composition on communication in friendships. *Journal of Black Studies, 17,* 418-437.

Hampshire, S. (1989). *Innocence and experience.* Cambridge, MA: Harvard University Press.

Han, G., & Park, B. (1995). Children's choice in conflict. *Journal of Cross-Cultural Psychology, 26,* 298-313.

Han, S., & Shavitt, S. (1994). Persuasion and culture. *Journal of Experimental Social Psychology, 30,* 326-350.

Hanh, T. N. (1991). *Peace in every step.* New York: Bantam.

Hara, K., & Kim, M. S. (2001). *The effect of self construals on conversational indirectness.* Paper presented at the International Communication Association convention.

Hasegawa, T., & Gudykunst, W. B. (1998). Silence in Japan and the United States. *Journal of Cross-Cultural Psychology, 29,* 668-684.

Haslett, B. (1990). Social class, social status and communicative behavior. In H. Giles & W. Robinson (Eds.), *Handbook of language and social psychology.* Chichester, UK: Wiley.

Haslett, B., & Ogilvie, J. (1988). Feedback processes in small groups. In R. Cathcart & L. Samovar (Eds.), *Small group communication: A reader* (5th ed.). Dubuque, IA: William C. Brown.

Hass, R., Katz, I., Rizzo, N., Bailey, J., & Moore, L. (1992). When racial ambivalence evokes negative affect. *Personality and Social Psychology Bulletin, 18,* 786-797.

Hayano, D. (1981). Ethnic identification and disidentification. *Ethnic Groups, 3,* 157-171.

Hayashi, R. (1990). Rhythmicity, sequence and synchrony of English and Japanese face-to-face conversations. *Language Sciences, 12,* 155-195.

Hayashi, R. (1996). *Cognition, empathy and interaction.* Norwood, NJ: Ablex.

Hayden, T. (2002). *Irish on the inside.* New York: Verso.

Hecht, M. (1978). The conceptualization and measurement of communication satisfaction. *Human Communication Research, 4,* 253-264.

Hecht, M., & Ribeau, S. (1984). Ethnic communication. *International Journal of Intercultural Relations, 8,* 135-151.

Hecht, M., Ribeau, S., & Alberts, J. (1989). An Afro-American perspective on interethnic communication. *Communication Monographs, 56,* 385-410.

Hecht, M., Ribeau, S., & Sedano, M. (1990). A Mexican-American perspective on interethnic communication. *International Journal of Intercultural Relations, 14,* 31-55.

Hegi, U. (1997). *Tearing the silence: On being German in America.* New York: Simon and Schuster.

Heider, F. (1958). *The psychology of interpersonal relations.* New York: John Wiley.

Heine, S., Lehman, D., Markus, H., & Kitayama, S. (1999). Is there a universal need for positive self regard? *Psychological Review, 106,* 766-794.

Henley, N., Hamilton, M., & Thorne, B. (1985). Womanspeak and manspeak. In A. Sargent (Ed.), *Beyond sex roles.* New York: West.

Henry, W. (1990, April 9). Beyond the melting pot. *Time,* pp. 28-31.

Herman, S., & Schield, E. (1961). The stranger group in a cross-cultural situation. *Sociometry, 24,* 165-176.

Herskovits, M. (1950). *Man and his works.* New York: Knopf.

Herskovits, M. (1955). *Cultural anthropology.* New York: Knopf.

Hewstone, M., & Brown, R. (1986). Contact in not enough. In M. Hewstone & R. Brown (Eds.), *Contact and conflict in intergroup encounters.* Oxford, UK: Blackwell.

Hewstone, M., & Giles, H. (1986). Stereotypes and intergroup communication. In W. B. Gudykunst (Ed.), *Intergroup communication.* London: Edward Arnold.

Hewstone, M., & Jaspars, J. (1984). Social dimensions of attributions. In H. Tajfel (Ed.), *The social dimension* (Vol. 2). Cambridge, UK: Cambridge University Press.

Hirokawa, R., & Miyahara, A. (1986). A comparison of influence strategies utilized by managers in American and Japanese organizations. *Communication Quarterly, 34,* 250-265.

Ho, D. (1976). On the concept of face. *American Journal of Sociology, 81,* 867-884.

Hocker, J., & Wilmot, W. (1991). *Interpersonal conflict* (3rd ed.). Dubuque, IA: William C. Brown.

Hockett, T. (1958). *A course in modern linguistics.* New York: Macmillan.

Hodges, H. (1964). *Social stratification.* Cambridge, MA: Schenkman.

Hofman, T. (1985). Arabs and Jews, blacks and whites: Identity and group relations. *Journal of Multilingual and Multicultural Development, 6,* 217-237.

Hofstede, G. (1979). Value systems in forty countries. In L. Eckensberger, W. Lonner, & Y. Poortinga (Eds.), *Cross-cultural contributions to psychology.* Lisse, Netherlands: Swets & Zeitlinger.

Hofstede, G. (1980). *Culture's consequences.* Beverly Hills, CA: Sage.

Hofstede, G. (1991). *Cultures and organizations.* London: McGraw-Hill.

Hofstede, G. (2001). *Culture's consequences* (2nd ed.). Thousand Oaks, CA: Sage.

Hofstede, G., & Bond, M. (1984). Hofstede's culture dimensions. *Journal of Cross-Cultural Psychology, 15,* 417-433.

Hogg, M. (2001). Self-categorization and subjective uncertainty resolution. In J. Forgas, K. Williams, & L. Wheeler (Eds.), *The social mind.* New York: Cambridge University Press.

Holmes, J., & Rempel, J. (1989). Trust in close relationships. In C. Hendrick (Ed.), *Close relationships.* Newbury Park, CA: Sage.

Holtgraves, T. (1997). Styles of language usage. *Journal of Personality and Social Psychology, 73,* 624-737.

Holtgraves, T., & Yang, J. (1992). The interpersonal underpinnings of request strategies. *Journal of Personality and Social Psychology, 62,* 246-256.

Honess, T. (1976). Cognitive complexity and social prediction. *British Journal of Social and Clinical Psychology, 15,* 22–31.

Honeycutt, J. M., Knapp, M. L., & Powers, W. G. (1983). On knowing others and predicting what they say. *Western Journal of Speech Communication, 47,* 157-174.

Honig, B. (2002). *Democracy and the foreigner.* Princeton, NJ: Princeton University Press.

Hornsey, M., & Hogg, M. (2000a). Assimilation and diversity. *Personality and Social Psychology Review, 4,* 143-156.

Hornsey, M., & Hogg, M. (2000b). Subgroup relations. *Personality and Social Psychology Bulletin, 26,* 242-256.

Howell, W. S. (1982). *The empathic communicator.* Belmont, CA: Wadsworth.

Hoyle, R., Pinkley, R., & Insko, C. (1989). Perceptions of social behavior: Evidence of differing expectations for interpersonal and intergroup behavior. *Personality and Social Psychology Bulletin, 15,* 365-376.

Hraba, J., & Hoiberg, E. (1983). Origins of modern theories of ethnicity. *Sociological Quarterly, 24,* 381-391.

Hu, H. (1944). The Chinese concept of "face." *American Anthropologist, 46,* 45-64.

Hubbert, K., Gudykunst, W., & Guerrero, S. (1999). Intergroup communication over time. *International Journal of Intercultural Relations, 23,* 13-46.

Huber, G., & Sorrentino, R. (1996). Uncertainty in interpersonal and intergroup relations. In R. Sorrentino & E. Higgins (Eds.), *Handbook of motivation and cognition* (Vol. 3). New York: Guilford.

Hui, C. H. (1988). Measurement of individualism-collectivism. *Journal of Research on Personality, 22,* 17-36.

Huo, Y., Smith, H., Tyler, T., & Lind, E. (1996). Superordinate identification, subgroup identification, and justice concerns. *Psychological Science, 7,* 40-45.

Hwang, A., Francesco, A., & Kessler, E. (2003). The relationship between individualism-collectivism, face, and feedback and learning processes in Hong Kong, Singapore, and the United States. *Journal of Cross-Cultural Psychology, 34,* 72-91.

Hwang, J., Chase, L., & Kelly, C. (1980). An intercultural examination of communication competence. *Communication, 9,* 70-79.

Hymes, D. (1974). Ways of speaking. In R. Bauman & J. Sherzer (Eds.), *Explorations in the ethnography of speaking.* Cambridge, UK: Cambridge University Press.

Ignatieff, M. (1994). *Blood and belonging: Journeys into the new nationalism.* New York: Farrar, Straus and Giroux.

Ignatieff, M. (1998a). *Virtual war: Kosovo and beyond.* New York: Metropolitan Books.

Ignatieff, M. (1998b). *The warrior's honor: Ethnic war and the modern conscience.* New York: Metropolitan Books.

Ignatieff, M. (2001). *Human rights as politics and idolatry.* Princeton, NJ: Princeton University Press.

Imahori, T., & Cupach, W. (1994). A cross-cultural comparison of interpretation and management of face. *International Journal of Intercultural Relations, 18,* 193-220.

Infante, D. (1987). Aggressiveness. In J. McCroskey & J. Daly (Eds.), *Personality and interpersonal communication.* Newbury Park, CA: Sage.

Infante, D. (1988). *Arguing constructively.* Prospect Heights, IL: Waveland.

Inkeles, A. (1974). *Becoming modern.* Cambridge, MA: Harvard University Press.

Islam, M., & Hewstone, M. (1993). Dimensions of contact as predictors of intergroup anxiety, perceived outgroup variability, and outgroup attitude. *Personality and Social Psychology Bulletin, 19,* 700-710.

Ittelson, W., & Cantril, H. (1954). *Perception, a transactional approach.* Garden City, NY: Doubleday.

Jackman, M., & Jackman, R. (1983). *Class awareness in the United States.* Berkeley: University of California Press.

Jackson, J. (1964). The normative regulation of authoritative behavior. In W. Grove & J. Dyson (Eds.), *The making of decisions.* New York: Free Press.

Jackson, L., Esses, V., & Burris, C. (2001). Contemporary sexism and discrimination. *Personality and Social Psychology Bulletin, 27,* 48-61.

Jaffee, L., & Polanski, N. (1962). Verbal inaccessibility in young adolescents showing delinquent trends. *Journal of Health and Social Behavior, 3,* 105-111.

Jampolsky, G. (1989). *Out of darkness into the light.* New York: Bantam.

Janis, I., & Mann, L. (1977). *Decision making.* New York: Free Press.

Johnson, D. (1986). *Reaching out* (3rd ed.). Englewood Cliffs, NJ: Prentice Hall.

Johnson, D., & Johnson, F. (1982). *Joining together* (2nd ed.). Englewood Cliffs, NJ: Prentice Hall.

Johnson, F. (2000). *Speaking culturally: Language diversity in the United States.* Thousand Oaks, CA: Sage.

Johnson, J., & Lecci, L. (2003). Assessing anti-white attitudes and predicting perceived racism. *Personality and Social Psychology Bulletin, 29,* 299-312.

Johnson, R., & Ogasawara, G. (1984). Group size and group income as influences on marriage patterns in Hawaii. *Social Biology, 31,* 101-107.

Johnstone, L., & Hewstone, M. (1991). Intergroup contact. In D. Abrams & M. Hogg (Eds.), *Social identity theory.* New York: Springer.

Jones, T., & Remland, M. (1982). *Cross-cultural differences in self-reported touch avoidance.* Paper presented at the Eastern Communication Association convention.

Jussim, L., Coleman, L., & Lerch, L. (1987). The nature of stereotypes. *Journal of Personality and Social Psychology, 52,* 536-546.

Kagan, S., Knight, G., & Martinez-Romero, S. (1982). Culture and the development of conflict resolution styles. *Journal of Cross-Cultural Psychology, 17,* 225-248.

Kanagawa, C., Cross, S., & Markus, H. (2001). "Who am I?" The cultural psychology of the conceptual self. *Personality and Social Psychology Bulletin, 27,* 90-103.

Kang, K. (1997, June 29). Chinese in the southland. *Los Angeles Times,* pp. A1, A40.

Kanouse, D., & Hanson, L. (1972). Negativity in evaluations. In E. Jones, D. Kanouse, H. Kelley, R. Nisbett, S. Valins, & L. Petrullo (Eds.), *Attribution.* Morristown, NJ: General Learning Press.

Karlins, M., Coffman, T., & Walters, G. (1969). On the fading of social stereotypes. *Journal of Personality and Social Psychology, 13,* 1-16.

Karniol, R. (1990). Reading people's minds. In M. Zanna (Ed.), *Advances in experimental social psychology* (Vol. 23). New York: Academic Press.

Kashima, E., & Hardie, E. (2000). The development and validation of the relational, individual, and collective self-aspects (RIC) scale. *Asian Journal of Social Psychology, 3,* 19-47.

Kashima, E., & Kashima, Y. (1998). Culture and language. *Journal of Cross-Cultural Psychology, 29,* 461-486.

Kashima, Y. (1989). Conceptions of persons. In C. Kagitcibasi (Ed.), *Growth and progress in cross-cultural psychology.* The Hague: Swets & Zeitlinger.

Kashima, Y., Siegel, M., Tanaka, K., & Kashima, E. (1992). Do people believe behaviors are consistent with attitudes? *British Journal of Social Psychology, 31,* 111-124.

Kashima, Y., Yamaguchi, S., Kim, U., Choi, S., Gelfand, M., & Yuki, M. (1995). Culture, gender, and the self. *Journal of Personality and Social Psychology, 69,* 925-937.

Katz, D., & Braly, K. (1933). Racial stereotypes of 100 college students. *Journal of Abnormal and Social Psychology, 28,* 280-290.

Keesing, R. (1974). Theories of culture. *Annual Review of Anthropology, 3,* 73-97.

Kegley, J. (1997). *Genuine individuals and genuine communities.* Nashville, TN: Vanderbilt University Press.

Kellermann, K. (1986). Anticipation of future interaction and information exchange in initial interactions. *Human Communication Research, 13,* 41-65.

Kellermann, K. (1993). Extrapolating beyond: Processes of uncertainty reduction. In S. Deetz (Ed.), *Communication yearbook 16.* Newbury Park, CA: Sage.

Kellermann, K., & Reynolds, R. (1990). When ignorance is bliss: The role of motivation to reduce uncertainty in uncertainty reduction theory. *Human Communication Research, 17,* 5-75.

Kelley, H. H. (1967). Attribution theory in social psychology. *Nebraska Symposium on Motivation, 15,* 192-238.

Kelley, H. H. (1972). Causal schemata and the attribution process. In E. Jones, D. Kanouse, H. Kelley, R. Nisbett, S. Valins, & B. Weiner (Eds.), *Attribution: Perceiving the causes of behavior.* Morristown, NJ: General Learning Press.

Kelly, G. (1955). *The psychology of personal constructs.* New York: Norton.

Kelman, H. (2002, May/June). Interview by Kurt Salzinger. *Psychology Today,* p. 34.

Kennedy, R. (2003). *Interracial intimacies: Sex, marriage, identity, and adoption.* New York: Pantheon.

Kennerley, H. (1990). *Managing anxiety.* New York: Oxford University Press.

Kim, H., & Markus, H. (1999). Deviance or uniqueness, harmony or conformity? *Journal of Personality and Social Psychology, 77,* 785-800.

Kim, M. S. (1994). Cross-cultural comparisons of the perceived importance of conversational constraints. *Human Communication Research, 21,* 128-151.

Kim, M. S., Aune, K., Hunter, J., Kim, H., & Kim, J. (2001). The effects of culture and self construals on predispositions toward verbal communication. *Human Communication Research, 27,* 382-408.

Kim, M. S., Hunter, J., Miyahara, A., Horvath, A., Bresnahan, M., & Yoon, H. (1996). Individual- vs. culture-level dimensions of individualism and collectivism. *Communication Monographs, 63,* 29-49.

Kim, M. S., & Kitani, K. (1998). Conflict management of Asian- and Caucasian-Americans in romantic relationships in Hawaii. *Journal of Asian Pacific Communication, 8,* 51-68.

Kim, M. S., Sharkey, W., & Singelis, T. (1994). The relationship between individuals' self construals and perceived importance of interactive constraints. *International Journal of Intercultural Relations, 18,* 128-151.

Kim, M. S., & Wilson, S. (1994). A cross-cultural comparison of implicit theories of requesting. *Communication Monographs, 61,* 210-235.

Kim, U. (1994). Individualism and collectivism: Conceptual clarification and elaboration. In U. Kim, H. Triandis, C. Kagitcibasi, S. Choi, & G. Yoon (Eds.), *Individualism and collectivism.* Thousand Oaks, CA: Sage.

Kinder, D., & Sanders, L. (1996). *Divided by race: Racial attitudes and democratic ideals.* Chicago: University of Chicago Press.

King, M. L., Jr. (1958). *Stride toward freedom.* New York: Harper & Row.

King, M. L., Jr. (1963). Letter from Birmingham jail. In *Why we can't wait.* New York: Harper & Row.

Kingston, P. (2000). *The classless society: Studies in social inequality.* Stanford, CA: Stanford University Press.

Kitano, H., Fujino, D., & Sato, J. (1998). Interracial marriages. In L. Lee & N. Zane (Eds.), *Handbook of Asian American psychology.* Thousand Oaks, CA: Sage.

Kitano, H., Young, W., Chai, L., & Hatanaka, H. (1984). Asian American interracial marriage. *Journal of Marriage and the Family, 46,* 179-190.

Kitayama, S., & Burnstein, E. (1988). Automaticity in conversations. *Journal of Personality and Social Psychology, 54,* 219-224.

Kitayama, S., Markus, H., Matsumoto, H., & Norasakkunkit, V. (1997). Individual and collective processes in the construction of the self. *Journal of Personality and Social Psychology, 72,* 1245-1267.

Kleg, M. (1993). *Hate, prejudice, and racism.* Albany: State University of New York Press.

Klopf, D. (1984). Cross-cultural apprehension research. In J. Daly & J. McCroskey (Eds.), *Avoiding communication.* Beverly Hills, CA: Sage.

Kluckhohn, F., & Strodtbeck, F. (1961). *Variations in value orientations.* New York: Row, Peterson.

Knapp, M., Ellis, D., & Williams, B. (1980). Perceptions of communication behavior associated with relationship terms. *Communication Monographs, 47,* 262-278.

Knowner, R. (2002). Japanese communication in intercultural communication: The barrier of status related behavior. *International Journal of Intercultural Relations, 26,* 339-361.

Knutson, T., Hwang, J., & Deng, B. (2000). Perception and management of conflict. *Intercultural Communication Studies, IX*(2), 10-31.

Kochman, T. (1981). *Black and white: Styles in conflict.* Chicago: University of Chicago Press.

Kochman, T. (1990). Force fields in black and white communication. In D. Carbaugh (Ed.), *Cultural communication and intercultural contact.* Hillsdale, NJ: Lawrence Erlbaum.

Kosmitzki, C. (1996). The reaffirmation of cultural identity in cross-cultural encounters. *Personality and Social Psychology Bulletin, 22,* 238-248.

Kramarae, C. (1981). *Women and men speaking.* Rowley, MA: Newbury House.

Krauss, R., & Fussell, S. (1991). Constructing shared communicative environments. In L. Resnick, J. Levine, & S. Behrend (Eds.), *Perspectives on socially shared cognition.* Washington, DC: American Psychological Association.

Kraut, R., & Higgins, E. (1984). Communication and social cognition. In R. Wyer & T. Srull (Eds.), *Handbook of social cognition* (Vol. 3). Hillsdale, NJ: Lawrence Erlbaum.

Kroonenberg, P., & Kashima, Y. (1997). Rules in context. *Journal of Cross-Cultural Psychology, 28,* 463-480.

Kurman, J. (2001). Self-enhancement: Is it restricted to individualistic cultures? *Personality and Social Psychology Bulletin, 27,* 1705-1716.

Kurman, J., & Sriram, N. (2002). Interrelationships among vertical and horizontal collectivism, modesty, and self-enhancement. *Journal of Cross-Cultural Psychology, 33,* 71-86.

Kwan, K., & Sodowsky, G. (1997). Internal and external ethnic identity and their correlates. *Journal of Multicultural Counseling and Development, 25*(1), 51-67.

Ladd, P. (2002). *Understanding deaf culture.* Clevendon, UK: Multilingual Matters.

LaFrance, M., & Mayo, C. (1978). Cultural aspects of nonverbal behavior. *International Journal of Intercultural Relations, 2,* 71-89.

Laing, D. (1961). *The self and others.* New York: Pantheon.

Lakoff, R. (1990). *Talking power.* New York: Basic Books.

Lampe, P. (1982). Interethnic dating. *International Journal of Intercultural Relations, 6,* 115-126.

Landis, D., & Boucher, J. (1987). Themes and models of conflict. In J. Boucher, D. Landis, & K. Clark (Eds.), *Ethnic conflict.* Newbury Park, CA: Sage.

Langer, E. (1978). Rethinking the role of thought in social interaction. In J. Harvey, W. Ickes, & R. Kidd (Eds.), *New directions in attribution research* (Vol. 2). Hillsdale, NJ: Lawrence Erlbaum.

Langer, E. (1989). *Mindfulness.* Reading, MA: Addison-Wesley.

Langer, E. (1997). *The power of mindful learning.* Reading, MA: Addison-Wesley.

Larkey, L., Hecht, M., & Martin, J. (1993). What's in a name? *Journal of Language and Social Psychology, 12,* 302-317.

Latin, D. (1977). *Politics, language, and thought.* Chicago: University of Chicago Press.

Lay, C., & Verkuyten, M. (1999). Ethnic identity and its relation to personal self-esteem. *Journal of Social Psychology, 139,* 288-299.

Lazarus, R. (1991). *Emotion and adaptation.* New York: Oxford University Press.

Lebra, T. S. (1987). The cultural significance of silence in Japanese communication. *Multilingua, 6,* 343-357.

Lee, C., & Gudykunst, W. (2001). Attraction in initial interethnic encounters. *International Journal of Intercultural Relations, 25,* 373-387.

Lee, F. (2003, January 8). Does class count in today's land of opportunity? *New York Times,* pp. A17, A19.

Lee, H., & Boster, F. (1991). Social information for uncertainty reduction during initial interactions. In S. Ting-Toomey & F. Korzenny (Eds.), *Cross-cultural interpersonal communication.* Newbury Park, CA: Sage.

Lee, R. (1999). *Orientals: Asian Americans in popular culture.* Philadelphia: Temple University Press.

Lee, S. (1990, July 12). [Interview on *48 Hours,* CBS Television.]

Lennox, R., & Wolfe, R. (1984). Revision of the self-monitoring scale. *Journal of Personality and Social Psychology, 46,* 1349-1364.

Leung, K. (1987). Some determinants of reaction to procedural models for conflict resolution. *Journal of Personality and Social Psychology, 53,* 898-908.

Leung, K. (1988). Some determinants of conflict avoidance. *Journal of Cross-Cultural Psychology, 19,* 125-136.

Leung, K. (1997). Negotiation and reward allocation across cultures. In P. Earley & M. Erez (Eds.), *New perspectives on international industrial/organizational psychology.* San Francisco: Jossey-Bass.

Leung, K., & Chan, D. (1999). Conflict management across cultures. In J. Adamopoulos & Y. Kashima (Eds.), *Social psychology and cultural context.* Thousand Oaks, CA: Sage.

Levin, J., & Levin, W. (1980). *Ageism: Prejudice and discrimination.* Belmont, CA: Wadsworth.

Levine, D. (1979). Simmel at a distance. In W. Shack & E. Skinner (Eds.), *Strangers in African societies.* Berkeley: University of California Press.

Levine, D. (1985). *The flight from ambiguity.* Chicago: University of Chicago Press.

Levine, R., Sato, S., Hashimoto, T., & Verma, J. (1995). Love and marriage in eleven cultures. *Journal of Cross-Cultural Psychology, 26,* 554-571.

LeVine, R. A., & Campbell, D. T. (1972). *Ethnocentrism: Theories of conflict, ethnic attitudes, and group behavior.* New York: John Wiley.

Levine, T., Bresnahan, M., Park, H., Lapinski, M., Wittenbaum, G., Shearman, S., Lee, S., Chung, D., & Ohashi, R. (2003). Self construals lack validity. *Human Communication Research, 29,* 210-252.

Levy, S., Plaks, J., Hong, Y., Chiu, C., & Dwede, C. (2001). Static versus dynamic theories of the perception of groups. *Personality and Social Psychology Review, 5,* 156-168.

Li, H. Z. (1999a). Communicating information in conversations. *International Journal of Intercultural Relations, 23,* 387-410.

Li, H. Z. (1999b). Grounding and information communication in intracultural and intercultural dyadic discourse. *Discourse Processes, 28,* 195-215.

Li, H. Z. (2001). Co-operative and intrusive interruptions in inter- and intra-cultural dyadic discourse. *Journal of Language and Social Psychology, 20,* 259-284.

Lieberson, S. (1985). Unhyphenated whites in the United States. *Ethnic and Racial Studies, 8,* 158-180.

Liem, R. (1997). Shame and guilt among first- and second-generation Asian Americans and European Americans. *Journal of Cross-Cultural Psychology, 28,* 365-392.

Lilli, W., & Rehm, J. (1988). Judgmental processes as a basis for intergroup conflict. In W. Strobe, A. Kruglanski, D. Bar-Tal, & M. Hewstone (Eds.), *The social psychology of intergroup conflict.* New York: Springer.

Lim, T., & Choi, S. (1996). Interpersonal relationships in Korea. In W. Gudykunst, S. Ting-Toomey, & T. Nishida (Eds.), *Communication in interpersonal relationships across cultures.* Newbury Park, CA: Sage.

Linville, P., Fisher, G., & Salovey, P. (1989). Perceived distributions of the characteristics of in-group and out-group members. *Journal of Personality and Social Psychology, 57,* 165-188.

Lippmann, W. (1922). *Public opinions.* New York: Macmillan.

Lippmann, W. (1937). *The good society.* Boston: Little, Brown.

Littlefield, R. (1974). Self-disclosure among Negro, white, and Mexican-American adolescents. *Journal of Counseling Psychology, 21,* 133-136.

LoCastro, V. (1987). *Aizuchi:* A Japanese conversational routine. In L. Smith (Ed.), *Discourse across cultures.* Englewood Cliffs, NJ: Prentice Hall.

Locke, D. (1992). *Increasing multicultural understanding.* Newbury Park, CA. Sage.

Loewry, E. (1993). *Freedom and community.* Albany: State University of New York Press.

Longmore, P. (1987). Screening stereotypes. In A. Gartner & T. Jol (Eds.), *Images of the disabled, disabling images.* New York: Praeger.

Loveday, L. (1982). Communicative interference. *International Review of Applied Linguistics in Language Teaching, 20,* 1-16.

Luhtanen, R., & Crocker, J. (1992). A collective self-esteem scale. *Personality and Social Psychology Bulletin, 18,* 302-318.

Lukens, J. (1978). Ethnocentric speech. *Ethnic Groups, 2,* 35-53.

Lynberg, M. (1989). *The path with heart.* New York: Fawcett.

Maas, A., & Arcuri, L. (1996). Language and stereotyping. In C. Macrae, C. Stangor, & M. Hewstone (Eds.), *Stereotypes and stereotyping.* New York: Guilford.

Mackie, D., Queller, S., Stroessner, S., & Hamilton, D. (1996). Making stereotypes better or worse. In R. Sorrentino & E. Higgins (Eds.), *Handbook of motivation and cognition* (Vol. 3). New York: Guilford.

Madon, S., Guyll, M., Aboufadel, K., Montiel, E., Smith, A., Palumbo, P., & Jussim, L. (2001). Ethnic and national stereotypes. *Personality and Social Psychology Bulletin, 27,* 996-1010.

Major, B., & Crocker, J. (1993). Social styles. In D. Mackie & D. Hamilton (Eds.), *Affect, cognition, and stereotyping.* San Diego, CA: Academic Press.

Maltz, D., & Borker, R. (1982). A cultural approach to male-female miscommunication. In J. Gumperz (Ed.), *Language and social identity.* New York: Cambridge University Press.

Markus, H., & Kitayama, S. (1991). Culture and the self: Implications for cognition, emotion, and motivation. *Psychological Review, 98,* 224-253.

Markus, H., & Kitayama, S. (1994a). A collective fear of the collective. *Personality and Social Psychology Bulletin, 20,* 568-579.

Markus, H., & Kitayama, S. (1994b). The cultural construction of self and emotions. In S. Kitayama & H. Markus (Eds.), *Culture, self, and emotions.* Washington, DC: American Psychological Association.

Markus, H., & Kitayama, S. (1998). The cultural psychology of personality. *Journal of Cross-Cultural Psychology, 29,* 63-87.

Markus, H., Kitayama, S., Mullally, P., Masuda, T., & Fryberg, S. (1997). *Of selves and selfways.* Stanford, CA: Stanford University Press.

Marris, P. (1996). *The politics of uncertainty.* New York: Routledge.

Marshall, R. (1997). Variance in levels of individualism across two cultures and three social classes. *Journal of Cross-Cultural Psychology, 28,* 490-495.

Martin, J., Krizek, R., Nakayama, T., & Bradford, L. (1996). Exploring whiteness. *Communication Quarterly, 44,* 125-144.

Matsumoto, D., Kudoh, T., & Takeuchi, S. (1996). Changing patterns of individualism and collectivism in the United States and Japan. *Culture and Psychology, 2,* 77-107.

Matsumoto, D., Wallbott, H., & Scherer, K. (1989). Emotions in intercultural communication. In M. Asante & W. Gudykunst (Eds.), *Handbook of international and intercultural communication.* Newbury Park, CA: Sage.

Matsumoto, D., Weissman, M., Preston, K., Brown, B., & Kupperbusch, C. (1997). Context-specific measurement of individualism-collectivism at the individual level. *Journal of Cross-Cultural Psychology, 28,* 743-767.

May, R. (1977). *The meaning of anxiety.* New York: Washington Square Press.

Maynard, S. (1997). *Japanese communication.* Honolulu: University of Hawaii Press.

McArthur, L. (1982). Judging a book by its cover. In A. Hastorf & A. Isen (Eds.), *Cognitive social psychology.* New York: Elsevier.

McConahay, J. B. (1986). Modern racism, ambivalence, and the modern racism scale. In J. Dovidio & S. Gaertner (Eds.), *Prejudice, discrimination, and racism.* New York: Academic Press.

McConnell-Ginet, S. (1978). Address forms in sexual politics. In D. Butturff & E. Epstein (Eds.), *Women's language and styles.* Akron: L&S Books.

McFall, R. (1982). A review and reformulation of the concept of social skills. *Behavioral Assessment, 4,* 1-33.

McGinn, N., Harburg, E., & Ginsburg, G. (1973). Responses to interpersonal conflict by middle class males in Guadalajara and Michigan. In F. Jandt (Ed.), *Conflict resolution through communication.* New York: Harper & Row.

McPherson, K. (1983). Opinion-related information seeking. *Personality and Social Psychology Bulletin, 9,* 116-124.

Mesquita, B., Frijida, N., & Scherer, K. (1997). Culture and emotion. In J. Berry, P. Dasen, & T. Saraswathi (Eds.), *Handbook of cross-cultural psychology* (2nd ed., Vol. 2). Boston: Allyn & Bacon.

Messick, D., & Mackie, D. (1989). Intergroup relations. *Annual Review of Psychology, 40,* 45-81.

Miller, G., & Steinberg, M. (1975). *Between people.* Chicago: Science Research Associates.

Miller, G., & Sunnafrank, M. (1982). All is for one but one is not for all. In F. Dance (Ed.), *Human communication theory.* New York: Harper & Row.

Miller, J. (1984). Culture and the development of everyday social explanations. *Journal of Personality and Social Psychology, 46,* 961-978.

Miller, L. (1994). Japanese and American indirectness. *Journal of Asian Pacific Communication, 5,* 37-55.

Mizutani, O. (1981). *Japanese: The spoken language.* Tokyo: Japan Times.

Monteith, M., Sherman, J., & Devine, P. (1998). Suppression as a stereotype control strategy. *Personality and Social Psychology Review, 2,* 63-82.

Morales, E. (2002). *Living in Spanglish: The search for Latino identity in America.* New York: St. Martin's.

Morisaki, S., & Gudykunst, W. (1994). Face in Japan and the United States. In S. Ting-Toomey (Ed.), *The challenge of facework.* Albany: State University of New York Press.

Morling, B., Kitayama, S., & Miyamoto, Y. (2002). Cultural practices emphasize influence in the United States and adjustment in Japan. *Personality and Social Psychology Bulletin, 28,* 311-323.

Morris, M., Menon, T., & Ames, D. (2001). Culturally conferred conceptions of agency. *Personality and Social Psychology Review, 5,* 169-182.

Morris, M. L. (1981). *Saying and meaning in Puerto Rico.* Elmsford, NY: Pergamon.

Morrison, T. (1992). *Playing in the dark: Whiteness in the literary imagination.* Cambridge, MA: Harvard University Press.

Morsbach, H. (1976). Aspects of nonverbal communication in Japan. In L. Samovar & R. Porter (Eds.), *Intercultural communication: A reader* (2nd ed.). Belmont, CA: Wadsworth.

Mullen, B. (1991). Group composition, salience, and cognitive representations. *Journal of Experimental Social Psychology, 27,* 297-323.

Mullen, B. (2001). Ethnophaulisms for ethnic immigrant groups. *Journal of Social Issues, 57,* 457-476.

Mullen, B., & Johnson, C. (1993). Cognitive representations in ethnophaulisms as a function of group size. *Personality and Social Psychology Bulletin, 19,* 296-304.

Mullin, B., & Hogg, M. (1998). Dimensions of subjective uncertainty in social identification and minimal intergroup discrimination. *British Journal of Social Psychology, 37,* 345-365.

Mummendey, A., & Wenzel, M. (1999). Social discrimination and tolerance in intergroup relations. *Personality and Social Psychology Review, 3,* 121-152.

Nagata, D. (1993). *Legacy of silence.* New York: Plenum.

Nakamura, H. (1960). *The ways of thinking of eastern peoples.* Tokyo: Japanese National Commission for UNESCO.

Nakane, C. (1970). *Japanese society.* Berkeley: University of California Press.

Nakane, C. (1974). The social system reflected in interpersonal communication. In J. Condon & M. Saito (Eds.), *Intercultural encounters with Japan.* Tokyo: Simul.

National Opinion Research Center. (1991). Race relations responses to general social survey. Reported in *Los Angeles Times,* January 9, 1991, p. A 15.

Nayo, L. (1995, July 7). Making monsters of ordinary men. *Los Angeles Times,* p. B 7.

Neuberg, S. (1989). The goal of forming accurate impressions during initial interactions. *Journal of Personality and Social Psychology, 56,* 374-386.

Ng, S., Liu, J., Weatherall, A., & Loeng, C. (1997). Younger adults' communication experiences and contact with elders and peers. *Human Communication Research, 24,* 82-108.

Nilsen, A. (1977). Sexism as shown through the English vocabulary. In A. Nilsen, H. Bosmajian, H. Gershuny, & J. Stanley (Eds.), *Sexism and language.* Urbana, IL: National Council of Teachers of English.

Nilsen, A., Bosmajian, H., Gershuny, H., & Stanley, J. (Eds.). (1977). *Sexism and language.* Urbana, IL: National Council of Teachers of English.

Nisbett, R. (2003). *The geography of thought.* New York: Free Press.

Nishiyama, K. (1971). Interpersonal persuasion in a vertical society. *Speech Monographs, 38,* 148-154.

Noesjirwan, J. (1978). A rule-based analysis of cultural differences in social behavior. *International Journal of Psychology, 13,* 305-316.

Noller, P. (1980). Misunderstandings in marital communication. *Journal of Personality and Social Psychology, 39,* 1135-1148.

Norasakkunkit, V., & Kalick, S. (2002). Culture, ethnicity, and distress measures: The role of self-construal and self-enhancement. *Journal of Cross-Cultural Psychology, 33,* 56-70.

Norenzayan, A., Choi, I., & Nisbett, R. (2002). Cultural similarities and differences in social inference. *Personality and Social Psychology Bulletin, 28,* 109-120.

Nozick, R. (1974). *Anarchy, state, and utopia.* New York: Basic Books.

Nuessel, F. (1984). Ageist language. *Maledicta, 8,* 17-28.

Obuchi, K., Chiba, S., & Fukuhima, O. (1996). Mitigation of interpersonal conflicts. *Personality and Social Psychology Bulletin, 22,* 1035-1042.

Oetzel, J. (1998). The effects of ethnicity and self construals on self-reported conflict styles. *Communication Reports, 11,* 133-144.

Oetzel, J., Ting-Toomey, S., & Chew, M. (1999). *Face and facework in conflicts with parents and siblings: A cross-cultural comparison of Germans, Japanese, Mexicans, and U.S. Americans.* Paper presented at the National Communication Association convention.

Oetzel, J., Ting-Toomey, S., Masumoto, T., Yokochi, Y., Pan, X., Takai, J., & Wilcox, R. (2001). Face and facework in conflict: A cross-cultural comparison of China, Germany, Japan, and the United States. *Communication Monographs, 68,* 235-258.

Oetzel, J., Ting-Toomey, S., Yokochi, Y., Masumoto, T., & Takai, J. (2000). A typology of facework behaviors in conflicts with best friends and relative strangers. *Communication Quarterly, 48,* 397-419.

Ogawa, N., Gudykunst, W. B., & Nishida, T. (2004). *Self construals and collective self-esteem in Japan and the United States.* Paper presented at the International Academy for Intercultural Research conference.

Ogden, C., & Richards, I. (1923). *The meaning of meaning.* New York: Harcourt, Brace.

Okabe, R. (1983). Cultural assumptions of east and west. In W. B. Gudykunst (Ed.), *Intercultural communication theory.* Beverly Hills, CA: Sage.

Okamura, J. (1981). Situational ethnicity. *Journal of Ethnic and Racial Studies, 4,* 452-465.

O'Keefe, D., & Sypher, H. (1981). Cognitive complexity measures and the relationship of cognitive complexity to communication. *Human Communication Research, 8,* 72-92.

Olsen, M. (1978). *The process of social organization* (2nd ed.). New York: Holt, Rinehart & Winston.

Omi, M., & Winant, H. (1986). *Racial group formation in the United States.* New York: Routledge.

Operario, D., & Fiske, S. (2001a). Ethnic identity moderates perceptions of prejudice. *Personality and Social Psychology Bulletin, 27,* 550-562.

Operario, D., & Fiske, S. (2001b). Stereotypes: Content, structures, processes, and context. In R. Brown & S. Gaertner (Eds.), *Intergroup processes.* Oxford, UK: Blackwell.

Optow, S. (1990). Moral exclusion and injustice: An introduction. *Journal of Social Issues, 46* (1), 1-20.

Orbe, M. (1998). *Constructing co-cultural theory: An explication of culture, power, and communication.* Thousand Oaks, CA: Sage.

Oyserman, D., Coon, H., & Kemmelmeier, M. (2002). Rethinking individualism and collectivism: Evaluation of theoretical assumptions and meta-analyses. *Psychological Bulletin, 128,* 3-72.

Palmore, E. (1982). Attitudes toward the aged. *Research on Aging, 4,* 333-348.

Park, R. E. (1930). Assimilation. *Encyclopedia of the Social Sciences, 2,* p. 282.

Park, R. E. (1950). Our racial frontier in the Pacific. In R. Park (Ed.), *Race and culture.* New York: Free Press.

Patai, R. (1976). *The Arab mind.* New York: Scribner.

Pavlenko, A., & Blackledge, A. (2003). *Negotiation of identities in multilingual contexts.* Clevendon, UK: Multilingual Matters.

Peck, M. S. (1978). *The road less traveled.* New York: Simon & Schuster.

Peck, M. S. (1987). *The different drum: Community making and peace.* New York: Simon & Schuster.

Peck, M. S. (1993). *A world waiting to be born: Civility rediscovered.* New York: Bantam.

Peng, F. (1974). Communicative distances. *Language Sciences, 31,* 32-38.

Perrucci, R., & Wysong, E. (2002). *The new class society: Goodbye American dream.* New York: Rowman & Littlefield.

Pettigrew, T. F. (1978). Three issues in ethnicity. In Y. Yinger & S. Cutler (Eds.), *Major social issues.* New York: Free Press.

Pettigrew, T. F. (1979). The ultimate attribution error. *Personality and Social Psychology Bulletin, 5,* 461-476.

Pettigrew, T. F. (1982). Cognitive styles and social behavior. In L. Wheeler (Ed.), *Review of personality and social psychology* (Vol. 3). Beverly Hills, CA: Sage.

Pettigrew, T., & Tropp, L. (2000). Does intergroup contact reduce prejudice? In S. Oskamp (Ed.), *Reducing prejudice and discrimination.* Mahwah, NJ: Lawrence Erlbaum.

Pilusuk, M. (1963). Anxiety, self-acceptance, and open-mindedness. *Journal of Clinical Psychology, 19,* 386-391.

Planalp, S., Rutherford, D., & Honeycutt, J. (1988). Events that increase uncertainty in relationships. *Human Communication Research, 14,* 516-547.

Plaut, V. (2002). Cultural models of diversity in America. In R. Shweder, M. Minow, & H. Markus (Eds.), *Engaging cultural differences.* New York: Russell Sage.

Plaut, C., & Markus, H. (2002). *Essentially we're all the same: Ideological challenges to diversity in America.* Unpublished paper, Stanford University.

Pogrebin, L. C. (1987). *Among friends.* New York: McGraw-Hill.

Powers, W., & Lowry, D. (1984). Basic communication fidelity. In R. Bostrom (Ed.), *Competence in communication.* Beverly Hills, CA: Sage.

Prather, H. (1986). *Notes on how to live in the world and still be happy.* New York: Doubleday.

Pratto, F., Sidanius, J., Stallworth, L., & Malle, B. (1994). Social dominance orientation: A personality variable predicting social and political attitudes. *Journal of Personality and Social Psychology, 67,* 741-763.

Pritchard, M. (1991). *On becoming responsible.* Lawrence: University of Kansas Press.

Purdie, V., Steele, C., & Crosby, J. (2000). *Implications of models of difference for African American college students.* Unpublished paper, Stanford University.

Putnam, L., & Wilson, C. (1982). Communication strategies in organizational conflicts. In M. Burgoon (Ed.), *Communication yearbook 6.* Beverly Hills, CA: Sage.

Putnam, R. (2000). *Bowling alone: The collapse and revival of American community.* New York: Simon & Schuster.

Pyszczynski, T., & Greenberg, J. (1981). Role of disconfirmed expectancies in the instigation of attributional processing. *Journal of Personality and Social Psychology, 40,* 31-38.

Rahim, A. (1983). A measure of styles of handling interpersonal conflict. *Academy of Management Journal, 26,* 368-376.

Ralston, D., Vollner, G., Srinvassan, N., Nicholson, J., Tang, M., & Wan, P. (2001). Strategies of upward influence. *Journal of Cross-Cultural Psychology, 32,* 728-735.

Regan, T. (1983). *The case for animal rights.* Berkeley: University of California Press.

Renteln, A. (1988). Relativism and the search for human rights. *American Anthropologist, 90,* 56-72.

Rhee, E., Uleman, J., & Lee, H. (1996). Variations in collectivism and individualism by group and culture. *Journal of Personality and Social Psychology, 71,* 1037-1054.

Richards, Z., & Hewstone, M. (2001). Subtyping and subgrouping. *Personality and Social Psychology Review, 5,* 52-73.

Roach, C., & Wyatt, N. (1988). *Successful listening.* New York: Harper & Row.

Rockquemore, K., & Brunsma, D. (2002). *Beyond black: Biracial identity in America.* Thousand Oaks, CA: Sage.

Rodriguez, R. (1982). *Hunger of memory.* New York: Bantam.

Rogers, C. (1980). *A way of being.* Boston: Houghton-Mifflin.

Rokeach, M. (1951). A method for studying individual differences in "narrow-mindedness." *Journal of Personality, 20,* 219-233.

Rokeach, M. (1960). *The open and closed mind.* New York: Basic Books.

Roloff, M. (1987). Communication and conflict. In C. Berger & S. Chaffee (Eds.), *Handbook of communication science.* Newbury Park, CA: Sage.

Roosens, E. (1989). *Creating ethnicity.* Newbury Park, CA: Sage.

Root, M. (Ed.). (1995). *The multiracial experience.* Thousand Oaks, CA: Sage.

Rose, A. (1965). The subculture of aging. In A. Rose & W. Peterson (Eds.), *Older people and their social world.* Philadelphia: F. A. Davis.

Rose, T. (1981). Cognitive and dyadic processes in intergroup contact. In D. Hamilton (Ed.), *Cognitive processes in stereotyping and intergroup behavior.* Hillsdale, NJ: Lawrence Erlbaum.

Rosenthal, P. (1984). *Words and values.* Cambridge, UK: Cambridge University Press.

Rosenthal, R., Hall, J., DiMatteo, M., Rogers, P., & Archer, D. (1979). *Sensitivity to nonverbal communication.* Baltimore, MD: Johns Hopkins University Press.

Ross, L. (1977). The intuitive psychologist and his shortcomings. *Advances in Experimental and Social Psychology, 10,* 174-220.

Ruben, B. (1976). Assessing communication competency for intercultural adaptation. *Group and Organizational Studies, 1,* 334-354.

Ruben, B., & Kealey, D. (1979). Behavioral assessment of communication competency and the prediction of cross-cultural adaptation. *International Journal of Intercultural Relations, 3,* 15-48.

Rubin, M., & Hewstone, M. (1998). Social identity theory's self-esteem hypothesis. *Personality and Social Psychology Review, 2,* 40-62.

Rubin, T. I. (1990). *Anti-Semitism: A disease of the mind.* New York: Continuum.

Ruscher, J. (2001). *Prejudiced communication.* New York: Guilford.

Ryan, C., Park, B., & Judd, C. (1996). Assessing stereotypes accuracy. In C. Macrae, C. Stangor, & M. Hewstone (Eds.), *Stereotypes and stereotyping.* New York: Guilford.

Ryan, E., Hewstone, M., & Giles, H. (1984). Language and intergroup attitudes. In J. Eiser (Ed.), *Attitudinal judgment.* New York: Springer.

Sachdev, I., & Bourhis, R. (1990). Bilinguality and multilinguality. In H. Giles & W. Robinson (Eds.), *Handbook of language and social psychology.* Chichester, UK: Wiley.

Safilios-Rothschild, C. (1982). Social and psychological parameters of friendship and intimacy for disabled people. In M. Eisenberg, C. Giggins, & R. Duval (Eds.), *Disabled people as second class citizens.* New York: Springer.

Saleh, S., & Gufwoli, P. (1982). The transfer of management techniques and practices: The Kenya case. In R. Rath et al. (Eds.), *Diversity and unity in cross-cultural psychology.* Lisse, The Netherlands: Swets & Zeitlinger.

Sanders, J., & Wiseman, R. (1991). *Uncertainty reduction among ethnicities in the United States.* Paper presented at the International Communication Association convention.

Sanders, J., Wiseman, R., & Matz, I. (1991). Uncertainty reduction in acquaintance relationships in Ghana and the United States. In S. Ting-Toomey & F. Korzenny (Eds.), *Cross-cultural interpersonal communication.* Newbury Park, CA: Sage.

Sarat, A. (2002). The micropolitics of identity-difference. In R. Shweder, M. Minow, & H. Markus (Eds.), *Engaging cultural differences.* New York: Russell Sage.

Scherer, K., Banse, R., & Wallbott, H. (2001). Emotion inferences from vocal expression correlates across languages. *Journal of Cross-Cultural Psychology, 32,* 76-92.

Schlenker, B. R. (1986). Self-identification. In R. F. Baumeister (Ed.), *Public self and private self.* New York: Springer.

Schmidt, K. L. (1991). *Exit, voice, loyalty, and neglect: Responses to sexist communication in dating relationships.* Unpublished doctoral dissertation, Arizona State University.

Schneider, J., & Hacker, S. (1973). Sex role imagery and the use of the generic "man" in introductory texts. *American Sociologist, 8,* 12-18.

Schwartz, S. (1990). Individualism-collectivism: Critique and proposed refinements. *Journal of Cross-Cultural Psychology, 21,* 139-157.

Schwartz, S. (1992). Universals in the content and structure of values. In M. Zanna (Ed.), *Advances in experimental social psychology* (Vol. 25). New York: Academic Press.

Schwartz, S., & Bardi, A. (2001). Value hierarchies across cultures. *Journal of Cross-Cultural Psychology, 32,* 268-290.

Scollon, R., & Scollon, S. (1981). *Native, literacy, and face in interethnic communication.* Norwood, NJ: Ablex.

Scollon, R., & Wong-Scollon, S. (1990). Athabaskan-English interethnic interaction. In D. Carbaugh (Ed.), *Cultural communication and intercultural contact.* Hillsdale, NJ: Lawrence Erlbaum.

Scotton, C. (1993). *Social motivations for code-switching.* New York: Oxford University Press.

Sears, D. (1988). Symbolic racism. In P. Katz & D. Taylor (Eds.), *Eliminating racism.* New York: Plenum.

Sellers, R., Smith, M., Shelton, J., Rowley, S., & Chavous, T. (1998). Multidimensional model of racial identity. *Personality and Social Psychology Review, 2,* 18-39.

Selznick, P. (1992). *The moral commonwealth.* Berkeley: University of California Press.

Sennett, R. (2003). *Respect in a world of inequality.* New York: Norton.

Shea, C. (1997, June 20). University of California investigates new approaches to changing behavior. *The Chronicle of Higher Education,* p. A15.

Shearer, A. (1984). *Disability: Whose handicap?* Oxford, UK: Blackwell.

Sherif, M. (1966). *In a common predicament.* Boston: Houghton Mifflin.

Shon, S., & Ja, D. (1982). Asian families. In M. McGoldrick, J. Pearce, & J. Giordano (Eds.), *Ethnicity and family therapy.* New York: Guilford.

Sidanius, J., & Pratto, F. (1999). *Social dominance: An intergroup theory of social hierarchy and aggression.* New York: Cambridge University Press.

Sieburg, E. (1975). *Interpersonal confirmation.* ERIC Document Reproduction Service No. ED 098 634.

Sillars, A., Coletti, S., Parry, D., & Rogers, M. (1982). Coding verbal conflict tactics. *Human Communication Research, 9,* 83-95.

Simmel, G. (1950). The stranger. In K. Wolff (Ed. & Trans.), *The sociology of Georg Simmel.* New York: Free Press. (Original work published 1908)

Simon, R. (1993). Old minorities, new immigrants. *Annals of the American Academy of Political and Social Sciences, 530,* 61-73.

Sinclair, S., Sidanius, J., & Levin, S. (1998). The interface between ethnic and social system attachment. *Journal of Social Issues, 54,* 741-758.

Singelis, T., Bond, M., Sharkey, W., & Lai, C. (1999). Unpacking culture's influence on self-esteem and embarrassability. *Journal of Cross-Cultural Psychology, 30,* 315-341.

Singelis, T., & Brown, W. (1995). Culture, self and collectivist communication. *Human Communication Research, 21,* 354-389.

Singelis, T., & Sharkey, W. (1995). Culture, self construal, and embarrassability. *Journal of Cross-Cultural Psychology, 26,* 622-644.

Singhal, A., & Nagao, M. (1993). Assertiveness as communication competence. *Asian Journal of Communication, 3,* 1-18.

Skevington, S. (1989). A place for emotion in social identity theory. In S. Skevington & D. Baker (Eds.), *The social identity of women.* London: Sage.

Smith, D. (1987). *The everyday world as problematic.* Boston: Northeastern University Press.

Smith, P., & Bond, M. (1993). *Social psychology across cultures.* New York: Harvester.

Smock, C. (1955). The influence of psychological stress on the intolerance of ambiguity. *Journal of Abnormal and Social Psychology, 50,* 177-182.

Snyder, M. (1974). Self-monitoring of expressive behavior. *Journal of Personality and Social Psychology, 30,* 526-537.

Snyder, M., & Haugen, J. (1995). Why does behavioral confirmation occur? *Journal of Experimental Social Psychology, 30,* 218-246.

Sorrentino, R. M., & Short, J. A. (1986). Uncertainty orientation, motivation, and cognition. In R. M. Sorrentino & E. T. Higgins (Eds.), *Handbook of motivation and cognition.* New York: Guilford.

Spickard, P. (1989). *Mixed blood.* Madison: University of Wisconsin Press.

Spitzberg, B., & Cupach, W. (1984). *Interpersonal communication competence.* Beverly Hills, CA: Sage.

Sprecher, S., Aron, A., Hatfield, E., Cortesa, A., Potapova, E., & Levitskaya, A. (1994). Love: American style, Russian style, and Japanese style. *Personal Relationships, 1,* 349-369.

Stangor, C., Sechrist, G., & Jost, J. (2001). Changing racial beliefs by providing consensus information. *Personality and Social Psychology Bulletin, 27,* 486-496.

Stanley, J. (1977). Paradigmatic women. In D. Shores & C. Hines (Eds.), *Papers in language variation.* Tuscaloosa: University of Alabama Press.

Staub, E. (1989). *The roots of evil.* New York: Cambridge University Press.

Stephan, C. W., & Stephan, W. G. (1992). Reducing intercultural anxiety through intercultural contact. *International Journal of Intercultural Relations, 16,* 89-106.

Stephan, W. G. (1985). Intergroup relations. In G. Lindzey & E. Aronson (Eds.), *Handbook of social psychology* (3rd ed., Vol. 2). New York: Random House.

Stephan, W. G., Boniecki, K., Ybarra, Q., Bettencourt, A., Ervin, K., Jackson, L., McNatt, P., & Renfro, C. (2002). The role of threats in racial attitudes of blacks and whites. *Personality and Social Psychology Bulletin, 28*, 1242-1254.

Stephan, W. G., & Finlay, K. (1999). The role of empathy in improving intergroup relations. *Journal of Social Issues, 55*, 729-744.

Stephan, W. G., & Rosenfield, D. (1982). Racial and ethnic stereotyping. In A. Millar (Ed.), *In the eye of the beholder.* New York: Praeger.

Stephan, W. G., & Stephan, C. W. (1985). Intergroup anxiety. *Journal of Social Issues, 41*, 157-166.

Stephan, W. G., & Stephan, C. W. (1989). Antecedents of intergroup anxiety in Asian-Americans and Hispanic-Americans. *International Journal of Intercultural Relations, 13*, 203-219.

Stephan, W. G., & Stephan, C. W. (1996). Predicting prejudice: The role of threat. *International Journal of Intercultural Relations, 20*, 409-426.

Stephan, W. G., & Stephan, C. W. (2000). An integrated threat theory of prejudice. In S. Oskamp (Ed.), *Reducing prejudice and discrimination.* Mahwah, NJ: Lawrence Erlbaum.

Stephan, W. G., & Stephan, C. W. (2001). *Improving intergroup relations.* Thousand Oaks, CA: Sage.

Stephan, W. G., Stephan, C. W., & Gudykunst, W. B. (1999). Anxiety in intergroup relations: A comparison of AUM theory and integrated threat theory. *International Journal of Intercultural Relations, 23*, 613-628.

Stevens, L., & Fiske, K. (1995). Motivation and cognition in social life. *Social Cognition, 13*, 189-214.

Stewart, J. (1990). Interpersonal communication. In J. Stewart (Ed.), *Bridges not walls* (5th ed.). New York: McGraw-Hill.

Stewart, L. P., Stewart, A., Friedley, S., & Cooper, P. (1990). *Communication between the sexes* (2nd ed.). Scottsdale, AZ: Gorsuch Scarsbrick.

Stone, C. (1974). *Should trees have standing?* Los Altos, CA: Kaufmann.

Strobe, W., Kruglanski, A., Bar-Tal, D., & Hewstone, M. (Eds.). (1988). *The social psychology of intergroup conflict.* New York: Springer.

Sudweeks, S., Gudykunst, W. B., Ting-Toomey, S., & Nishida, T. (1990). Relational themes in Japanese-North American relationships. *International Journal of Intercultural Relations, 14*, 207-233.

Sugimoto, N. (1997). A Japan-U.S. comparison of apology styles. *Communication Research, 24*, 349-369.

Sumner, W. G. (1940). *Folkways.* Boston: Ginn.

Sunnafrank, M. (1991). Interpersonal attraction and attitude similarity. In J. Anderson (Ed.), *Communication yearbook 14.* Newbury Park, CA: Sage.

Sunnafrank, M., & Miller, G. R. (1981). The role of initial conversation in determining attraction to similar and dissimilar others. *Human Communication Research, 8*, 16-25.

Suro, R. (1998). *Strangers among us.* New York: Knopf.

Sussman, N., & Rosenfeld, H. (1982). Influence of culture, language and sex on conversational distance. *Journal of Personality and Social Psychology, 42*, 66-74.

Swain, C. (2002). *The new white nationalism in America.* New York: Cambridge University Press.

Swim, J., & Campbell, B. (2001). Sexism: Attitudes, beliefs, and behavior. In R. Brown & S. Gaertner (Eds.), *Intergroup processes.* Oxford, UK: Blackwell.

Swim, J., Hyers, L., Cohen, L., & Ferguson, M. (2001). Everyday sexism. *Journal of Social Issues, 57,* 31-54.

Swim, J., & Stangor, C. (Eds.). (1998). *Prejudice: The target's perspective.* San Diego, CA: Academic Press.

Tajfel, H. (1969). Social and cultural factors in perception. In G. Lindzey & A. Aronson (Eds.), *Handbook of social psychology* (2nd ed.). Reading, MA: Addison-Wesley.

Tajfel, H. (1978). Social categorization, social identity, and social comparisons. In H. Tajfel (Ed.), *Differentiation between social groups.* London: Academic Press.

Tajfel, H. (1981). Social stereotypes and social groups. In J. Turner & H. Giles (Eds.), *Intergroup behavior.* Chicago: University of Chicago Press.

Tajfel, H., & Turner, J. (1979). An integrative theory of intergroup conflict. In W. Austin & S. Worchel (Eds.), *The social psychology of intergroup relations.* Monterey, CA: Brooks/Cole.

Tak, J., Kaid, L., & Lee, S. (1997). A cross-cultural study of political advertising in the United States and Korea. *Communication Research, 24,* 413-430.

Takata, T. (1987). Self-depreciative tendencies in self-evaluation through social comparison. *Japanese Journal of Experimental Social Psychology, 27,* 27-36.

Tamir, L. (1984). The older person's communicative needs. In R. Dunkle, M. Haig, & M. Rosenberg (Eds.), *Communications technology and the elderly.* New York: Springer.

Tannen, D. (1975). Communication mix and mixup or how linguistics can ruin a marriage. *San Jose State Occasional Papers on Linguistics,* 205-211.

Tannen, D. (1979). Ethnicity as conversational style. In *Working papers in sociolinguistics* (Number 55). Austin, TX: Southwest Educational Development Laboratory.

Tannen, D. (1990). *You just don't understand.* New York: Ballentine.

Tannen, D. (1993). Commencement address at State University of New York at Binghamton. Printed in *Chronicle of Higher Education,* June 9, 1993, p. B5.

Tata, J. (2000). Implicit theories of account giving. *International Journal of Intercultural Relations, 24,* 437-454.

Taylor, C. (1991). *The ethics of authenticity.* Cambridge, MA: Harvard University Press.

Taylor, C. (1992). Multiculturalism and the politics of recognition. In A. Gutmann (Ed.), *Multiculturalism and the politics of recognition.* Princeton, NJ: Princeton University Press.

Taylor, S., & Fiske, S. (1978). Salience, attention, and attribution. In L. Berkowitz (Ed.), *Advances in experimental social psychology* (Vol. 11). New York: Academic Press.

Tempest, R. (1990, June 12). Hate survives a holocaust: Anti-Semitism resurfaces. *Los Angeles Times,* pp. H1, H7.

Thai, H. (1999). "Splitting things in half is so white." *Amerasia Journal, 25*(1), 53-88

Thomas, D., & Meglino, B. (1997). Causal attribution in intercultural interaction. *Journal of Cross-Cultural Psychology, 28*, 554-568.

Thomas, K. (1983). Conflict and its management. In M. Dunnette (Ed.), *Handbook of industrial and organizational psychology.* New York: John Wiley.

Thompson, L. (1993). The impact of negotiation on intergroup relations. *Journal of Experimental Social Psychology, 29*, 304-325.

Thompson, T. (1982). Disclosure as a disability management style. *Communication Quarterly, 30*, 196-202.

Thompson, T., & Siebold, D. (1978). Stigma management in normal-stigmatized interaction. *Human Communication Research, 4*, 231-242.

Tinder, G. (1980). *Community: Reflections on a tragic ideal.* Baton Rouge: Louisiana State University Press.

Ting-Toomey, S. (1985). Toward a theory of conflict and culture. In W. Gudykunst, L. Stewart, & S. Ting-Toomey (Eds.), *Communication, culture, and organizational processes.* Beverly Hills, CA: Sage.

Ting-Toomey, S. (1986). Conflict styles in black and white subjective cultures. In Y. Kim (Ed.), *Current research in interpersonal communication.* Beverly Hills, CA: Sage.

Ting-Toomey, S. (1988). A face negotiation theory. In Y. Kim & W. Gudykunst (Eds.), *Theories in intercultural communication.* Newbury Park, CA: Sage.

Ting-Toomey, S. (1989). Identity and interpersonal bonding. In M. Asante & W. Gudykunst (Eds.), *Handbook of international and intercultural communication.* Newbury Park, CA: Sage.

Ting-Toomey, S. (1991). Intimacy expression in three cultures. *International Journal of Intercultural Relations, 15*, 29-46.

Ting-Toomey, S. (1994). Managing intercultural conflicts effectively. In L. Samovar & R. Porter (Eds.), *Intercultural communication: A reader* (7th ed.). Belmont, CA: Wadsworth.

Ting-Toomey, S., Gao, G., Trubisky, P., Yang, Z., Kim, H., Lin, S., & Nishida, T. (1991). Culture, face maintenance, and styles of handling conflict. *International Journal of Conflict Management, 2*, 275-296.

Ting-Toomey, S., & Kurogi, A. (1998). Facework competence in intercultural conflict. *International Journal of Intercultural Relations, 22*, 187-226.

Ting-Toomey, S., Trubisky, P., & Nishida, T. (1989). *An analysis of conflict styles in Japan and the United States.* Paper presented at the Speech Communication Association convention.

Ting-Toomey, S., Yee-Jung, K., Shapiro, R., Garcia, W., Wright, T., & Oetzel, J. (2000). Ethnic identity salience and conflict styles in four ethnic groups. *International Journal of Intercultural Relations, 23*, 47-81.

Tominaga, J., Gudykunst, W. B., & Ota, H. (2003). *Perceptions of effective communication in Japan and the United States.* Paper presented at the International Communication Association convention.

Tracey, K. (2002). *Everyday talk: Building and reflecting identities.* New York: Guilford.

Trafimow, D., Triandis, H. C., & Goto, S. (1991). Some tests of the distinction between the private self and the collective self. *Journal of Personality and Social Psychology, 60,* 649-655.

Triandis, H. C. (1975). Culture training, cognitive complexity, and interpersonal attitudes. In R. Brislin, S. Bochner, & W. Lonner (Eds.), *Cross-cultural perspectives on learning.* Beverly Hills, CA: Sage.

Triandis, H. C. (1977). *Interpersonal behavior.* Monterey, CA: Brooks/Cole.

Triandis, H. C. (1980). Values, attitudes, and interpersonal behavior. In M. Page (Ed.), *Nebraska Symposium on Motivation* (Vol. 27). Lincoln: University of Nebraska Press.

Triandis, H. C. (1983). Essentials of studying culture. In D. Landis & R. Brislin (Eds.), *Handbook of intercultural training* (Vol. 1). Elmsford, NY: Pergamon.

Triandis, H. C. (1984). A theoretical framework for the more efficient construction of cultural assimilators. *International Journal of Intercultural Relations, 8,* 301-330.

Triandis, H. C. (1988). Collectivism vs. individualism. In G. Verma & C. Bagley (Eds.), *Cross-cultural studies of personality, attitudes, and cognition.* London: Macmillan.

Triandis, H. C. (1989). The self and social behavior in differing cultural contexts. *Psychological Review, 96,* 506-517.

Triandis, H. C. (1990). Cross-cultural studies of individualism-collectivism. In J. Berman (Ed.), *Nebraska Symposium on Motivation* (Vol. 37). Lincoln: University of Nebraska Press.

Triandis, H. C. (1994). *Culture and social behavior.* New York: McGraw-Hill.

Triandis, H. C. (1995). *Individualism & collectivism.* Boulder, CO: Westview.

Triandis, H. C., Bontempo, P., Villareal, M., Asai, M., & Lucca, N. (1988). Individualism-collectivism: Cross-cultural studies of self-ingroup relationships. *Journal of Personality and Social Psychology, 54,* 323-338.

Triandis, H. C., Brislin, R., & Hui, C. H. (1988). Cross-cultural training across the individualism-collectivism divide. *International Journal of Intercultural Relations, 12,* 269-289.

Triandis, H. C., Leung, K., Villareal, M., & Clack, F. (1985). Allocentric vs. idiocentric tendencies. *Journal of Research in Personality, 19,* 395-415.

Triandis, H. C., & Trafimow, D. (2001). Culture and its implications for intergroup behavior. In R. Brown & S. Gaertner (Eds.), *Intergroup processes.* Oxford, UK: Blackwell.

Trilling, L. (1968). *Beyond culture.* New York: Viking.

Tuan, M. (1998). *Forever foreigners or honorary whites.* New Brunswick, NJ: Rutgers University Press.

Tucker, M., & Mitchell-Kernan, C. (1995). Social structure and personality correlates of interethnic dating. *Journal of Social and Personal Relationships, 12,* 341-361.

Turner, J. C. (1982). Towards a cognitive redefinition of the social group. In H. Tajfel (Ed.), *Social identity and intergroup relations.* Cambridge, UK: Cambridge University Press.

Turner, J. C., Hogg, M., Oakes, P., Reicher, S., & Wetherall, M. (1987). *Rediscovering the social group.* Oxford, UK: Blackwell.

Turner, J. H. (1988). *A theory of social interaction.* Stanford, CA: Stanford University Press.

Turner, J. H. (2002). *Face to face: Toward a sociological theory of interpersonal behavior.* Stanford, CA: Stanford University Press.

Tyler, T., Lind, E., Ohbuchi, K., Sugawara, I., & Huo, Y. (1998). Conflict with outsiders. *Personality and Social Psychology Bulletin, 24,* 137-146.

Tzeng, O., & Jackson, J. (1994). Effects of contact, conflict, and social identity on intergroup hostilities. *International Journal of Intercultural Relations, 18,* 259-276.

Uleman, J., Rhee, E., Bardoliwalla, N., Semin, G., & Toyama, M. (2000). The relational self. *Asian Journal of Social Psychology, 3,* 1-17.

U.S. Census Bureau. (1997). *Interracial marriages.* Washington, DC: Government Printing Office.

van Dijk, T. (1984). *Prejudice in discourse.* Amsterdam: Benjamins.

Varonis, E., & Gass, S. (1985). Nonnative/native conversations: A model for negotiation of meaning. *Applied Linguistics, 6,* 71-90.

Vassiliou, V., Triandis, H. C., Vassiliou, G., & McGuire, H. (1972). In H. Triandis, *Analysis of subjective culture.* New York: John Wiley.

Verkuyten, M., & Hagendoorn, L. (1998). Prejudice and categorization. *Personality and Social Psychology Bulletin, 24,* 99-110.

Vlastos, G. (1991). *Socrates, ironist and moral philosopher.* Ithaca, NY: Cornell University Press.

VonHippel, W., Sekaquaptewa, D., & Vargas, P. (1995). On the role of the encoding process in stereotype maintenance. In M. Zanna (Ed.), *Advances in experimental social psychology* (Vol. 27). New York: Academic Press.

Vorauer, J., & Kumhyr, S. (2001). Is this about you or me? *Personality and Social Psychology Bulletin, 27,* 706-719.

Wallace, A. (1952). Individual differences and cultural uniformities. *American Sociological Review, 17,* 747-750.

Wallbott, H., & Scherer, K. (1986). How universal and specific is emotional experience? *Social Science Information, 25,* 763-796.

Ward, J. (2002). Conversation and culture. In The Market Segment Group (Ed.), *Portrait of the new America* (a supplement to *Forbes*). New York: Forbes Custom Communications Partners.

Waterman, A. (1984). *The psychology of individualism.* New York: Praeger.

Waters, M. (1990). *Ethnic options.* Berkeley: University of California Press.

Watson, O. (1970). *Proxemic behavior: A cross-cultural study.* The Hague: Mouton.

Watson, O., & Graves, T. (1966). Quantitative research in proxemic behavior. *American Anthropologist, 68,* 971-985.

Watters, E. (1995, September 17). Claude Steele has scores to settle. *New York Times Magazine,* pp. 45-47.

Watts, A. (1951). *The wisdom of insecurity.* New York: Pantheon.

Watts, A. (1966). *The book: On the taboo against knowing who you are.* New York: Pantheon.

Watzlawick, P., Beavin, J., & Jackson, D. (1967). *The pragmatics of human communication.* New York: Norton.

Wegner, D., & Vallacher, R. (1977). *Implicit psychology.* New York: Oxford University Press.

Weiner-Davis, M. (1992). *Divorce busting.* New York: Summit Books.

Weiss, W. (1970). Selective acculturation and the dating process. *Journal of Marriage and the Family, 32,* 273-278.

Wheeler, L., Reis, H., & Bond, M. (1989). Collectivism-individualism in everyday social life. *Journal of Personality and Social Psychology, 57,* 79-86.

White, S. (1989). Back channels across cultures. *Language in Society, 18,* 59-76.

Wiemann, J. M., & Backlund, P. (1980). Current theory and research in communication competence. *Review of Educational Research, 50,* 185-199.

Wiemann, J. M., & Bradac, J. (1989). Metatheoretical issues in the study of communicative competence. In B. Dervin (Ed.), *Progress in communication sciences* (Vol. 9). Norwood, NJ: Ablex.

Wiemann, J., Chen, V., & Giles, H. (1986). *Beliefs about talk and silence in cultural context.* Paper presented at the Speech Communication Association convention, Chicago.

Wiemann, J. M., & Kelly, C. (1981). Pragmatics of interpersonal competence. In C. Wilder-Mott & J. Weaklund (Eds.), *Rigor and imagination.* New York: Praeger.

Wilder, D. A. (1993). The role of anxiety in facilitating stereotypic judgment of outgroup behavior. In D. Mackie & D. Hamilton (Eds.), *Affect, cognition, and stereotyping.* New York: Academic Press.

Wilder, D. A., & Shapiro, P. (1989). Effects of anxiety on impression formation in a group context. *Journal of Experimental Social Psychology, 25,* 481-499.

Wilder, D. A., & Shapiro, P. (1991). Facilitation of outgroup stereotypes by enhanced ingroup identity. *Journal of Experimental Social Psychology, 27,* 431-452.

Wilder, D. A., & Simon, A. (1996). Incidental and integral affect as triggers of stereotyping. In R. Sorrentino & E. Higgins (Eds.), *Handbook of motivation and cognition* (Vol. 3). New York: Guilford.

Williams, A., & Giles, H. (1996). Intergenerational conversations. *Human Communication Research, 23,* 220-250.

Williams, J. (1984). Gender and intergroup behavior. *British Journal of Social Psychology, 23,* 311-316.

Wilson, T. (2002). *Strangers to ourselves: Discovering the adaptive unconscious.* Cambridge, MA: Harvard University Press.

Wink, P. (1997). Beyond ethnic differences. *Journal of Social Issues, 53*(2), 329-350.

Winkler, K. (1997, July 11). Scholars explore blurred lines of race, gender, and ethnicity. *The Chronicle of Higher Education,* p. A11.

Winter, G. (2003, January 21). Schools resegregate, study finds. *New York Times,* p. A14.

Wolfe, A. (1998). *One nation, after all.* New York: Viking.

Won-Doornink, M. (1985). Self-disclosure and reciprocity in conversation. *Social Psychology Quarterly, 48,* 97-107.

Worchel, S., & Norwell, N. (1980). Effect of perceived environmental conditions during co-operation on intergroup attraction. *Journal of Personality and Social Psychology, 38*, 764-772.

Wright, E. (1997). *Class counts: Comparative studies in class analysis.* New York: Cambridge University Press.

Wylie, R. (1979). *The self-concept.* Lincoln: University of Nebraska Press.

Yamada, H. (1990). Topic management and turn distributions in business meetings: American versus Japanese strategies. *Text, 10*, 271-295.

Yamaguchi, S. (1994). Collectivism among the Japanese. In U. Kim, H. Triandis, C. Kagitcibasi, S. Choi, & G. Yoon (Eds.), *Individualism and collectivism.* Thousand Oaks, CA: Sage.

Yamaguchi, S., Kuhlman, D., & Sugimori, S. (1995). Personality correlates of allocentric tendencies in individualistic and collectivistic cultures. *Journal of Cross-Cultural Psychology, 26*, 645-657.

Yankelovich, D. (1981). *New rules: Searching for self-fulfillment in a world turned upside down.* New York: Random House.

Yeh, C., & Huang, K. (1996). The collective nature of ethnic identity development among Asian-American college students. *Adolescence, 31*, 645-661.

Yik, M., Bond, M., & Paulhus, D. (1998). Do Chinese self-enhance or self-efface? *Personality and Social Psychology Bulletin, 24*, 399-406.

Yinger, M. (1994). *Ethnicity.* Albany: State University of New York Press.

Yoshida, T., Kojo, K., & Kaku, H. (1982). A study of the development of self-presentation in children. *Japanese Journal of Educational Psychology, 30*, 30-37.

Yuki, M., & Brewer, M. (1999). *Japanese collectivism versus American collectivism: A comparison of group loyalty across cultures.* Paper presented at the Asian Social Psychology convention.

Zajonc, R. (1980). Feeling and thinking. *American Psychologist, 35*, 151-175.

Zebrowitz, L. (1996). Physical appearance as a basis for stereotyping. In C. Macrae, C. Stangor, & M. Hewstone (Eds.), *Stereotypes and stereotyping.* New York: Guilford.

Zebrowitz, L., & Collins, M. (1997). Accurate social perception at zero acquaintance. *Personality and Social Psychology Review, 1*, 204-233.

Zentella, A. (1985). The fate of Spanish in the United States. In N. Wolfson & J. Manes (Eds.), *Language and inequality.* New York: Mouton.

Zerubavel, E. (1991). *The fine line.* New York: Free Press.

Zoglin, R. (1993, June 21). All you need is hate. *Time,* p. 63.

INDEX

ABOUT THE AUTHOR

William B. Gudykunst is a professor of speech communication and Asian American Studies at California State University, Fullerton. He became interested in intercultural communication while working as an Intercultural Relations Specialist with the U.S. Navy in Yokosuka, Japan. His work focuses on developing a theory of interpersonal and intergroup effectiveness (anxiety/uncertainty management theory) that can be applied to improving the quality of communication and helping people adjust to new cultural environments, as well as explaining similarities and differences in communication in Japan and the United States.

He is the author of *Asian American Ethnicity and Communication,* and coauthor of *Culture and Interpersonal Communication* (with Stella Ting-Toomey), *Communicating With Strangers* (with Young Yun Kim), *Bridging Japanese/North American Differences* (with Tsukasa Nishida), and *Ibunkakan Komyunikeishon Myumon: Nichibei Kanno Sougorikai Notameri* (*Introduction to Intercultural Communication: Developing Mutual Understanding Between Japanese and North Americans,* with Tsukasa Nishida), among others. He also has edited or coedited numerous books including *Communication in Japan and the United States, Intergroup Communication, Theorizing About Culture and Communication,* and *Handbook of International and Intercultural Communication* (with Bella Mody), among others. He is a past editor of the *International and Intercultural Communication Annual* and *Communication Yearbook,* and a Fellow of the International Communication Association.